Nafisa
Enjoy!

signature

5-22-2023

DANCE WITH THE DEVIL

COLLECTOR'S EDITION

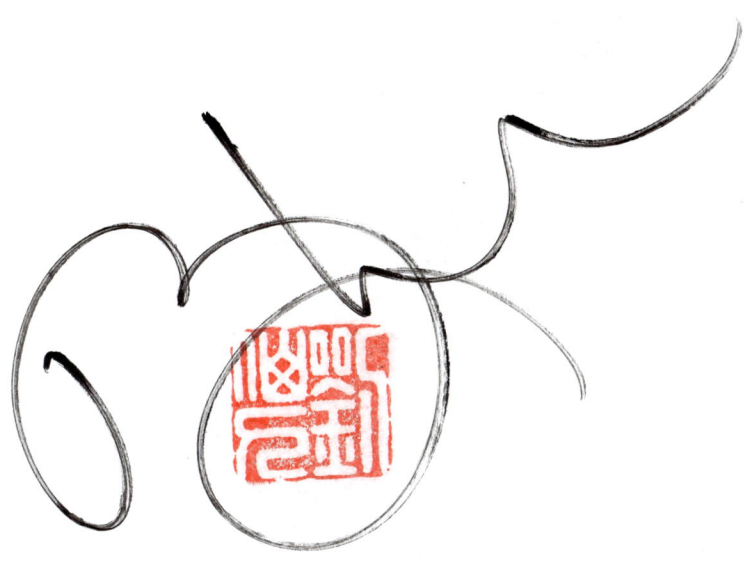

Bernie Lau

DANCE WITH THE DEVIL
COLLECTOR'S EDITION

THE MEMOIRS OF AN
UNDERCOVER NARCOTICS DETECTIVE

BERNARD LAU MEDIA

Dance with the Devil—Collector's Edition

The Memoirs of an Undercover Narcotics Detective

All rights reserved © 2011 by Bernard Lau

No part of this book may be reproduced or transmitted in any form or by any means, graphic, electronic, or mechanical, including photocopying, recording, taping, or by any information storage retrieval system, without the permission in writing of the publisher.

The names and characteristics of persons portrayed in this book have been changed to protect their privacy.

Bernard Lau Media

For information address:

Bernard Lau Media

   c\o

Richard Opheim

6204 N.E. 185th St.

Kenmore, WA 98028 U.S.A.

www.bernielau.com

ISBN-13: 978-1466239302

Cover: Caden Lau

Interior: Richard Opheim

Edited by Richard Opheim

For Nancy, Keith, Zachary, Caden and Kam

and in memory of

Antonio Lopez Montoya

Acknowledgments

There are many people who've helped me throughout the years and their unconditional friendship has played a big part in the making of this book. Wayne and Noriko Gorski, Michell Knight, Bob and Linda Oslin and Steve Shoji are all true friends who stood by me during my darkest hours.

Special thanks goes to family members Jan C. War, Jane Medeiros, Abel Medeiros and John Medeiros.

I must also thank Richard Opheim—my invaluable editor—for his unwavering friendship and support. Without his editorial expertise, there would be no "Dance with the Devil."

And last, but not least, I'd like to thank my son Caden for putting up with me while he did the cover design.

Contents

Acknowledgments vii

Foreword xiii

Preface to the Collector's Edition xiii

I French Bastard in a Chinese Mind   1

1 A Bastard is Born 3

2 Land of the Free 7

3 Turning Chinese 11

4 Bad Dog 19

5 Tohei 25

II A Girl in Every Port   31

6 A Higher Power 33

7 Sub School 39

8 Submariner 43

9 Crisis in the Bering Sea 53

10 A Girl in Every Port 63

11 Showing the Flag 69

12 Operation West Wind 73

13	Nalani	77
14	A Prayer Answered	81
15	Roots	87
16	Escape Training Tank	93

III Dance with the Devil   99

17	Campus Cop	101
18	Field Training	105
19	Probie	111
20	Rookie	115
21	Hippie Girl	119
22	The First Sin	125
23	Jip Joint	129
24	Precognition	133
25	Mayhem	139
26	The War on Drugs	145
27	Making Detective	159
28	Dance With the Devil	165
29	Busted	173
30	Johnny Medeiros	177
31	Bird Dog	187
32	The Great Meth Lab Bust	195
33	Blown	201
34	Bobby C.	211

35 Tea Party	215
36 Johnny Rotten	223
37 Tina	231
38 The Razor's Edge	235
39 First Toot	245
40 Little 'Ho'	257
41 Concerned Citizen	261
42 New Sheriff in Chinatown	273
43 Internal Investigation	277
44 Benjamin Ng	279
45 Off the Edge	281
Glossary	291
Appendix A: Fake I.D. Cards	297
Appendix B: Dr. Liebert's Letter	299

Foreword

At the age of 16, I sat down and made a list of everything that I wanted to accomplish in my life. Perhaps unlike most people, I've actually fulfilled every one of those youthful ambitions, though things didn't always turn out exactly the way I planned.

Several years ago, I decided to write down what had happened to me in the process of fulfilling the plan that I'd laid out for my life. I've tried to recall the events as accurately as possible and to spare no embarassing details in telling the story, even if it sometimes shows me in a less-than-flattering light. That was the way it was and there's no use pretending otherwise.

Part One tells the story of my childhood as an orphan in France and the culture shock I experienced after being adopted by a Chinese family in Hawaii. It was while I was growing up in Hawaii that I first came into contact with aikido, which has been so important in my life.

In Part Two, I tell about my career in the Navy. During my first term of enlistment, at the height of the Cold War, I was a submariner. I became a Navy diver as well, and during my second hitch, I was assigned to be an instructor at the Escape Training Tank at Pearl Harbor. All the while, I continued my aikido training and participated in various kinds of eastern meditation practices.

Part Three is about my career in law enforcement, first in the University of Washington Police Department, then in the Seattle Police Department. During my 15 years as a police officer, I worked patrol, undercover vice, and for most of my career, undercover narcotics. I retired on medical disability in 1983, only 42 years old.

This book is the story of my life up until my retirement, a life that has had its share of sadness and happiness. I hope you'll find it entertaining and enlightening.

Bernie Lau, June, 2011

Preface to the Collector's Edition

Why a "Collector's Edition," you might ask! During the first 42 years of my life, I was involved in so many surreal and unusual situations that some readers of my memoir, "Dance with the Devil," may have questioned its authenticity. However, for many of these events of which I wrote, I'm fortunate to have photographic documentation.

It's said that a picture is worth a thousand words. Over the years, I've shown and shared many of my pictures with personal friends and acquaintances. Most of them have suggested that I put together a collection and offer it to the reading public in order to share these photos of my past experiences with others who may be interested. Having done this, I now offer you a very special "Collector's Edition" of my memoir, "Dance with the Devil." I hope you'll find its contents—both text and photographs—interesting and entertaining.

Bernie Lau, September, 2011

Part I

French Bastard in a Chinese Mind

1

A Bastard is Born

It was 1940, and northern France was swarming with German troops. Sometime in early September, a 20-year-old by the name of Renée Marthe Mulier and a 21-year-old named Lucien Gervais stole off into the woods by themselves. Maybe they had a cheap bottle of red wine, some crusty bread, a moldy cheese, and an apple. Alone and hidden from view, they escaped the madness and horror of the war around them and lost themselves in a brief moment of lust.

In a month or two Renée realized that she, an unmarried woman, would be giving birth to a bastard child.

Renée, her mother, Marthe, and her sister, Jacqueline, all lived in a tiny 5th-floor apartment in Lille. Just to survive, they worked at whatever jobs they could find. Marthe worked nights as a cleaning lady, scrubbing floors on her hands and knees in a large office building. Renée worked as a waitress in a club for Nazi officers. Food of any kind was scarce. In fact, everything was scarce. Things like clothing, that used to be easy to buy, were now being diverted to the Third Reich. Neither Renée nor her mother had the means to take care of a baby.

On June 8, 1941, shortly after midnight, Bernard Daniel Mulier came into the world, feet first. Being born out of wedlock, I was a genuine bastard child, and a bastard I'd think of myself for the rest of my life.

When he heard that Renée had had a baby, Lucien immediately denied being the father, swearing to his parents that he'd never had sex with her.

I was baptized in a Catholic church and immediately put in an orphanage located several miles outside of Lille, there to be raised alongside other unwanted newborns from the surrounding countryside.

The orphanage, located in a little red brick house, was run by Maman and Papa Germain, the only names I ever knew them by. They were a happy old couple, and I never heard them speak an unkind word to any of us orphans. There were six or seven of us; a cross-section of misfits, outcasts, and rejects.

My first memories are of being in a dark, damp, moldy cellar along with the other frightened children, listening to the awful rumbling of the American bombs falling nearby. I remember being fascinated by reflections from the slimy trails of the snails as they fled their once-happy homes in the niches of the cellar walls. That was the way the world was then; even the snails were trying to get away.

During the five-plus years I spent in that orphanage, I can't remember anyone ever being adopted. I guess in wartime, nobody thinks about adopting a child. Just day-to-day survival is enough of a challenge.

The main problem was that there was hardly any food since most of it was confiscated by the Germans. We had old, crusty pieces of bread with a thin layer of lard on the surface. No butter or jam, just lard. We often ate marrow, and that was good. I loved to suck the marrow out of those big old cow bones. Sometimes there were beets; I loved the sweetness of raw sugar beets.

The orphanage near Lille, France

And once in a while, we got rabbit. The next day, I'd see the rabbit's hide nailed to a dilapidated fence in back of the house. Later, an old man dressed in torn, weathered clothing would come by and sharpen the kitchen knife in exchange for several hides.

Growing children need protein for proper bone and cell development. Protein, vitamins, vegetables ... but no, none of these were available to us during the war. Milk? No way. But wartime or not, we always had a lot of cheap red wine. It was mixed with water before being served to us children; one part water to one part wine. They did that either to make sure the water, which we got out of a big wooden tank in back of the house, was safe to drink or to make the wine go farther. Or both.

Maman Germain holding the author, with two orphan girls

So there I was: a breech baby, rejected by my parents from birth, malnourished, and a habitual wine drinker. Children exposed to such factors can have severe physical and mental problems in later life and are even considered to be at risk for developing criminal behavior. My prospects were not good.

I remember once, a week before Christmas, when I was two or three years old. Outside the tiny, red brick house, it was dark and snowing. It was cold outside, and inside it wasn't much warmer. I was all alone in the living room. There was no Christmas Tree with hanging balls and shiny ornaments, but there was a tiny homemade manger scene set up on a table. It made me curious.

I remember grabbing the edge of the table and standing on my toes so I could get a better look at it. What caught my eye first was a makeshift crib with something white and shiny inside. It was a tiny Baby Jesus, maybe two inches long, just lying there. I stretched out my arm, reached in, and picked it up for a closer look. The whiteness fascinated me. Holding him in my hand, I gazed in wonder. I put him to my lips to taste what he was made of and ... wonderful sweetness!

Looking around, I saw there was no one else in the room; we were alone. It was just me and the sweet-tasting Baby Jesus. Slowly, I stuck the Baby Jesus in my mouth and bit off his head. As I stood there next to the table, I leisurely chewed on the crunchy, sugary head and savored the taste of unbelievably delightful sweetness. Imagine that! The first time I'd ever tasted pure sugar was when I bit the head off of Baby Jesus, who'd been lying there, all alone in that makeshift manger, waiting for his birthday.

I put the now-headless figure back into his crib, hoping that no one would notice what I'd done. I was still standing in front of the table enjoying the sweet aftertaste, when suddenly, my face flushed, my mood changed, and I got angry. I started to pace around the living room. My thoughts were strange and confused. I picked up a chair and, with all my might, flung it through the living room window, sending shattered glass flying in all directions. I didn't care; I was mad and wanted to destroy things.

Alarmed by the noise, Maman and Papa Germain rushed into the living room and saw the broken window with the chair still hanging in the window frame. No harsh words were spoken; Papa Germain simply picked me up by the back of my shirt, carried me out the back door, put me on the ground, and slammed the door as he went back inside. I was locked out in the freezing cold.

I cried, I yelled, I kicked at the door, I threw a tantrum. I sobbed and pounded on the door, pleading to be let back in. Before long, I'd peed my pants and the frozen pee had stuck to my legs. I kept screaming and yelling till my voice went hoarse, but it didn't do me any good. There I was, two and a half years old, and I'd already managed to get myself thrown out of an orphanage several days before Christmas. Baby Jesus got his revenge!

The Germains were poor people and the Occupation made things worse. Once, I remember Papa Germain leading me by the hand to the outhouse, located in a field several yards behind the orphanage. In his other hand he was holding a burlap sack. I could hear crying and meowing coming from the sack, and I saw the squirming shapes of newborn kittens through the burlap as they struggled desperately to get out. We got to the outhouse and he opened the door. A terrible stench filled the air as he held the sack of helpless, frightened kittens over the hole and then let it drop down into the muck. After a short while, there were no more meows.

One of the Germains' many chores was to put all six of us to bed. No, we didn't have six beds; there were two and that was all. Three or four to a bed, no other choice. I do remember times when I was allowed to sleep with the Germains in their bed on the second floor. Was that because I was somehow their favorite, or could it have been that they wanted to keep me out of trouble? I was what the French call a *petit diable* ("little devil"—a child who misbehaves).

Older boys in the neighborhood frequently came over to play or just hang around. Often, they would entertain themselves at our expense. I remember once, when they thought it would be funny to roll me up in the living room rug. One boy held me down on the edge of the rug while the other two rolled me up. My hands were pinned to my sides, my entire body trapped in the rug. I was breathing in dust and surrounded by darkness. I felt sheer panic and horror. I fought to breathe, unable to move or cry out. Finally, after ten minutes or so, I was unrolled. The three boys were laughing and making fun of me; I'd soiled myself. That was when I was barely four years old.

Another time, the older boys were playing with a can of gasoline. One boy poured a small amount of gasoline on the ground while another one lit it with a match. It ignited with a "whoosh." Somehow the open can of gasoline caught on fire too. The oldest boy tried to grab hold of the can and throw it away, but some of the gasoline splashed on his hands. He screamed and dropped the can, splattering flaming liquid in all directions. A little landed on me, catching my shirt on fire and resulting in a severe burn to my chest. In time it healed, but I still have the scar.

Then there was the time they mounted a small generator on the frame of an old bicycle. The bicycle had been turned upside down so the pedals could be turned by hand. As they were turned, the generator produced an electrical charge. I was standing there, watching politely, when all of a sudden, two of the boys grabbed me and held my arms. Another one wrapped electrical wires around both my wrists. Then they started turning the bicycle pedals, sending an electrical current through my body. I tried to scream and break free, but couldn't move. All I could do was stand there, grit my teeth, and make animal-like sounds as the electricity coursed through my body. I remember that the pain was intense and there was a sickening taste of copper in my mouth.

Frightened and angry at being abused by the older children, I left the orphanage and headed for Lille, two miles away, where Renée lived with her mother and sister. I'd been to their apartment before, but always in the company of an adult. Now there was no one to guide me, and I had to find the building all by myself, which I did somehow. Tired, cold, hungry, and frightened, I climbed the five flights of stairs up to her apartment and knocked on the door. Soon I'd be inside, safe from further torment, and my mom would take care of me.

I knocked again, louder this time. Moments later, the door opened. I looked up and there, standing in front of me, was Renée. I smiled at her as she looked down at me, but she didn't say a word. Stepping out onto the landing, she looked around to see if anyone else was there.

"*Qui t'a amené?*" (Who brought you?)

"*Personne. Je suis tout seul.*" (Nobody. I'm all by myself.)

Hearing that, she got mad. She yelled at me; I was a bad boy for leaving the orphanage by myself, I was in big trouble, and I was going to be punished. She grabbed me roughly by the arm, dragged me inside, led me down a long, dark hallway, and stood me in front of a large window overlooking a courtyard. She told me to stay there and not move. So I stood there for what seemed like hours, gazing down at some pigeons fluttering around in the courtyard.

2

Land of the Free

One bright, sunny afternoon, when I was five and a half years old, Renée showed up at the orphanage to tell me that we'd soon be going to America.

After the war ended, some American troops stayed in France for several years. It seems that, during that time, while working in the night club in Lille (which now catered to American officers), Renée met a young, good-looking Air Force lieutenant from Hawaii, and they'd dated frequently until he went back to the States. She told me many years later that, after he left France, she didn't get any letters from him for over a year. No letter, no postcard, no nothing. Then one day, she got a letter out of the blue asking her to come to America and marry him.

While he was stationed in France, the good-looking young lieutenant had been dating another French girl with a view towards marriage. However, on one of their dates, during dinner, this gal accidentally spilled some coffee onto her saucer. Then she picked up the saucer and slurped the spilled coffee off it. Well, that was the end of any hope she had of being married to the lieutenant. He decided, right then and there, that she was low-class and not good enough for him. He must have felt real embarrassed to be seen in public with a gal who slurped coffee right off her saucer. But if she hadn't slurped the spilled coffee, he'd most likely have married her instead of Renée, and I'd have stayed in France. Imagine that—the slurp that changed my destiny.

Anyway, Renée was thrilled by the proposal of marriage. France wasn't in good shape following the war. Times were tough, food was still being rationed, and the thought of flying off to a place like Hawaii and starting a new life must have seemed like a fairy-tale to young Renée—a Cinderella story! She decided to take a chance on a better future and said yes to his proposal.

Years later, she told me that she'd meant to leave me in the orphanage and go to Hawaii without me, but the lieutenant convinced her to bring me along. He'd said he wouldn't mind having to raise me. So when it was time to leave, Renée showed up at the orphanage to get me, just like he'd told her to.

Thinking back, it was kind of funny. There was nothing to do to get me ready for the trip. No packing because I didn't have any clothes of my own. All of us little bastards shared the few items of clothing that were available. So with the clothes on my back as my only possessions, I left the orphanage with Renée, bound for Hawaii.

We crossed the English Channel by boat, which made me really sick. Later, we walked up some steep steps and into a huge tube-like thing with large silver wings, where we sat down next to some other people. I heard a loud, frightening noise, and the tube-like thing lifted off the ground. Looking out a small window, I saw that we were up in the sky, flying, like a big bird.

After a long while, the big metal tube was on the ground again. Renée took my hand and carefully led me down some steep stairs into a large, crowded building. I just stood there, not saying a word. Too many strange things had happened in such a short period of time. Until only yesterday, I'd still been living at the orphanage that had been my home since I was born. I'd been taken away from the only parents I'd ever known, Maman and Papa Germain.

We went into the arrival terminal, where we were met by an odd-looking man, very unlike folks back in France. He was tall and skinny and his skin was sort of dark. His hair was black and his eyes ... There was something about those eyes. They were strange, weird, actually; sort of slanted. I'd never seen such a strange-looking man in my entire life. And another thing; he smelled like flowers. (Probably his aftershave.)

Next thing I knew, Renée and this strange-looking man were hugging and kissing. Then something even stranger happened. Renée looked down at me and told me to give the guy a hug! I pulled my hand out of Renée's grip and took a few steps backwards. Holding my arms stiffly to my sides, I said, "*Non, je ne veux pas!*" (No, I don't want to.) Renée squatted down next to me, put her hand on my shoulder, looked sternly at me, and said: "*Bernard, c'est ton papa. Embrasse-lui.*" (Bernard, this is your dad. Give him a hug.)

Papa? This alien-looking man? This guy that didn't even speak the same language as us? His French was limited to "*Je t'aime*" (I love you), and a few other words which, I guess, were supposed to be romantic. Again, she tried to get me to give my "papa" a hug and a kiss. Now, I may have only been five and a half years old, but I was old enough to know that he was definitely not my *papa*.

Next, this man took Renée and me, via taxi (I'd never ridden in a car, let alone this yellow thing, called a "taxi"), to some fancy hotel in New York City. Renée, I, and the strange man walked up to the front desk, where he asked for a room for the night. The desk clerk took one look at the three of us and told him that he could and would not rent us a room, absolutely not. The reason was that he was not a white man.

Back in 1947, in the United States of America, the "Land of the Free," no first class hotel would rent a room to a "mixed-race" couple since at that time in U.S. history, it was against the law to do so. From the 1860s until the late 1950s, most states (not just the southern states) had laws prohibiting non-white men from marrying white women. The federal government had a law, known as the Mann Act, prohibiting non-white men from transporting white women across state lines.

But this Chinaman was about to transport a white woman not just across some state line, but all the way across the entire United States of America, and then he was going to continue on with her to the Territory of Hawaii, and on top of that, he was going to marry her!

I believe that being refused a room had a profound psychological effect on him for the rest of his life. Here he was, bringing his French bride-to-be and her five and a half-year-old bastard kid all the way from France, only to be looked down on and refused a room at a first class hotel. Talk about being embarrassed; talk about the anger and humiliation he must have felt on that night. "Losing face:" a very bad thing for Chinese folks! Reginald Lau, the Chinaman, would now spend the rest of his life proving to everyone that he was not only as good as anyone else, but actually better.

Following several failed attempts at getting a room at other respectable hotels in New York City, the former United States Army Air Force lieutenant was finally able to rent a room at some run-down hotel located in the "colored" part of town in the Bronx. Welcome to America, Renée Mulier and bastard son; welcome to America, the Land of the Free! Oh, yeah, that's if you're white, that is.

The following day, Reginald (everyone called him "Reggie"), Renée, and I boarded a flight from New York City to Honolulu, Hawaii, where we were met by Reggie's brother-in-law, another strange-looking Chinaman, who went by the name of Leighton Chu. Uncle Leighton drove us to his house, which was located at 1258 Nihoa Street in upper Honolulu, and we spent the night there.

The next day, Reggie drove us to an area of Honolulu called "Chinatown." Sitting in the back seat, I looked out the car window and what do you know? Everyone looked like Reggie. Tall, dark-skinned, mostly skinny, and they all had alien, slanted eyes. What kind of people were they, and where had they all come from? Until a couple of days ago, the only people I'd ever seen were French people. White skin, mostly brown or blond hair, normal, round eyes. Another thing—French people didn't go around smelling like some flower. (They actually smelled rather bad because they didn't bathe very often.)

Wedding photo, Renée and Reggie

I was left in the car while Renée and Reggie went into a Catholic church and got married. Years later, Renée would reveal to me that before she was "allowed" to become the wife of Mr. Reginald Lau, she had to sign a marriage contract. It was either sign or be sent back to France on the next plane. The marriage contract which, by the way, was written in English, a language she didn't speak at the time, read:

> "I, Renée Marthe Mulier of Lille, France, upon signing this legal document, followed by legal marriage to Reginald Karn Fan Lau, hereby agree that, as the wife of Reginald Karn Fan Lau, I shall perform all duties as follows:
>
> - Cook and prepare all meals,
> - Take care of future children
> - Maintain the household in good order
> - Perform wifely sexual duties as required and as requested.
>
> I agree to obey all said wishes and demands of my husband, Reginald K. F. Lau. Honolulu, T.H., 1947."

After Renée got married to Reggie Lau, we spent a week in Honolulu. Then we took a flight to a place called Hilo Town, located on the island of Hawaii—the "Big Island," as they call it. We were met at the airport by several relatives of Reggie and driven to a large, white two-story house located at 1321 Kinoole Street, where we were introduced to the rest of the Lau clan.

1321 Kinoole St.

Being suddenly whisked away to Hilo from Lille was a big change for Renée and me. Nobody else in the house spoke French (Reggie's French was very basic), and we didn't speak English or Chinese. I'd been used to having lots of French kids my age around to play with. Now there were only Chinese adults.

Besides Reggie, the other people in the house were:

• Kam Hoon Goo Lau, Reggie's widowed mother. (We called her "Nanny.") She was always nice to me. She could only speak Chinese, but always had a smile for me, patted me on the head, and never spoke harshly to me or scolded me.

- Ralph Lau, Reggie's older brother, owner of the family business, "Hilo Dry Goods," and wife Beatrice. When Reggie went off to fight in the war, their father had turned ownership of Hilo Dry Goods and other family properties over to Ralph. After that, Reggie had to work for his brother as the bookkeeper, and there was unspoken resentment between them.

- Karn Song Lau, Reggie's brother, and wife Emma. He had a store called "The Candy Box" in Hilo. It was the first one of its kind in Hilo Town. He produced and sold chocolate candies that contained macadamia nuts.

- Nit Lin Lau, Reggie's sister, single. Worked as an accountant in downtown Hilo.

- Nit Wan Lau, Reggie's sister, single. She had arthritis and stayed at home.

- Nit Me Lau, Reggie's sister, married to Leighton Chu.

- Nit Ung, Reggie's sister, and husband, Souy Hoy Wong, a high school teacher.

3

Turning Chinese

One of the hardest things for me to adjust to in Hawaii was the food. I'd suddenly gone from stale bread, red wine diluted with water, and an occasional rabbit to an endless supply of food: steamed rice, noodles, beef, pork, chicken, *lop chung* (Chinese sausage), steamed buns, hot tea, all sorts of Chinese vegetables, tangerines, apples, pears, lychee, pineapple, and mango. Then there was soda pop, cake, ice cream, Chinese cookies, and so on. For a starving orphan, learning to eat three big meals a day was a challenge, and though I'd later learn to love Chinese food, it was hard to get used to it at first.

Also, at the orphanage, I hadn't been taught to chew my food properly. As a result, I often gagged when I tried to swallow. No matter, though. Reggie immediately made it a rule that I was to remain at the dinner table until I'd completely eaten every bit of food off my plate, and I mean every single grain of rice. The longest I stayed at the dinner table struggling to finish my dinner was two and a half hours. Two and a half hours of sitting at the large dining table all by myself, chewing and gagging.

Every so often, when chicken was served for dinner, my aunts Nit Lin, Nit Wan, Nit Me, and Nit Ung, (I called them Nit One, Two, Three and Four—not to their faces, of course), the Nit Sisters, would have their fun by making me eat the "Pope's Nose." That, by the way, is the chicken's ass. The witty Nits always got a good laugh out of that. "Here, let's give little Bernard the Pope's Nose! Ha, ha, ha!"

Nit Lin, Nit Wan, Nit Me

I was served the chicken's ass every time chicken was served for dinner, without fail, and chicken was served often. But thanks to Reggie and the Nit Sisters, I now totally enjoy eating Chinese food, and yes, that includes the "Pope's Nose" (especially grilled on a skewer). Put any kind of Chinese food in front of me and I'll eat every bit of it with great relish whether it's grilled chicken ass, fried fish lips, boneless or deep-fried chicken feet, or eyeballs and cheeks of steamed rock cod ... It's all good, even when I have no idea in hell what it is that I'm eating.

The family always ate dinner together at a big table that seated eight people. There were strict rules about how I was to conduct myself:

- Request permission prior to sitting at the dinner table.

- Sit straight in my chair, eyes always on my plate.

- Absolutely no talking.

Order of eating was as follows:

1. Meat

2. Rice

3. Vegetables

4. Repeat until food is all eaten.

There was to be no drinking of milk to wash down my food.

Cutting of meat was to be done as follows:

1. Take fork in left hand

2. Take knife in right hand

3. Cut a portion of the meat

4. Put knife down

5. Transfer fork to right hand

6. Pick up meat and put in mouth

7. Chew meat 15 times before swallowing

8. Repeat above procedure

Once dinner was finished, I had to request Reggie's permission to leave the table: "May I please be excused?" Then I went to the kitchen to wash the dishes, dry them with a towel, and put them away.

Later, when I was around 8 or 9 years old, Reggie would make me chew a big chunk of dried abalone every night while I was drying the dishes. Ever try chewing a chunk of dried abalone? For an 8-year-old it's no easy task. Reggie's reasoning was that I'd learn to chew better. Of course, he made me not only chew, but swallow the damned thing as well. And he never let me choose the piece I wanted; he always made sure I got the big one.

A few months after our arrival, Reggie legally adopted me, and I went from being "Bernard Daniel Mulier" to "Bernard Mulier Lau," all quickly accomplished with the signing of some legal document. That was good, I guess, as I was now a naturalized U.S. citizen and couldn't ever be deported back to France. I was no longer a little French bastard; I was Bernard Lau, the legal son of Reginald Lau who would now try to bring me up as a respectable Chinese boy.

To start my transformation into the perfect Chinese son, the first thing Reggie did was change me from being left-handed to being right-handed. The reason was that Chinese kids are not left-handed. So now that I was being brought up Chinese, I'd have to be right-handed.

Some experts believe that forcing a child to change from being left-handed to being right-handed can impair mental development, and sure enough, from that time on, I tended to get confused when doing any sort of physical activity. I had difficulties with reading and couldn't retain what I learned in school. I couldn't even remember my multiplication tables (still can't) or add or subtract numbers in my head. Even now, I have to use my fingers and toes.

I was no longer allowed to use a pillow in bed. Reggie's reasoning was that men in the military don't use pillows, so why should I?

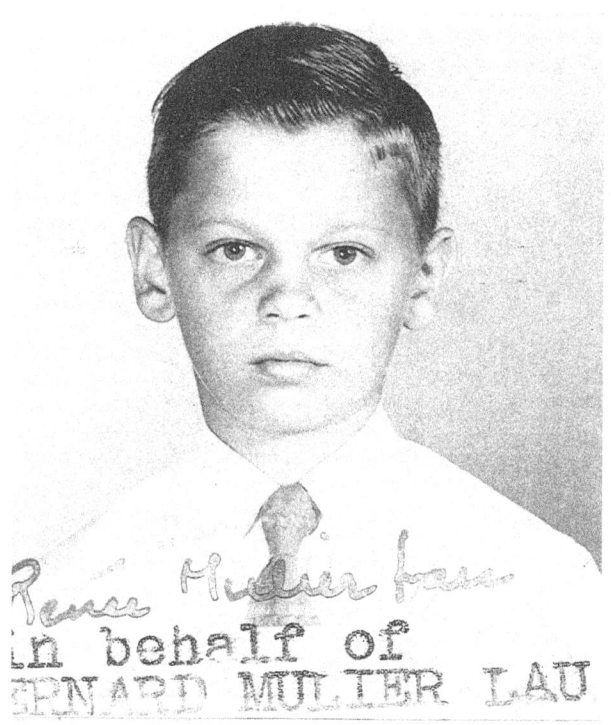

The author when he first came to the U.S.

ested in listening to her explanations. In time, she learned to handle Reggie's verbal abuse with the aid of a bottle of Muscatel.

The first time he spanked me was because of something I said. I remember Reggie poking his head into the kitchen, where his mother and Renée were cooking, and saying, "Good stuff. Smells good!" I'd followed Reggie to the kitchen door and, in my little six-year-old voice, I repeated what I'd heard him say: "Good stuff. Smells good!" Well, next thing I knew, I was picked up by the back of my shirt, dragged into the living room, thrown across Reggie's lap, pants pulled down, and spanked. Spanked for what? For repeating what I'd just heard Reggie say. After that, I never felt comfortable around him.

I was ordered to always look directly into Reggie's eyes whenever I spoke to him or he to me. "God damn it, Speed,[1] look me in the eyes when I talk to you!"

Reggie ruled his household with an iron hand. His rules were absolute, and there were a lot of them, such as the ones for answering the phone. I was to say "Hello, this is 3155, Lau's residence, Bernard Lau speaking. Whom do you wish to speak to?" If the phone call was for me, I was allowed exactly three minutes for the call. Reggie had placed a clock next to the phone for that purpose.

I had to be in bed by eight o'clock sharp every night. There I lay awake listening to Reggie cussing Renée out for whatever it was he thought she'd done wrong that day. He belittled her, told her how stupid she was, called her a dumb *haole*.[2] Sometimes Renée would try to justify herself, but Reggie wasn't inter-

Me, Reggie, and Renée, shortly after arrival in U.S.

---
[1] He started calling me "Speed" because I took so long to eat.
[2] A Hawaiian word meaning "white person" or "outsider."

For more routine spankings, Reggie used a leather slipper. By the age of seven and from then on, he spanked me quite often. He'd make me bend over my bed and have at it. Sometimes he did it five times, sometimes ten. With each whack I was required to count out the number. "One! Two! Three! ..." I'd scream and cry. I'd sob, plead, and try to cover my butt with my hands because it hurt so much. Reggie just grabbed my hands and kept hitting me, adding another whack each time I tried to protect myself.

As I got older, following the discipline, Reggie would sit me down and lecture me. I don't know which I hated more, the spankings or those damn lectures. I developed the trick of mentally visualizing a flag on a tall flag pole. I focused on the flapping of the flag. No special flag, just a flag waving in the wind on a tall flagpole. That was how I tuned out Reggie's lectures.

I remember one in particular—the "solid foundation" lecture. Reggie would tell me how I had to have a solid foundation by doing good in school. He'd say something like, "When you build a house, you have to build the house on solid ground. If you build a house on sand, then the house won't last and will eventually fall down. That's why you have to have a solid foundation." Boy, I hated that lecture. House on a solid foundation. Why? So you can beat the crap out of a kid?

Even a minor infraction, like not doing my homework right or not standing or sitting properly (that is, military fashion), could get me a spanking. Reggie had a military mentality. Discipline was the order of the day, and that meant every day!

At six years of age, I was enrolled in St. Joseph's, a Catholic school. Meeting other kids my own age and hanging out with them, I started learning to speak English. Unfortunately (from Reggie's point of view), the kind of English that I was learning there was what we in Hawaii call "Pidgin." Reggie didn't like Pidgin. He prided himself on his ability to speak "correct" English. Whenever I'd forget and say something in Pidgin, I'd get a spanking. Finally, to save me from bad English, Reggie took me out of the Catholic school and enrolled me in Hilo Riverside School.

The author and classmates at Hilo Riverside School

When I was around eight years old, Reggie moved us into a house located at 15B Lanihuli Street.

15B Lanihuli St., Hilo, Hawaii

I now had a new baby brother named Craig who was only a few months old.

Once, when Renée had taken me and Craig shopping with her and we got back to the house, she had to carry some groceries upstairs and left me alone in the car with Craig. Back in those days, there was always a cigarette lighter mounted on the dashboard. Push the knob in, wait a few seconds, and the knob popped out. You pulled the knob out and you had a red-hot, glowing branding iron in your hands.

I pushed the lighter in, waited a few moments, pulled it out, and without a thought, pressed the glowing end of it onto the right shin of Craig's leg. Craig screamed. Renée came running down to the car and saw what I'd just done. I was scared as hell. I pleaded with Renée not to tell Reggie about this. What would he do to me? Craig was Reggie's first son, and to the Chinese, the first-born son is very important. I guess I got spanked, though I don't have any memory of it.

Craig Lau

Craig, was one of the nicest, most caring people I've ever met. Later, he became a steward for Pan Am and, in the early 80s, he died of AIDS. Of course, no Chinese kid could be gay, so he died of "hepatitis." He was Reggie's first male child, so he was given the "jade ring" when he turned 18, according to Chinese custom. He liked to cook, travel, and shop for Asian collectibles (sort of like me). Craig was only half-French, but he seemed more "French" than Reggie's other sons, Marc and Lance. They turned out to be more "Chinese" in personality.

Much later in Honolulu, I met one of Craig's roommates. The guy was probably 20 years older than Craig and, well, we've all seen really "gay-type" individuals; the type that speak with a lisp, the hand gestures, and body language … That was Craig's roommate. I was present when Reggie met him, and he acted like nothing was out of the ordinary. Me, I was chuckling to myself.

Around the time I was ten years old, Reggie went to Fort Benning, Georgia for some sort of officers' school. Renée, Craig, and I went to Long Beach, California, along with Renée's sister, Jacqueline, and her husband, Uncle Jan, who was Dutch. Long Beach was OK. Endless beach; the Pike was very cool. I collected empty soda bottles on the beach and turned them in for 5 cents each. Not too bad a way to make a little change.

Once again, I went to a Catholic school. St. Anthony, it was called. I had a nun for a teacher, Sister Barbara, who was an old witch. Used to keep me after school a lot. I never did my school work; never really could learn for some reason. I'd try to study every so often, but no luck. I couldn't remember anything, so I just quit trying.

One day, Uncle Jan brought home a cute little newborn lamb, and we named it "Kiki." That little lamb played with me just like it was a puppy. I used to feed him with a baby bottle, and he used to lie next to me while he slept. It might sound strange to say that we were friends, but after all, what's a friend if it isn't someone you get along with and enjoy being with?

Usually Renée or her sister did the cooking, but one evening, Uncle Jan made dinner. We were all sitting at the table in the living room, when Jan brought in a large platter and placed it on the table. There, right in front of me, on a serving platter, lay Kiki. My uncle had killed, butchered, and roasted little Kiki in a sauce with mushrooms, onions, and carrots. Poor little Kiki. No one ate dinner that night except my uncle. I was just lucky that Reggie wasn't there. I know he'd have made me eat Kiki, and I'm sure I'd have thrown up.

In 1951 we went back to Hilo and lived at 15B Lanihuli Street again. It was a pretty nice house built over a garage with an open basement, so that the residents could hang up their clothes to dry. (This was before dryers were available.) It rained a lot in Hilo, so an open basement was a good thing. Renée washed all the clothing by hand in the basement sink, using a wooden washboard.

Later, Reggie bought her a washing machine. It didn't have a spin cycle, so you had to feed the washed clothes through two rubber rollers to squeeze out the water. Then the clothes would be hung on a line in the basement for several days till they were dry.

Every Sunday Reggie would take the trash to a garbage dump. The dump was just an open field owned by the county, located on the outskirts of town. I was in the basement one Sunday afternoon helping Reggie gather up the trash to take to the dump, when I saw him take the old washboard and shatter it with his foot. When I asked him why he'd broken the washboard, his answer was, "I paid good money for that washboard, and nobody else is going to use it." You see, there were always poor folks at the dump, going through the garbage, looking for things that could be used.

After returning to Hawaii from Long Beach, Reggie had me go to summer school. Before starting I took a test and got a score of 55%. After two months of private tutoring, I took the test again, and this time I got 45%. Reggie was livid; he screamed at me; "How the hell can you get a lower grade after two months of tutoring? How the hell is that possible?" To this day, I can't really explain it. I never was any good at test-taking. But he taught me a lesson that I took with me for the rest of my life: pass the test, no matter what.

So I went back to Riverside School and had to repeat the 4th grade. I was embarrassed as hell, and my embarrassment continued all the way through high school because, every day, I had to meet the kids I started 1st grade with, and they were now a class ahead of me.

About three years after moving back to Lanihuli Street Reggie bought a half-acre lot above Hilo Town. It had been a sugarcane field before, and he had to have it bulldozed and cleared. A lot of the clearing had to be done by hand, and I was to put in many years of hard work on that. He later bought a lot of tropical plants and giant hapuu ferns to landscape the property. Really looked nice.

It became my job to keep up the yard. I weeded, mowed, and watered twice a week. With no shortage of food and working like a slave in the fields, I began to bulk up. Without trying to, I was getting stronger and tougher.

I also became Reggie's houseboy. I had to set the table before meals, clear the table following meals, wash and dry all the dishes, and put them away. And I was given the task of cleaning the bathroom every Saturday. Following that, once a month, I had to wax the oak floors in the living and dining rooms by hand. During the summer I had to work in the yard all day.

Reggie would come home for lunch at ten o'clock. I'd hear him driving up to the house when he was still a half mile or so away, and the sound always made me feel nauseous. After he entered the house, I had to go back inside, present myself before him, and say "Hello, Dad." When it was time for Reggie to go back to work, I had to go up to him again and say "Goodbye, Dad." I'd catch hell if I forgot to do that.

I was the babysitter for my three brothers, Craig, Lance, and Marc. I hated babysitting. I remember one night, when Reggie and Renée were out for the evening, I had to babysit all three of my brothers at the same time. Marc, the youngest, wouldn't stop crying. He was maybe a year old, and he was driving me crazy. I never could stand the sound of kids crying; it drove me up the wall. I yelled at Marc, I shook his stroller, and finally, I took him out of the stroller, held him up, and shook him. I now know that it's a big no-no to shake a kid, but back then, that's what I did.

When I was in intermediate school, Reggie ordered me to try out for the basketball team, so I did. About ten minutes into the tryouts it was my turn to show how well I could do some simple drills that we'd just been shown. Not only did I not do well; I was pathetic. I was so bad that everyone just laughed at me. I remember shaking my head and leaving the gym, deeply shamed. I'm sure that Reggie was very unhappy too, when his Army Reserve buddy, Mr. Nakamura, the basketball coach, told him about my dismal performance.

The author babysitting his three brothers

You see, Chinese folks like to brag about their kids. It's a game of one-upmanship. Someone says, "Well, my son is a doctor." And the other person will say, "Well, my kid's a lawyer;" that sort of thing. But when it came to me, Reggie didn't have anything to brag about. In fact, what he had on his hands was a kid who was flunking out of school and wasn't any good at sports. Reggie must have been at his wits' end with me.

Throughout my school years, I'd get Cs, Ds, and Fs on my report card. I just couldn't retain anything I read. I used to think to myself, "When I die, I hope they cut my brain open to see what was wrong with me." I knew I wasn't like the "normal" kids. I did go out for track in high school, and I was pretty fair at the 880-yard dash, which we ran barefoot. I was good in wood shop; I made a small working guillotine and a coffin. Cool projects!

I didn't quite fit in with the local kids: I was a *haole* with a Chinese name. Lots of folks were confused by that. Often on the first day of school the teacher would call out the roll, and when she got to "Bernard Lau," I'd raise my hand. Expecting to see a Chinese kid, she'd ignore me and continue to look around the classroom, calling out "Bernard Lau ... Bernard Lau?"

4

Bad Dog

Several times, Reggie bragged to me about his sexual exploits. For instance, he told me that when he was young and used to take girls out on dates, if the girl didn't want to put out, he'd drive her way out in the country and tell her to get out of the car. Then, every ten minutes or so, he'd drive by to taunt her and see if she'd changed her mind yet about having sex. Nice going, Reggie. In today's world, we call that "date rape."

Lt. Lau

He had no problem telling his teenage son how, when he was stationed in France, he used to go to brothels. He bragged to me that, although the GIs would have to form a line outside a whorehouse and wait their turn to get in, he and his fellow officers would get to go to the head of the line because "rank has its privileges."

He also told me about how, when they went to night clubs, there was a game they sometimes played with the bar girls. They'd balance a silver dollar on its edge and tell the gal that she could keep it if she could pick it up with her pussy. This was just after the war, and there was still food rationing. Some of the gals working in those clubs were desperately poor and would do almost anything for money. Reggie added that, sometimes, his fellow officers would "play a joke on the gals:" they'd heat up the silver dollar with a cigarette lighter. He thought that was funny.

According to Reggie, the Chinese were best at everything and that included torture. He told me in detail how they'd put bamboo slivers under the fingernails of their captives and then gently tap on the end of the bamboo. Then they'd set fire to it. He also described different methods of Chinese water torture. I don't know why he used to tell me about stuff like that. I guess it made him feel powerful and important.

Once, when I was 15 years old, I made the mistake of talking back to Reggie. It was a nice, sunny day in Hilo, and I'd been ordered to mow the lawn. I started mowing, but a short time later my friend Michael and his dad showed up and invited me to go swimming with them. I figured, hey, why not? I could continue mowing when I got back from swimming. No big deal, right? Wrong.

Several hours later, swimming over with, I was back mowing the lawn. Reggie came home, went into the back yard, saw that I hadn't finished, and demanded to know why. I explained that Michael and his dad had come by and invited me to go swimming. I looked him in the eyes and said, "What's the big deal?"

Well, I guess that was the wrong thing to say. He started chewing me out, calling me a son of a bitch, and somehow the words "Well, if I'm a son of a bitch, you must be the bitch because you're my dad" came out. For the first time in my life, I'd talked back to Reggie. I said it right to his face, looking him square in the eyes, just like he'd trained me to do. He cursed me, saying, "You're not my son," and then came across with a fast right hook that hit me square in the mouth.

Tasting blood in my mouth, I stumbled back a few steps and saw flashes of colors I'd never seen before. I put my right hand up to my mouth; my lip was swelling rapidly. I shook my head a few times and tried to focus on Reggie who was standing a few feet in front of me. Standing straight and clenching my teeth, I made a fist with both hands and stared at him defiantly. I was pissed and ready to do battle. It didn't matter if he kicked my ass or not; I wasn't taking any more of his abuse.

I think he realized that I was ready to fight because, cursing under his breath, he turned and stomped back into the house. I just stood there spitting blood from my mouth. I started the lawnmower up again and continued mowing. I was mad and, biting down on my cut lip, I got madder and madder.

Then I had an idea. I started hitting myself in the mouth with my closed fist and kept hitting harder and harder while I continued to mow the lawn. After I finished mowing, I went into the bathroom and looked at myself in the mirror. My lip was swollen and discolored with hints of blue and purple, but no more bleeding. "Great job, Bernard," I thought to myself. I was satisfied that I'd made it look really bad.

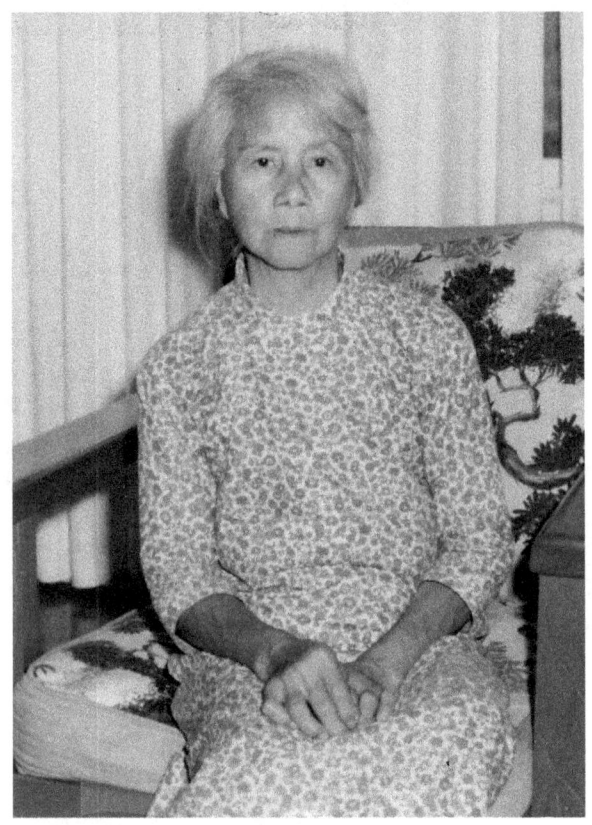

Nanny

You see, it was Mother's Day, and we were going to Reggie's mother's house for dinner. All the family members would be there to celebrate. Yep, the entire Lau clan would be there, and they'd be asking, "What happened to Bernard's lip?" I was going to enjoy this, and I did. Reggie caught hell from his mom. Nanny had always had a soft spot for me and didn't approve of the way Reggie treated me. I remember that night I had chicken ass with black bean sauce. Boy, did it taste good!

When I was 15, I met a gal in school called Gloria, who lived in a foster home because her mom didn't want her. One evening I got invited over to her house, and she kissed me right on the lips. It was the first time

I'd ever kissed a girl. My head spun, I got weak in the knees, and couldn't talk. It was a magical moment. When I got home, Reggie looked at me and, seeing I was in a daze, demanded to know if I'd been drinking or taking drugs.

Age 16

After Gloria, there was Lillian, a beautiful Hawaiian-Chinese-Filipino girl. Lillian and two of her sisters also lived in a foster home with an elderly couple. I went steady with her for some time. Then I had a crush on another Filipino girl named Lourdes. I hung out with her a few times, but could never tell her that I liked her. I was kind of shy around girls and couldn't express my feelings to them.

Reggie never cared much for the company I kept. He thought the orphan girls I went out with were "low-class." But, for some reason, I wasn't interested in the *haole* girls from rich families that belonged to the local yacht club. Once, he said to me, "You know, Bernard, when it comes to the people you hang around with, the gals you go out with, you don't scrape the bottom of the barrel; you scrape under the barrel." Well, maybe the reason I scraped under the barrel was because that's where I too, bastard that I was, came from.

Reggie tried to do his part, though. When I started going out with girls, he gave me the lecture about sex. Actually he didn't have much to say. He just brought out a broom (green handle, I recall) ripped open a packet of Trojans and unrolled a condom onto the broom handle. Then he took it off and threw it away. That was it; all a kid needs to know.

When I was 16 or 17 years old, I had a dog named "Buddy." He was mixed breed; what we in Hawaii call a "Poi dog." I didn't tie him up, but he usually stayed around the house anyway. Well, one nice, sunny day, I rode my bicycle over to my friend Michael Frenz's house, which was located maybe a mile and a half up the street. Michael's dad, a tough German guy from the old country, owned and operated Frank's Foods and provided beef, hot dogs, sausages, etc., to the local markets in and about Hilo Town. At the Frenzs', I often rode Mike's horse, "Big Red." Mr. Frenz had acres of pasture land for the cattle he raised, and I'd gallop all over on Big Red, riding without a saddle.

This particular day, my dog Buddy followed me from a distance as I rode my bike to Mike's house. I never noticed him. A few days later, an angry Mr. Frenz drove up to our house and called Reggie out. "Mr. Lau," Mr. Frenz yelled out; "Your dog killed two of my ducks. (Mr. Frenz had several ducks running loose on his property.) Mr. Lau, you gotta pay for my two dead ducks. You owe me a total of $8.00."

Reggie didn't argue with Mr. Frenz. He just got the $8.00 from his room and paid him. Mr. Frenz pocketed the money and drove off, leaving the two dead ducks at Reggie's feet.

I was there watching all this, but I didn't say a word. I figured that if Mr. Frenz said he saw my dog Buddy chasing his ducks, then it must have been true. OK, I thought; "bad doggy." Now, I'd have to put him on a leash. No more running away, chasing and killing ducks. But Reggie had other ideas.

"Bernard, you get your damn dog tied up on that clothes line pole. Tie that dog up tight, so he has no room to move around." I did as Reggie ordered and tied Buddy up to the metal pole, leaving maybe two inches of slack in the rope. That done, Reggie instructed me on how Buddy was to be punished for being a "duck killer."

"Bernard, I want you to tie one of the ducks around your damn dog's neck, and I want you to whip him with the other duck." I stood there, stunned and unable to say a word. I was thinking: "Reggie wants me to whip my own dog with a dead duck? Hey, Buddy's my pal; we play together, we have fun together. I can't whip Buddy. No way."

I picked up one of the ducks, but then I hesitated. Reggie got pissed and started yelling at me. "God damn it, you either do as you're told, or I'll whip that dog myself." Reggie picked up the dead duck and started to whip Buddy with it. Buddy panicked and tried to get away, but he was tied up so tight he could hardly move. Reggie kept on whipping Buddy. Buddy rolled his eyes and started to yelp in terror. Then Reggie stopped and turned to face me. He handed me the duck and ordered me to shove it into Buddy's mouth. He told me to whip Buddy ten times every 15 minutes for the next two hours, then he stomped off into the house.

I stood there in front of Buddy. I felt sick to my stomach. I couldn't hit my own dog. Buddy was my friend. But I was afraid that if I didn't, Reggie would come up with something even worse. Slowly, I picked up one of the dead ducks and tied it around Buddy's neck. He looked up at me with big, sad eyes. He had no idea what it was all about.

Buddy was a dog, damn it. It's natural for dogs to hunt and kill game. So, OK, Buddy shouldn't have gone off and killed two of Mr. Frenz's ducks. But what good was it going to do to tie him up and whip him for the next two hours with a dead duck?

Standing in front of Buddy, I put the other duck into his mouth. I said, "No. Bad dog!" and started hitting him with it. Buddy was going crazy trying to get away. He was yelping, he was trying to slip the rope from around his head, but he only managed to choke himself. He was in a state of utter panic. I counted out: "seven—eight—nine—ten," as I hit him.

I threw the duck down, crying and cursing Reggie. I wanted to hit something.

I continued to hit Buddy with the dead duck every 15 minutes. Finally, the two hours were up. I just walked off down Pohakulani Street, leaving Buddy tied up with the dead duck around his neck. I was gone for over an hour, just walking around and crying.

Finally, I came back, went into the back yard, and walked over to where Buddy was. I tried talking softly, tried to pet him and say how sorry I was for having beaten him. Buddy, however, wanted no part of me and tried to get as far away from me as he could. He was no longer my friend. He was frightened of me.

Reggie came out of the house and ordered me to leave Buddy tied up with the duck around his neck overnight. I did as ordered.

The next morning, I went out to untie him from the tree. As I got near him, he kept his head down and shook in fear. After I untied him, he didn't run off; he just lay there with his head on the ground, looking up at me and shaking. He wouldn't eat his food or drink his water. He just lay there under the tree I'd tied him to, lay there with his eyes closed and his head on the ground.

Buddy died a couple days later, still lying under that tree, frightened and alone. I carried his body into the back yard, dug a deep hole, and buried him. With a small, homemade wooden cross I marked his grave and said my final goodbye.

I should probably say something good about Reggie, so, OK, here goes. Reggie was a good provider, the best any little bastard child could hope for. He brought me back to good health and got my buck teeth fixed. He attempted to give me an education. Maybe he meant well, but he was a military man and ran his household as such. His own father had been a wife-beater and a mean drunk, and I guess, compared to that, he wasn't so bad.

Capt. Reginald Lau

5

Tohei

It was a beautiful hot summer day at Hapuna Beach, which is on the west side of Hawaii along the Kona Coast. The annual Boy Scout summer camp was in session, and each week, scout troops from various parts of the Big Island would spend an entire week camped out at Hapuna Beach in pup tents, living right there on the most beautiful beach on the island. It was half a mile long and 200 feet wide with no rocks and no trash; just pure white sand.

I was only 14 years old at the time, but I was the camp's swimming and lifesaving instructor. It was one of the best instructor jobs. While the other instructors and scout masters were teaching compass-reading, survival skills, tracking, knot-tying, and other merit badge subjects, I stayed nice and cool in the warm, clear water of the Pacific Ocean.

During the day it was all classes and study, but come dark, we'd sit around the bonfire, listening to the local Hawaiians tell legends about Pele the Volcano Goddess, Lono the Shark God, and the angry, fallen Hawaiian warriors of the great King Kamehameha, whose earthbound spirits lingered still in a cave at the south end of the beach.

Later, we'd run around in the warm darkness of the night, playing capture the flag, or sending the tenderfoot scouts on a "snipe hunt." It worked like this: each tenderfoot (probationary boy scout) was given a burlap sack and told to hold it open at ground level. Meanwhile, the older scouts were supposed to beat the brush and scare the snipes into the bag. After making sure the tenderfeet understood that they had to stay perfectly still with their burlap sack held open until the snipes ran inside, the older scouts went back to the campfire and had a good laugh.

What fun times those were, growing up in Hawaii.

Walking alone along the beach one afternoon, I noticed a group of maybe a dozen Japanese boys gathered in a semi-circle at the north end of the beach, doing what looked like some sort of a martial art. Intrigued, I went over and watched them, trying to stay unnoticed. A slightly older Japanese fellow, maybe in his late 20s or early 30s, seemed to be the center of attention.

Noticing that I was watching, he invited me to come and join the group. I approached cautiously. Although I'd grown up on the Big Island, the locals still considered me a *haole*, and these kids were all Japanese or a mixture of the local melting pot of various races.

This man, who I guessed was the *sensei* (teacher), had a pleasant smile on his face. "Come, you try hit me," he said to me. I looked around at the group for a few seconds. Everyone was smiling; some of them were actually chuckling and elbowing each other. I didn't feel in any way threatened, so, looking back at the instructor, I planted my feet, made a fist with my right hand, and threw a punch at his face.

Next thing I knew, I was flipped onto my butt and ended up on the warm sand looking up at this guy, who, by the way, was still smiling. He was totally at ease, totally relaxed, and confident. Reaching out his hand, he helped me up and once again said, "You try hit me one more time please."

I stood for a few seconds, brushing the sand off my butt, and while doing so, thought to myself, "OK, man, you're asking for it; this time I'm gonna hit you." I focused on him, put my chin down, puckered my lips, clenched my right fist, paused, and with double the force, power, and speed, I again threw a punch at his face. But when my fist reached the spot where his face should have been, there was no longer anything there. I felt a slight touch on my wrist, lost my balance, and was once again flipped onto my butt.

Damn it, I thought, how the heck does he do that? Must be some sort of *jujutsu* trick. I'd heard talk in school about Japanese *jujutsu*, but had never witnessed it personally.

The Japanese boys standing around were all looking down at me and laughing, not in a disrespectful way, but having a good time seeing the *haole* boy get flipped onto his butt, not once, but twice.

Standing up without any assistance this time, I again brushed the warm Hapuna sand off my butt. The man who'd just flipped me came up and, still smiling, introduced himself.

"My name Koichi Tohei. I from Japan. I teacher of aikido." He continued, "Aikido non-fighting Japanese art for self defense. Aikido for defend only, not for hurt attacking person. Protect yourself, but no hurt other person. Aikido good for develop mind and body. Aikido be very good for you. Where you live?" he asked me.

"I live in Hilo, on the other side of the island," I answered.

"Ah, Hilo, very good. Next week I go Hilo Town for teach aikido there. You come my class, please. I teach you; you please come. I teach at tea house in Hilo. I invite you come my class."

The boy scout summer camp would be over in a few days so I decided to go.

"OK, sir," I answered, "I'll be there. Where'd you say you'd be teaching; at a tea house?"

"Yes. Here; I give you what day, time, and tea house location." Mr. Tohei extended his hand and we shook; all the while, he was smiling and totally at ease. Making a slight bow of respect and thanking him for the invitation, I turned and walked off towards the water, wondering what the heck had just happened moments earlier.

Little did I realize at the time that fate had just placed me on the path of aikido, and that it was to become a part of me for the rest of my life.

After returning to Hilo several days later, I told my best friend Michael Frenz about my aikido experience at Hapuna and meeting Tohei. He was interested too, so we both went to the tea house, which was located on the grounds of a 30-acre Japanese garden called "Queen Liliuokalani Park and Gardens."

The door was shut and there were no windows. I knocked twice, gently. Seconds later, the sliding door opened, and there, standing before us, was a short, heavy-set Japanese man sporting a crew cut and dressed in some sort of Japanese garb: a white judo jacket and baggy black trousers (called a *hakama*). This guy looked like something right out of a Japanese samurai movie.

Shoryoan Teahouse

"What you guys want?" were the first words out of his mouth. I started explaining to this samurai-looking guy that, a week earlier, I'd been invited personally by

Mr. Tohei to an aikido class that he'd be teaching here at the tea house. The samurai guy started saying something not overly-welcoming, when suddenly, Tohei appeared.

Recognizing me immediately, he smiled a broad smile and said, "Ah, so. I happy see you come. I remember you, Hapuna Beach before, yes? Yes, I remember you. Please, you come in. Your friend too, come in."

As Michael and I entered the tea house, Tohei turned and spoke briefly to the samurai guy. It sounded like he was scolding him, and the broad smile briefly vanished from Tohei's face. We followed him into the tea house, where we were formally introduced to the samurai guy, plus three other Japanese adults.

Tohei *sensei* and the four Hilo black belts, 1955

The samurai guy turned out to be Mr. Nonaka, a newly-promoted black belt who would soon become the chief instructor of aikido in Hawaii. Next, we met Mr. Nagata, also a black belt, who was the current chief instructor. The two other gentlemen, Mr. Iwasa and Mr. Takaki, were also black belts.

Wow, Tohei, the teacher, and four other Japanese guys who were all black belts. I was impressed. Here we were, two skinny *haole* kids, setting foot in a Japanese teahouse and being introduced to four aikido black belts who were the initial cadre of aikido instructors outside of Japan.

This was in the year 1955. Michael and I were in fact the first two *haole* boys in Hawaii, and in the greater United States for that matter, to be introduced to the self-defense art of aikido.

Following the introductions, we were each handed a white judo uniform (called a *gi*) to change into. However, we didn't get any of those neat *hakama* that made you look like a samurai because they could only be worn after you made black belt. Darn it. Well, patience, Bernard; that would come in time.

Quickly, we changed and joined the Japanese guys in the *tatami* room of the tea house. *Tatami*, which are made out of rice straw, measure about 3' x 6'. In Japan and Hawaii, they're used in lieu of gym mats in martial arts training halls. The area of the *tatami* room in the teahouse was equivalent to 12 tatami, making it around 12' x 18'. That may seem small to a Westerner, but for a traditional Japanese *tatami* room, that's on the big side.

My *gi* jacket fit fine, but my trousers only came to my knees. No matter though, all this was too exciting. Class was ready to start. Tohei clapped his hands together, signaling the four Japanese black belts to line up and go into the *seiza* (kneeling) position, facing him. Michael and I followed suit and knelt down directly behind the black belts. Tohei knelt facing us, made a bow, and we all bowed back. He began by speaking to the four Japanese guys in Japanese, but soon switched to English, maybe for the benefit of Michael and me.

He instructed us in the proper method of aikido breathing, and we practiced the breathing exercise for about five minutes. My knees and ankles were starting to hurt, and soon, both my feet fell asleep and started to hurt like hell. Eventually, Tohei clapped his hands. We bowed to him and tried to get up. My feet had fallen asleep, and I wobbled as I tried to stand. Michael didn't fare much better. Tohei looked over at us and smiled slightly.

Next, he led us in a sort of strange wrist-twisting exercise. This was followed by movement exercises, which Tohei made look somewhat like ballet. The guy sure was smooth; he must have been a good dancer.

Finally, came the part where we were taught aikido techniques. Tohei motioned for Nonaka to step up in front of him and throw a punch. Nonaka did as instructed and was immediately thrown on his rear. It was the same exact trick he'd pulled on me at Hapuna Beach. He demonstrated the technique several times, and then we were all told to practice among ourselves.

Well, Michael and I tried, but we had absolutely no idea where to start. Tohei came over and attempted to walk us through, but it was no good; we were hopeless. It was going to take some serious training for either of us to ever be able to perform the technique.

What got me was, he made it look so simple.

Several other techniques were demonstrated and the time passed. Finally, Tohei clapped twice and we knelt facing him. This time, we were instructed in meditation exercises, and once again, my legs hurt and my feet fell asleep. One final clap by Tohei. Then we all bowed to him, bowed to each other, and that was it. Class was over.

Tohei noticed that I'd brought a camera with me and asked if I wanted to have my picture taken with him. I said, "Yes," and he told Michael to take the picture. I stood to the left of him, straight and tall. However, he had something else in mind. He took hold of my right wrist and put some sort of a lock on it. That hurt! He told me to jump up as he applied the wrist lock. Hey, I thought, I don't need to be told. You put the lock on me and twist; I'm jumping up! Michael snapped a shot, the flash bulb went off, and I could smell the burning outer film on the burnt bulb.

Even after 55 years, I've somehow been able to keep a copy of that photograph in my possession. The 2" x 2" black and white negative has long since been lost, but the photo remains. It brings back memories of a time when, back in Hilo Town, in a tiny Japanese tea house on the grounds of the Queen Liliuokalani Park and Gardens, a skinny, 14-year-old boy whose *gi* trousers were too short for him became the first *haole* to take up aikido and was instructed by none other than Tohei *sensei* himself.

Following my introduction to the world of aikido that first night, I soon joined the Hilo Aikido Club. The training was headed by Chief Instructor Kiyoshi Nagata *sensei* and was held twice weekly in a large building down by the waterfront, known as the "Cow Palace." This extremely spacious one-story building was a martial arts training center and housed a boxing ring and a roped-off area for the practice of aikido.

First aikido lesson, 1955

The training area measured 15' x 24', which amounted to 20 *tatami*. A single mat, back in 1955, cost $5. Today, that single *tatami* shipped from Japan will start at $200.

Aikido training at the Cow Palace was held twice weekly in the early evening hours. During the first few months of my training, Tohei *sensei* often conducted the classes. He taught me and other beginners the first 50 basic techniques of aikido.

Sometimes on weekends, Tohei and another instructor would go to Honokaa Town, some forty miles to the north of Hilo along the Hamakua Coast. Often, I was invited to accompany them. I'd ride in the back seat, Tohei in the passenger seat, and either Mr. Nagata or Mr. Nonaka would drive.

Those were exciting days for me. There I was, a 14-year-old *haole* kid riding in a car with the famous Tohei *sensei* and other ranking black belt aikido instructors. I realized, even back then, how great a privilege it was for me. Aikido history was being made, and I was allowed to be a part of it.

We'd go to a judo *dojo* (martial arts training hall) in Honokaa, change into our *gis*, and Tohei would teach the class. I was often used as his *uke* (in aikido, the attacker and the one who takes the fall). Training would last three hours, and then we'd be taken out to lunch. I felt very special and privileged to be in such company.

Tohei was 33 years old, handsome, charismatic, and held the rank of 8th *dan* (8th-degree black belt). He was treated as royalty wherever he went. No request of his was ever denied, and he could do no wrong. He was attended to all day, and at night, he was always taken out to dinner, then drinking and merry-making. He was, after all, the personal emissary of Osensei, the one chosen to spread the teachings and philosophy of aikido to the United States.

He remained in Hilo Town for several months before returning to Honolulu, where he spent several more months teaching and spreading the arts of aikido. After that, he returned to the Hombu Dojo in Tokyo, where he was Chief Instructor for a year or two before returning to Hawaii again.

Tohei *sensei* in Hilo

I continued my aikido training, attending Tohei's classes twice a week at the Cow Palace. There weren't many students at the time, maybe eight or nine. There was Mr. Nagata, Mr. Nonaka, Mr. Iwasa, Mr. Takaki, Mr. Jimmy Uweki, a Portuguese guy who was also taking karate at the Honganji Buddhist Church in Hilo, a few other Japanese guys, Michael Frenz, and myself. That was the beginning of aikido in Hilo.

Tohei had also started an aikido group in Honolulu around the same time. Among the first students in that group were Yokiso Yamamoto, Sadao Yoshioka, Howard Sato, Bob Aoyagi, the Hirao brothers, who ran a *mochi*[1] shop near Aala Park at the foot of Hotel Street, Larry Mehau, a Honolulu police lieutenant, Meyer Goo, who would later become my mentor, Dr. Wakataki, an important backer of the Waialea Dojo, and a handful of other locals.

In early 1958, Tohei *sensei* returned to Hilo Town to continue the spread of aikido throughout the Hawaiian Islands.

---

[1] A traditional Japanese sweet made of pounded rice.
[2] One who practices aikido.

In June, under the direction and watchful eyes of Tohei himself, several aspiring *aikidoka*,[2] including myself, took their first test in aikido. One by one, Tohei called out the names of the 50 basic attack and response techniques in Japanese, and we had to demonstrate each one to his satisfaction. Remembering all the names of the techniques in Japanese was actually more difficult for me than performing the techniques themselves! Anyway, I passed and was promoted to 3rd *kyu*[3] and presented with a "Certificate of Rating in Aikido" by Tohei *sensei* himself.

In spite of having been in aikido for approximately three years and having passed 3rd *kyu*, I still didn't know how to use aikido techniques in a practical, self-defense situation. In aikido training, except for *randori*,[4] all attacks and the responses to them are pre-arranged.

I continued practicing aikido in Hilo till the tsunami hit on May 23, 1960. The tsunami was so forceful that it completely destroyed the Cow Palace.

3rd *kyu* certificate

---

[3]*Kyu* means "rank." In the U.S., holders of the rank of 3rd *kyu* wear a blue belt.
[4]Free-style attack of many on one.

Part II

A Girl in Every Port

6

A Higher Power

When I was 16, I sat down in my bedroom, took out a sheet of paper and wrote down what I wanted out of my future:

- Graduate from high school
- Join the Navy
- Submarine duty
- Navy Diver
- Go to Japan
- Meet the founder of aikido
- Get out of the Navy
- Honolulu Police Officer
- Undercover narcotics detective

Writing those things down on paper gave me a roadmap to the future. It's just like when you want to go on a trip. If you know where you want to go, you have to map out the route, or you may not get there. Life is the same way. The secret to getting what you want out of life is to have a clear idea of where you're going.

Knowing where you want to go is the first step; the next question is "how."

All through my school years, my grades were real bad. So bad, it didn't look like I was going to even graduate from high school. Then fate intervened.

On May 23, 1960, a great tsunami hit Hilo. 61 people lost their lives and the town was wrecked. Entire neighborhoods were washed away by the 35-foot waves. It wasn't the first time that Hilo had been hit with a tsunami, nor would it be the last. As always, the residents buried their dead, cleaned up the mess, and rebuilt the town. But this time, many structures weren't rebuilt, and much of the area that had been in the path of the incoming wave was left as open grass fields.

School was cancelled, no final exams were given, and there was no graduation ceremony that year. Later, they just sent us our diplomas in the mail.

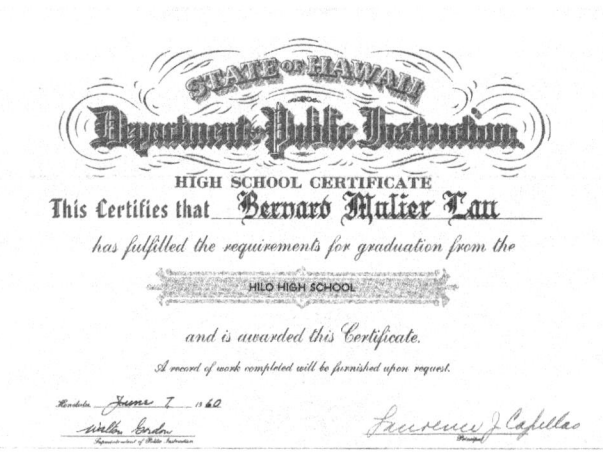

OK, that was number one on my list. Next thing, I ran down and enlisted in the Navy for four years. Goodbye, Reggie; hello, world.

But before I could report to the induction center, I got a letter from the French government. I'd turned 18, and it was time for me to report for duty in the French Army. The notice informed me when and where to report and also that my pay would be about 10 bucks a month. The draft notice, written in French, also warned me that failure to report for duty at the designated time and place would result in a warrant being issued for my arrest and that it would be a grave matter to disregard said notice.

Most likely, the French government wouldn't have sent someone all the way to Hawaii to arrest me if I hadn't reported, but if, in the future, I'd ever visited France or any territory subject to France (say, Tahiti), I'd have been arrested on the spot. So I had a choice between being classified as a deserter from either the French or the U.S. armed forces.

Inquiries were made, forms filled out, oaths given, and being as I was a naturalized U.S. citizen and about to enter the U.S. Navy, I was granted an exemption from French military duty.

Sign up with any branch of the military, and you start off by getting basic training—boot camp. This is where the military begins to turn boys into men. But after life with Reggie, boot camp wasn't all that bad! First thing was, I got all my hair cut off. Next, I got a bunch of shots, which made me sick for a day or two. Then I got my uniforms and my sixty-day training period began.

There was a lot of classroom time, a lot of waiting in line for chow, and a lot of guard duty at night. Tons of inspections, memorization of the general orders, and calisthenics, lots of calisthenics. I got to know recruits from all parts of the United States. Before I knew it, two months had gone by, and boot camp was over.

Next came "A School," as it was called; basic schooling in a certain trade or field. I wanted to be an electrician, so I was assigned to Electrical School, which was located in San Diego, not far from where I'd gone to boot camp. Basic Electrical School would last three months.

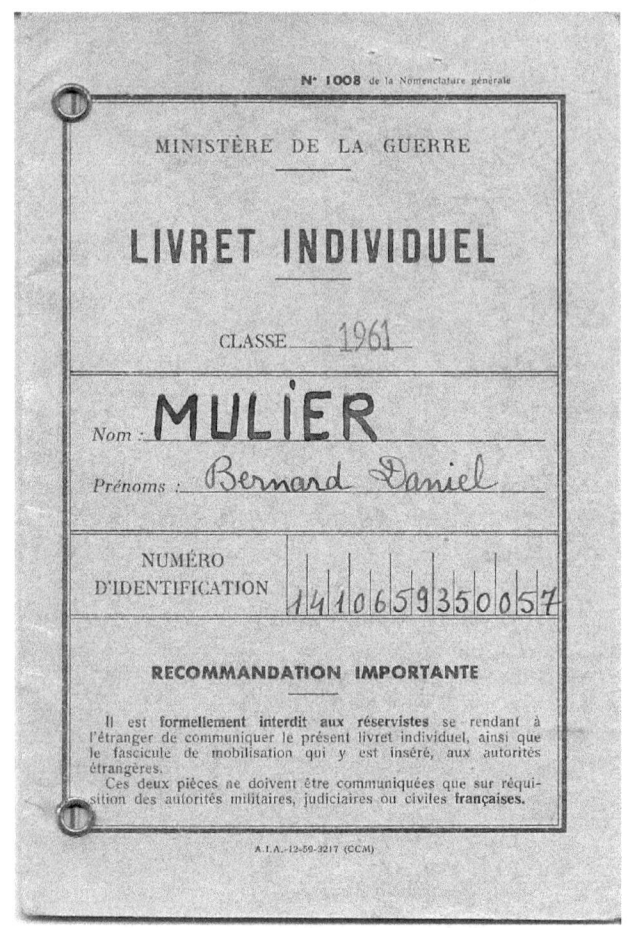

Service record book (French military)

About two-thirds of the course was classroom lectures. The other third was practical demonstrations and hands-on experience, such as disassembly of motors, etc. I also attended review classes at night, knowing that I'd need every bit of help I could get to pass the course. Every Friday, a test was given covering the material studied that week. You were allowed to fail one test. If you failed a second, you were dropped from the school and, most likely, shipped off to a destroyer, wherever the Navy needed you. Being assigned to a destroyer meant scraping paint, swabbing decks, and a lot of other unpleasant work.

I was never good at school or taking tests, so I studied extra hard. I had to graduate from Electrical School before I could go on to the next item on my list: Submarine School. I studied hard, but my test scores were low; in fact, they were barely passing. By the second month, I'd already failed one test. If I failed another, I'd be dropped from the school.

During the third week of the third month, the subject of the week was Electrical Math. No matter how hard I studied, I just couldn't understand Electrical Math.

It was a Thursday morning, and the test would be tomorrow. I knew in my heart that there was no possible way I was going to pass. Thursday afternoon—smoke break. I didn't smoke, but I went out and shot the breeze with the other students. I was standing there with five or six guys, when all of a sudden, out of the blue, a guy standing next to me said, without looking at me, "You know, guy, they rotate those test booklets every week so that one class can't give the following class the answers. But I heard that one of those test booklets has a mark next to the correct answer. (Answers were multiple choice.) There's a microdot next to the correct answer, but you can't see it unless you look at it from an angle. They always give that booklet to the guy in the window seat." Saying nothing else, the guy just walked off. Don't know who he was; he wasn't one of the guys in my class.

I stood there, focusing on the gray cement floor; my mind was racing, my heart was pounding. I was trying to make sense of what the stranger had just told me. Test booklet, secret microdot next to the correct answer, booklet by the window. My seat wasn't located by the window; it was directly across from and facing the window. Damn it. We were all assigned seats the first day of each week and some other guy already had the window seat. How would I be able to switch seats with him? I'd have to find a way, or I'd flunk out of school.

That evening, I attended night class as usual, but I couldn't concentrate. I kept thinking about how I could work it out. Somehow, I had to get into that seat. I tossed and turned in my bunk all night. My entire Navy career, my entire future rested on my sitting in that seat.

The next morning, I walked into class, nervous as hell, but I didn't let it show. I took a deep breath, held it in, paused, and let it out slowly. I was ready. The instructor was at his desk, getting ready to hand out the test booklets. I stood tall, smiled, approached the instructor, and said, "Morning, Chief. Ah, Chief, you know, me being from sunny Hawaii and all that, any chance of me sitting by the window to take the test? You know, I need that sunlight!"

The chief looked up at me; "Well, Lau, it don't matter to me, if it don't matter to the guy who's assigned to that seat." I tried to stay calm and relaxed. My heart was pounding. "OK. Thanks, Chief!" I walked over to the guy sitting by the window.

"Hi, guy. Hey, you know, being I'm from Hawaii, I always do better when I have sunlight. Mind if we change seats? Chief said it was OK with him, if you didn't mind."

The guy looked up at me and said, "Well, Bernie, it's OK with me if the chief says it's OK." We swapped seats.

I sat with my back to the window; the sun did feel good on my back. I stayed calm, trying to relax and control my breathing. Several minutes went by before the chief finally walked around and placed a test booklet in front of each student.

"OK, men, you got your test there in front of you. Scratch paper's inside for you to work out the problems. You got 45 minutes to answer as many questions as you can. If you get stuck on one problem, go on to the next. When you finish, walk up and hand me the booklet with all the scratch paper you worked your problems out on. After that, you're free till 1300 this afternoon."

The chief stood next to his desk, looking down at the stopwatch.

"OK, men, start. You have 45 minutes. Good luck!"

I held my breath and, slowly, opened the test booklet. Looking down at the questions and answers, I placed my left arm on the table and took up my pencil in my right hand. Leaning slightly forward, I looked at the margin to the left of the answers. At first, I didn't see anything unusual. I concentrated and focused; I squinted my eyes looking for the dots. Yes! I saw them; faint, ever so faint. The dots were virtually invisible to the naked eye. Unless you were looking for them, you'd never see them.

Another deep breath. OK, time to start. I realized that I needed to be careful. I couldn't answer too many questions correctly, or the chief would get suspicious. But too many wrong answers, and I'd fail the test. Another problem; I needed to fill up the enclosed scratch paper with numbers and problems, as if I were actually working out questions and formulas. I had to make it look like I knew what I was doing, so I took my time and did the best I possibly could at cheating on that Electrical Math Test.

"45 minutes; time's up! Hand in your test booklets. Scratch paper too." I walked up and handed my booklet to the chief.

"How do you think you did, Lau?"

"Well, Chief, I think I passed. Hope so, at least."

It was a sleepless weekend. I wouldn't know till Monday morning what the course of my future would be. Monday morning in class, I was back in my regular seat. The chief finally came into the classroom, stood at his desk, and said; "Congratulations. You all passed!"

Then, looking at me, he said; "Congratulations, Lau. I didn't know if you were gonna pass or what. You must have studied a lot."

"Yes, sir; I did (which was true)."

Looking back, all I can think of is that, once again, some Higher Power must have intervened. How else could it be possible that a guy I never saw before would just walk up to me and tell me about the booklet with the microdots, and this on the week when I was sure to fail the test?

Also, the lesson I learned from Reggie, "Never fail a test," stood me in good stead too, I guess. I felt bad about cheating, but I would have felt worse if I'd flunked out and been unable to finish the plan that I'd mapped out for myself. And in my own defense, I'd like to mention that, during the last week of school, when we had to take a final test covering the entire eight-week course, including Electrical Math, I passed, and that time I didn't cheat!

7

Sub School

After graduating from Electrical School, I was handed travel orders to report to Groton, Connecticut within two weeks.

I was happy beyond words: I was headed to Sub School!

Submarine duty is completely voluntary; you have to request it. If your request is approved, you next have to undergo rigorous testing. Not just anyone can become a submariner; it's special duty and submariners are the elite of the naval fleet. So after arriving, I was subjected to batteries of psychological and physiological tests, to see if I was fit material to be a submarine sailor. I passed each and every one of them with flying colors and was accepted into Submarine School.

At the school, I was confronted with the unbelievable task of memorizing the basic construction and operation of submarines. In addition to classes during the day, there were lots of nightly homework assignments. Happily, I was able to pass the course.

During the final week, my travel orders came through. I was to report on such and such a date to the commanding officer aboard the USS Bluegill SSK 242 ComSubPac Subase Pearl Harbor, Hawaii. I was to be stationed aboard a sub out of Pearl Harbor!

I couldn't believe it. That was the exact assignment I'd requested.

During the three months of Sub School, there was no socializing, fun or excitement. We just attended classroom lectures, did our homework assignments, studied at night, and every third night, were required to stand a four-hour watch in some vacant, freezing parking lot. The school was only a few yards away from a large river, and it wasn't just cold, it was bitter cold.

It was our last weekend before graduation, and soon, we'd all be heading out to our next duty stations. We had the weekend off, and several of my classmates were going to New York City for the day. I'd never been to New York City, so here was my chance. They offered to let me ride along if I chipped in a few bucks for gas. No problem; gas was 25 cents a gallon back then. I gave them two bucks.

We left mid-morning on Saturday. Wow. Me going to New York City. Imagine that! I'd have to remember to get some postcards to send to friends back home. Little ol' me, sending post cards from New York City. My friends in Hawaii would be impressed.

It happened to be a sunny day, and the forecast was for a warming trend. Great! I wore dark slacks (no wearing jeans back then) and a colorful aloha shirt. It was, of course, a short-sleeved aloha shirt since you don't need long sleeves in the tropics. No need for a jacket either, I figured. Radio said the weather was going to be warm and sunny all day.

Off we drove to New York City, which turned out to be about an hour's drive from the school. After we got into town, they let me out in an area called "Times Square," which is in the center of Manhattan. They told me that Times Square was where the action was, where it was all "happening" (whatever that meant). I exited the vehicle, making certain we all knew which street and intersection it was because that was where I was going to be picked up at midnight.

"Twelve o'clock on this corner, Bernie. We'll pick you up."

"Great, guys, enjoy the day. See you here at midnight."

I waved, and they drove off to wherever they'd decided to go.

I always liked to explore by myself. Most sailors just want to find some tavern and start drinking. I wasn't drinking at all back then, not even beer. Didn't have any interest in alcohol. What I did have an interest in, however, was sex. Here I was, a 20-year-old sailor about to be stationed aboard a Navy submarine, and I was still a virgin. Yep, still a virgin at 20 years of age. I was a disgrace to the U.S. Navy. Damn, Bernie; what's wrong with you?

I didn't know anything about Times Square, or New York, for that matter, and I had no plan; I just walked around aimlessly. It was almost noon, the sun was out, the weather was warm, and I was comfortable in my colorful aloha shirt. I was happy, carefree, and smiling.

One thing about Times Square; there sure were a lot of porn shops. Nothing like that in Hawaii. Being a healthy, 20-year-old male, I was, of course, horny, and for some reason, the more I looked through the store windows at those dirty magazines, the hornier I got. I felt a little ashamed. I mean, people weren't supposed to enjoy looking at dirty pictures or magazines. Wasn't that some sort of a sin? But, damn, I kept looking. Block after block, I window-shopped dirty magazines. I didn't dare enter the stores, though. No way. I mean, this was all new to me, and it was overwhelming.

Suddenly, a Negro gentleman approached me.

"Where you from peckerwood?" he asked. Peckerwood. I'd never heard that term before, and I wondered what it meant. Maybe it was because of my colorful aloha shirt. Maybe he meant to say "woodpecker," as in "a colorful bird." Yeah, that's what he must have meant.

I answered, "Hawaii, sir. I'm from Hawaii."

I thought of this Negro as a gentleman because, unlike the other people hanging around in Times Square that day, he was dressed in a suit, wearing a hat and, on top of that, smoking a pipe. I'd never seen anybody smoking a pipe before. Folks in Hilo don't smoke pipes (and they don't wear suits, either).

Actually, all my time growing up, I honestly never saw a Negro person. For whatever reason, there weren't any Negroes in Hilo Town.

"Boy, you lookin' to get laid?" this Negro gentleman asked. Had he just said "get laid?" You see, ever since I'd been 12 or 13 years old, every day, every night, one thing had always been on my mind: getting laid. I'd had the chance once. I'd taken a girl I really liked to a movie, put my arm around her shoulder while we were watching the movie, and she'd grabbed my hand and put it on her breast. I still remember the sensation—wow! She was a foster child, sort of like me, a local girl, 15 years old at the time. She was so pretty. Damn, I wished I'd had the nerve to have sex with her!

The Negro gentleman spoke to me again; "Boy, where your mind be at? I'm talkin' to you. If you be lookin' to get laid, I can find you some real fine pussy, damn good pussy." I thought a few moments, not really knowing what to say or how to answer. Was I finally going to have sex? The idea excited me.

"Aaah, yes. Yes, sir. I would like a girl."

"Well, boy, tell you what; you come with me, and I'll take you to some gal I be knowin'. She'll give you all the pussy you want, best goddam pussy in town. Maybe she'll even suck that little white dick of yours, if you ask her nicely. But we gotta get on the train, see. Her place be a ways out of town. But don't worry; you gonna like her. She treat you real fine."

Well, I gave the guy a dollar to buy two train tickets and we boarded the subway. About 15 minutes later, way the hell out of New York City, some place called "Harlem," I think it was, we got off the train. After walking for another ten minutes or so, we went into a large apartment complex. No elevators in the building, so we walked up five flights of stairs.

"OK, boy, she's right there in Room 502. Just go knock on the door and ask for Betty. Don't worry, she'll take good care of you. But, I gotta have the money first. Five bucks, I need for you to give me the five bucks first." I took out my wallet.

"Ah, sir, all I got is a twenty-dollar bill. Do you have change?" (Twenty bucks was worth about a hundred bucks back then in 1961—more than enough money for an afternoon of fun in Times Square.)

"No, boy, I ain't got no damn change. But tell you what; you wait right here and I'll run down and get you some change real quick-like. Won't take but a minute."

I wasn't so sure about that. I mean, what if he took my twenty and didn't come back? All I had was the twenty-dollar bill. Oh, yeah, I also had a shiny, new dime in my right front pocket. My reason was screaming at me, "Bernard, do not give this guy your twenty-dollar bill; he will not come back with your change!" But at the same time, the head of my dick was screaming, "Give this guy the twenty, damn it; he said he'd be right back with your change, didn't he?" I was torn between the two; I wanted to have sex so bad, but on the other hand, I didn't want to get ripped off. What should I do? ... OK; a compromise. I'd just explain to him that all I had was that twenty-dollar bill and, in case my ride didn't show up at midnight, I really needed to have some money to take the train back to Groton or I'd be AWOL.

I told all that to the Negro gentleman, and he seemed to understand and guaranteed me that he'd definitely be right back with my change. OK. He went off to get my change, and I went up and knocked on the door of apartment 502 and asked for Betty.

But there was no Betty in apartment 502; just some pissed-off older Negro guy who opened the door, looked at me, and said, "What the fuck you knocking on my door for, white boy?"

For some reason, the Negro gentleman never came back, and the naive, young sailor boy from sunny Hawaii, wearing a bright aloha shirt, slowly made his way back to Times Square. Dumb peckerwood!

Now, I didn't have any money at all, except for one thin dime in my right front pocket.

I hung around in Times Square until 3:00 A.M., and my pre-paid ride never showed. (Thanks, guys.) Somehow, the weather had turned freezing, and I was shivering uncontrollably in my colorful Aloha shirt. There was only one thing left to do: turn myself in to shore patrol.

As luck would have it, I spotted two sailors in uniform walking my way. On their left upper arms was a black band with two large white letters—"SP." I gave them my name and ID and explained my situation. I asked if there was any way I could get back to the base by Monday morning in time for graduation.

"Got any money on you?" One of them asked me.

"No, sir, just a dime," I replied.

"Well, that's money, isn't it, sailor? So don't say you got no money, understand? First thing is, don't bullshit!"

"Yes, sir."

"Here, call this number. They'll send a van to pick you up. A dime's all you need, sailor." (Phone calls were only a dime, back then.)

I went to a phone booth and dialed the number. I explained my situation and the voice on the other end ordered me to stand by. A van would be there in 20 minutes.

I stood and waited for the van while the two shore patrol officers watched over me. I guess I was the most exciting incident they'd had that night—a sailor whose ride didn't show up.

Finally, a black van arrived and took me to a receiving facility, where I was told to stand tight; a ticket would be issued to me on Monday morning. I pleaded with the officer in charge; "But, sir, I need to be on base by 0600 hours, Monday!"

"Sorry, sailor. This is the weekend. No can issue tickets on Saturday or Sunday. You just sit tight."

Still wearing my slacks and aloha shirt, I climbed into a top bunk, where I had the next two days to go over in my mind the events of my liberty in New York City.

8

Submariner

Somehow, I did just barely make it back to base in time for graduation, and following the ceremonies, I was handed my travel orders which read:

"Bernard M. Lau, EM3, 4917243. You are hereby ordered to report to the Commanding Officer, USS Submarine BLUEGILL, SSK 242, COMSUBPAC, Subase, Pearl Harbor, Hawaii, no later than ____."

The sub was an SSK; a "Hunter/Killer" submarine. A sub that hunted down and killed enemy subs—how neat!

So, departing New London, Connecticut, I headed for Hawaii.

A week later, I found myself standing at the end of the gangplank that would take me from the solid ground of the U.S. Naval Submarine Base at Pearl Harbor to my future home aboard the USS Bluegill. Just 12 short steps across that gangplank.

I paused, put down my sea bag, and stood there for a few minutes, taking it all in, looking over the awesome black submarine bearing the numbers "242" on her sail. It was to be my home for the next three and a half years.

Taking a deep breath, I picked up my sea bag, walked to the foot of the gangplank, stopped, saluted the guard on duty at the other end, and intoned, "Permission to come aboard." The guard returned my salute and responded, "Permission granted." Such a procedure is required before boarding any U.S. naval vessel. You don't just walk aboard, and if you did, you'd most likely get arrested.

I showed him the orders for me to report to the USS Bluegill for duty. The guard welcomed me aboard, logged down my information in the duty log book, and said, "Go down the mess hall hatch located just back of the sail (conning tower) and report to the COB.[1] He'll assign you a bunk and show you the boat."[2]

I went below decks, reported to the COB, and joined the crew of the Bluegill.

Back in the early days, submarines were named after fish, hence "Bluegill." "SS" stood for "silent service" and the "K" stood for "killer." I believe the Bluegill was one of only two hunter/killers in the entire U.S. Naval fleet at the time.

As a hunter/killer, Bluegill had an enlarged bow within which were 36 hydrophones used for detecting enemy submarines. She was a WWII-type diesel-electric submarine. Three 1600-horsepower engines ran generators which provided power to two huge electrical motors which turned the two propellers while simultaneously charging the sub's two banks of batteries. However, the diesel engine used up air when op-

---

[1] Chief of the Boat—the highest-ranking enlisted man aboard a sub, whose word even the captain respected. The Chief was responsible for and oversaw all day-to-day operations aboard the submarine.
[2] Submarines are called boats, not ships.

erating, so when running submerged, the sub had to use battery power. There was a third alternative, called "snorkeling," which meant that the sub ran submerged on diesel power with air provided to the engines by a 26-foot-long tube.

After reporting for duty, I was assigned mess duty, which was to last for one month. This was the normal assignment for all enlisted men who were not petty officers (E-4 and above).

A new sailor on a submarine first had to "qualify" before being accepted as part of the crew. To qualify you had to draw schematic blueprints of all systems on the boat from memory and have knowledge of their workings. Propulsion, hydraulic, high pressure air, diesel engine, electrical, etc. This learning process usually took six months. When ready, the seaman attempting to qualify was given a written and an oral exam, followed by a walk-through of the boat with a qualified officer. The officer could point out any valve, nut, or bolt and request a detailed explanation of whatever system that particular item might belong to and what its purpose was.

Memorizing schematic drawings and blueprints of electrical, hydraulic, pneumatic, and propulsion systems was difficult. I was haunted by my (as yet undiagnosed) learning disability, and it took me several extra weeks of study to qualify. Finally, I passed all the exam requirements and was awarded a set of the coveted dolphin insignia, indicating that I was now a qualified submariner.

But, due to my difficulties in learning information critical to the operation of the sub, the other crew members considered me a screw-up, and I was assigned tasks that didn't require advanced knowledge of electrical systems. I was typically assigned such duties as battery-well maintenance: taking readings of the batteries, watering the battery cells if required, and keeping them free of acid build-up. I was also assigned lookout watch whenever we ran on the surface. When submerged, I stood four-hour watches at the helm, which involved steering the boat on a certain course and heading via the compass. At other times, I was assigned to operate the bow planes, which were used to maintain the depth and level of the submarine.

Standing watch

Fresh water was a problem aboard a submarine. Once the initial supply was used up, more had to made by onboard distillation of salt water. The process was simple. Seawater was heated to the boiling point, producing steam. The temperature was kept low enough so that the salt didn't vaporize; it stayed in the boiling seawater. Meanwhile, the steam, which didn't have any salt in it anymore, was condensed back into fresh water. The problem was, we had to make thousands of gallons at a time, and it was a long, hot, humid process.

Because of the limited supply of fresh water, we weren't allowed to take showers while at sea and were allotted only one gallon of water per man per day for personal use. No shaving, no washing of the body. I'd brush my teeth, then rinse my face and use a damp cloth over the rest of my body. You washed your face one day, your arm pits the next day, maybe the crack of your ass the following day.

How submariners looked when deployed

In addition to not being able to wash properly, the quality of the air itself was bad. Once we submerged, the air, laden with diesel fumes, had to be recirculated. Did it end up smelling foul? Hell, yes! In addition to the diesel fumes, when you have a crew of 70 men and nine officers, you've got a total of 158 stinking armpits! Since everyone stank, we got used to it. But when we returned to port after a long deployment, the other sailors noticed it. That's why we submariners were called "sewer pipe sailors."

Submariners were the only sailors in the entire U.S. naval fleet allowed to wear boots. On a sub, if an emergency occurred when you were 300-500 feet below the surface of the ocean, there wasn't time to mess around bending over and tying your shoe laces. Sometimes, seconds is all you've got. Sub sailors normally slept in their clothes, and it wasn't our habit to change clothes every day. At sea, we'd wear the same clothes for weeks on end. What a way to live. But I wouldn't have traded it for the world.

Sub sailors got the best food in the entire Navy. The sub's galley was open 24 hours a day, and you could grab a meal or a snack whenever you wanted. While in port, we were allowed to cook a meal anytime we so desired, for ourselves or for a guest. Talk about impressing some gal friend of yours: "Hey, hon! How'd you like to come down and have dinner with me on my submarine?" Every Friday, steak and lobster was served. Rock lobster that is; none of that East Coast stuff. Every meal was "all-you-can-eat," and you got your steak cooked however you wanted it. The Navy did this to compensate for the difficulties and dangers we faced aboard a submarine.

If you qualified as a sub sailor, you were elite and nobody messed with you. You were *la crème de la crème*, even if you stank like hell each time you came back to port.

Shortly after I arrived, the Bluegill underwent repairs in dry dock. It was another three months before she was overhauled and back in the water. Following dry dock, sea trials were conducted for a month, during which time all systems in the sub underwent thorough testing.

Once at sea, the Bluegill went into a three-section routine of four and eight. We were on watch or job assignment for four hours at a time, and then we'd be off for the next eight hours unless, of course, there were repairs to be made on equipment or you were assigned to some other detail. That meant you were normally on duty for eight hours out of every 24. If you were qualified, then you were free to do whatever you wanted during your free time.

Of course, activities aboard were limited. There isn't really much to do aboard a submarine when you're not on watch, except read, study, watch movies, which were shown once a day, or sleep. Being technically housed and living in a "sewer pipe," approximately 15 feet wide, 10 feet tall, and 130 feet long, there isn't much room for activities.

The first and most forward compartment was the forward torpedo room. This was where live torpedoes were stored and fired from. The forward torpedo room housed six torpedo tubes and also contained an underwater escape compartment. In the event of an emergency while submerged, crew members of a stricken or disabled submarine could make their escape from the sub to the surface of the ocean. (All submarine personnel in the Pacific Fleet were required, every few years, to go through a day's worth of "Submarine Escape Training" at the Submarine Escape Training Facility located at Pearl Harbor.) The forward torpedo room also served as a sleeping compartment and was where 16 mm. films were shown nightly.

Next, came the forward battery compartment, also known as "Officers' Country." This area served as the sleeping quarters for the captain, his fellow officers and also the COB. The Bluegill's officers had their meals prepared and served in this compartment by stewards; usually black or Filipino enlisted men. These guys had attended Navy steward training specifically for the purpose of preparing meals for and catering to naval officers.

Directly under the forward battery compartment was the area which housed the sub's large battery cells, in which the submarine's electrical power was stored. Many hot, sweaty, tedious hours would I spend there, watering the hundred and four individual battery cells.

Next, came the control room, which served as the nerve center of the submarine and was usually "rigged for red" (illuminated by red lights only) whenever the sub was submerged. Orders to dive or surface, change or set course, increase or decrease speed, or whatever else necessary in the operation of the submarine were all given from here. Above the control room was the conning tower, which housed the boat's two periscopes and was also where the sub was steered from.

Next, came the mess hall and galley area, where the crews meals were prepared and served. Below the galley was a refrigerated compartment.

Just aft of the galley was the after battery compartment. This was where the majority of the Bluegill's crew bunked. The old subs didn't allow you the luxury of having your own private bunk. The first bunk I was assigned was either the lower last bunk or the middle bunk in a rack of five bunks stacked on top of each other. But basically, it was whatever bunk was unoccupied! "Hot bunking" was the norm. When you weren't in your assigned bunk, some other crew member would be using it. Once in the rack (bunk), if I wanted to turn over or even turn my face from side to side, I literally had to get completely out of the bunk and slide in again, lying on the side I wanted to lie in or facing the direction I wanted to face in. That's how close the bunks were stacked on top of one another. When you've got 80 men all living within a 130-foot length of pipe, space is precious.

Located directly under the berthing space was a second battery well.

Aft of the after battery compartment came the forward engine room, followed by the aft engine room. There were three 1600-horsepower diesel engines. They were hot, loud and reeked with diesel fumes—not something you'd want to hang out around.

Next, came the maneuvering room, which was the electrical center of the boat and from where the actual speed and direction of the sub were controlled. The maneuvering room only had space for a small bench where the electricians (usually two or three) sat out their watch, answering signals for speed and direction changes being sent from either the bridge, when running on the surface, or from the conning tower or control room, when running submerged.

What I remember most about the maneuvering room were the senior electricians on watch who passed the time eating pickled hard-boiled eggs and sitting there farting, trying to see who could chase the other guys out of the compartment. These guys would come to sea bearing quart-size jars of pickled eggs just for this game of "Bet you can't stand my fart!" Put a bunch of grown men into a confined space for weeks or months at sea with not much to do, and that was what you got.

Another thing these guys would do: if they came upon you reading a paperback, they'd take the book and rip out the last few pages, so you'd never know how the story ended. A fine bunch! Or, following a long deployment, say, to an exotic port, the engine men would pick out some newlywed kid, hold him down and one of them would suck on the kid's neck, making hickeys. The poor kid would then have to try to explain these hickeys to his wife; "But honey, it was really the engineers. They were the ones who put the hickeys on my neck..." Good luck with that!

After the maneuvering room, came the aft torpedo room, which was similar to the forward torpedo room. Live torpedoes were stored there, and it was equipped with four launch tubes.

Today, the diesel-electric submarine no longer exists. They've all been decommissioned; some scrapped, some sunk, and others put into mothballs.

Looking back, I'm proud to have served aboard a "real" sub.

Years ago, when the USS Bluegill was finally decommissioned, she was sunk off the island of Maui in deep waters. Guess that was a better fate for her than being cut up for scrap metal.

My first year aboard the USS Bluegill was spent working at qualifications, dry dock and sea trials. I took advantage of training opportunities, attending three months of diver's training, and upon graduating, qualified as a SCUBA and 2nd Class Hard Hat Diver. I also enrolled in naval photography training and became the Bluegill's official photographer.

2nd Class divers were trained in SCUBA (Self-contained under-water breathing apparatus) and the MK V (Mark V) Deep Sea Diving Dress (surface-supplied air) in order to perform submerged submarine lookouts, underwater maintenance, propeller changes, hull repairs on both surface ships and submarines, and search and salvage operations in depths of up to 190 feet. They were also trained in rescue chamber operations and in the use of munitions (primer cord and blasting caps) plus mechanical and chemical cutting equipment for salvage, battle damage repair, and underwater construction projects.

One afternoon, when I was in the mess hall, I heard a voice from topside calling, "Down ladder!"(the correct warning to be given by anyone coming down from topside). First a sea bag dropped down, then a young guy climbed down the ladder. Stepping into the mess hall, he turned, looked around and smiled naively. "Hi, my name's Nate Johnson." He was a 5'6" tall, 140-lb., dark-eyed mulatto. The rest of us gathered round and began to introduce ourselves.

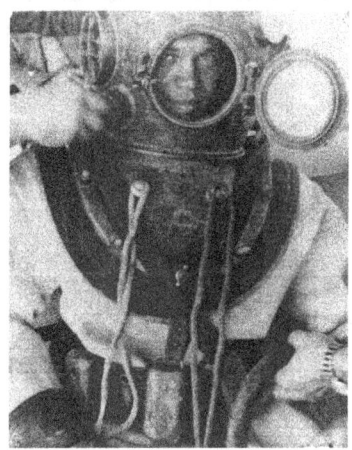

Wearing the MK V Deep Sea Diving Dress

Suddenly, an Engineman 1st Class petty officer (E-6) named Ivan walked into the mess area from aft. He was a southern white male in his late 20s, around 5'5" tall. Ivan's job was to operate and maintain the Bluegill's three diesel engines, which meant that he was constantly over, under, around, and inside the engines. He looked dirty as hell. Spots of oil and grease covered his hands, face, and hair from head to toe, and he always had a dirty oil rag in hand. He had a bad temper, a foul mouth, and never had anything nice or pleasant to say to or about anyone. He was so foul that his nickname was "Shit-house Ivan," and he was proud of being called that.

Ivan saw this young, innocent-looking kid all decked out in his fresh, white sailor's uniform, and without skipping a beat, he went up to him and said "Hi, kid; I'm Shit-house Ivan," put his arms around him, and laid a huge kiss on him, right on the lips! Nate panicked and tried to break away. Next, Ivan sucked on Nate's neck, making a large hickey. He then stepped back, grinned, and said, "Welcome aboard, kid!" Then he walked off.

That was Nate's introduction to life on the Bluegill.

When not at sea, most of the other sailors spent their time hanging out in bars and drinking beer. I, on the other hand, had found out the whereabouts of the main aikido *dojo* on Oahu, the Hawaii Aiki Kwai. One evening, I grabbed my *gi* and a white belt (proper etiquette when entering a new *dojo*) and just showed up for class.

The chief instructor at the time was a gruff-looking Japanese guy in his 50s, sporting cauliflower ears. His name was Yukiso Yamamoto, and he didn't exactly like *haole* boys, or anyone else, for that matter. I soon learned that he was a 5th-*dan* black belt. The guy could take you down and choke you out in a microsecond. His aikido was a pleasure to watch; powerful, yet smooth. Never smiling, Yamamoto was a true man of *budo*.[3]

As I went in to the *dojo*, I was immediately confronted by Yamamoto *sensei* himself, who asked me who I was and what I wanted there. I explained about my prior training in Hilo Town and about my training with Tohei *sensei*. I'd brought along my 3rd-*kyu* certificate, signed by Tohei himself. Yamamoto looked it over, and his stern face seemed to register surprise. He made a gruff sound, looked at me, and said; "OK, you wear blue belt with your *gi*. Change in back of building."

15 minutes later, I was back and once again practicing aikido. It felt like I'd come home. It was good to be on the mats, even though I was the only *haole* in the entire dojo. No matter; aikido is the Way of Harmony, to make all people of the world one "family." It was an attractive idea to me, who'd always been an outsider.

The Hawaii Aiki Kwai, as it was called back then, had been specifically built for aikido training. Walking in the front door, you came upon a section of seats overlooking the entire training area. To the left, a staircase led down to the mats. The mats were wrestling mats, not *tatami*, and easier to fall on. The training area was huge. The changing rooms, bathrooms, showers, etc., were located to the rear of the building. Above the bathroom and changing area was a second level, a private room which had been built especially for Tohei *sensei* and was later used by other high-ranking visiting instructors from Japan. There was a back door that led from that private room to the mats; however, in all the years that I trained at that *dojo*, I never once ventured into or looked in that back room. It remained "off limits" to everyone except Tohei *sensei* and other visiting instructors.

Manoa Falls *misogi* practice

I did the best I could to train two to three evenings a week. Later, I also attended Sunday morning training at the Waialae Dojo under Sadao Yoshioka *sensei*, and once a month, I went to *misogi* training at Manoa Falls,

---
[3] Japanese martial arts

where we'd stand under the waterfall, chanting "to-ho-ka-mi," or practice slashing 1,000 times with a *bokken* (wooden sword). Those were good days of which I have fond memories.

My main training partner was a local boy named Alex Tripp. My mentor, Meyer Goo, also trained with us and kept the *haole*-hating Japanese guys from bothering me. Meyer was also doing Chinese gung fu, and no one messed with him.

Due to being assigned to the Bluegill, there were periods of several months at a time when I couldn't practice. When back in port, however, I'd go to the *dojo* and train as much as I could. Eventually, I passed *shodan* (1st-degree black belt), given by Yamamoto *sensei* and then *nidan* (2nd-degree black belt), given by Yoshioka *sensei*. The certificates were signed by Osensei himself.

The author, Tohei *sensei* and Yamamoto *sensei*

In the summer of 1962, after some maneuvers in the Southeast Pacific, Bluegill paid a goodwill visit to the port of Mazatlan, Mexico. This was before anyone knew much about Mazatlan, Cancun, or any of those places that would, in the coming years, become prime tourist destinations.

Following our arrival, we opened the sub to visitors. Within a half hour, a crowd of over 200 locals lined up, all wanting to come aboard. The visitors entered the sub via the aft torpedo room hatch and climbed down a ladder into the torpedo room. Then they walked the entire length of the Bluegill and exited via the forward torpedo room hatch. Being there was only one passageway to get from one end to the other, controlling such a large flow of visitors was not a problem.

I remember being up on deck, watching the crowd, when I spotted a young local gal towards the back of the visitors' line, waiting with her mother. The instant I laid eyes on her, I was struck by her beauty. There she was amongst 200-plus other Mexicans waiting to come aboard the Bluegill. More than anything else at that moment, I wanted to meet this young beauty.

I walked over to the girl and her mother, introduced myself as a member of the Bluegill crew, and invited them aboard as my personal guests. Then I took them both to the head of the line and gave them a guided tour of the sub. Of course, they were surprised and pleased. In return, they invited me to their home the following day for lunch.

Though neither the girl nor her mother spoke a word of English, and I didn't speak Spanish, we got along fine. The girl's name was Miriam, and I immediately fell head-over-heels in love with her. For the entire week that the sub was in port, Miriam, her mother, and I met every day and spent the entire day together. I gave Miriam a set of my dolphins, a gesture to show her how much I cared for her. She was, after all, "the one;" the one I wanted to share my future life with. Deeply in love for the first time in my life, all I could do was think about her night and day.

After the Bluegill departed Mazatlan, Miriam and I wrote back and forth to each other for about a year, she in Spanish and me in English. Of course, we had to have someone translate our letters, but no matter, we kept writing to each other. One of Miriam's grandmothers sent me a handkerchief upon which was stitched an image of a sailing ship, the sailing ship that would bring "Bernardo" back to Mazatlan, back to his true love, Miriam. The black thread sewn into the handkerchief outlining the sailing ship was made from a strand of Miriam's hair. It was like something out of a story-book romance. But sadly, it was not to be.

Miriam

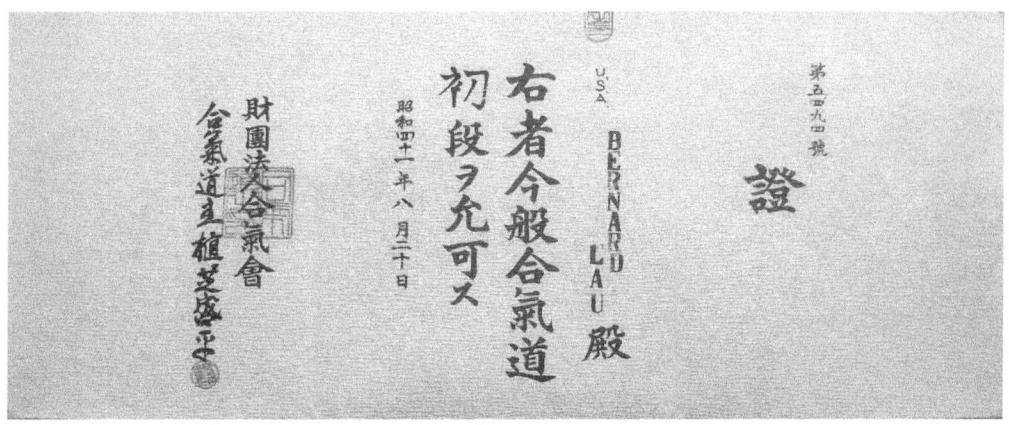

Shodan certificate signed by Osensei

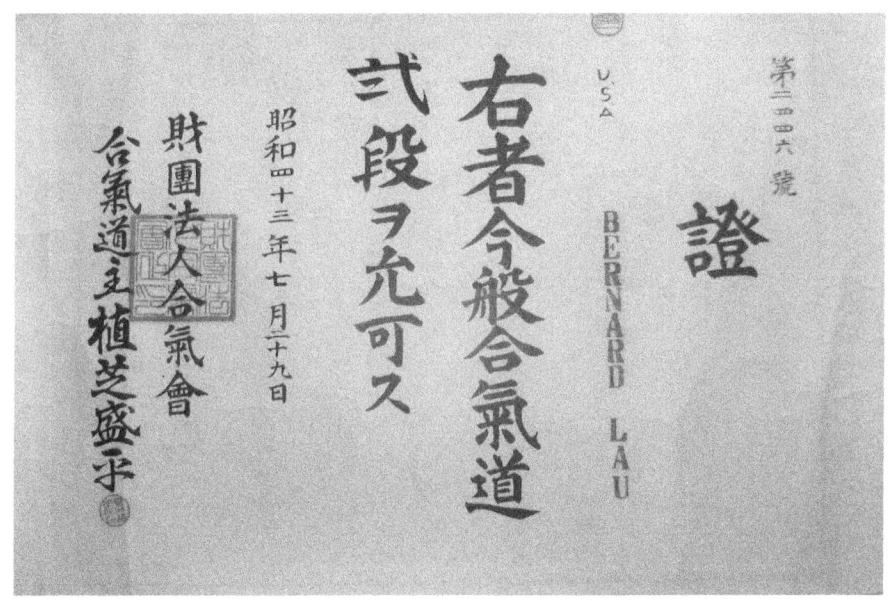

Nidan certificate signed by Osensei

9

Crisis in the Bering Sea

A few months later, I was off duty and relaxing in the crew barracks at Subase Pearl Harbor, when suddenly, a 1st Class petty officer from the USS Bluegill came running into the barracks shouting, "This is it guys; we're going to war. This is the real thing. Let's go, we're loading up!"

We'd all seen the news about the "Cuban Missile Crisis" on local TV. It was a face-down between Premier Nikita Khrushchev, who'd gone toe-to-toe with Adolf Hitler for seven months at Stalingrad without blinking, and President John F. Kennedy, who'd hurt his back in the war.

For the next 24 hours, the Bluegill took on provisions of every sort: powdered eggs, fresh produce, potatoes, coffee, cans upon cans of food, boxes of steaks, and, yes, we also loaded armed torpedoes to the max. This could be it: war with Russia.

The Bluegill's identification numbers were quickly painted over, good-byes were spoken to loved ones, and the crew being all present and accounted for, the order was given: "All back one-third!" We slipped out of Pearl Harbor, or "Papa Hotel," as the entrance to Pearl Harbor was code-named, and sailed off into the darkest night I'd ever seen.

Several miles out to sea, the captain ordered, "All ahead full, turn off all running lights." The Bluegill continued out into the deep waters of the Pacific Ocean. Soon she submerged and vanished, destined for ...? Where? No one knew; not even Captain Barry, the CO.

Moments before departure, the captain had been handed a large, sealed manila envelope, which was not to be opened for 24 hours. 24 hours; that's a long time not knowing the Bluegill's mission or destination, knowing only that war with Russia was possible. The following evening, word finally came over the PA system.

"Men, this is your captain. I've just unsealed and read the official ComSubPac orders for our mission. The orders read as follows:

'Officers and enlisted men aboard United States Ship Bluegill SSK 242, you are hereby ordered to proceed submerged and undetected at maximum speed, observing total and absolute radio silence, on course heading of (deleted) upon where you shall remain within three miles off shore of the Russian naval base located at [Kamchatka], remaining submerged except when necessary to recharge your ship's batteries, which shall be done via snorkel. You are to remain submerged and undetected. In the event of war, you men of the USS Bluegill are hereby ordered to fire torpedoes upon and destroy as many Russian naval vessels as you possibly are able to. Should this act of defending the United States of America become necessary, may God be with you and with us all. ComSubPac.'"

So now we knew. The orders were for a suicide mission. All alone out there in the Bering Sea, three miles off the coast of the Soviet Union, there was no way we'd be able to fire all of our torpedoes and escape. The Bluegill was not fast enough to outrun a Russian surface ship, nor could she dive deep enough to escape detection and eventual destruction. As soon as she fired her first torpedo, the entire Far Eastern Russian Fleet would know our exact location, and within minutes, we'd be hunted down and sunk.

The mood of the crew aboard the Bluegill was somber; we all had families and loved ones awaiting our return. None of us wanted to die; not this way, at least.

At top submerged speed, we headed on towards the gates of Hell.

Up until the second week, our sailing through the Pacific was uneventful. The seas had stayed calm. We stood our watches, we repaired equipment that needed repairing, we ate our meals, and hit the rack. Not much happened, nor was there much talking. We all had a lot to think about. At the beginning of the second week, however, sea conditions started to change drastically. Traveling 50 feet below the surface of the ocean, making 12 knots, the ocean swells were starting to be felt. Not much at first; just slow gentle swells. But the further north we got into the Bering Sea, the more the ocean above us started to turn angry, as if to warn us, the crew of the USS Bluegill, that we weren't welcome, that this part of the ocean belonged not to us, but to the U.S.S.R. We had no choice; we sailed on.

Soon the Bluegill was being tossed around like a cork. Bunks were quickly latched to angle in towards the bulkhead, so that men trying to sleep wouldn't be thrown out. The entire crew started getting seasick, and the smell of vomit began to permeate the already stagnant air. I remember being on watch in the control room, manning the bow planes, which meant I had to watch a leveling bubble on a gauge and keep the Bluegill leveled out. I became violently sick and threw up all over myself. Everyone else was getting seasick and throwing up too. It was like being on an amusement park ride, only worse, because this ride would last for days without letting up.

Cooking in the galley soon became impossible because nothing would stay on the grill. Bologna sandwiches became the meal from then on. Anything not tied down became airborne. At one point, the stainless steel ladder in the galley, which was normally hung on hooks, came loose, was flung with great force, and smashed into one of the cooks, opening a large gash in his head. A corpsman (medic) came to his rescue and was somehow able to stitch him up, which wasn't easy on that roller coaster ride.

The Bluegill had been patrolling submerged at her assigned location in the Bering Sea for several days, when suddenly, word came from the sonar man on duty that he was picking up a mechanical squeaking sound. Something nearby was definitely squeaking. Another sub, perhaps? Soon the sonar man had analyzed the sound and reported that it wasn't coming from another submarine or surface ship, but from the Bluegill herself. At a certain RPM, a squeaking sound was being emitted from one of our propeller shafts. This was not good news at all, for if a squeaking sound could be picked up by our own sonar, it could also be picked up by Soviet hydrophones, which were often positioned in waters surrounding Soviet naval bases. To be detected would mean certain death for the USS Bluegill and her crew and maybe the start of WWIII.

Before any repairs could be attempted, the cause of the squeaking propeller shaft had to be ascertained. The captain and Bluegill's engineers put their heads together in an attempt to figure it out. Was there some sort of damage to the propeller or shaft? The only way to tell for sure was by visual inspection, and that meant that somebody had to go over the side, into the freezing Bering Sea. And it needed to be done quickly. The time was 16:47 hours (4:47 P.M.), and it would soon be dark, making visual inspection all but impossible.

So now the only question was, who? Who would be called on to "volunteer" to go over the side and visually inspect the sub's shafts and screws? I'd been aware of the squeaking and knew that something needed to be done fast. Even before being asked, I already knew that I'd be the one called on. After all, I was the only qualified diver aboard. Yep, it would be me, Petty Officer 3rd Class Electrician screw-up Bernard Lau, whose only present assignments aboard the boat were to stand lookout watches while surfaced or man the helm or bow planes when submerged and to water the batteries as necessary. I'd be the one called on by the captain and depended on by the crew of the submarine Bluegill, the U.S. Navy, and the United States of America to keep the Bluegill from being discovered by the Soviets and giving Khrushchev a reason to turn the world into a smoldering heap of radioactive slag.

I was standing watch in the control room, still seasick, but no longer throwing up (as nothing was left in me to throw up). But I had the "dry heaves" (not fun). Captain Barry came to my watch location, looked down at me for a moment, and said "Petty Officer Lau, how'd you like to go for a swim?" I stood up, looked at Captain Barry, and without hesitation, replied, "No problem, Captain. I'll suit right up!"

I got the diving equipment out of a storage locker. There was only a single SCUBA tank, a regulator, face mask, a set of fins, and a wet suit top, but no bottom. I knew this dive was going to be a cold one, but I had no idea how cold.

Once I had my diving gear in hand, Captain Barry gave the order to surface. "Oogha, oogha, oogha;" three blasts from the sub's klaxon sounded, followed by "Surface, Surface, Surface!" shouted, as usual, by the diving officer on watch. Moments later, the Bluegill was on the surface, being tossed about like a soda pop bottle.

Having by now put on my wet suit top, I carried my SCUBA tank, fins, and face mask from the control room up a stainless steel ladder to the conning tower, where the periscopes were located. From the conning tower, I climbed up another stainless ladder to the bridge area, which exposed me to the bitter, freezing Bering Sea. Climbing down from the bridge via an oval-shaped opening, I stepped onto the main deck of the Bluegill, which was made of one-inch by three-inch slats of teak.[1]

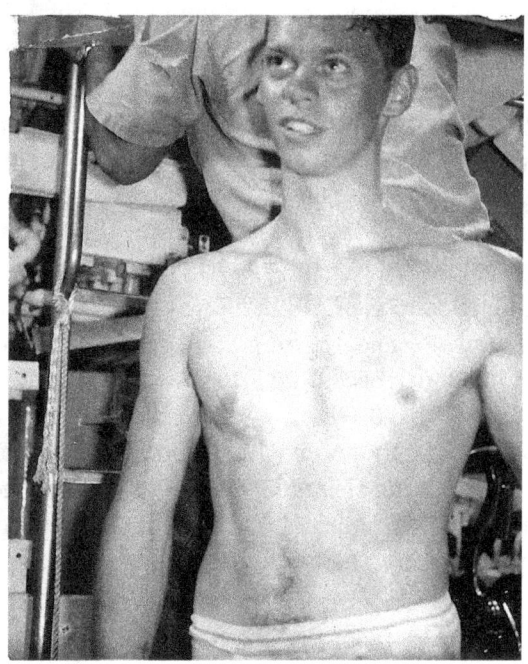

Before Bering Sea dive

With the COB holding onto me with one hand, his other hand holding on to a railing, I donned my SCUBA tank and put on my fins. That done, I spat in my face mask to keep it from fogging up and placed it snugly over my face. I was ready to go, or so I thought. Meanwhile, the COB handed me a line, which I wound around my right hand. This was to act as my safety line, my only lifeline to the surface. With the COB still holding onto me, I carefully stepped forward to the edge of the sub's deck. I placed my left hand over

---

[1] The rationale for using teak was as follows: if a submarine is depth-charged and destroyed, it's better if the enemy can't be sure whether or not they've succeeded. Teak is a heavy wood that sinks and leaves no traces on the surface, so if the sub were destroyed, the only thing an enemy would expect to see would be an oil slick. On the other hand, we could release oil and try to make the enemy think they got us.

my mask to keep it from coming off as I hit the water, took one final deep breath, and jumped into the 15-foot swells.

I'd mistimed my jump—I jumped just as the sub was being lifted up by the swell. It took a while to hit the water (I think it was about a 12-foot drop), but as soon as I hit, I quickly sank some 20 feet into the 36-degree F. water, and my body went into thermal shock. I was breathing at a rate of 120 breaths per minute. (That amounts to two complete in-and-out breaths per second.) I clamped down on my regulator mouthpiece to keep from losing it and fought my way to the surface. Immediately, I found the large swells to be a problem. But no matter the danger that faced me, I had to make that visual inspection, or we'd be discovered and sunk.

I signaled to the COB that I was OK. Slowly, fighting the swells and freezing cold, I swam aft to the Bluegill's "turtleback," the aft-most section of the submarine. I was 20 feet away from the hull. With the swells the way they were, I didn't dare get any closer for fear of getting slammed into the sub. I signaled the COB that I was heading down, flipped, and swam down towards the sub's shafts and propellers.

I was now about 15 feet down. Visibility was good, but as soon as I got the shafts and props level with my line-of-sight, they'd disappear. With the 15-foot swells, the Bluegill was bobbing madly on the surface and the distance of the submarine's up-and-down movement ranged from 15 to 20 feet. To make matters worse, I was starting to get sucked into the area of the shafts and props. The up-and-down motion was creating a backwash, a downward current that was drawing me in.

The sub crashed down in the water again. I had less than 10 seconds to inspect the shafts and props before being sucked in and plastered by the sub in the downward phase of its movement. As I looked carefully at the shafts and props, I could see no damage. Everything looked fine.

Still at a depth of 15 feet, I righted myself and started kicking and flailing my arms in a backwards motion to escape being crushed to death. My mind and body were shutting down from the cold. I let go of the safety line. I was on my own in the middle of the Bering Sea, nearing hypothermia. I was about to die.

I shut my eyes and transported my mind, body, and spirit to another place. Years ago, through aikido training, I'd learned the art of centering, of not allowing whatever madness surrounded me to take hold. My mind and I were now in a *dojo*. I was seated in *seiza* and centered on my "one point." The world around me no longer existed. Time seemed to pass. I heard voices calling out to me . . .

"Bernie, Bernie; look up!"

I opened my eyes and found that I was only a few feet from the hull of the Bluegill. Looking up, I saw the COB flat on his stomach, one hand grasping his safety line, the other reaching down for me.

"Here, catch this line."

A line was thrown to me. Though my hands were totally numb, I somehow managed to take hold of it. With the help of the rescue crew, I was pulled from the clutches of the sea and onto the deck of the Bluegill. I was back in the world of the living.

I looked up at the graying sky and noticed that it had started to snow. "How beautiful!" I thought. Then I lost consciousness. With me safe aboard, the Bluegill quickly submerged.

I opened my eyes and found myself in the control room. My SCUBA tank was no longer strapped to my back, and my wet suit top, my mask, and fins had been stripped off. The boat's corpsman was saying something to me, but it wasn't making any sense. He handed me a bottle of brandy and told me to drink. After breathing deeply, I took a large swig of the medicinal brandy. I was instructed to take another swallow, and then I was ordered to take a hot shower, as my body temperature had become critically low. Following the shower, I was tucked into a bunk, where I slept for the next ten hours.

When I finally awoke, I learned that I'd somehow been able to inform the COB and Captain Barry that I'd seen no damage to the propellers or the shafts. Based on my observation, and after further analysis, it was determined that the squeaking noise must have been due to contraction of the lignum vitae housing of one of the shafts, caused by the freezing temperature of the sea. The squeaking only occurred when it turned at a certain RPM, and the only solution at the time was to avoid running the shaft in that particular range of RPM.

Several days passed and another incident occurred. The Bluegill was now staying hidden beneath the surface at a depth of 150 feet, except, of course, when the sub's batteries needed to be recharged. She would then come up to snorkel depth (26 feet). Also, every few hours, the captain would bring the Bluegill to periscope depth (65 feet), in order to scan the horizon and the surrounding sea. The swells in the Bering Sea were now averaging 20+ feet. The Bluegill was taking a pounding each time she came up to snorkel or to periscope depth.[2]

It was during one of those times when she had her periscope up that she was hit by two continuous 20-foot swells and, as a result, took a list of 48 degrees and remained there for almost 15 seconds. The raised periscope reacted like a whip antenna. This managed to shift the scope's delicate mechanism off track by a fraction of an inch, just enough to keep it from being lowered into its housing tube. With the periscope sticking up out of the water at a height of three to six feet, it presented itself as an object that could be picked up on Soviet radar from shore, surface vessels, or aircraft.

A submarine is unable to dive to a safe depth when its periscope is in the up position. If she were to try, the O rings that surround the periscope, which are designed to keep seawater from entering, wouldn't hold up against the increasing pressure.

Once again, there was a serious crisis in the making. This time, Captain Barry and the engineers quickly figured out why the periscope couldn't be lowered and knew what had to be done to fix the problem. The periscope had to be set back into its guide track. And it had to be done quickly; there was no time to waste. The inspection plate on the periscope housing had to be removed so that someone could be lowered, feet-first, by block and tackle, down into the housing, where he could, hopefully, realign the periscope in its track, which, by the way, could only be accomplished by this individual using his feet.

Now, the periscope well hadn't been designed for a person to be lowered into it. The inside diameter of the housing was only 14 inches, which meant that whoever went in would have to be of slender build, non-claustrophobic, and good with his feet. Once again, that turned out to be me.

I was slender and willing to face any assignment, no matter how dangerous. My childhood experience of being rolled up in a rug had made me frightened of being trapped in small spaces, but no way could I allow my fear to be witnessed by my fellow shipmates or Captain Barry. I had to present myself as the brave and carefree sailor who laughed in the face of danger.

Aboard the Bluegill, I'd been looked on as something of a screw-up when it came to my electrical specialty. I was seen as someone who wasn't all that bright, and sometimes that was true. But I wasn't a coward, and this was a chance to redeem myself in the eyes of my comrades.

Again, Captain Barry stood before me and said, "Bernard, just a few days ago, you were called upon and undertook a dangerous inspection of our propeller shaft and acquitted yourself in the manner that's expected of any submariner. Without hesitation or concern for your own safety, you jumped into the Bering Sea, into swells of 15–20 feet and water that was 36 degrees F. Once again, I'm asking you to get us out of a jam. We know of no other solution than to lower someone down into the periscope well and have him attempt to make the required adjustment so that the periscope can be lowered. If we don't get that periscope lowered soon, there's a good chance that we'll get picked up on Soviet radar within the hour. Should the USS Bluegill be discovered several miles off the Soviet coast and forced to surface, there's no telling what Khrushchev

---

[2]U-boats had originally been designed by the Germans for the purpose of chasing merchant ships, which typically sail in calm waters. They were never meant to be operated in extreme environments, like the Bering Sea.

might do. The Russians locating and capturing an American submarine just a few miles off their coast could trigger World War III. Nikita Khrushchev would finally have the excuse he needed to push the button."

I stood at attention in front of Captain Barry, looked him in the eyes, and said, "Captain Barry, sir; no problem, sir. I'll do it!"

Quickly, I stripped down to my skivvies. The inspection plate was removed as a block and tackle was rigged in the conning tower to help lower me into the housing unit. Schematic drawings and ship's blueprints were laid out. The COB advised me as to the best possible action to be taken in replacing the periscope onto its track.

"Lau, I honestly don't know if this is going to work, but we gotta give it a try. There's no other solution we can come up with. Once you're lowered to the bottom of the well, place your right foot next to the guide track, then carefully push inwards and back. We're talking a small fraction of an inch to reset the track, so go easy."

I had my instructions, and I was ready to go down the tube. Helping hands guided first my legs and then the rest of my body into the well. As I was being lowered, I had to raise my arms above my head since there wasn't enough room for me to keep them at my sides. I was scared as hell, but my personal feelings didn't matter. The Bluegill and her crew were facing an emergency. A job needed to be done, and I was going to do it to the best of my ability, fear or no fear!

With terror pounding at my heart, I smiled as I was being lowered into the total darkness of the periscope well housing. I closed my eyes and worked at getting my breathing under control. Soon I felt my feet touch the bottom of the well. My right foot felt for and found the periscope track. I took my time. Carefully, slowly, I applied pressure inwards and to the rear, as I'd been instructed. Though the well was totally dark, I kept my eyes tightly shut in order to better concentrate, and focused entirely on the feel and movement of my right foot.

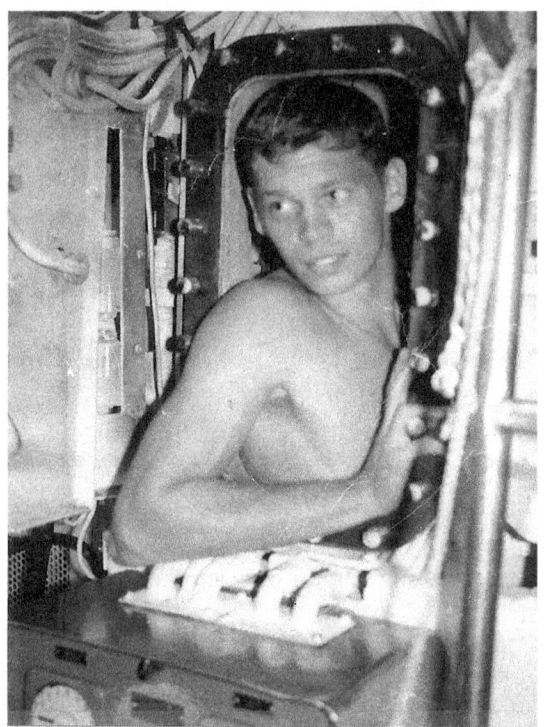

Descent into periscope well

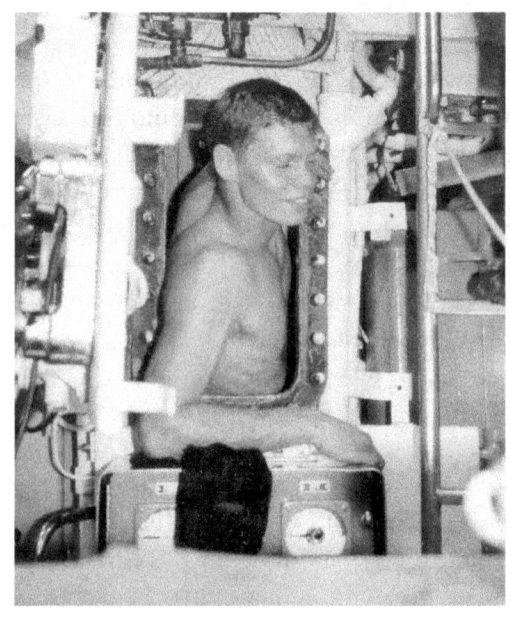

Coming out of periscope well

When I thought I'd accomplished the required re-alignment, I yelled to the guys above to haul me up. I heard the sound of the chain as it passed through the block and tackle. With my arms still held over my head, I grabbed on to the rope that had been tied around my waist. Slowly I was hauled up to where both my arms were once again level with the inspection plate opening. Several hands grabbed me and pulled me out of the well. I'd been confined in the tube for 15 minutes, and now that I was out, I could no longer move my limbs. My upper body circulation had been cut off by being in the tight enclosure of the well.

In the conning tower, Captain Barry slowly pulled down on the lever controlling the movement of the periscope. Silently, it lowered. The unorthodox repair job had worked!

As for my fears of confinement, I left them down in the darkness of the periscope well. I no longer cared about such things. I'd gone through a lot over the past few days, and as a result, I'd learned to face my fears and finally let them go.

Months later back in port, in appreciation for a "job well done," Captain Barry handed me a black and white photograph of himself sporting a beard. The photograph had been taken soon after our return from patrol. It was inscribed:

"To Bernard Lau—Thanks for pulling Bluegill out of a pinch more than once."

It was signed "J.H. Barry."

I was unaware that Captain Barry had also written a personal letter to Reggie and Renée back in Hilo, commending me for what I had done. However, neither of them ever spoke of it to me. Years later, Renée mailed me the letter which to this day I retain with great pride, as I remember how it might just possibly be that I, a bastard from a small orphanage in Lille, France, actually saved the world from WWIII.

Several days following the repair of the periscope, a Soviet destroyer was spotted several miles away heading towards our location. The Bluegill had silently come up to periscope depth in order to have a quick 360-degree observation. Within seconds, Captain Barry spotted the destroyer and immediately ordered the Bluegill to dive to a depth of 300 feet. Every non-vital piece of equipment aboard the sub was ordered turned off. No circulating air, no lighting, no nothing. The Bluegill rigged for "zulu quiet." That meant that every man not at a critical station had to sit quietly and stay still. No talking was allowed, not even whispering. Rigged for red in order to conserve battery power, we hovered there at 300 feet, hot, sweating, and praying not to be discovered.

At first, the sound of the propellers was faint. Soon, however, it grew louder and louder, till the destroyer was passing directly overhead; "Swish-swish-swish-swish-swish!" The danger slowly passed and the destroyer continued on. Fortunately for us, it hadn't activated its sonar and was not actively pinging. Had the destroyer's sonar been in operation, the Bluegill would certainly have been detected and forced to surface, or she might have been depth-charged and sunk.

Weeks later, when the Cuban Missile Crisis finally came to an end, the Bluegill headed back to Pearl Harbor. Prior to stepping ashore, everyone aboard was required to sign an official form stating we wouldn't reveal our mission off the coast of the U.S.S.R. to anyone for a period of 20 years. If anyone was ever discovered doing so, that individual could face years of federal penetentiary time.

It's been over 45 years since our secret mission off the Soviet coast. To this day, there exists no official record of the USS Bluegill ever being in Soviet waters. The crew of the USS Bluegill and I, however, know better. We were there, and we came very close to starting World War III.

USS Bluegill—SSK-242

10

A Girl in Every Port

About a year later, orders came down from ComSubPac that the Bluegill was next in line for a WestPac assignment. That meant that we'd soon be headed to the western Pacific for a six-month deployment. The crew was excited. Assignments like these were the basis for the Navy's most famous advertising slogan: "Join the Navy and See the World!" The sub was loaded with provisions, spare parts, and whatever else necessary for the duration.

A week later, we left Pearl Harbor and headed out to sea. An hour after leaving, all hands went below decks. We secured the boat and dove to a depth of 250 feet. We continued at this depth for approximately ten hours, at which time we surfaced and continued on a westerly course. In a week or so, we'd be in Japan.

I remember going topside on the deck of the Bluegill in my clean, pressed white sailor uniform. We were five miles off the coast, preparing to enter U.S. Fleet Activities Yokosuka, a large U.S. naval base and dry dock at the entrance to Tokyo Bay. The sight of Japanese fishing boats, the smells, the sounds of this strange land ... It was all new and exciting.

After the Bluegill had docked and secured, all crew members except those on watch were allowed to go ashore on liberty. It was Friday afternoon, and liberty ended on Monday morning at 0600 hours sharp, at which time all crew members on liberty were required to be back aboard. No exceptions, no excuses.

Prior to going ashore, each crew member was handed two penicillin tablets to be taken before engaging in any sexual activity. The idea was that the penicillin tablet would reduce the possibility of sexually-transmitted diseases. Back in the early 1960s, for some reason, condoms were not readily available to the crew. I don't remember anyone aboard the Bluegill being in possession of one.

Yokosuka, 1961

Where you have sailors on liberty, you have prostitutes. There were hundreds of cute young Japanese girls waiting to get their hands on our Yankee dollars. Directly across the street from the base were dozens of bars, each housing anywhere from 10 to 20 girls, each ready and willing to service American sailors. This four-block area, known as "Thieves' Alley," was full of bars and girls, and the girls working in those bars were all warm and friendly to us sailors. There were no attitudes and no games. The girls knew exactly what a bunch of horny sailors were looking for, and they were more than willing to oblige us.

Most of the bars offered different themes. There were go-go bars, Western bars, bars that catered to blacks, bars that catered to Filipinos, and there was a special bar, "The Starlite," that catered only to submarine sailors. If you weren't a submariner, you weren't allowed to enter. No exceptions!

Girls in any bar immediately knew if you were a submariner, as our uniforms always smelled of diesel. The bar girls working in "Thieves Alley" sought us out since, on top of our monthly wage, we got $90 extra per month (a lot, back then) for hazardous duty pay. They quickly figured out that us sub sailors had a lot more money to spend than sailors on surface ships.

The girls working at the Starlite didn't bicker with you or push you to spend money, like at most of the other bars. They treated us special because we *were* special. We were, after all, submariners, the elite sailors of the U.S. fleet (and we made more money). The girls there knew how to take care of us and make us feel welcome and at home. We could sit and chat with them, buy them drinks if we wanted to, but there was never any pressure. If you met a gal you liked and wanted to take her home for sex, that too was not a problem; all you had to do was ask her. So if you were a submariner, the Starlite Bar was where you headed every time you went on liberty. It was like our second home. You didn't need to go bar-hopping because you knew that there wasn't a better bar in all of Yokosuka, not one among all the hundred bars of Thieves' Alley.

I was 20 years old at the time and had never had sex. Imagine that; me, a 20-year-old submarine sailor and still a virgin. So, how exactly did I "lose my cherry" (have sex for the first time) and finally become a "man?" Well, my very first night at the Starlite, I fell for one of the girls working there. She was a petite, fine-looking 18-year-old Japanese girl with a great personality. We met, shared several beers, chatted, and later she took me home. Once home, "Noriko" immediately prepared a scalding bath for me to soak in; after I'd first scrubbed myself clean, that is. While I was soaking, she prepared a Japanese meal which consisted of rice, soup, pickled radish and fish heads. Being that I'd been raised in a Chinese family, I was used to eating strange food, so I truly enjoyed it.

During the meal, my lovely young Japanese companion introduced me to a drink called "sake." Ah, yes; sake. The nectar of the Gods and creator of fools. The sake was served warm and didn't have much of a flavor, but after sipping several small cups, I was no longer able to defend myself against Noriko's sexual advances. What a night it turned out to be. First a scalding hot Japanese bath, then a delicious meal, along with "sacred sake," and then I became a man! I was "Made in Japan" and was now a true submarine sailor.

I stayed with Noriko until early Monday morning, at which time she called me a taxi. Being it was the first time that I'd been with a woman, she wanted no money.

"My gift for you, Baa-nee. Now you not cherry boy any more. You come see me again, OK?"

And with that I got in the cab and was driven back to the base.

The Bluegill stayed in Yokosuka Harbor for a week, then headed out to sea again. Our next port of entry was Subic Bay, the Philippines. "Olongapo" was the name of the small town just outside the base, and it turned out to be a wild place. Olongapo looked nothing like Yokosuka; the streets were dirty and the bars were on the shabby side. From what I hear, conditions have changed over the past 48 years. Now, the streets of Olongapo are paved.

At most there were maybe a dozen bars there, averaging three or four girls (prostitutes) in each. American music was played loud and San Miguel beer was served warm, so it wasn't all that refreshing. I remember my first day of liberty in Olongapo. I drank one bottle of beer, walked out into the hot Philippine sun, and fell down drunk on my ass. The combination of warm beer, hot sun, and me not having ever drunk alcoholic beverages till I arrived in Japan was all it took. I was drunk on one beer. Pathetic!

Most girls in the bars I didn't find all that attractive. Every so often, you'd run across a Filipino gal that was kind of pretty, but you had to be careful because, in the Philippines, a lot of boys impersonated girls, and they were good at it. You might think that you could tell the difference, but the fact is, no, you can't; not always. Binney Boys; that's one name for them. There were stories about sailors who hooked up with someone they thought was a gal, only to find out later that—oh, hell, no!—she's a him. These "girls" would usually come up with some reason they didn't want to have sex with you, but they were willing to give you the best damn blow job you could ever wish for.

I did find one cute Filipino gal to have sex with. How it happened was, I'd been drinking beer and kicking back in some open-air shack located off the main drag of Olongapo, when one of my electrician buddies from the Bluegill came walking by with a tiny, cute Filipino gal. After they took a seat at my table, my buddy looked at me and said, "Bernard, this gal is wild in the sack! Why don't you go with her and have yourself a good time?" I was rather surprised and caught off-guard by his generous offer, but being he outranked me and his "friend" was very cute, how could I refuse?

Arm in arm, we walked back to her house, located just around the corner. She was friendly, charming, and yes, she liked having sex. She was my second sexual experience. I was quickly learning what having sex was all about and starting to enjoy it.

From the Philippines, the Bluegill sailed off to Kaohsiung, Taiwan, where I looked up a bar girl that a friend of mine from Hawaii had once dated. This friend had given me a photograph of her along with her name (Miss "Lee") and the name of the bar she worked in. It didn't take me long to locate her. I hopped into a pedicab, told the driver the name of the bar, and within ten minutes, I was sitting next to her, enjoying conversation and a cold beer. She was a bit older than my first two sexual encounters (21); tall, slender and very pretty.

The way it worked in Taiwan was, if you wanted to rent yourself a sexual companion for a few hours or for the day, you just paid the bar a fee. I handed over a five-dollar bill, and Miss Lee and I left quickly, walking hand-in-hand. She took me to a small restaurant, where we had a great meal for two dollars, including beer. After that, we went to a "by-the-hour" room located nearby. I showered, she took a long bath, and then we lay in bed naked and had sex. What I found funny was that while we were having sex, this gal and I talked about my friend back in Hawaii. She remembered him and spoke highly of his sexual powers.

Miss Lee

Back aboard the Bluegill, strange things were going on. Once it was dark, small boats containing two occupants would show up alongside and take aboard one crew member at a time. There was someone rowing the boat, and there was a gal sitting in the rear waiting to service whoever came aboard. Once a sailor was aboard, the boat would be rowed out several hundred yards and sit there while the gal and the sailor engaged in sex.

Once word got out, numerous boats started showing up alongside the Bluegill at all hours of the night. Money was always accepted in exchange for sexual favors, but trade for American goods, such as coffee, silverware, blankets, or whatever items could be "acquired" from the Bluegill, was favored. The gals really liked American coffee and cigarettes.

I laugh when I recall this one particular engine man who went out on one of the bum boats and ended up trading a pocket knife and a pair of his dirty old socks for a blow job! This is God's honest truth. A pocket knife and a pair of dirty socks in exchange for a blow job while on a bum boat in the middle of Kaohsiung Harbor.

For whatever reason, the COB chose to overlook what was going on. "Sailors will be sailors," I guess. But orders finally came down that coffee and blankets were not to be bartered for sex. Running out of coffee at sea would be devastating since most sailors can't function without it.

One sad thing about Kaohsiung was the homeless kids, girls and boys, paddling around the harbor on small rafts made of bamboo. There were about a dozen of them, living on the water. They'd paddle right up next to the sub and hold out their skinny little arms, begging for whatever we'd give them. We were ordered to break out the fire hose and keep them away from the side of the boat. They'd retreat, paddling a few hundred yards away, just out of reach of the hose. Most of them were Eurasian; the father a U.S. serviceman, the mother a prostitute. Good-looking kids, really; sort of like the kids in Hawaii. But in the Orient, such mixed-race kids are usually outcasts, and nobody wants anything to do with them.

While in Taiwan, I took a train from Kaohsiung to the capital city of Taipei and visited the National Palace Museum. It was quite a treat to see all those rare and wonderful treasures from China's past; a once-in-a-lifetime opportunity. Anyway, it sure beat getting drunk in some bar with a bunch of sailors. I stayed sober, went sightseeing, had a beer if I felt like it; I had not a care in the world. 20 years old, touring the Orient on a submarine, money in my pocket … Yeah, those were good times.

From Taiwan, the Bluegill sailed off to Hong Kong Harbor, where I felt totally at home. Once on liberty, I went walking all around that exciting and mysterious city where five million Chinese folks all live together in a 426 square mile area. Hong Kong had an energy that none of my fellow crew members understood. To them, it was just another place to get drunk and laid, but I didn't go into a bar once the whole time we were there. There was way too much to see and experience. Star Ferry, Hong Kong Harbor, Wanchai, the back alleys, Victoria Peak, with its fantastic view, and Aberdeen Harbor, where I enjoyed a fabulous meal of fried fish and lobster at a floating restaurant called "The Sea Palace."

To get to the Sea Palace, you had to hire a small rowboat, usually rowed by an old grandmother or a woman with a baby strapped to her back.[1] Once there, you were taken to an array of tanks where live seafood was kept. A cook's helper would scoop out a fish, lobster, or some other sea creature for you to check out. Whatever you chose, he'd take it to the kitchen and tell them how you wanted it cooked.

For dinner, I had steamed lobster, sea bass, sauteed salt-and-pepper shrimp, and the house special, fried rice. I also treated myself to a glass of fine white wine. It was a perfect meal.

I did have sex one time while I was in Hong Kong. It happened early one evening, when I was wandering around the waterfront apartment area; I suddenly heard someone calling to me from overhead.

"Hey, sailor boy; where you from?"

---

[1] They were "boat people," some of whom, it's said, have never stood on dry land.

I looked up and saw two Chinese gals leaning out over a 2nd-floor balcony.

"Sailor boy, you come up for tea with us!"

I thought to myself, "What the hell, why not?" I walked up two flights of stairs and was greeted by the young Chinese beauties. Both were dressed in those tight, sexy "Suzie Wong"-type dresses, the ones that cling to the female body and have high collars.

"Sailor boy, come in, please; we share tea with you, OK?"

The apartment was clean and well-furnished. I was served steaming, hot, aromatic oolong tea and Chinese finger pastries. As we sat drinking tea, they asked about my life in the Navy and also wanted to know about America. Were there many Chinese in America, and how much money did people make? As the evening wore on, they spoke of their own lives growing up in China, and how they'd both fled the Chinese mainland in search of freedom and a better life. Time went by. I relaxed and enjoyed the company of the two exotic Chinese beauties, drank tea, and engaged in pleasant conversation. It was the perfect evening, or so I thought.

Suddenly, both gals stood up in front of me and started to undress, all the while looking coy and enjoying the surprised expression on my face. I was speechless; this was totally unexpected. There had been no prior sign from either of them that this tea-drinking session would lead to sex and certainly not with both at the same time!

"Sailor boy," they cooed, "Come, come; we go bedroom now!"

Oh, my God! Was this really happening? While growing up, I'd often fantasized about having sex with two females at the same time, but I never imagined that I'd ever have the opportunity to experience a threesome. I stood up as they approached. Each one took hold of one of my hands. The two "Dragon Ladies" then guided me into their decadent chamber of lust. I was too weak to resist!

As the evening continued on, those two exotic beauties did things to me, taught me things that were, well ... Never mind! All I can say is, it turned out to be one of the most interesting and educational evenings of my life.

11

Showing the Flag

One afternoon, in the Bluegill's control room, Captain Barry entered, laid out a map in front of me and said, "Bernard, how'd you like to go to Saigon?" I replied, "Saigon, what's Saigon, Captain?"

"Saigon, Bernard, is the capital of South Vietnam."

That didn't help me much. Like most Americans at the time, I didn't even know where Vietnam was. This was in 1963, and although there were already 16,000 U.S. military personnel stationed there, not many people had actually heard of Vietnam.

Three days later, the Bluegill found herself at the mouth of the Mekong River and started her 20-mile journey upriver to Saigon. We were escorted by two heavily-armed Vietnamese Navy river craft, and we'd been re-certified in combat arms before the trip. The river and adjacent shore felt eerie, like something wasn't right. We weren't fired on, but after we'd gone in about ten miles, we started to see dead bodies floating by. Sometimes just one, other times several. We didn't stop to investigate; we just continued upstream at a speed of 8 knots.

Part of the Bluegill's mission in Vietnam was to show the flag. Literally. At night, whenever the Bluegill passed near a fishing boat or other vessel in the Mekong River, the two topside lookouts on the bridge would turn on a very bright spotlight and shine it on the American flag, which flew just aft of the conning tower. The spotlight was held on the flag until we'd passed the Vietnamese vessel. Now at the time, the Bluegill was painted black and there was no moon, so what the occupants of the other vessels must have seen was this illuminated American flag mysteriously passing by in the darkness, like some kind of supernatural phenomenon. What a sight it must have been, and imagine some poor fisherman trying to explain it when he got back to his family! But we were ordered to "show the flag," so we did. Kind of a crazy way to fight a war, I think. We lost over 54,000 men in Vietnam, and in 1975, we finally left in disgrace.

20 miles upriver, we entered Saigon Harbor and were greeted by a full Vietnamese Navy Band. This official honorary greeting was the first ever accorded a U.S. submarine. Once securely moored, the Bluegill's personnel were allowed to go ashore. Again we were required to be back aboard by 0600 hours the following morning.

South Vietnamese Navy band greets the Bluegill

Saigon was a fantastic city and totally different from Taiwan or Hong Kong. What I instantly liked about the people was that most of them spoke French. It didn't sound exactly like the French I knew; it was more of a "sing-song" French. It was interesting to listen to, and I enjoyed walking along Tu Do Street and talking to the people there. Many of them were surprised and pleased to learn that I too could speak French.

We were in Saigon on a goodwill tour, which was intended to demonstrate to the government and people of South Vietnam that the United States of America backed the government of South Vietnam in the fight against the Communist "Viet Cong," as they were called.

Capt. Barry, Pres. Diem, Me, Amb. Nolting

At one point, South Vietnam's President Ngo Dinh Diem visited the Bluegill, along with the U.S. Ambassador Frederick Nolting, for an official inspection. For some reason, President Diem preferred to speak in French during his tour of the Bluegill, so I was assigned by Captain Barry to be part of the welcoming entourage and to act as the official interpreter. There I was, just a few inches from President Diem while he toured the Bluegill from bow to stern, with bodyguards in tow. The Vietnamese press took photographs and shot newsreel footage of the event; photos and movies of me, Bernard Lau, standing next to President Diem as I pointed out various gauges and workings of the Bluegill.

Several days later, while walking aimlessly through the streets of Saigon, I happened to come upon two lovely Vietnamese schoolgirls leaving a Catholic school. They both wore the traditional school girl uniform, a white *ao dai* (traditional Vietnamese women's dress) with a straw hat. They were sisters and, maybe, 17 and 18 years old. Our eyes met; I smiled. They smiled and stopped to talk in French. I was captivated by their exotic beauty and their seductive, sing-song voices. I invited them for coffee at a nearby French coffee house, and surprisingly, they both accepted. We sat at a table outdoors, and I ordered Vietnamese-style coffee for myself, while they ordered Coca Cola. We also enjoyed fresh strawberries and pastries as we talked.

Catholic school girls in Saigon

Soon it was time to go. As I got up to leave, the older of the two invited me to their house for a home-cooked Vietnamese meal. How could I refuse such an invitation? After all, these weren't bar girls or prostitutes; they were two young students enrolled at a Catholic school who, for whatever reason, found me worthy of being introduced to their family.

It seems that they'd recognized me from the previous day's Saigon Daily News, which ran an article and photos on President Diem's visit aboard the Bluegill and showed me standing next to him as he toured the submarine. The entire family was impressed and honored to have me as a guest in their home. It turned to be out a very enjoyable evening for everyone.

With Vietnamese bar girl in Saigon

Standing next to Diem in Vietnamese newspaper photo

During our last evening in Saigon, I went out hunting for a sexual companion. "A girl in every port," goes the saying, and no way was I about to miss out experiencing Vietnamese "companionship!" I found a bar on Tu Do Street, entered, sat at the bar, and ordered a glass of the local beer. Within minutes, a pretty, but hard-looking Vietnamese "hostess" took a seat next to me. I ordered her a drink, we talked a while, and I ended up walking her home, where we quickly undressed to enjoy an evening of sex.

Once finished, I went to wash up, as was my usual habit. To my annoyance, there wasn't any soap to be found in the entire house. How could that be? Everybody's got at least one bar of soap in their house! Since I never used a condom during sex, I needed to wash my pecker off. Standing in the bathroom, I looked around one last time, hoping to find the non-existent bar of soap. There was none. However, I did find a half-filled tube of Tartar Control Colgate Toothpaste. Being fully aware of the importance of proper hygiene following sexual activity, especially in Exotic Foreign Ports, I lathered up my now limp "friend" with the "Tartar Control" Toothpaste and rinsed off. One thing was now certain: I wouldn't be getting any cavities on my pecker.

Before departing Saigon and heading back down the Mekong River, we planned to do a "routine" dive: submerge and resurface. The purpose was to provide a show for the locals and the press and demonstrate what our sub could do since they'd never seen a submarine before.

The higher the salinity of water, the more energy it takes for a sub to dive. A junior officer aboard the Bluegill was given the task of diving the boat, and for some reason, he made his calculations based on the salinity of the water while we were at sea, before we'd entered the river. But the Mekong River near Saigon was brackish, which meant that it had less salinity than seawater and was less buoyant.

Emergency surfacing in Saigon Harbor

The dive officer gave the order, "Dive, dive," and the ballast tanks were opened. River water entered the tanks, thus giving the boat a negative buoyancy and allowing it to submerge. Due to the junior officer's miscalculation, the Bluegill sank like a rock. In just ten seconds we hit bottom, and we hit hard. The river was only 60 feet deep! The collision alarm sounded: "Emergency Surface." This resulted in an emergency blow of all ballast tanks. Instantly, the tanks were filled with 3200 PSI high-pressure air, and the Bluegill shot to the surface of the river like a rocket.

The news footage taken by the local media showed the Bluegill submerging. Then you saw the periscope shudder as we hit bottom. Next, came the expeditious surfacing. It may have been an impressive show for the citizens of Saigon, but it was a very dangerous mistake. Had the hull been punctured, we would have flooded.

The dive sequence made the newspapers and nightly TV news for several weeks following our departure. The public certainly had been impressed. But as a result of our maneuver, the Bluegill got her bottom sonar dome smashed beyond repair.

Smashed sonar dome

We immediately returned to the port of Yokosuka and went into dry dock for repairs. Replacement of the damaged sonar dome could only be carried out with the submarine completely out of the water, and it took two weeks. Two weeks of liberty in "Thieves Alley" and the Starlite Bar. Nobody complained about that.

During those six months of WestPac deployment, I had the privilege of visiting six different countries: Japan, Okinawa, the Philippines, Taiwan, Hong Kong, and finally, South Vietnam. I got to meet and interact with countless individuals from different cultures, from presidents to prostitutes. For me, a dumb kid from the small town of Hilo, it turned out to be a wonderful learning experience.

12

Operation West Wind

Following a period of leave and maintenance, the Bluegill began a busy schedule of local operations. During this time, ASW (Anti-submarine warfare) exercises were conducted jointly with the HMS Royalist and various U.S. Pacific Fleet units.

From February 1st to 20th, 1964, I was assigned to a photographic team made up of three individuals from Naval Intelligence, who were to be brought aboard the Bluegill for the purpose of photographic reconnaissance in a highly classified location. The captain, of course, knew where we were going, but neither I nor any of the other crew of the Bluegill were ever informed as to where the reconnaissance had taken place. All I know is that it took the Bluegill seven days to reach the objective, and we remained submerged and undetected for six days while the reconnaissance was carried out. On the 14th day, we suddenly departed and sailed back to Pearl Harbor.

Once ashore, I had the privilege of being involved in the post-analysis of hundreds of recon photos, which was carried out at Naval Intelligence Headquarters in Pearl Harbor, and for which I was awarded a letter of commendation from the Bluegill's captain.

In March, 1964, the Bluegill took part in amphibious exercises with a Navy UDT.[1] The Bluegill's new captain, Captain Robish, asked the UDT to allow me to train with them in the exercise. The exercise involved having the Bluegill take a five-man UDT out to sea at night after which the UDT was to exit the Bluegill while she was submerged at a depth of 65 feet (periscope depth) via the submarine escape hatch located in the forward torpedo room. The members of the UDT climbed into the escape chamber and secured the

Ship's photographer

---

[1] Underwater Demolition Team. By 1983, all UDTs were merged with the SEALS.

bottom hatch leading to the torpedo room, then flooded the escape chamber with seawater, leaving just eight inches of air at the top for us to breathe. The chamber was then pressurized to the same pressure as the water outside the sub, allowing personnel in the chamber to open the outer hatch leading to the open ocean. Then, one at a time, we took a deep breath, submerged, and exited the chamber into the sea.

Once outside, we swam up to the surface, as we exhaled the expanding air in our lungs. Not exhaling would have caused an embolism and instant death. During the exit procedure, a rubber UDT raft was released from the deck of the Bluegill. Once on the surface, the raft inflated automatically from a pressurized flask similar to a small SCUBA tank. When the UDT had reached the surface and the raft had inflated, all six of us got in and sat straddling its sides. A line was secured to the Bluegill's periscope from the raft.

Shortly thereafter, a signal was given to the captain via the periscope, and the Bluegill got underway, still maintaining periscope depth and pulling the raft along behind. So there I was, riding on a six-man raft in the middle of the Pacific Ocean at night, several miles off the Hawaiian Islands, being pulled around by a submerged submarine. It was one of the most exciting nights of my life!

We continued on for several hours until we came close to an isolated beach off the western side of Oahu. Through the lens of the periscope, a red signal light was flashed at the UDT, and the tow line was released from the periscope without the Bluegill stopping or even slowing down.

The Bluegill continued on, lowered her periscope, and then vanished. We were on our own now. Slowly, quietly, we paddled towards land. Our objective was to come ashore undetected at a designated location.

Several hours later, we arrived and went ashore on the designated beach and were met by another recon unit. We teamed up and proceeded to capture an "enemy installation" a half-mile inland, which we did successfully.

At the time, I didn't realize that this covert exercise with the UDT was in preparation for an actual operation. The same team would later repeat the procedure in an unfriendly geographical location and conduct surveillance in preparation for an amphibious landing of U.S. forces. The location of that landing is still classified, but it probably had something to do with the war in Indochina. It was called "Operation West Wind."

USS Bluegill

13

Nalani

When we weren't at sea, we were in Oahu. I was still writing to Miriam in Mazatlan, but, every so often, I also wrote to a gal in Laupahoehoe named Nalani that I'd met when I was 16. She used to write me when I was in boot camp. When you're away from home for the first time, it's a little lonely, so I'd written back to her, and we'd kept in touch.

One day, I got a letter from her saying she'd be graduating from high school in a few weeks and inviting me to her graduation. So I figured, "Why not?" The only girl in my life was my other pen pal, Miriam, but she was far away, and I was a 22-year-old sailor. I was, as the saying goes, "young, dumb and full of cum."

I hopped a military flight from Honolulu to the Big Island and hitched a ride to Laupahoehoe Town. I booked myself a room at the Laupahoehoe Hotel and then went over to see Nalani. She was delighted to see me and said she'd come over to my room that evening. Six o'clock rolled around and, sure enough, there was a knock on my door. We quickly undressed and hopped into bed, where I started to put on a condom that I'd brought with me all the way from Honolulu for this very special occasion, because I didn't want to get her pregnant. Well, Nalani looked at me and said in no uncertain terms, "If you use that, you can't have sex with me." I asked, "Is it safe?" and she answered, "Yes, it's safe." There I was with my dick in my hand; I had me a boner that was throbbing and ready to go, but the gal wouldn't let me use a rubber. What's a guy to do when your dick's that hard, and you got this fine, cute, young 17-year-old gal laying there in front of you, all naked and all willing and ready to have sex with you? So, yeah, I had sex with her without the use of a condom. What an orgasm that was! I still remember it, even though it's been nearly 50 years.

The following day, I flew back to Pearl Harbor. Months later, I received a letter. It was from Nalani. I thought, "How nice; she's still thinking about me." I read it once. Hoping I'd misread it, I read it a second time. I paused at every word, praying to myself: "Please, God; don't let it be what I think it is." The letter read;

"Hi, Frenchy.[1] I hope all is well with you on that submarine of yours in Pearl Harbor. Not much to do here, you know. Laupahoehoe is really a small town! I haven't yet decided what to do, now that I've graduated. Last week, I went to a luau. Some friends of my mom and dad were having a party for one of their kids, so they went and invited me to go along. I must have gotten food poisoning, because I started throwing up. I feel a lot better now. When can you come to visit me again? Write back, Frenchy, and send

---
[1] My nickname among the locals.

me some pictures of yourself in that cute sailor uniform. Love and kisses;

Nalani"

Somehow, my gut told me right away. I knew that it wasn't food poisoning. She was pregnant! My mind went blank; I couldn't think. Then, after a few moments, I began to think straight again. Why was I worrying? It couldn't be mine. She'd told me it was safe, so the child couldn't possibly be mine.

Feeling better, I exhaled a sigh of relief. I didn't write her back. I did call Reggie and explain the situation and that I was sure that I couldn't be the father. I based my thinking on the fact that she'd told me that it would be safe to have sex without a condom.

A few weeks later, her parents drove from Laupahoehoe to Reggie's house on Pohakulani Street in Hilo. They explained to Reggie that, since they were soon going to be in-laws, they thought it only proper to introduce themselves. Reggie wasn't having any of it. He said that I'd told him the child wasn't mine and, no, I wasn't getting married to their daughter and, in a burst of anger, ordered them out of his house. As I mentioned, Reggie was prejudiced against what he considered to be low-class people. Nalani's family was of Portuguese, Puerto Rican and Indian descent, all peoples that Reggie despised. No way was the Lau family name going to get connected with such low-class people. Absolutely not!

A week later, I was sitting in the mess hall of the Bluegill, enjoying a cup of orange Tang, when suddenly a fellow seaman yelled down from topside, "Hey, Lau, get up here. There's a shore patrol officer up here needing to talk to you." I went topside and was immediately confronted by two shore patrol officers, both sporting sidearms. Standing next to them was a naval officer. What the hell had I done?

The officer stepped up to me and asked if was Petty Officer Second Class Bernard Lau, to which I answered, "I am." The officer informed me that I was being sued by a girl in Laupahoehoe Town, Hawaii for paternity payments. He then handed me a legal envelope. (My fellow seamen were standing around taking it all in.) The officer further informed me that I'd best find an attorney and get the matter taken care of or I could end up going to the brig. The three men gave me a final look of disgust, turned and departed.

I stood there, dumbfounded. I was just a kid from Hilo Town, and I hadn't quite understood all the legal terminology. Paternity? Brig time? Not knowing what to do and more than a little scared, I called Reggie. Reggie hired my uncle, Bob Lau, a licensed attorney, to represent me in the pending paternity suit. I was instructed to have no contact whatsoever with Nalani or any of her family.

A month or so later, I got a call from her on the phone in the Bluegill. She told me that the child was, in fact, mine, and how could I say it wasn't? I repeated her own words to her, how she'd sworn that it was OK to have sex without a condom. She said that she'd sincerely thought it was safe, since she'd just had her period a few days prior. She claimed that I was the first person she'd ever had sex with and that she hadn't had sex with anyone since. She also told me that she'd had to move to Oahu and was living with her aunt, only ten miles from where I was.

Back in the late 1960s, it was a disgrace to be an unwed mother in Hawaii, a disgrace to the girl and to her entire family. To save face, her parents had shipped her out of Laupahoehoe Town and off to Oahu. Nalani was, at that time, about four or five months pregnant.

Listening to her explanations and pleading, I began to think that the child could be mine. She said she wanted to see me, and I didn't have the heart to tell her to get lost. I felt that history was repeating itself. 22 years ago, in France, another "sperm donor" had produced a bastard child (me), and now it was all happening again.

Nalani pleaded with me to meet her at a certain location just above Honolulu, on Liliha Avenue. I knew the location, but I'd been specifically instructed by Reggie and my attorney, Uncle Bob, not to have any contact with her. I told her I'd have to think it over; I couldn't give her an answer just yet. I needed time to think.

I thought of Miriam, of Miriam and me getting married, of her being my wife, the wife of a Honolulu Police officer. At that point, we'd been writing each other for quite some time. We'd exchange letters at least once a month, and the letters were becoming more and more romantic. Miriam didn't say outright that she was in love with me, but she'd definitely said that she liked me and was thinking of a possible future in Hawaii. Every time I got a letter from her, I ran around trying to find someone who could translate it for me, usually in a Mexican restaurant in Honolulu. Miriam had been on my mind constantly since I'd met her 18 months previously. I'd never in my life felt so in love with a girl, nor have I ever since.

Two days went by, and Nalani called me again. I talked with her for several minutes and agreed to see her the following afternoon. The next day being Saturday, I'd have the weekend off, and I guessed I should finally have a face-to-face talk with her, in spite of Reggie's orders and my attorney's advice. I'd come to accept the idea that the child was, in fact, of my making. Deep down, I must have known it all along, but I hadn't wanted to accept it.

Walking down the pier, I found my car, parked with others belonging to the crew of the Bluegill. It was a 1929 Model A Ford coup with a rumble seat in the rear. Several years previously, I'd bought it off a submariner from another boat who was being relocated to the East Coast. I drove out the main gate of the Pearl Harbor Naval Base and off towards Honolulu, just 10 miles away. On Liliha Avenue, I turned left and continued on for a mile and a half. Up ahead, I saw a small park and made a right turn into the parking lot.

I spotted Nalani sitting on a bench under a tree, where we'd agreed to rendezvous. Nalani was a pretty girl; short, cute, with a small body. Except for her protruding belly, she looked great. No doubt about it, though; she was pregnant. I got out of my coup and walked over to her. Seeing me, she got up and said, "Hi, Frenchy!" I said, "How you doing?" Dumb question. How did I think she was doing? She was pregnant! We hugged. It was the first time I'd ever hugged anyone who was pregnant with my child.

I took in a deep breath, held it, then exhaled. I was at a loss for words. What was there to say? She took hold of my hand and led me to the bench where we sat down. She began by saying that she knew for sure that the child she was carrying was mine. I replied that I knew, that I no longer had any doubts, but that I didn't want to get married. I'd support the child, but I didn't want to get married. I was only 22 and in no way ready to become a father and a husband. I wasn't ready for the responsibility.

I took her hand in mine, looked into her eyes and said, "Look. The Bluegill is leaving port in a month, headed for Vallejo, California. We're due for a three-month overhaul. During that time, we'll be in dry dock. I won't be in Pearl Harbor; I'll be in California until I get discharged in July. I don't know what to say, but I won't be here when the child's born."

She put her head down and started to cry. I felt bad.

"You mean, I have to go through these final months all by myself? Have the baby all by myself? I'm scared, Frenchy. I don't want to be alone going through this. I don't want to have the baby alone."

"Look, I can't say for sure, but maybe, I don't know, maybe after the baby's born, maybe you and the baby can fly out to California..." I couldn't just walk away from her. I grew up without parents, all alone, and it had sucked. It hadn't been fair. I didn't want that to happen to our child.

"The deal is, I agree to having you join me in Vallejo after the baby is born, until I get my discharge. I don't know that'll happen after that. But I definitely don't want to get married. You and the child can live with me. I'll take care of you both; I'll provide financial support, but I don't want to get married. Can you agree to that condition? Live together without getting married?"

Still crying, she looked up at me, nodded and said, "Yes, Frenchy. That would be OK with me. We don't have to get married. Thank you, Frenchy." We were both too choked up to say anything else. But after a while, I wondered to myself, "What the hell did I just say?"

We continued to meet while the Bluegill was being prepared for departure. Nalani would sneak out from her aunt's house once or twice a week to meet me, and we'd go for a drive in my Model A. We drove to the beach, to Diamond Head and to the park. We didn't discuss marriage. That topic wasn't open for discussion.

Painfully, I had to come to terms with the fact that I'd never see Miriam again. I forced myself to write her a letter explaining how I'd screwed up and, through carelessness and stupidity, thrown away any hope of a future for us together, a future that we'd both been looking forward to so much. It was a hard letter to write. After writing the letter, there was still the unbearably painful task of actually dropping it into the mail slot.

As I let it slip from my fingers, I pictured Miriam, happy at receiving another letter from "Bernardo," then reading the sad news. She would be deeply hurt, as would also her mother and brother. It would be as though the entire household were in mourning. I'd caused it; it was my fault. Four unguarded minutes of lust that had forever changed the lives of so many people.

Nalani and I continued our secret rendezvous which, of course, weren't secret for long. Her parents flew to Honolulu to try to talk some sense into her, to tell her not to see me again. Meanwhile, I caught royal hell from the Chinaman. As soon as Reggie heard that I was seeing her, he boarded an inter-island flight to Honolulu and located my whereabouts in no time.

It so happened that I was having dinner with my aunt and uncle at their apartment. The table had been set, the food served, the French wine poured and we were about to start eating when, suddenly, there was pounding on the door. Not polite knocking, but heavy pounding. My uncle got up, opened the door and there, standing in the doorway, was Reggie, angrier than I'd ever seen him before.

He took one step inside, pointed at me and then at the door, saying, "Outside." Shaking, I went out. Reggie started cussing me out and poking me in the chest with the finger of his right hand. My uncle and aunt just stood there, speechless. We were all stunned by Reggie's behavior. Without saying goodbye to my aunt and uncle, I left the apartment and followed Reggie.

For the next hour, we walked the streets of Waikiki, as he yelled at me, threatening me with bodily harm if I ever had contact with "that tramp" again. I was too frightened to say a single word in my defense; I just endured the barrage of verbal insults and threats. Then, as suddenly as it had started, it was over. Reggie just turned and walked away. I didn't see or hear from him again for years.

The next day, Nalani phoned me, and I told her what had happened. "We can't meet anymore," I said. "Everyone is too upset, so let's just cool it for now." The Bluegill would soon be departing for her overhaul. I told her that I'd send for her once the baby was born.

14

A Prayer Answered

Several weeks later, the USS Bluegill sailed to Vallejo. After we arrived, she went into dry dock, and I never went to sea aboard her again. It was sad, but it was time for me to get out of the Navy.

However, first things first. I rented a small house and, with the help of my fellow electricians, I completely repainted the exterior. I phoned Nalani, who informed me that I was now a daddy and that I had a son, Keith Brian Lau. I told her that I was ready for her and the baby to come over.

Being we still weren't married, I guess he was technically a bastard, but he had a mother and a father and I wasn't going to allow him to be placed in any stinking orphanage. No way. I told Nalani that I'd be sending airfare for them to fly to San Francisco and join me.

I bought a used car and, the following week at the scheduled time, I went out to the airport to pick up my new family. There they were, Nalani and a baby, my son, Keith, all wrapped up in a blue blanket. I drove them to the little, freshly-painted, white house on the hill, and we put Keith in his crib.

First thing, we all went sightseeing in San Francisco, and I recall driving up Nob Hill and climbing up the Tower. From the observation area, there was a 360-degree view of the city and surrounding countryside. Having just arrived from Hawaii a few days earlier, Nalani and the baby didn't have warm enough clothing for the San Franciscan climate. Keith didn't even have little booties for his feet. It was cold, but Keith was a well-behaved baby and he didn't cry.

That evening, on returning from San Francisco, Nalani fed him and put him back in the crib next to our bed. We ate dinner and turned in for the night. Sometime later, she got up to check on Keith. I woke up with her shaking me and saying, "Bernard, wake up, wake up. Something's wrong with Keith. He's turning blue!" I got out of bed and looked down at Keith. He was just lying there in his crib, not moving or making a sound. It was too dark to see what color he was. Nalani took him out of the crib and held him close. "Bernard, Keith's freezing cold. Something's wrong. What do we do? We need to get him to a doctor, right now."

I put my clothes on, she wrapped him up tightly in a baby blanket and we drove off to the Navy hospital located in Oakland, some 20 miles away. We took him into the Emergency Room and, luckily, a doctor and a nurse were there. They took one look at Keith and immediately rushed him to the ICU. We were told that he was dying. They asked us what had happened, and we said we had no idea. All of a sudden, he'd just stopped moving for no reason.

After the doctor examined him, he told us that it was pneumonia. Keith was put in an incubator and we were taken to the admitting office for registration where Nalani and I were asked for our IDs. I showed them my Navy ID. "And Mrs. Lau's, too, please. I need to see her Navy Dependent's ID Card." "Ah, ma'am, we're not actually married." "Sir, we can't treat this child if the two of you aren't married. Your son cannot be admitted."

I couldn't believe my ears. We weren't married, so Keith couldn't be admitted to the hospital? "My son is dying! Damn it, he's dying. He needs help! I don't want him to die!" "Sir, I understand how you feel, but being that you and the mother aren't married, and even though he's your son, we cannot admit him to the hospital unless you are married to the mother."

I was about ready to burst into tears. Nalani looked at me. "Bernard, what are we going to do? We can't just let him die! Bernard, please, what can we do? Please do something!" Now, it sounds cruel, but military health care is strictly for the military. You might think it would be great public relations for the military hospitals to offer care to as many people as possible, but, in reality, that just won't work.

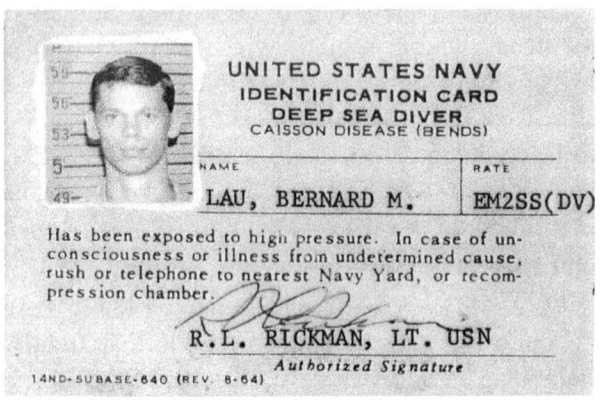

Nobody in the military pays anything for health care. There are no bills, just reports of what person got what treatment. Congress authorizes enough money to take care of the military, and that's it. If the hospitals began caring for all the bastard children of soldiers and sailors, the system would break down.

I looked at the admitting nurse. "Ma'am, we can't just take our son out of the ICU and go home. He'd die before morning. Isn't there something that can be done?"

"Well, sir, the two of you could get married, then we could admit him."

"Ma'am, I just arrived from Hawaii about a month ago on a submarine. I'm stationed in Vallejo at the Naval Shipyard. Nalani and the baby just got here a week ago. We're new here. Could you please tell us what to do? We don't know about these things. We don't know anything about having a baby or how to care for one. Plus we don't understand all of this legality or why it's necessary. I can't just let my son die because I'm not married to his mother. That's not right! What would you do if you were in our shoes? There's got to be some way to make it legal so that Keith can be treated."

"Well, sir, if I may make a suggestion, marriage here in California requires some legal work. Forms have to be filled out, blood samples taken... all that would take time. However, you could drive down to Reno and get married within an hour of arriving."

"You mean, we could be married and drive back?"

"Yes, sir. Folks do that every day. Drive down to Reno and get married. It's a legal marriage and is recognized as such in all states. Get married in Reno, drive back, show us the marriage certificate, let us make a copy of it and that's all it takes. We'll accept a copy of your marriage certificate for Keith's admittance until your wife gets her Dependent's ID card. We can do it, no problem. So what do you say; you two want to drive down to Reno and get married real quick-like? You'll eventually want to get married anyway if you're going to stay in the Navy. With a newborn child, you're going to be needing full medical coverage and for your wife"

"OK, ma'am. How far is Reno? I don't know anything about California. I've never been out here before."

"Well, it's an easy drive. You can drive down in the morning, get married and be back by tomorrow evening. Meanwhile, we'll do everything we can for Keith. He's very sick. I don't want to frighten you, but the doctor isn't sure he'll survive till morning. But I promise you, we'll do everything we can for him."

"Thanks, ma'am." We went to look at Keith in the incubator. He was so tiny, so helpless. I shut my eyes and said a prayer, "Please, God, please let Keith live. Don't let him die. It's not his fault that he was born and this happened to him. Please, God, I ask this of you; please let him live!"

Then, we headed out and drove back to the base. I reported to the Bluegill petty officer on duty and explained the circumstances.

"No problem," he said. He'd inform the chief and take care of everything.

"Don't worry, Lau. You guys go on down to Reno and get married."

I thanked him, and then we drove back to our tiny house and got ready for the trip to Reno. I stopped at a service station to fill up the tank, and they gave me a map and directions. We were off. Several hours later, we arrived in Reno, Nevada at 10:30 in the morning.

We were now in Reno, where you could get married in a hurry. But just how did one go about getting married in Reno? Two kids, far away from Hawaii. We didn't know the first thing about getting married in Reno. I drove up to a service station to get more gas and asked the station clerk,

"Can you tell me how my lady friend and I can get married? I mean, we really need to get married. My kid's in the hospital in Oakland."

"So, you want to get married? Well, you're in the right town for that. Just find yourself a Justice of the Peace, any Justice of the Peace. There's signs for 'em all over the place. Just drive around—you'll see. Oh, yeah; good luck and congratulations. Wait a minute... better yet, just drive on up to the courthouse and find some judge there to marry you. It'll be cheaper."

"Thanks, sir. I'll do that. The courthouse it is."

I got back into my car and explained to Nalani that what we needed to do was to go to the courthouse and find a judge. So away we went and managed to locate the courthouse. Entering the building, we asked the receptionist in the lobby about finding a judge to marry us and were directed to an office located on the 2nd Floor. We headed up to the office, went in and asked the gal behind the desk if there was a judge available because we wanted to get married.

"Have a seat, sir. The judge will be with you in a few minutes."

15 minutes later, we were ushered into the inner office, where we were introduced to an older man with graying hair.

"Morning, folks. I'm Judge Hather, Thomas Hather. What can I do for you this morning?"

"Morning, Mr. Hather—I mean, Judge Hather." We shook hands.

"Ah, sir, my friend and I, well, we want to get married. Can we get married right now? Is that possible?"

"Certainly," he answered. "I do marriages every day. Not a problem; it only takes a few minutes—won't hurt a bit! Fee is $50 paid up-front. Got $50, son?"

"Yes. Yes, sir. I do." I start to reach for my wallet.

"Hold up there, son. We need to get some paperwork filled out first. How old is your friend, there? She needs to be 18 years old in this State of Nevada. She 18?"

"Yes, sir, she is."

"Good, then, no problem. Just hand the receptionist your IDs, and she'll fill out the necessary documents. I'll look them over, and then we can go about getting you two married and on your way."

I took out my wallet, removed my Navy ID Card and handed it over to the receptionist. The receptionist looked over at Nalani and said, "Uh, ma'am, I need your identification, too."

Nalani looked at me. "Bernard, I don't have my ID with me. I left it back at the house in my bags. It's in Vallejo!"

The receptionist went to talk to the judge. Then the judge called us back into his office. "Have a seat, kids. Mr. Lau, I need identification from your friend, here. If she doesn't have any ID, I can't marry you."

"But, sir, we drove all the way from Vallejo to get married. My friend here is 18 years old; she just graduated from Laupahoehoe High School in Hawaii, on the Big Island. She's 18."

"Well, son, if you say so. But the law states that we need identification from both parties; otherwise, we can't marry you. Sorry, Mr. Lau; that's the law in the State of Nevada."

"But, sir, you can call her parents in Hawaii, and they'll confirm her age. Could you do that, please?"

"Sorry, Mr. Lau. I'd need the identification of the people vouching for her. I'd still need somebody's ID."

We left the courthouse, not knowing what to do or say. Our son was in the hospital, in the ICU; he might die. I needed to be married to get him admitted. We were in Reno, but couldn't get married because Nalani didn't have her ID. We sat in the car, trying to figure out what to do next.

Why me, Lord? All I'd wanted was to get laid. Was that so terribly wrong? Would I be plagued with misfortune for the rest of my life, just because of a few minutes of sex? OK, think, Bernard; the guy in the service station said there's lots of justices of the peace in Reno. Maybe, just maybe, I could find one that would marry us. There's got to be one! I couldn't give up on my son; he was depending on me.

We spent the rest of the day going from one justice of the peace to another; no luck. It was 4:30 in the afternoon and at 5:00, everyone would be closing. I decided to try Judge Hather again; he was my last hope.

We returned to the courthouse, walked up to the 2nd Floor and entered the Judge's office again. "Please, ma'am, could we just have a few minutes with the Judge? Its important. Our child is dying in the Navy hospital, and they won't admit him. We can't go back to Vallejo without getting married. We just can't!"

"Wait here, Mr. Lau. Let me talk to Judge Hather." She went into the office and shut the door behind her. Minutes later, she came out and said, "OK, Judge Hather will see you."

We went in and the Judge asked us, "What's this about your son being in the hospital?"

"Yes, sir, my son has pneumonia. He's only a month old. He and his mom just arrived here from Hawaii a week ago. The Navy hospital said they couldn't admit him if we weren't legally married. She has to be a Navy wife in order for him to get treatment..."

"OK, Mr. Lau, just slow down and take a deep breath. Why didn't you mention all this to me, about you son being in the hospital, when you first came into my office this morning? Tell you what, I'll marry you kids right now. Both of you raise your right hands."

"Do you, Bernard, take Nalani to be your lawful wedded wife..." So, that's how Nalani Medeiros and I finally got married. One minute I was single and carefree, thirty seconds later, I found myself officially married and legally responsible to a wife and a dying child. I thanked the judge, paid the clerk the required fee, and then the new "Mrs. Lau" and I drove back to the Naval Hospital in Oakland where we were informed by the doctor in charge that Keith had been near death, so near death in fact, that a Catholic priest had been summoned, and he had administered Keith the last rites.

Once Keith was hooked up to IVs and put under an oxygen tent, his condition quickly improved. Thank you Lord. OK, you might ask, so why didn't I explain to the judge the circumstances surrounding the urgency of why Nalani and I needed to get married in the first place? Looking back, I was frightened and confused. I had a new born son who was dying, and, although I didn't want to be married, I needed to do so or my son would most likely die. I was too young and naive at the time to realize that rules could be bent when lives were at stake.

Another thing—why didn't we take Keith to another hospital? Why not have taken him in an ambulance to a Catholic hospital, for example, where many charity cases go. There were plenty around, and they'd most likely have been quite willing to work out a payment plan. Easy enough to do! But somehow, it didn't occur to us (or to the admitting nurse at the Navy hospital, either, for that matter). In a state of panic, a suggestion was made, and I jumped on it.

The moral of the story is: when you're young, you do dumb things.

June 8, 1964, my 23rd birthday, Vallejo Naval Shipyard. My first hitch would be over in about a month. I'd served my four-year tour of duty with the U.S. Navy and would soon be getting my honorable discharge. Finally, I'd be free to pursue the next item on my list. "Officer Bernard Lau, Honolulu Police." Being stationed on the Bluegill, I often saw Honolulu Police officers walking the beat in Chinatown, in Waikiki or just driving by in their police cruisers. Soon, I, too, would be walking the beat, in a police uniform, and wearing the distinctive badge of the Honolulu Police. Yeah, I'd be a Honolulu cop, patrolling Hotel Street, the infamous Hotel Street, with its bars and porn shops, where all the prostitutes, drunks and low-lifes congregated round the clock. I could hardly wait.

"Bernard, Bernard, wake up! It's time to go to work. You don't want to be late for roll call. And don't you have an appointment with Mr. Brown? Remember, we talked last night about you re-enlisting?"

"What time is it, Nalani? Am I late?"

"No, its only seven, but if you want to eat breakfast first, you gotta get out of bed right now."

I got out of bed, freshened up in the bathroom, ate my breakfast, kissed Keith goodbye and then I was off to the shipyard.

Becoming a Honolulu Police Officer would take time. There would be, maybe, up to six months of written examinations, physical agility testing, background checks... what was I going to do? I didn't really want to re-enlist. I'd enjoyed it for the time I was in, but now I wanted to go on to other things. Deep down, I knew I'd have to enlist for another four years. There was no getting around it. I didn't want to, but I had to, unless I wanted to desert Keith and his mom. That I knew I could never do. There was no way I could just walk away from my son.

Quietly, I knocked on the door of the office of the XO, Lt. Commander Brown. The door opened. "Petty Officer Lau. C'mon in; have a chair. Did you make up your mind yet?"

"Mr. Brown, are you certain that I'll get the billet we talked about?"

"Bernie, the Navy likes to hang on to good personnel, so I've pulled a few strings. I can offer you a four-year tour of duty at the Submarine Base Escape Tank Training Facility at Pearl Harbor. It's an instructors assignment, and you'll be one of 12 divers assigned to the facility. Your duties would be to teach submarine escape procedures to submarine personnel in the Pacific Fleet. It's one of the best assignments in the entire U.S. Navy; no going out to sea and duty only once every 11 days, meaning you'll be at home with your wife and son all but two or three nights a month. You'll also receive hazardous duty pay, since it's a diving billet. The Diving Tank is a very sought-after assignment, and there are lots of Navy divers out there who'd kill to be stationed there."

"Sir; if I re-enlist, are you certain that I'll be stationed at the Diving Tank? I don't want to re-enlist and end up somewhere else!"

"Bernie, this is for real; you have my word on it. I'll even have the paperwork, along with your travel orders, ready for you to read over prior to signing; how's that?"

"Well, sir; if you can do that, then I'll re-enlist; as soon as I see those orders, that is."

"Good. Didn't want to lose you to civilian life. Navy needs good men like you. Congratulations!"

"Thank you sir!"

A week later, I was handed my next duty assignment at the Diving Escape Training Tank at Pearl Harbor. I raised my right hand, took the Oath and was sworn in for another four years of duty with the U.S. Navy. Four more years!

15

Roots

It wasn't until the age of 16 that I was finally told that my real father was alive and well and living in France.

I recall the day being a bright Sunday afternoon. I was walking through a hallway from my bedroom to the living room, when Reggie suddenly appeared, his left hand stretched out towards me and holding a piece of white paper.

"Here. Here's your dad's address," were his words. "Go ahead and write to him."

Now hold on, Reggie, I thought to myself, you say my "dad," my real dad, is alive and living in France? Hell, all those years, I thought he'd been killed in the war.

I reached out and took the white piece of paper. Reggie turned and walked off without saying another word. "Lucien Gervais" and an address in Lille, France was all that was written. I stood there for several minutes, confused and unable to think.

Years later, I asked Renée why she'd never told me that my real dad was alive and living in France. Her answer was, "Well, Bernard, you never asked!"

Had I known all those years that my real dad was in fact alive, I'm certain that living under Reggie's rule would have been a lot easier. I wouldn't have felt as alone as I did.

I wrote to Lucien, and over the years, we exchanged letters. Along with his letters, Lucien would often send me drawings. He was a talented artist. He once sent me a drawing of a submarine, as I had mentioned to him that I wanted to someday join the Navy and become a submariner.

In June of 1964, I re-enlisted in the U. S. Navy for another four years and received a $2000 re-enlistment bonus. I used the money to fly to France and finally meet Lucien Gervais, the dad I never knew.

Arriving in Lille, I located his home address, which turned out to be in a loft over a storefront. I climbed the stairs and knocked on the door. Seconds later, the door opened, and there standing in front of me, was Lucien, my real father. I reached out and shook his hand. "*Bonjour, Lucien. Je suis Bernard, ton fils.*" (Hello, Lucien, I'm Bernard, your son.) We hugged. It felt so good to finally be embracing my real father. How different Lucien's energy felt compared to Reggie.

He invited me into his home, which was, as mentioned, a loft with one huge room. He then introduced me to his wife, Ana, a short, plump middle-aged woman wearing thick glasses and a sweet smile. I was also introduced to Lucien's two sons, one 12 years old and the other 16. These two boys were my half-brothers, definitely my half-brothers, as they sported large ears, like I had when I was younger! Lucien informed me that I also had a sister named Cathérine. She was 14 and lived with her mother, Lucien's first wife, and I was told that I'd be able to meet her later on that afternoon.

Lucien invited me to sit with him at the kitchen table while his wife Ana brought out several glasses, a bottle of red wine, cheese, salami, and a loaf of french bread. We had 23 years of catching up to do.

He started off by apologizing to me for denying that I was his son when I was born. I raised my hand and stated that it didn't matter to me. All that took place years ago, and the only important thing now was that we finally get to meet each other; I didn't care about the past. We toasted, drank wine and talked.

That was a great day for all of us. Finally, after 23 years, I got to meet my real dad, and Lucien got to meet his son, Bernard, whom he'd never seen, but had always wondered about. Wine depleted, small talk done for the moment, Lucien suggested that we walk down to the local bistro for an afternoon drink. I agreed and followed him outside.

The neighborhood bistro was two blocks away. Lucien ordered a glass of Pernod for himself and for me. We toasted to my homecoming and bottoms up went the Pernod. Yuk! I'd never drunk any kind of liqueur before. This Pernod was rank, tasted like that Nyquil you took for colds. Damn, I thought, how can Lucien stand drinking this stuff? Oh well, he probably wasn't drinking it for the flavor, but for its alcoholic content.

He then showed me the bookshop where he worked, which turned out to be just a small hole-in-the-wall shop with a bunch of dusty old books. I don't know exactly what it was that Lucien did in the shop; most likely, it was sweeping and tidying up. Well, no matter. I had come to France to meet my father, not to pass judgement. It didn't even matter that he too had left me in that orphanage and never once visited me. I didn't care; this was my father, and that was all that mattered.

Lucien and I looked a lot alike. He had those big ears and he was left-handed, like I used to be before I became "Chinese," and was changed from left to right. He painted in oils, almost always choosing sad clown-faces as his subjects. There must have been 15 or so paintings of sad clowns hanging on the wall of his loft. Not one face wore a smile, not one happy clown in the entire bunch.

Like me, Lucien was born with the "gift" of ADD. He was creative, he had a quick mind, he was a talented artist, he was a womanizer, liked to flirt, to joke around, but he was also a dreamer of things that might have been. His mind jumped around and he couldn't sit still.

His first wife was very beautiful and came from a good family. She dressed well, was financially secure, kind, and easy to talk to. She and Lucien had a beautiful daughter together—Cathérine Gervais, my little sister—who I was soon to meet.

We returned to the loft, where Ana informed us that Cathérine would be dropping by soon. She mentioned that Cathérine was very excited to finally be meeting her big brother from America, who was a navy diver and submariner.

I asked Lucien where the bathroom was. He took me over to the kitchen sink behind a partially-closed curtain and explained that since the lavatory downstairs was broken, I had to pee in the sink. I looked him and grinned. "What a joker," I thought. But it was no joke; I was in fact supposed to urinate in the kitchen sink. Meanwhile, Lucien had left the kitchen and pulled the curtain shut. I was left alone, and I had to pee bad. OK, whatever. I still didn't believe it, but, hey, I had to go. So if Lucien was playing a joke on me, it would be his fault if I pissed in his sink. Don't blame me!

I gritted my teeth and looked up at the ceiling. OK, Bernard, let's do this. I had to stand on my toes to get over the edge of the sink. I unzipped my pants and aimed towards the drain. Lucien and his wife and my two brothers were a few feet away on the other side of the thin curtain, and I was feeling a bit uncomfortable. Here I was, all the way from America to pee in the kitchen sink of my father's home.

Just as I started to pee, I heard, *"Bernard, Bernard, mon frère, c'est moi, Cathérine!"*

Unbeknownst to me, Cathérine had just arrived, and she was ducking her head under the curtain ... *merde!*

But anyway, it was a day filled with joy. I finally got to meet my real father, my brothers, and my kid sister. I was totally happy and thankful. Lucien's wife went out and bought food for everyone: boiled potatoes, sliced beef, a *baguette* (French bread), some cheese and another bottle of red wine. We all squeezed around the small kitchen table and ate, talked, and laughed.

With Lucien Gervais, half-brother and half-sister

At dinner, I asked Lucien if it was possible to visit the little red brick house, the orphanage where I'd spent the first five and a half years of my life. Was the house still there? Yes, Lucien answered, he would take me to see it the next day. What about Maman and Papa Germain, I asked, were they still alive? Yes, both were still alive and living in a retirement home not far from there. I would get to see them tomorrow too.

Over the years, I'd kept in touch with Maman and Papa Germain, sending them souvenirs from Japan and other places I'd visited while in the Navy. I didn't really know how to write in French, though. The grammar and spelling must have been horrible, but Maman Germain was able to read the letters, somehow. Since I couldn't read French, I always had to have her letters translated for me.

The next day, Lucien borrowed a car from a friend of his. I say "car," but it looked like a small tin shed mounted on a frame with four wheels. Whatever it was, it ran, and there was enough room for four people, so that was all that mattered.

The first stop was the little red brick orphanage, located only eight minutes away from Lucien's loft. We pulled up in front, and I hurriedly jumped out of the car and walked around the house very slowly. In the back of the house, I saw the old wooden water tank, and a ways from the house, was the old outhouse, barely standing, where Papa Germain had dropped a burlap sack of tiny meows into the smelly darkness. I could almost hear the helpless little cries as I walked towards it.

I walked back to the house and knocked on the front door. After a minute, I was about to knock again, when I heard my name being called: *"Bernard, Bernard; tu es revenu!"* A heavy, elderly lady from next door was hobbling towards me all excited with her arms raised. "Bernard, Bernard; you've come back!" I had no idea who the lady was, but I smiled and spoke to her in French. Turned out she lived next door since before the war and remembered who I was. It had been 17 years since I'd left! How did she recognize me after all that time? Of course; it must have been my ears. After a brief conversation with the neighbor lady, I took several photos of the little brick house, and then we were on our way once again.

As I mentioned, Maman and Papa Germain were living in a retirement home. It had been 17 years since I saw them, but I had their address since I'd kept in touch over the years, and Lucien located it without any trouble. We pulled into the parking area. I got out, while Lucien stayed in the car. I found the reception desk and was told that the Germains lived in Room 107. Just as I started to walk down the hall, I saw Papa Germain standing there a few feet away from me. I recognized him instantly; he was still wearing that black beret he used to wear when I was a child. He saw me, and a look of utter surprise came over his face. He turned around and hobbled down the hallway, flailing his arms and calling out at the top of his voice, *"Maman, maman; c'est l'Américain. L'Américain est ici!"* (Maman, the American is here!)

The door to 107 flew open, and an old lady with white hair came running out. *"Bernard, Bernard; c'est toi!*" We embraced and she kissed me on both cheeks. Papa approached; we shook hands, then I gave him a long hug. We were all in tears. Maman took my hands into her own frail hands and led me down the hall to her room without taking her eyes off me for a second. We went inside. The room was small, but not tiny. It contained a bed, a dresser, several chairs, and a coffee table. It was very clean and tidy.

I told Maman that Lucien was in the parking lot, and Papa immediately got up to go get him. Soon Papa Germain and Lucien entered the room. Greetings were exchanged and they began a conversation that touched on Lucien's childhood, his first and second wives, his present life, and his children.

Then the conversation turned to me. I was asked about my own family history in America and my present life in the Navy. They were very surprised to learn about my often dangerous assignments as a submariner and a diver.

Papa was quiet. I never remembered him talking much; I guess he was just like that. Maman offered us juice and cookies, and we continued to talk.

and ordered food and beer, which was served in short order. We sat, chatted, ate, drank, laughed, and blessed the day for allowing us to once again share in each others' company and family love.

Some hours later, the time had come to take Maman and Papa back to the retirement home. As we were heading back in the tin vehicle, I started to sob uncontrollably. I was so happy to meet them again and so sad to have to say goodbye again so soon.

Soon we pulled up to the entrance of the retirement home and we all got out of the car, except for Lucien. I walked back to the front door with Maman and Papa Germain, where we paused, faced each other, kissed, and hugged. We said our final goodbyes looking deep into each others' eyes, wishing each other the best of health, knowing that we'd never see each other again. Our meeting had been a miracle.

With Papa and Maman Germain

With Maman and Papa Germain and Lucien Gervais

Then it was lunch time, and I suggested to Lucien that we should all go to lunch. We climbed into the tiny tin vehicle and headed off to a luncheon spot favored by Lucien, a beautiful outdoor café. We were soon seated

I had several days left in Lille before I had to depart for Paris and then off to the U.S. and Hawaii, where four more years of military obligation awaited me. I could have seen Maman and Papa Germain again, maybe, before I left France, but I decided against it. That would have been too emotional. That day we had enjoyed a wonderful reunion, and our time together could not have gone any better. It was better to just say goodbye and leave it at that. Returning to these places and people in my past had taken an emotional toll on me, one that I hadn't expected. It was just difficult to be there for a brief moment after all those years and then suddenly have to once again say goodbye forever.

The day of my departure arrived too soon. I was to board my train back to Paris at 1:00 P.M. We spent the morning walking the streets of Lille, taking in the shops and streets of the city. 12:45 found us at the train station. At five minutes before departure, we all kissed, hugged, and held each other for the very last time.

Cathérine and I suddenly found ourselves alone together. Strangely, it seemed like nothing existed except the two of us. The train was about to depart, and I kept holding Cathérine ever so tightly, and she me, not wanting to let go. I reached into my pocket and brought out my set of dolphins, the ones I'd worked so hard for in order to qualify as a submariner. I placed them in Cathérine's tiny hands, and for one final moment, looked deep into my little sister's eyes and whispered, "I love you very much, little sister. Take care of yourself and have a wonderful life." As the train departed the station ever so slowly at first, Cathérine walked along side, keeping me in view. Soon the train gathered speed. I kept looking back at Cathérine's disappearing figure and waved to her one last time.

16

Escape Training Tank

Submariner's dolphins with 2nd Class Diver's helmet

Escape Training Tank

Usually, a hard-hat Navy diver pulls duty aboard a surface vessel, say a salvage ship or a submarine rescue vessel. You've got Navy divers out there and you've got sub sailors wearing dolphins, but you've only got a handful of U.S. Navy divers wearing dolphins in the entire U.S. of A. Navy fleet. Yes, those were the days! I'd walk around the sub base and heads would turn; "Navy diver and a submariner!"

My assignment was to teach submarine sailors escape techniques at the escape training tank.

Built in 1932, the 100-foot-tall Pearl Harbor Submarine Diver Training Tower was used for over 50 years to instruct sailors in submarine escape techniques. The tower was basically a vertical tube filled with 280,000 gallons of fresh water and used to simulate a sailor's ascent from a disabled submarine. Sailors would don a Steinke Hood in an airlock beneath the water-filled chamber, a flood valve would be opened, and the chamber would fill with water. Then it would be pressurized until the pressure equaled the pressure of the water outside. Once the sailors exited the airlock chamber, the buoyant air pressure in their Steinke Hoods allowed them to rise quickly to the surface.[1]

Inside the Escape Training Tank

While stationed at the Escape Training Tank, I continued to practice aikido, and around 1965 I got a chance to go to Japan again via a military flight and train at the Aikido Headquarters in Tokyo for several weeks. Just prior to my departure, Yamamoto *sensei* gave me a bottle of whisky to deliver to Osensei. I also took an 11 x 14 black and white portrait photograph of Osensei, taken professionally at a Honolulu studio during his visit to Hawaii back in 1961, which I intended to have personally autographed.

An old friend of my aikido mentor Meyer Goo, named Virginia Mayhew, whom I had met while training in Honolulu, was now living in Tokyo and training daily at the Hombu Dojo. I made contact with Virginia and mentioned that Yamamoto *sensei* had given me a bottle of whisky for Osensei. Virginia passed this information on, and a time was set aside for a meeting.

The following day I was told to get the whisky and be prepared to meet Osensei. Wow! Was I excited. I, just a nobody from Hilo, Hawaii, a *haole* boy at that, was going to meet the world famous "Osensei," Morihei Ueshiba, the Founder of aikido. I took the brandy and, hidden away under my shirt in a business envelope, the portrait of Osensei.

Several tough-looking, unsmiling Japanese aikido instructors came and led me to the residence attached to the *dojo*. In the front room, sitting behind a desk, was Osensei. There he was, three feet in front of me, right there; Osensei himself! It's difficult to express in words what I felt at that very moment. It was as if I was standing before God himself. My head felt light, and I had to make an effort just to relax and breathe. I felt a pleasant warmth engulf me slowly; I felt peace radiating through the twinkling eyes of Osensei. There was only Universal Love being transmitted. It was "beautiful," if I can use that word. I can think of no other to describe the feeling at that moment.

I bowed to Osensei, voicing a greeting from myself and from Yamamoto *sensei*. I raised the bottle of whisky very slowly towards Osensei, who extended both his arms and accepted it. He spoke to me in Japanese for several minutes, thanking me especially for the fine bottle of whisky and asking me to thank Yamamoto *sensei* when I returned to Hawaii. He also asked me to please continue aikido training, and I answered that I would. Osensei smiled; he was in a happy mood. I told him that I'd brought his portrait with me

---

[1] In 1983, the tower was drained for the last time and converted into a crow's nest conference room by Rear Admiral Jack Darby. Today's modern nuclear-powered submarines run too deep for any possible escape of the crew in case of accident. Normal submarine rescue was previously limited to 500 feet, maximum. Nuclear subs operate at depths of over 1,200 feet.

and respectfully asked if he would be so kind as to sign it for me. He reached out and accepted the photograph, and right there in front of me, wrote his name with a brush and ink and placed two of his official seals on the calligraphy. There it was; done!

He looked up at me and, saying that his hand was a bit shaky that morning, apologized for accidentally allowing part of his thumb to touch the ink on his signature, thus leaving a small partial print. I smiled and thanked him for the autograph, saying that my best wishes were with him and thanking him for sharing his aikido with the world. Bowing respectfully, I was led out of the residence, taking a treasure with me.

That afternoon Virginia asked if I'd gotten the chance to meet Osensei yet. I said yes and told her and about how he'd autographed his portrait and affixed his seals.

Signed portrait of Osensei

"Bernie," she said, "you're fortunate to have possession of such a treasure! Signed photographs of Osensei are only given to special people. The high-ranking Hombu instructors who watch over Osensei don't allow just anyone to get one."

I looked at Virginia and with a wink and a smile said "Oh, I'm so sorry. I guess I should have known better, but I'm just an ignorant *gaijin* (foreigner). How foolish of me!"

"Ha-ha. Nice going, Bernie," she said and hugged me.

Around 1967 on the island of Oahu, I heard talk of a new meditation practice, known as "TM" or Transcendental Meditation, being taught by a great holy man from India. He was called "Maharishi Mahesh Yogi," and the word was that this wonderful guru, this teacher of the Beatles and Mia Farrow, would be holding a meditation seminar in Honolulu. I'd seen photos of the Maharishi, a bearded man from India, shown sitting, always with a serene smile on his face, and I'd felt strangely drawn to him. Being involved in the practice of aikido, I had a strong interest in meditation techniques. And the greatest teacher of meditation in the entire world would be conducting a public seminar right there in Honolulu.

There was, of course, a required donation of $50 in order to attend. $50 was a great deal of money back then, especially for a sailor. However, I knew that meeting this greatest of all gurus from India would be a once-in-a-lifetime opportunity.

With $50 in hand for donation money, I drove to the location of the seminar. As I entered the hall, I saw, seated on a raised platform, the saint himself, the Maharishi Mahesh Yogi. There he was, in the midst of a thousand offerings of tropical flowers, sitting with that captivating smile on his face and eyes that radiated peace and harmony. There were no seats in the hall where the Maharishi was to give his lecture; everyone was seated on the floor, as would have been the norm in an *ashram* in Mother India. Sitting on the floor gave the gathering an air of mystery, of something unknown. Had there been chairs to sit on, the whole feeling would have been totally different, totally western, and not as "cool" as sitting on the floor.

I made my way to the front of the gathering. I didn't care if I was cutting in line; I needed to sit at the feet of this great enlightened guru. There I sat, three feet from His Holiness, from the Saint. I gazed up in admiration; the Maharishi looked down at me and smiled. The great Maharishi had actually looked at me and smiled. I felt bliss; I was trapped into his energy. I knew instantly that I would have to become initiated into the teachings of this great guru. It was my destiny.

For the next hour, the Maharishi spoke to those in attendance, people from all walks of life. His voice was soothing, his strange, exotic Indian accent making his words all the more mysterious. I still don't remember a word he said during the seminar; it was all mumble-jumble to my ears, but that didn't matter because I was there at his feet. I'd felt his energy, and the Maharishi himself had looked directly at me. That alone was enough. Following his hour-long lecture, I was allowed to stand at the side of the great teacher.

I immediately signed up for the great honor of being initiated into the teachings of TM, and thus, I was told, my life would change. There would be great peace and future wealth, my life would be transformed, and I'd no longer experience suffering. Once I received my secret mantra and started practicing TM, I'd be on the path to achieving "universal bliss." I was given a date, location, and instructions about what to bring with me. I was also told the amount of the "donation" required in order to purchase my own personal secret mantra.

Three days later, I drove up to a residence located near Diamond Head in Waikiki, walked up to the house, and knocked on the door. An elderly Japanese woman greeted me and asked if I had the required items with me and the "donation." Let's see, one brand-new white handkerchief, a half cup of uncooked white rice, flowers, and oh yes; that all-important donation. $100 cash, to be exact. All these I gladly handed over to her.

With the Maharishi

She took the sacred items from me and led me into a room, a large closet, actually, where, on the wall, was hung a large picture of His Holiness, the Maharishi. There were flowers everywhere and the smell of exotic incense filled the air. She sat me down, looked into my eyes, and paused for a few moments. Then she leaned close to me and whispered a two-syllable word into my ear; a "word" which, to me, had absolutely no meaning. I was told to very quietly repeat the word back to her, to make sure I had it right. This I did, and having done so, the elderly woman went on whispering to me, telling me that this word was mine and mine alone and to never reveal it or say it to anyone else because, if I did, its power to transform me would be lost forever. I smiled, thanked her, and left, rushing back to my home on the base.

I went into my bedroom and sat myself down in the lotus position to begin my transformation. I repeated my mantra over and over again, as I had been instructed to do. In my mind, I pictured a wheel turning in a circle and mentally recalled my secret mantra. Over and over, I repeated this meaningless two-syllable word, maybe several thousand times in the space of a half hour. I felt bliss and calmness overcoming my body. I felt drugged. I felt relaxed. Wow!

In the beginning I did TM every morning and evening. In time, however, I began to slack off, and now, some 45 years later, I hardly ever do it. Yeah, repeating the mantra relaxed me; I felt a sort of high. But my life remained a life like everyone else's. A life faced with challenges; sometimes filled with joy, sometimes with heartbreak and loss.

I've discovered since then that any word can be used as a "mantra" during meditation. I found this out by substituting other words for the secret mantra I'd been given. Words such as "Holy Mary, Mother of God," "Hello, there," "Hilo, Hawaii," "Doo-doo" and even "Hot Dog!" They all worked as well and helped me to feel a slight high and a sense of relaxation. All I had to do was pick a phrase and keep repeating it to myself for a period of time, say about a half hour.

I "donated" $100 in cash, some white rice, a brand new handkerchief, and a bunch of fresh flowers in return for some secret magical word that has absolutely no meaning to me whatsoever. Was it worth it? Yeah, I guess it was because now I have a photograph of me standing next to the billionaire guru from India, the late Maharishi Mahesh Yogi, who passed on "with a great big smile on his face!"

OM!

Part III

Dance with the Devil

17

Campus Cop

Following my honorable discharge from the U.S. Navy, we caught a flight to Seattle, Washington, where I'd been invited to stay with Nate Johnson's parents. (Nate Johnson was the poor kid who was kissed by Shit-house Ivan way back when we were on the Bluegill.) Their residence, a large brick house, was located at 705 26th Ave S. in the Central District, smack in the middle of the "colored" part of town.

At the time racial tensions were running high. Sometimes I'd come out in the morning, and there would be a sign reading "blue-eyed devil" on my car.

First thing I did was to start looking for a job, which meant applying to the Seattle Police Department. On the scheduled date and time and at the scheduled location, I took the written portion of the test for the position of police officer. One week later, I was notified that I had "not passed." Bummer! I was never good at taking tests.

Next, I took the test for Seattle Fire Department and passed with a high score. On the physical test, I got a 93%. But I didn't want to be a fireman; I wanted to be a cop.

As luck would have it, Nate's Dad told me that the University of Washington was accepting applications. The following week I was back taking another written exam for the position of University of Washington police officer. I opened the exam booklet, and damn me if it wasn't the exact same one I'd taken and failed when I tested for the SPD. I hadn't passed because I didn't answer enough questions correctly in the allotted time.

This time I picked up the pace and answered more questions. Since I'd taken the same exam before, I remembered a lot of the questions and answers and didn't have to think too long about which answers were correct. I was one of the first to complete the written test. I got up, handed in my test booklet and answer sheet, and walked out of that classroom, confident that I'd passed. I was right. The following week, I received notice that I'd passed the written.

Next, came the physical agility portion of the testing procedure. I passed with a score of 92% out of 100. Hell, I'd just gotten out of the U.S. Navy, where I'd been a SCUBA and deep-sea diver and a diving instructor, in charge of the early morning PT (physical training) section of the diving school. I was also actively practicing aikido. I was slim, trim, and could run like the wind.

I went through the basic Police Academy training, which lasted for a period of 3 months. Then I returned to the University of Washington Police Department for assignment.

The year was 1968; the era of the Vietnam War, large-scale civil unrest and riots, and the Black Panther movement. Police were being shot at (yes, in Seattle, too), and ROTC buildings were being bombed. It was the era of the hippies, sex, drugs, rock and roll, marijuana, blotter acid, pills, heroin, black lights and velvet paintings, Jimmy Hendrix, Janis Joplin, the Doors, and let us not forget, Richard Nixon. Life was interesting.

UW Police Academy graduating class

One night I'd gone into the office and was in the lunch room having my dinner, when all of a sudden, BOOM! The loudest explosion that Seattle had ever heard took place not 200 yards from where I was sitting. The SDS had set off a large bomb in the plaza area of the University of Washington. Running up to the blast site, I saw a crater measuring 15 feet across and 10 feet deep. The blast was so powerful that store front windows two miles away were blown out. The bomber was never identified or apprehended, but the rumor was that it had been that violent faction of the SDS known as the "Weathermen." It was their way of protesting against the ROTC program on campus.

Several months later, Trim Bissell, of the Bissell Brush family, was arrested on the UW campus in the act of placing a live bomb on the porch of the Air Force ROTC building. Bissell, who was a member of the Weathermen, jumped bail and was on the run for many years before being nabbed in Eugene, Oregon, where he was employed, under an alias, as a physical therapist.

For an ex-sailor, a kid from Hilo, Hawaii, this chaos was fascinating.

Demonstrators took to throwing bottles and rocks at the Seattle Police riot squad. These demonstrators would then run onto the UW campus to an area known as "Hippie Hill," which they knew didn't come under Seattle police jurisdiction. The demonstrators continued using this tactic for several nights, which frustrated the riot squad to no end. On about the third or fourth night the demonstrators were once again performing this maneuver and, after throwing rocks and bottles at the riot squad, they ran into the bushes located at the top of "Hippie Hill," where suddenly, they were attacked and badly assaulted by a group of about eight to ten white males.

UW policeman, 1968

Word soon got back to the UW police that students were getting their heads cracked by vigilantes. A half-dozen UW police officers responded and, with guns drawn, rounded up the suspected vigilantes, who were still hiding in the bushes at the top of Hippie Hill. The suspects were ordered to lay flat on the ground and not move. However, one of them reached behind him with his right hand. A rookie UW police officer, fearing that this suspect was reaching for a gun, struck him in the mouth, full force, with a riot baton. Blood and teeth erupted from the suspect's mouth; his jaw had been broken and most of his teeth were knocked out. Well, as luck would have it, this small band of supposed vigilantes turned out to be detectives from the intelligence unit of the Seattle Police Department. The "vigilante" had just been reaching for his police ID.

Another time a heavy-set, white female demonstrator was arrested for throwing rocks at the riot squad. She was arrested by the UW police, and a UW police lieutenant and I were assigned to transport the arrestee from the UW campus to the county jail for booking. Her hands were handcuffed behind her back, and she was seated in the back of my police cruiser. The UW lieutenant was also seated in the back, directly behind me, with the female suspect to his right. I drove off campus via a rear exit to avoid running into the riot in progress.

As we were heading up 23rd Avenue on the east side of Capitol Hill, the UW lieutenant suddenly began yelling at the female, calling her a "cunt," "fucking commie," "fat, fucking bitch," and other similar vulgarities. I was surprised to hear this type of language from the lieutenant since, until then, he'd always been a perfect gentleman, never cussing or swearing. As if the verbal abuse wasn't enough, the lieutenant next reached over, grabbed hold of this gal's large breasts, and started squeezing and violently shaking them. I glanced back at him, then looked at the face of the female demonstrator, now the victim of a sexual assault by the police. She looked at me with pleading eyes, no doubt hoping that I'd order the lieutenant to cease his verbal and sexual assault. But I turned my head and pretended not to see what was taking place. I was shocked, angry, and confused. "This is crazy," I thought. "What the hell is this lieutenant doing?"

The abuse continued till I drove into the Seattle police garage, at which time, the lieutenant sat back in an upright position, acting as if nothing out of the ordinary had happened.

What the lieutenant had done wasn't right. What the female demonstrator had done, throwing rocks at the police, wasn't right, either. My not intervening immediately was also not right; but had I taken any action against the lieutenant, I would have been labeled a "rat" (an officer who squeals on fellow officers). My career as a police officer would soon have been over and done with, and that wouldn't have been right either!

When the civil unrest finally quieted down, and especially during the summer months, when classes were not in session, being a campus cop became boring to the max. Eight hours, night after night, driving around campus all night long, locking up buildings, driving off campus to check UW property and parking lots, at times going an entire week without getting a single radio dispatch call, and trying to stay awake all night long in your patrol car without falling asleep ... Well, that wasn't my idea of being a cop. I craved action! I wanted to work narcotics. I wanted to be a detective someday. I wanted that living-on-the-edge type of feeling.

I applied and took the test for Seattle police officer a second time. And damn it, I failed the written test again. I'd have to wait another six months before being allowed to re-take the written test. Bummer! It wasn't really that difficult a test. I just had to focus, concentrate, and understand the questions. The math problems weren't that hard. I had my own way of figuring out some of the answers, like "How many yards are there in a mile?" Right offhand, I couldn't tell you. But in high school, I ran the 880-yard dash, which I knew was a half-mile race. 880 yards times two = 1,760 yards. So the answer was, there are 1,760 yards in a mile.

What to do about passing that Seattle police written exam? All I needed was to answer just seven or eight more questions correctly. That would give me a passing score, and I could then go on to the physical agility portion of testing. I had an idea; it was a long shot, but it just might work. The UWPD and SPD written tests were exactly the same. The UW had a testing center that was located off-campus, just outside the main gate. Now, if I could somehow talk the person in charge of testing into allowing me to take that police test again ... Well, that way I could jot down some of the math problems that I didn't know, some of the vocabulary words that I'd missed, and that would give me the additional number of correct answers necessary to pass the SPD test.

So I went into the testing office and somehow convinced the gal in charge of testing to let me re-take the test. I had a piece of paper with me on which to jot down questions and math problems that I knew I'd missed. I was taken to a large classroom, where I sat all by myself while the individual in charge of testing sat at her desk. Upon opening up the test booklet, I scanned for questions that I'd missed before. This was the fourth time that I'd gone over the same test booklet, and I was getting to know it rather well. I scanned the booklet and, without being noticed, jotted down the necessary information. Finishing my task within 15 minutes, I got up and exited the classroom. I didn't even bother to finish the exam. I'd gotten the necessary information, and now it was time to get out. In my mind, I saw myself as a spy getting information from some foreign government. My mission was to obtain a secret file and jot down critical information. I'd succeeded!

Now, I needed to study that critical information and, with the new-found knowledge, re-take the SPD exam, which I now had no doubt I'd pass. Then I'd go on to the physical agility testing phase, which I also knew I'd have no difficulty passing. I'd stayed lean and mean by exercising every day.

As the saying goes, "Third time's a charm." I took the test, passed the written with a high score, and just about aced the physical agility portion. I also passed the oral interview, background check, and medical examination. Back then, there was no polygraph testing. I'd have passed anyway; I was a young, clean-cut kid who'd just spent eight years in the Navy and two years with the UWPD. I was a prime candidate for becoming a Seattle police officer. My dream was coming true. It took a while, but I got myself hired on.[1]

---

[1] As a note of interest, I found out from a Seattle police sergeant assigned to recruiting that if I failed the written portion of the exam again, then, being that, on paper, I was "Chinese," and therefore a "minority," I qualified for the "Police Trainee" program which was designed to aid minorities, mostly blacks, in passing the written portion of the exam. Had I not passed this third time around, I most certainly would have taken up his offer. One way or another, I was determined to become a Seattle cop.

18

Field Training

I finally got a call informing me that I'd been accepted as a Seattle police recruit and was told the date and time to be present at the Seattle Municipal Building to be sworn in. One fine day in April of 1970, 40 other individuals and I were sworn in. I was now a real cop, a Seattle police officer. I'd never given up my dream, and finally, I'd made it. Seattle police officer "Bernard Lau; serial number 3354."

Next, came four and a half months of basic training. The first two months were held at the Seattle Police Academy, which was located in an old nunnery out in Issaquah.

The first day of class, we were introduced to Lt. Bob Holter of the homicide unit. We later learned that Lt. Holter had shot and killed a member of an organized crime family. From what we were told, things were a bit dangerous for him since there was the possibility of a reprisal. You don't just kill some mob guy and expect no reprisal. So there, in front of the class of 41 raw recruits, stood Lt. Holter; tall, tough-looking, and wearing a shoulder holster with a Colt .357 six-shot magnum revolver, the same make and model that Steve McQueen had carried in the movie "Bullit." I was impressed!

Lt. Holter started off by saying, "Men, I'm going to tell you something that you should never forget throughout your careers as police officers. Remember what I tell you, and it will make your police work a lot easier. Here it is: anyone is capable of anything at any time, no matter who that person might be." Holter went on explaining to us wide-eyed recruits, "Just because someone is a priest, a lawyer, a housewife, a scoutmaster, an 80-year-old grandmother, a six-year-old kid, even a cop, it doesn't automatically mean that they shouldn't be considered a suspect if the evidence points that way. Any individual, and I mean any individual, is capable of committing any crime."

"Never think 'it can't be him because he's not the type' or 'he's not capable.' There is no type of individual that is not capable. Priests have molested and raped altar boys, scoutmasters have molested the boy scouts in their troop, family members have molested and raped their own children and housewives have committed murder. Cops have gotten drunk and beaten up their wives, molested children, and committed murder. There is no one, not one individual on this planet, who isn't capable, under certain circumstances, of committing any crime, no matter how heinous. Who and what a person is, what occupation a person is involved in doesn't exempt that individual from being as capable as the next person of committing a crime. Never forget that, men, and in time, you'll understand what I'm saying. Good luck to each and every one of you, and I'll look forward to maybe working with you in the near future."

I attended classes, took notes, studied every night, did my homework assignments, and overall, did very well in my studies. I passed all the written tests with good scores. And because of my duties in the Navy, I never had a problem with the physical training. I could still run like the wind.

After the first two months of classroom work, each recruit was assigned to ride along on patrol with a seasoned officer as his FTO (Field Training Officer). Usually, this FTO was someone with five or more years of experience on the force. These "old timers" were going to teach us green recruits what real police work was all about. Back then, FTOs were like God. They had the power to wash you out of the recruit program at will and for whatever reason they chose. They basically owned you.

My very first FTO was Officer "Henson," who worked the day shift out of the Georgetown Precinct in West Seattle. He started off by telling me the following; "Hey, kid, forget all that book stuff they taught you in the Academy; that shit can get you killed! Keep your mouth shut, do as I tell you, and I'll teach you what real police work is all about." So my "real" training started. It would be a week before Officer Henson allowed me to sit behind the wheel and actually drive the police cruiser, but when he finally did, wow, what a feeling of excitement that was! I was instructed how to make traffic stops, how to fill out traffic citations and traffic accident reports, and how to safely pull over suspicious vehicles.

It was a sunny afternoon; my third week of riding with Henson. I was behind the wheel, driving in the vicinity of Alki Beach, when suddenly, he told me to pull over and park. I thought we were going to do a foot patrol along the beach, looking for kids drinking beer and all that. I was mistaken. Officer Henderson instructed me to come to the rear of the patrol vehicle, where he opened up the trunk. Then he took out his briefcase, closed the trunk, and laid the briefcase on top. He opened it and proceeded to show me a collection of various types of illegal drugs.

There was a lid of marijuana, there was heroin (it was the first time I'd ever seen heroin), there were pills of various shapes and colors, and a few tabs of what Henson said was acid. At first, I thought it was going to be one of those "show and tell" exercises, where us green recruits learned to identify different types of illegal drugs. Neat! But, no. Officer Henson explained to me that these drugs were reserved for "assholes." If some guy gave him a bad time, mouthed off, got smart with him, and acted like a prick, he simply planted the dope on him and charged him with possession of narcotics. He could deny it in court, but who would the judge believe? Henson, a police officer, or some puke asshole that had probably been arrested before and had a rap sheet? That said, Henson closed his briefcase and put it back in the trunk.

For a moment, I just stood there trying to make sense of what had just happened. I was confused, to say the least. Had I heard correctly when Henderson said he kept the drugs in case some "asshole" gave him a bad time, so he could plant the drugs on him and charge him with possession of narcotics? I went back to the police cruiser. Henderson got in on the passenger side, and we resumed patrolling West Seattle. He didn't say another word about the drugs.

I had one more week before I'd be reassigned to my second FTO. The topic of the drugs never came up again, and I'm glad to say I never witnessed Officer Henson plant drugs on anyone. I could have gone to one of the precinct supervisors and turned him in. He might have been fired, but I'd certainly have been flunked out of the police academy. Cops don't rat on other cops, no matter what.

My second FTO was Officer "Bill." Bill seemed like a good guy; easy-going, easy to talk to, and he told me to go ahead and call him "Bill." A few weeks into riding with Bill, we got a call from dispatch for us to take an assault report from a Miss Anderson. Seemed she'd been beaten up by her boyfriend and wanted to file a restraining order on him. I drove to the address location and, being as I was the officer in training, I ended up taking the report. In other words, I did the paperwork. It wasn't all that difficult.

I started in, "Miss Anderson, could you give me your full name and date of birth." She was 28 years old. I wrote down the information. I then had Miss Anderson write out a statement of what exactly had transpired. Who'd assaulted her, what injuries she may have received ... all the "just the facts, ma'am" kind of information.

Meanwhile, Officer Bill was sitting down next to Miss Anderson, trying to comfort her since she was still very upset and shaken by the assault. At one point he took hold of her hand and started to stroke it while telling her that everything would be fine and not to worry. Before long, he was starting to flirt with her.

I thought, "Here we go again!"

I finished taking the assault report, and Officer Bill told me to go wait in the patrol vehicle, saying he'd be right out. I sat in the patrol unit as instructed and read over the report for any errors I may have made in spelling or punctuation. Ten minutes went by before Officer Bill finally returned. He got in, I drove off, and we continued patrolling our West Seattle district. Bill informed me that after he got off shift, he was going go pay this "asshole boyfriend" a personal visit and, in no uncertain terms, tell him to "stay the fuck away from Miss Anderson, or else." I didn't say a word. I was still just a police recruit, assigned to this Field Training Officer Bill, and therefore, I wasn't allowed to voice any personal opinions unless asked.

The next day while on patrol, Bill informed me that he'd paid the asshole a visit and that the now-ex-boyfriend had gotten the message loud and clear. Bill went on to tell me that, later on that evening, he'd gone back over to Miss Anderson's residence to let her know that she didn't have to worry about her boyfriend any longer because he'd "taken care" of the problem. Bill added, "Yeah, Miss Anderson was very thankful and relieved, and we ended up having sex." (OK, Recruit Officer Lau, you want to keep your job, just drive and keep your damn mouth shut. You've worked too long and hard to become a Seattle police officer to throw it all away by ratting out another cop. Besides, you'll soon be reassigned to another FTO.)

The month over with, I got assigned to FTO Number Three; Officer "Bob." FTO Bob turned out to be an easy-going, laid-back kind of guy who took his job seriously. This time, the patrol area was the University District. On the last week of riding with FTO Bob, we were near the University Bridge. Officer Bob was driving, and he suddenly pulled into the Red Robin Restaurant parking lot.

I was thinking, "OK, time for a coffee break. Maybe I'll order one of their fine Hawaiian Teriyaki Burgers. I like the pineapple they put on them Hawaiian Burgers; reminds me of back home in the islands."

But no, we weren't there for a coffee break.

Bob looked over at me and said, "Bernie, next week you'll be returning to the Academy. How'd you like to get laid tonight?"

I looked at FTO Bob.

"What do you mean 'get laid?'"

Bob continued, "Well, there's this gal everybody calls 'Uniform Linda.' She'll screw anything that wears a uniform. Cops, firemen ... She don't care as long as they got on a uniform."

I thought it must be a joke. Yeah, sure; a joke. I mean, this being my final week of FTO training, it was his last chance to play a prank on Bernie, the naive recruit.

"Bob, you're joking, right?"

"No Bernie, I'm not joking, I'm telling you the truth. This gal Linda likes to fuck cops. Hell, probably half the department's screwed her!"

I didn't know what to say. It was way too weird. Bob wrote down a phone number on a piece of paper and handed it to me.

"Here, Bernie; go over to that phone and give Linda a call."

I said, "Bob, what am I supposed to say to this Linda gal; 'Hi, I'm Officer Lau, and I'd like to come over tonight and fuck you?!'"

"Bernie, just go call and tell her you're riding with Bob. Believe me, that's all you need to say."

I wasn't so sure about this. I still thought it might be a prank. I mean, come on, it couldn't be that easy to get laid. Call up some gal, some "Uniform Linda" I'd never met, tell her Bob said to call, and she'd invite me over for free sex? No way.

But, what the hell, Bob was my FTO, so I went over to the phone booth and, following his instructions, dialed the number. Several rings later, a sweet voice answered, "Hello, this is Linda."

"Hi, Linda. My name's Bernie. I'm a police officer. Aah, Bob said to give you a call."

"Oh, OK, great. I'd like to meet you, Bernie. Want to come by tonight?"

"Aah, OK, sure. Where do you live, and what time should I come over?"

"Have Bob tell you where I live. See you around nine tonight. That OK with you?"

"Sure, Linda, nine is fine. See you at nine."

My mind was reeling. This was all so strange. Was it really possible to just call up some gal I'd never met and make a date for free sex? There had to be a catch. She was probably fat and ugly. There had to be something wrong with this "Uniform Linda."

That evening I found myself knocking on her door with a bottle of red wine and a bunch of daffodils. I was a bit nervous. I couldn't believe what I was doing. Like I said, I didn't know what Linda looked like. I really hoped she wasn't a dog.

The door opened and there she stood before me. I couldn't believe it: Linda was cute!

"Hi, I'm Linda. You must be Bernie."

"Hi, Linda. Yes, I'm Bernie." We shook hands and I handed her the flowers and the bottle of wine.

"Oh, how thoughtful of you, Bernie; they're beautiful! Thank you. You didn't have to. How sweet of you! Come in, come in."

I followed Linda into her house. It was clean, tidy, and well-furnished. Linda looked to be around 24 years old, about 5' 3" with short brown hair.

"Bernie, shall we have a glass of wine?"

"Ah, yes, thank you. I don't drink much really; just a glass of wine now and then. I'm not really a drinker, but I am French, so I must have a glass of wine every so often. It's a French thing!"

"French? You're really French? I bet you're a great lover. *Voulez-vous coucher avec moi?* (Do you want to sleep with me)?"

I blushed. It seemed to be the one thing that every American knew how to say in French.

"Why, Bernie, you're blushing! How cute!"

"Ahh, sorry."

"That's OK, Bernie. Just relax and enjoy your wine." Linda poured us each a glass.

"Here, Bernie. Cheers to my first French lover!"

"Cheers. I'll drink to that!" We drank our wine and made small talk. I learned that Linda worked as a waitress at the University IHOP. She was from the Mid-West, originally, and had been in Seattle going on six years. We didn't talk about cops or sex, and I was grateful for that.

After the second glass of wine, she took my hand, winked at me, and said, "Bernie, want to go to the bedroom?"

"Ahh, sure," I said. I got up and followed her into the bedroom, all the while thinking to myself, "Is this really happening?" I stood at the foot of the large king-size bed and watched as Linda started to undress.

"C'mon, Bernie, don't be shy. Take your clothes off! I won't bite. Promise!"

I started to take my clothes off while looking at Linda's body. Very nice, slim build, tiny breasts with soft pink nipples, strong legs… Linda sure was cute, and I was getting very horny. Linda, now completely naked, climbed onto the bed.

"Come join me, my French lover boy."

I got on the bed and moved over towards her. We hugged. Her body was soft and smooth, and she smelled wonderful. We kissed and caressed. I got harder and harder, and then Linda reached down and took hold of me.

"My, my! You're pretty hard, Bernie! Ha-ha. You ready?"

"Ah, yes, I am."

I could hardly believe it, but all this was in fact real. Linda lay on her back, and I got on top of her. She reached for me again, I touched her. Boy, how wet she was. Linda arched her back slightly and, as she held me, she guided me inside her. Oh, my. God Damn! She was tight! I still couldn't believe it was happening.

I was in sexual heaven. We made love, we sweated, we moaned, we moved in sync with each other, and finally, we both climaxed at the same time!

After that, we just lay there, holding each other, as we attempted to bring our rapid breathing under control. As I was lying there in Linda's arms, thinking about how great it had been, how fantastic, and how she really knew what she was doing, I tried not to think about how she'd gotten to be so good at sex. She was no cheap slut. Uniform Linda was cute, well-mannered, well-dressed, pleasant to be with, a good conversationalist, and kept her home neat and tidy. She was even a good cook. She would have made a perfect wife, but for the fact that she was available for free sex to any cop or fireman who wanted her.

Believe it or not, some idiot cop once brought Uniform Linda to one of the annual police retirement parties that were held at the Police Range. There must have been 300 cops there—officers, sergeants, lieutenants, captains, majors, assistant chiefs—yep, and Linda had had sex with at least a third of those present. Now, can you just see all those nervous cops there who'd had sex with Linda introducing her to their wives? "Hon, I'd like you to meet 'Uniform Linda.' She likes to screw cops. Me? Oh no, I never did!"

Linda was like the department's therapist. Had a bad week, Officer? Stressed out? Just go see Linda. Wife mad at you for some unknown reason, won't sleep with you? Just go see Linda. Overly-horny following an exciting night of car chases, catching bad guys, or being involved in a shootout? Go see Linda. She was always available, always pleasant, and always ready and willing to provide personal therapy. You might have to wait a while if other stressed-out cops or firemen had booked an appointment ahead of you. But anyway, being in the caring arms of Uniform Linda sure beat seeing the department shrink or the chaplain. Linda was in fact easy to talk to. She listened, she comforted you, she held you close, gave you advice if you asked, and never charged you a dime for sex.[1]

My three months of FTO training over and done with, I returned to the Police Academy for the final two weeks. During that time, we recruits were asked to stand in front of the class and share with our fellow recruits what we'd learned about police work under the guidance of our individual FTOs. I wondered to myself what I should say. "Well, fellow recruits, I had an exciting few months. My first FTO showed me illegal drugs and told me they were for planting on assholes. My second FTO ended up threatening an assault suspect with bodily harm and then going over and having sex with the victim of that assault. My third FTO introduced me to Uniform Linda. Who's Uniform Linda, you ask? Well, never mind, but I kept her phone number, and no, you can't have it!" Did I share those experiences with the class? Well... no, I chose not to, and by keeping my mouth shut, I kept my job and graduated from the Seattle Police Academy in September of 1970.

Those were three interesting months, and I did in fact learn a lot about the real world of being a Seattle police officer.

---

[1] On occasion, Uniform Linda would show up at police roll call and stand in line with the officers getting ready to go on shift. Nothing was ever said to her about not doing so, and no sergeant ever barred her from showing up. She was sort of like a police mascot.

Seattle Police Academy—Class 64 (1970)

19

Probie

Following graduation from the Police Academy, I was assigned to the Downtown Precinct, evening shift, 8:00 P.M. to 4:00 A.M. (We worked 8-hour shifts back then and usually with a partner.) My very first time ever as a cop on the streets of Seattle, fresh out of the Academy, I was partnered up with Officer "Jim."

As soon as I met Officer "Jim," I got the feeling that he had a chip on his shoulder. Anyway, we called in to radio as "in service" and hit the streets with Officer Jim behind the wheel. We cruised over to Chinatown, then headed west on Jackson Street.

Suddenly, as if there was some sort of emergency, he pulled us over onto the curb behind an unoccupied parked vehicle. I looked over at him and asked, "What's happening? What's going on?" Officer Jim ignored my question and started cussing as he exited the police cruiser.

"Fucking dykes, fucking bitches, fucking lesbians. I hate them cunts."

He had his traffic citation book with him and was proceeding to fill out a parking citation on the parked vehicle. I got out of the car and walked up to him.

"What's going on?" I asked him again. Officer Jim answered, "Illegal parking. I'm gonna have this car towed."

From what I could tell, the "illegally parked" car wasn't actually parked illegally. I did notice that we were in front of the "Silver Slipper," a tavern that catered to lesbians. Suddenly, a half-dozen or more irate females came pouring out of the tavern towards us. They were yelling, cussing, and screaming at Officer Jim, calling him a "pig" and an "asshole."

I just stood there, not saying a word, not knowing what to do. What was going on? One minute, Officer Jim and I were driving peacefully down Jackson Street. The next minute, all hell was breaking loose. Angry females were yelling and screaming at Jim, and more still coming out of the tavern. I stood back, watching all this go down. I'd been on the street as a cop for ten whole minutes; that was all. The moment that I'd been dreaming of since I was 16 years old, my very first few minutes as a real Seattle police officer!

Officer Jim finished writing the parking citation and pushed a copy under the wiper blade of the vehicle. The gals continued to cuss at him as we got back into our vehicle. Just before I got in, I looked over at the angry lesbians. I raised both my hands and shrugged my shoulders as if to say, "Hey, ladies, this wasn't my doing. I had no part in it, and I don't know what's wrong with this officer." Several of the gals looked at me and nodded their heads as though saying, "It's OK, Officer. We understand. We know it wasn't you."

I got back into the patrol car. Officer Jim peeled out and headed over onto 1st Avenue. He looked over at me and said, "What's the matter, Bernie; you like dykes or something? You like queers?" Knowing that you can't argue with an idiot, I kept my mouth shut.

The rest of the shift, we responded to a few minor calls. We didn't say much to each other. Shift over, I turned in the paperwork and walked away without saying a word. I was hoping I'd never have to work with Officer Jim again. Please, Lord!

I changed into my civilian clothes, got my VW bus, and drove off to the Silver Slipper. Exiting my vehicle, I took a moment to center myself and walked into the tavern. I was immediately confronted by the bartender and several of her pals. Before they could speak, I raised my hands to show that I wasn't there to cause trouble. I said that I was there to offer my personal apology for the unprofessional and totally wrong behavior of Officer Jim. I went on to explain that I'd had absolutely no prior warning that this behavior on his part was going to take place.

Everyone was silent for a moment as what I'd said sank in. Then the bartender said, "Yeah, we figured as much from the look on your face. We could tell that you were surprised by his behavior. What's your name, Officer?"

"Lau, my name's Bernie Lau, and this was my first night on patrol since I graduated from the Police Academy. What a way to start my career, huh?"

"Well, Officer Lau, on behalf of the Silver Slipper and all us gals here, we appreciate your stopping by, and we accept your apology. I don't think any other officer would've stopped by to apologize, and we appreciate that. I hope you never become a creep, like that partner of yours. You're a good man. Stay that way. By the way, can we offer you a beer?"

"Yes, ma'am, I'd like that."

After having a beer, I left and headed home. I felt better for having apologized, even though it hadn't been my fault. Folks deserve to be treated with respect, no matter who they may be.

The following night, I was partnered up with Officer John Guich, and we got assigned to King Sector (Chinatown). The King Sector sergeant was Sgt. "Billy Smith," a white male in his early 30s, slim build, dark hair … Seemed like a nice enough guy. We checked in with radio dispatch as we began our shift; John was driving.

Ten minutes into our shift, we got a call, "King Sector cars, meet your sergeant at 7th and Yesler." We looked at each other; "Wonder what that's all about?" We pulled up to where the other patrol vehicles were parked on the I-5 Overpass, parked, got out of our car, and walked over to Sgt. Smith's car.

"Evening, Sarge. What's up?"

Sgt. Smith started, "Well, guys, I called you all here because this is my final night with the department. I'm getting fired tomorrow."

"Why, Sarge? What's going on?" I could see that Sgt. Smith was about to cry. He already had a few tears in his eyes.

"Well, it's all because of them damn 'ho's turned me in. That gal, Debby, that 'ho' that hangs around the little park near the Sun Ya Restaurant, well, she squealed on me. Every so often, I'd have her suck my dick, you know, her and a few of the others. I figured, hey, Chinatown is my sector. They wanna work in my sector, they gotta do me favors every now and then. It's all part of the game, you know. No big deal; two, three times a week I got a blow job from one of 'em. In return, I left 'em alone. You all know that; that's why I had you leave them 'ho's alone."

One of the officers spoke up. "Why'd she squeal, Sarge? What was her beef?"

"Well, Debby got this bright idea that if she was gonna suck my dick, I should be paying her. The fucking bitch!"

Sgt. Smith started to cry, but quickly got hold of himself and wiped the tears from his eyes.

"Well, I just wanted to let you guys know that it's been great working with you, and I'm gonna miss each and every one of you. Lau, you're new; wish I could have gotten to know you better."

One of the officers spoke out, "Hey, Sarge, you want us to take care of that Debby gal? You know, fuck 'er up or something?"

"No, guys. Thanks, but she's caused enough trouble as it is. No use any of you men getting fired over this too. Just leave her alone."

Sgt. Smith shook each of our hands and said, "Guys, I'm sure gonna miss this job. Gonna miss working with all of you. Take care!"

We all went back to our cars and drove off to resume our shifts. I looked over at John and said, "Damn, that's a bummer, Sgt. Smith getting fired like that."

"Yeah, Bernie, it is. But Sgt. Smith was stupid. Really dumb, actually. He was getting blow jobs while on duty, in uniform, in his patrol vehicle. Tell me that wasn't dumb!"

"Yeah, John, I guess you're right. And if it was about money, that gal wanting to get paid, well, Sgt. Smith should have just given her some money. I mean, I'm not saying what he was doing was OK, but if he was going to do that, he should at least have waited until he was off shift and out of uniform. Then he might have gotten some time off, but not lost his job."

"Well, Bernie, you're right, but doing it on duty, that was part of his trip. Smith enjoyed the feeling of power. Think about it—to be the sergeant in charge of an entire sector, Chinatown, of all places, and to be in uniform with a gun, a badge, in a patrol vehicle, and having some prostitute give you head ... Now, that's powerful. It was all about feeling powerful. The blow job was just a small part of it."

There was always something going on in Chinatown. On New Year's Eve, 1970, I think it was, the SPD vice squad conducted a raid on one of the gambling dens in the middle of a rather well-attended New Year's Eve party. Everyone at the party was searched for gambling tokens or other gambling paraphernalia, and anyone caught with them on their person was arrested and hauled off to jail. My partner and I were called in as backup.

As we entered, I saw several Chinese friends of mine. One of them was Ming L., who was there with his wife and parents. I went up to Ming, said "hi," and shook his hand. As we clasped hands, Ming slipped me a half-dozen Chinese gambling tokens that he and his parents had been holding. Nonchalantly, I took the tokens and pocketed them.

I couldn't see my friend Ming, his wife, and his parents being arrested on New Year's Eve, of all times, for such a minor offense. Spend New Year's Eve and New Year's Day in jail for possession of gambling tokens? I don't think so! So I did what I did and the Mings were released.

In all 20 men and women were arrested and hauled off to jail. These people had dressed formally for the celebration. The ladies were dressed to the hilt, some wearing their best gowns with fur wraps. It was quite a sight to witness them being hauled off to jail in the back of a dirty old police paddy wagon. Talk about disgrace.

The following week heads rolled, from the vice commander all the way down to the detectives who were responsible for the raid. Mayor Uhlman was pissed! Some of the people arrested were very influential, the type you don't want to mess with. Later, I heard that city politics may have played a role in the incident. Anyway, several supervisors from vice were suddenly transferred to less desirable units, such as patrol. Playing politics can be a dangerous game.

A year or so later, after I'd been transferred to narcotics, the day shift detectives I was working with decided to have lunch at Tai Tung Restaurant in Chinatown. Sgt. Sanford, three other detectives, and myself went into the restaurant and were shown to a large table. No sooner had we taken our seats than a waiter came over and placed a large serving of shrimp with lobster sauce in front of me. The waiter said, "*Sifu* ("Master," or "teacher" in Chinese), somebody order, but no want, so now I give for you." Then he walked away. Sgt. Sanford and the other detectives had surprised looks on their faces. One of them asked, "Hey, Bernie, what was that all about? What makes you so special?" I just smiled and said, "Hey, some of us got it, and some of you don't."

The waiter was Ming L.

20

Rookie

One of the first things a rookie cop learns is where to get free meals. Cops are on patrol for eight hours at a time, and being human, they need to eat. The three choices are: don't eat till you get home, bring a sack lunch, or eat out while on shift.

Cops overwhelming choose number three. But if you eat out five nights a week, it ends up costing you a lot of money, and that's if you only eat once during your eight-hour shift. Have two meals a shift, and you end up spending a major part of your monthly salary on food.

Here's how we dealt with the problem back in the early 70s: each patrol sector had its own favorite eating spots reserved for that sector's cars. These restaurants offered the district cars free or discounted eats. For example, there was a restaurant called "The Joker" that offered free food to police officers, but the officers had to eat whatever they were served. Often it was nothing more than spaghetti with a salad and coffee. But, hey, not too bad if it's free. And every so often, you got pork chops, mashed potatoes, gravy, and apple sauce.

There were two rules you couldn't violate: one was you couldn't hit up any one restaurant too often. The other rule was you couldn't infringe on another sector's eating spots.

Those restaurants that offered discounts or freebies to on-duty police officers liked the visual presence of the police. It kept trouble-makers away, which was well worth the restaurant's cost of a free meal. The officers got fed, the restaurants got the presence of Seattle's finest for 30 minutes. It was a fair trade.

One evening I was partnered up with a black officer named "Darrel Cartwright." Officer Cartwright was a large individual, maybe 6'2", and weighed at least 200 lbs. It was my understanding that Darrel had been a "jock" in high school. I could tell he was in top physical condition and not one to be messed with in a physical confrontation.

The night I got partnered up with Cartwright, I'd been out of the police academy for perhaps only a year. In other words, I was still very much a rookie. However, right off the bat, he treated me as an equal. We shook hands; "You Bernie? Hi, I'm Darrel, Darrel Cartwright. You'll be riding with me this evening. Let's go!"

During the early 70s, there was an undertone of racial prejudice within the department. The prejudice wasn't blatant. White officers didn't go around using racial slurs towards black officers. It was just that black officers were often passed over for promotion, that sort of thing.

The black officers formed themselves a "Black Officers' Union" within the Seattle Police Department. I didn't know any of the details or reasons why, but black officers getting together and forming their own "Black Officers' Union," well, there must have been good reason for doing so.

As for myself, a kid from Hilo, Hawaii, I got along with everyone. Black, White, Asian, or whatever ethnic background the individual came from. It made no difference to me, none whatsoever. In fact, I always felt more comfortable with "non-white" officers than I did with white officers.

The evening I got partnered up with Officer Cartwright, I thought "cool" and looked forward to an interesting evening. Here I was, a white police officer partnered up with a black police officer and patrolling the CD.

It didn't take me long to observe that Officer Cartwright was "connected," meaning that he knew just about everyone in the CD. He knew the drug dealers, the addicts, the pimps, the prostitutes, the gamblers, the merchants, the kids on the streets, the bums ... Darrel knew them all. Wherever Darrel Cartwright went, he was respected, or perhaps, just feared. No one dared mouth off to him. If they had, no doubt Darrel would have gotten up in their face and read them the riot act. He had no fear and took no bullshit from anyone.

During our shift, he had me drive around to one location after another and park, where he would then get out of our patrol vehicle and go chat with different people. After about an hour of this, he asked me, "Bernie, how you like your steak cooked?" I said, "I like mine real rare, why?" All he said was "That's all I need to know. You'll see." He then had me pull over to a phone booth, where he made a quick call. About a half hour later, he instructed me to drive to a certain address located along Cherry Street near 23rd Avenue. There he had me pull over and park.

I followed him as he got out of the squad car and went up the stairs. Without knocking, we walked inside and were greeted by a very attractive black female, perhaps 23 years old. Darrel introduced me to this young lady as his "partner" and instructed me to have a seat. I looked around. Lo and behold; there, in the middle of the living room, was a full-sized dining table complete with a white table cloth and a full dinner setting for two.

I looked over and asked Darrel, "What's this?" He just smiled and said, "Dinner, Bernie, just dinner." Then he added, "I do know how to treat my partners."

Darrel and I sat down and were served a full-course steak dinner with all the trimmings. I couldn't believe it. Here we were, two Seattle police officers in uniform, sitting down to a beautifully laid-out dinner for two and being attended to by a lovely young lady. I'll never forget that wonderful dinner in the middle of the CD.

Unfortunately, his "connections" were his downfall. I never saw or witnessed Darrel Cartwright do anything unlawful or shady, but eventually, he was set up in some sort of sting operation, arrested, booked into the city jail, and in time, fired.

I always enjoyed working with Cartwright whenever we were partnered up, for I knew I was safe. Sure, I was a white boy, a "pig," as we were often called by blacks back then, but no one ever dared to disrespect me when I was in the company of Officer Cartwright. And even though I was only a rookie at the time, Darrel Cartwright always treated me with respect. That's more than I can say for some of the white officers I ended up working with.

Officer John Hoffard, was another fine officer I had the pleasure of working with during my rookie days. Once while on uniform patrol, he and I arrested a guy for creating a disturbance at some local tavern up on Broadway Avenue. This individual, a somewhat drunk white male in his mid-30s, was placed in the back of our patrol vehicle behind the passenger seat. I was sitting behind Hoffard, who was driving.

On the way to the station, the drunk said to John, "Hey, Officer, your wife's a cocksucker." John glanced back at me, smiled and gave a nod. For whatever reason, the guy hadn't been handcuffed. So without any words spoken or emotions displayed, I reached over and put a lock on his left wrist. It wasn't long before I had this person sobbing like a baby.

I held the wrist lock all the way to the station. John pulled in, parked the patrol unit, then went around and opened the rear passenger door. I was still applying the wrist lock.

Just as John and I were removing the still-sobbing arrestee from the vehicle, a patrol sergeant happened to walk by. "Oh-oh," I thought, "Now, we're gonna get chewed out." The sergeant just looked at us and said, "Good work, men!"

Officer BERNARD LAU
PATROL DIVISION
PHONE 583-2300

THE CITY OF SEATTLE
DEPARTMENT OF POLICE
PUBLIC SAFETY BUILDING

EMERGENCY
PHONE 911

21

Hippie Girl

One night Officer John Guich and I were working third watch patrol (8:00 P.M. to 4:00 A.M.) in the Capitol Hill area. It was a quiet evening, and we hadn't gotten any calls since going on shift. We were about to take a coffee break when we got a call from radio dispatch.

"Car Three Boy Three, Bellevue has in custody a female arrested on one of our city warrants. Pick her up and deliver to our jail."

"Three Boy Three to radio. Any idea what the warrant is for?"

"That's a negative, Three Boy Three."

"Three Boy Three, received. On our way to Bellevue to transport one female to our jail."

Twenty minutes later, we arrived at the Bellevue Police Station and spoke with the desk sergeant.

"Evening, Sergeant. I'm Officer Lau, and this is my partner Officer Guich. We're here to transport some female arrested on one of our city warrants."

"Right. We got 'er right here in our holding cell. Hippy gal. She's scared shitless."

"What's the warrant for, Sergeant?"

"Dog leash violation." Officer Guich and I looked at each other and shook our heads. Talk about a chippy warrant!

"OK, let's get her." The sergeant walked us over to the holding cell and opened the door. Seated on the bench was a white female, approximately 18 years of age, tall, cute, with long blonde hair. Yep, she was a hippy all right.

"Evening, ma'am. I'm Officer Lau, Seattle Police, and this is my partner, Officer Guich. We're here to transport you to Seattle city jail on your outstanding warrant. What's your name, ma'am?"

The hippy girl looked up at us. Her eyes were red from crying; mascara was running down her cheeks. Sobbing, she said, "I'm 'Nancy.'"

"OK, Nancy. Everything's gonna be OK. Don't be scared."

"Officer, I've never been arrested before. I've never been in jail."

"Nancy, everything's gonna be fine. It's just a dog leash violation. Nothing to worry about."

"Yes, but I'm in jail, and you're gonna put me in another jail! I've never been locked up before. Please, can't I just go home?"

"You can go home as soon as you post bail."

"Post bail? I only have a few dollars on me. How much is bail?"

"I don't know, but we'll find out once we get up to the jail. OK, Nancy, time to go."

We drove Nancy back to the Public Safety Building in Seattle and took her up to the 7th Floor, where the women's section of the jail was located. Nancy was booked, her fingerprints were taken, and her mug shot.

I asked the female booking sergeant what the bail was on her warrant.

"Let's see, OK, dog leash violation. That's a bail of $25."

Leaning towards the booking sergeant, and in a low voice I said, "Sergeant, I know this is unusual, but when I get off shift, is it OK if I bail her out? I mean, it's only a dog leash violation. She's never been booked before, and she's pretty scared."

"Sure, Lau, that's not a problem. Once you're off duty, it's perfectly legal for you to bail her out. After all, like you say, it's not like she's a serial killer or anything like that. Tell you what, Officer; I'll have Nancy sit here on the bench until you get off shift. I won't throw her in with the general population. Dog leash violators! Like we don't have anything better to do up here."

Nancy was standing next to me all the while, listening to my conversation with the booking sergeant.

"Officer Lau, can you do that? I mean, are you really going to post bail for me? You're not just saying that, are you?"

"No, Nancy. I'll post your bail as soon as I get off shift. It'll be a while before I get off, but just sit tight. You don't have to go in there with all the other gals. That OK with you?"

"Officer Lau, I'll pay you back the money. I will. I promise!"

"That's fine with me, Nancy. I gotta get back to work now, so just sit tight for the next few hours."

"Thank you so much, Officer." As I left the booking counter, the booking sergeant looked at me, smiled, and winked.

"You take care, Officer."

"Ah, yes, Sergeant, I will. And thanks!"

"Don't worry, Officer; she'll be just fine here."

Officer Guich and I left the jail booking area and took the elevator back down to the police parking garage. Guich looked over at me and said, "Bernie, you dog, you!"

"What you mean, John? I'm just trying to help a damsel in distress, that's all. I mean, you saw how scared she was."

"Right, Bernie. Wouldn't have anything to with her being eighteen and cute as hell, could it?"

"Absolutely not, partner. How could you even think such a thing! Ha-ha."

Officer Guich and I finished off our shift and turned in our patrol vehicle and our paperwork to the shift sergeant. Then I headed down to the locker room and changed into my civilian clothes. I took my off-duty revolver out of my locker and tucked it into the holster on the right side of my trousers. Then I took the elevator down to the Warrants Office located on the 1st Floor of the Public Safety Building and posted Nancy's $25 bail. Being that the dog leash violation bail and fine were the same amount, $25, Nancy didn't have to show up in court if she didn't want to.

15 minutes after I posted her bail, the heinous dog-leash violator got off the elevator on the ground floor, where I was waiting for her.

"Officer Lau, thank you. I'm so grateful. And like I told you up in the jail, don't worry; I'll pay you back the money."

Nancy started to cry again. I walked up and put my arm around her shoulder and escorted her out of the Public Safety Building.

"Do you need a ride home?"

"Well, yeah; sorry, I mean … Would you please give me a ride to my house? I don't really have a way to get home."

"No problem."

Nancy held on to my arm as we walked up the steep hill towards the Diamond lot where I usually parked my green VW bus. She told me that she was from Wenatchee, across the mountains. She'd been in Seattle for a year and a half and lived at 711 Summit Avenue in a two-story house with a band called "Child." The band members all lived upstairs, and Nancy lived downstairs.

"So what kind of dog was it that landed you in jail, Nancy?"

"Oh, my dog. Her name's Lady and she's an Afghan with beautiful long, white hair. I let her run sometimes at Volunteer Park, you know. I play ball with her a few times a week when it's not raining. A few months ago this Seattle cop was driving through the park and saw me playing ball with Lady. He got out of his police car, came over, and wrote me a ticket for not having Lady on a leash. But how could she get her exercise if she had to stay on a leash? I tried explaining this to the officer, but he was a real jerk. He told me that he didn't care and that he'd haul me off to jail if I didn't sign the ticket."

"Yeah, believe me, Nancy, I know. Some cops are like that. Got a chip on their shoulders."

"So, Bernie, how come you're being so nice to me? I mean, you're not like most other cops. You, like, listen to what I have to say, you actually cared about my situation, and you posted my bail. You don't even know me. Do you make a habit of rescuing girls in trouble?"

"No, Nancy. I've never posted a bail for anyone before. You're the first. It's just that you looked so damn scared. And for them to throw you in jail for a stupid dog leash violation... That's a bit much. OK, well, let's get you home."

I drove Nancy up to where she lived on Summit Avenue. Pulling into a small parking area on the south side of the house, I turned off the engine.

"Well, there you are; finally home, safe and sound. Do you have a phone number? I'd like to take you out to lunch some time, if that's OK with you. That's if you're not married and don't have a boyfriend or anything like that."

"No, Bernie, I don't have a husband, boyfriend, or children. It's just me, my dog Lady, and the band."

"How many people are there in the band?"

"Four. Carol and Jennifer—they sing—and there's Jeffrey and Tom on guitar and keyboards."

"What about you, Nancy? You sing or anything?"

"No, Bernie, I don't sing or play anything. I'm just a groupie. We're just friends, that's all. What about you? Are you married?"

"Nope."

"So do you have a girlfriend?"

"Nope, no girlfriend. Just me in my little house in Mountlake Terrace."

"That's up north, right?"

"Yeah, it's about 12 miles north of Seattle. Nice and quiet; just the way I like it."

"Bernie, I know we sort of just met, but would you mind coming in and staying with me for a little while? I'm still a bit shook up from being in jail. Tonight was really scary for me. If you hadn't bailed me out, I'd still be in that jail this very moment. Hope you don't mind my asking."

"Well, it's late. Actually, early, about five o'clock, now. I'm tired. It's been a long day for me."

"You can crash on the couch if you want. If you don't mind, that is. The band never gets up before late afternoon."

"What will they say if they see me crashed on the couch when they wake up?"

"They don't care what I do or who I see, Bernie. I have my own life. Even though I hang around with them a lot, what I do is my business."

"Ah, well, OK. I guess I could crash on your couch. Sure you don't mind?"

"Bernie, I just asked, didn't I?"

"Yeah, you did. OK, I'll come in."

"Thanks, Bernie. I'll feel a lot better with you here."

Nancy and I went into the house. It was a big old house, a relic from a different era.

"Mind if I take a shower? Here, just take your shoes off and lay down here on the bed. On the covers is fine. Don't worry about it."

I took off my shoes and socks, took out my gun, and laid it on the night stand by the head of the bed. Nancy noticed the gun.

"You always carry a gun with you? It's not loaded, is it?"

"Ah, we cops always have to carry a gun off-duty, Nancy. A gun and a badge. It's required. And, yes, it's loaded."

"Is the safety on?"

"Revolvers don't have safeties, Nancy, but it's safe as long as you don't point it at someone and pull the trigger. It's not going to go off by itself, so don't worry."

"OK. It's just that I'm not used to being around guns. They scare me."

"A gun is just a tool for us police officers, just like a hammer is to a carpenter. Nothing to be afraid of."

"OK, if you say so. I'm going to take a shower now. Want the light turned off?"

"Yeah, please. I might doze off, so just kick me onto the couch when you're through with your shower."

"OK, I will."

I laid my head on the large soft pillow and went out like a light. Next thing I knew, Nancy was back in the bedroom, standing next to the bed. She was wearing leopard-skin-design panties and a matching bra. Damn, she looked good!

"Bernie, why don't you go take a shower, then you can go crash on the couch."

She seemed to be unconcerned that she was standing right next to me with almost nothing on, like it was normal to be that way in front of someone she'd just met several hours ago.

I got up, put my gun back in its holster and headed to the bathroom. I took a long, hot shower. I dried off and went back into the bedroom, wearing just my trousers, and, of course, my gun.

"OK, shower was great Nancy, I feel a lot better. So where's the couch?"

"Bernie, we're both adults, right? You mind sleeping in the same bed with me? There's no reason for you to sleep on the couch in the living room. Actually there is no couch in the living room."

"Well, OK. That is, if you don't mind."

"Just take off your pants and get into bed with me. But put the gun away first. I don't like guns."

Leaving my shorts on, I climbed into bed. Yes, it was happening again. First, there was Uniform Linda, now it was Nancy. I was finding myself in bed with another beautiful young gal that I'd just met on the job. I was never a pussy hound. I never went out of the way looking for sex. Of course, while I was in the Navy, deployed to those exotic Asian ports, pussy was always available; but that was just the way life was over there. All this sex being available every time I turned around here in Seattle was something new to me.

I pulled the covers up to my chin, turned on my left side, and lay there, looking at Nancy. She was no longer wearing the cute leopard-style panties and bra. She was completely naked. And, oh boy, I was getting hard. Nancy didn't say a word, she just moved toward me, grasped the waistband of my shorts, pulled them off me, and threw them on the floor next to the bed. Then she pulled me into her arms, held me close, and started to kiss me. She kissed my right ear lobe, started to nibble gently, and then stuck her tongue into my ear. Oh, my God. I was definitely getting turned on!

I closed my eyes. Damn; whatever she was doing was sending shivers up and down my spine. I cupped her left breast with my right hand. It was small and firm—perfect! I felt her nipple harden under my touch. I gently rolled the nipple between my thumb and index finger. Nancy started sighing. She let out a low moan and held me even tighter. She reached behind me with her left arm and started to rake my back ever so lightly with her finger nails. I tucked my head down and started kissing her breast and then her nipples. I breathed deeply as I got harder and harder.

Squeezing my eyes shut as hard as I could, I tried to control my breathing. Slow and deep, Bernie, slow and deep. My body started to tremble. Nancy reached down under the covers and, ever so gently, caressed my manhood. The next thing I knew, she had her warm, moist lips around my hardness. She engulfed me deeply and completely. My breathing was starting to get out of control. I gritted my teeth, sucked in another breath and moaned a deep, animal moan. Fuck, I couldn't stand it!

Nancy didn't say a word; she just continued to do what she was doing with focus and total concentration. My mind drifted. I was no longer lying on a bed; I went into a state of "non-thinking." I felt only sensations, I had no thoughts. Nancy was once again on her back, I was above her and deep into her and caught up in the slow rhythmic movement of her body. I felt heat building up inside the pelvic area and a powerful sensation of sexual energy slowly engulfed my entire being. I tried to hold on, tried not to allow it to complete its final burst of energy. "No," I said to myself, "Not yet, Bernie. Not just yet. Hold on a bit longer, not just yet!" I struggled to put my mind someplace else, but the orgasmic tsunami of my cumming had started deep within me, and now there was no stopping it. I exploded in bliss. I came hard and cried out like a wounded animal.

I shuddered for the longest time, panting, trying to catch my breath. I wrapped my legs around Nancy and locked her tightly against my body, crushing my hips into hers as her nails dug deeper into my back. I felt extreme pain as the sweat from sexual exertion mixed with the open wounds. I didn't stop her; I didn't want to, I loved the pain. I just gritted my teeth and endured the wonderful punishment of my flesh. Suddenly, my endorphins kicked in. Go ahead, Nancy; rip open my back, make my flesh bleed. I didn't care!

It was afternoon when I finally woke up. I was lying on my stomach.

"Morning, Bernie. Sleep well?" I lifted my head, and there, lying close to me, was Nancy, wearing nothing but a big grin.

"Morning, Nancy," I mumbled, laying my head back down on the pillow.

"So how did you sleep there, Officer Lau?"

"Sorry, Nancy, I can't remember."

"I made coffee, hon. Want some?"

"Yeah, sure. Thanks."

Later, as we lay in bed drinking coffee, Nancy said, "Bernie, thanks again for posting my bail, I can't thank you enough! I'll pay you back the money."

"Don't worry about it, Nancy. You just did! By the way, where's Lady?"

"Lady? Oh, she ran away about a week ago. Afghans are pretty dogs, but they're really dumb. I opened the front door one afternoon and she ran out. I looked for her for hours, but no luck."

"Well, I'll keep a lookout when I'm on patrol. Who knows? Maybe we'll find her."

"Bernie, I've already taken a shower. Why don't you rinse off and come back to bed. You don't work tonight, do you?"

"No, I'm off the next four days. What about your friends in the band?"

"Oh, them. They already got up and left. Won't be back till tomorrow afternoon, so we got the whole house to ourselves."

I looked at Nancy, gazing into her brown eyes, and realized that I'd really fallen for this lonely, 18-year-old hippy gal. I got out of bed to go shower off.

"Oh, my God, Bernie. I'm so sorry. Your back, it's all scratched up. I didn't realize I was scratching so hard!"

"It's OK, Nancy. Don't worry about it. The pain felt good actually. I don't mind."

"But Bernie, your back has blood all over it. Here, let me put something on it. I got ointment in the bathroom."

"OK, maybe after I shower."

But after I showered, I went straight back to bed and into Nancy's warm embrace. Laying on top of her, I took hold of both of her arms and pinned them to her sides so she couldn't move. I brought my head down and placed my mouth directly over her right nipple and blew on it gently. I felt the nipple harden as I placed the tip of my tongue on it and moved it ever so slowly in a circle. How I loved her tiny breasts!

Nancy, attempting to pull free of my grip, was starting to make faint animal sounds from her throat. Sexual control is sometimes wonderful and exciting, and I was thinking to myself, "No way, girl, it's my turn." I was enjoying tormenting this beautiful hippie girl. How precious she was, and how lucky I was!

In time I let go of Nancy's pinned arms, reached down around her soft, yet firm, legs, and brought my mouth and my lips to inches away from her soft blond bush. I paused a moment and gently blew my warm breath on her now musk-scented, moist pussy. Nancy started moving her pelvis, opening her legs wider. I heard a faint "please" from deep in her throat.

"Please, Bernie, please, please—I can't stand it any longer. Please, now!" I smiled and said to myself, "Not yet, Nancy. Not just yet."

Much later, I awoke with Nancy still asleep beside me. I decided not to wake her up. I slipped out of bed and went to the kitchen, where I got myself a cold beer out of the fridge. I popped open the cap and took a much-needed gulp of cold, refreshing beer. Then I went back to bed, where I lay on my side, gazing at my sleeping beauty.

"You're very beautiful, Nancy," I whispered to her as I leaned over and kissed her right cheek. I then laid my head next to hers and dozed off once again.

Back on patrol several nights later, my shift partner Howard Johns and I were patrolling the neighborhood of Summit Avenue, several blocks south of Nancy's residence. We pulled over a suspicious vehicle in which were three black males ranging in age from 15 to 17 years of age. I say "suspicious" due to the fact that they'd been cruising aimlessly through the neighborhood.

As I approached their vehicle, I observed a white Afghan dog in the back seat. I inquired as to the ownership of the dog and was informed by the driver that they'd "found the dog running loose around the neighborhood several weeks ago and were just looking for its owner." Well, perhaps they were and perhaps they weren't.

I informed them that I'd recently gotten a report of a lost Afghan dog in this exact neighborhood and that this particular dog answered the description. (I'd actually taken no such report.) Both the driver and passengers immediately said, "Go ahead, Officer; take the dog. It's not ours. We didn't steal her, we were just trying to find the owner."

I took the Afghan, placed her in the back of our patrol vehicle, and then allowed the three individuals to drive off without further investigation as to whether or not the driver possessed a valid driver's license. (Due to the driver's young age, I was certain that he didn't.) At the moment, my only interest was returning this Afghan to Nancy, and I hoped that it was in fact Nancy's dog, "Lady."

With the Afghan riding in the back seat of our patrol vehicle, Officer Johns and I drove up to Nancy's house, where I turned the dog over to her. It turned out that this particular Afghan wasn't Nancy's lost dog, "Lady," after all. Finding the exact same breed of dog as the one Nancy had lost, and so close to her residence at that, was an inexplicable coincidence. Still, Nancy was thrilled to have this dog as a replacement for Lady and immediately named her "Lady."

Once off shift, I returned to Nancy's house, where she and I once again shared hours of heated lust. We became very close and ended up going together for several years. In time, however, Nancy moved back to Wenatchee to live with her sister Jenny on a large ranch. There Lady would be free to run loose without fear of some police officer issuing Nancy a citation for a "dog leash violation."

22

The First Sin

Of all the officers I worked with, Dale Eggers was the one I was with the longest. Dale was tall, slender, easy-going, and loved to read Louis L'amour novels about the Old West. We got along fine and ended up being a great team.

Eggers had one problem though: his girlfriend "Bernice." She was a total psycho and extremely jealous. She once broke out the rear window of Dale's private vehicle because she'd caught him having sex with some other girl. Bernice was also an addict and would shoot up meth from time to time. Why is it that police officers are often times attracted to women plagued with emotional problems? I can't really say, but over the years, I witnessed many examples of this syndrome.

One evening following roll call, Eggers and I were called into the watch commander's office.

"Shut the door behind you, men," he said. "Have a seat. Lau, Eggers, I hear from your patrol sergeant that you're a good team. And I also hear that you enjoy working plain clothes detail. How would you two like to work undercover for a few months?"

Eggers and I looked at each other and grinned.

"Yes, sir. We'd enjoy that very much."

"Good then, it's done! We've had a lot of complaints recently from concerned citizens stating that come nightfall, the parks are being taken over by perverts. Especially Volunteer Park. Decent citizens and their kids can't use the park's public restrooms without being accosted by these low-lifes. I want you both to start hanging around there and see what's actually going on. Make an arrest if you see any illegal sexual activity. The chief is aware of what's happening in the parks and has in fact requested that you two work on this assignment. Good luck, men!"

So Eggers and I exited the watch commander's office and headed down to the locker room to change back into our street clothes. We checked out an undercover vehicle from narcotics and drove up to Capitol Hill, where Eggers let me out by the Water Tower in Volunteer Park. I walked down in front of the Art Museum while Eggers parked the car in stakeout.

It was still light out. A lovely, warm summer evening. Perfect for falling in love. On the north side of the museum was a walkway heading down to the men's public toilets. I turned and strolled down the path.

No sooner did I go into the restroom, step up to the urinal, and take a pee, than a white male entered the bathroom. He stood behind me and started to rub his groin up against my butt. I thought to myself, "No way, dude." As I turned around, he reached over and grabbed at my balls. I yelled out, "Hey, asshole; police. You're under arrest!"

The pervert was completely taken by surprise and attempted to explain his way out of getting arrested.

"What? I'm under arrest? For what? I didn't do anything. I was just waiting to pee. Don't be so uptight!"

I responded, "Save it, dude. You're under arrest for rubbing your groin against my butt and grabbing my nuts."

I cuffed him, read him his rights, and took him back to our undercover vehicle. Dale and I then drove him back to the police station and booked him for indecent liberties.

Then we went down to the patrol room, where I wrote up my arrest report. Dale was telling some officers who happened to be in the area how I hadn't even been in the rest room for two minutes, and a guy walked in and grabbed my nuts.

As I was filling out the report, the watch commander happened to walk by. Noticing Eggers and me, he asked, "Hey, guys, aren't you supposed to be out arresting degenerates in the park?"

Looking up from my paperwork I answered, "Well, boss, we weren't out there for but two minutes, and we already made an arrest."

A surprised look came over the commander's face, which turned into resolve.

"Good work, men. Now, get out there and get me another one. Let's see how many of these guys you can lock up before your shift is over."

"Will do, sir. We'll see what we can do."

By the third night, Eggers and I were bringing in so many gays that the duty sergeant was starting to complain to the watch commander about being swamped with paperwork. We were then instructed to limit our arrests to eight per night.

"Lau, you and Eggers bring me eight arrests per shift, and then you guys are free to go home. Eight per shift, then call it a night."

Volunteer Park wasn't our only hunting ground. Back in the early 70s, Pike Street in Seattle was known as the prostitution area. Sometimes as many as eight prostitutes worked one block. These gals would walk up to any male they saw and proposition him. It didn't matter if the individual was in the company of his wife or girlfriend; the prostitutes would just walk up and say, "Hi, honey, want a date?" If the guy's date complained, the prostitute would just say, "Shut the fuck up, bitch. I'm not talking to you." Sometimes the guy's date wouldn't mind the proposition and the lucky guy (or date?) would end up having a threesome for the evening.

Yes, back in the early 70s, Seattle was a bit on the wild side. The 1400 block of First Avenue, located at the west end of Pike Street, was nothing but seedy, decadent, XXX-rated book stores selling hard core pornographic magazines, black and white photo sets depicting extreme bondage, and 8 mm. pornographic movies. There were also illegal under-the-counter sales of child pornography; "kiddy porn," as it was called. There were sex toys of every imaginable creation. There were vibrators with variable RPMs; some even had remote control switches. There were rubber dildoes of every shape, size, color, and flavor.

Then there were the movie arcades ("pan rooms") that featured private viewing booths where individuals went in and viewed 8 mm. pornographic movies in private or, as happened more often than not, with another male. After dark, those arcades were so teeming with lewd homosexual activity, you almost needed a traffic cop to direct foot traffic. The viewing booths were filthy. Totally nasty would be a better description. Ejaculated sperm and spit dripped from the walls and puddled on the floor along with wadded-up kleenex tissue. The smell of sperm and body odor was nauseating and overpowered you the moment you entered the viewing booth. Gays, perverts of all kinds ... You name it, they'd all gather there once the sun went down; all huddled together, like a bunch of vampires sucking on each other. The scene was surreal and disgusting.

On one occasion while working undercover, I came upon a young white male masturbating as he stood viewing a pornographic film. I decided to have some fun. I looked at the young man and asked him if he was up to having a threesome with a buddy of mine. The kid's eyes lit up. Wow! He could hardly wait.

We left the arcade and walked over to my undercover vehicle, where Eggers was waiting in the driver's seat. I made introductions, then Eggers drove off. The kid was sitting next to Eggers with me sitting next to him with my left arm around his shoulder. As we rode along, Eggers and I talked about all the nasty sexual things we were going to do to each other once we got to my place. The kid was going crazy with anticipation—until, that is, we drove into the police garage, which was filled with patrol vehicles. He looked over at me. I smiled, kissed him on the cheek, and said, "Gotcha." You should have seen the look on the poor kid's face.

Whenever Eggers and I worked the pan rooms, we usually tried to make it into a game; otherwise, it would start getting to us. Going into darkened, nasty-smelling pan rooms night after night and dealing with every type of imaginable pervert out there was not an easy assignment. I don't know many police officers or undercover detectives who would be willing to do what we did. But someone had to do it, and that "someone" would usually turn out to be me.

As Eggers and I were cleaning up 1st and Pike Street, an article appeared in the Seattle Times written by a columnist named Rick Anderson. In the article Anderson described the situation on 1st Avenue as it stood in 1972. There were a lot of businesses that catered to pornography, and most of it was gay. Anderson went into detail about the multitude of arrests that Eggers and I had made in the pan rooms, mentioning me by name. At the end of the article, Anderson wrote,

> "This is how the city handles it now. Thousands of man hours rounding up these lawbreakers. I'm sure it's comforting to know that while you sleep, the police are hard at work protecting you. As for the burglar in your front room, well, they'll get to him just as soon as they can."

In other words, the police shouldn't have been pursuing "victimless crimes" when burglars were breaking into peoples' homes at an alarming rate. In response to Anderson's article, the Chief of Police sent out the following memo:

> "A great deal of public attention has been directed recently to vice enforcement and I'm sure many of you are being asked to justify the Seattle Police Department's position. There have been accusations that we are spending a disproportionate amount of time enforcing laws that are considered 'unpopular restrictions on public morals.' Our critics are also expressing concern that other, more important services are being neglected. Once again, we are in the position where law enforcement has to deal with the 'real world.' Police officers know from actual experience that blatant vice activities are a threat to public safety. The facts are obvious: Homosexual seductions in public facilities involve innocent victims, including small children and teenagers. Prostitution, gambling and drug traffic not only victimize the residents of the community where it is allowed to flourish, but also attracts the dregs of humanity into those cities that condone such activities. Tolerance of vice problems breeds corruption ... we know this from bitter experience. We also know that the enforcement of vice laws is an extremely sensitive area of responsibility and requires a high degree of professionalism. I know you all recognize that a police department cannot afford the stigma of entrapment or brutality in its enforcement efforts. This does not mean we back off from enforcing existing vice laws, only that we are scrupulously professional in the manner in which we discharge our responsibility. It is not inconceivable that some laws regulating vice activities will be changed in the future. So be it ... but until that time arrives, we will protect this community from activities that are corrupt and illegal. It is interesting to read that, in Copenhagen, Denmark, the citizens are not happy with their international reputa-

tion as a vice center and are supporting a police 'crackdown' on such activities as live sex shows. Our citizens would be well-advised to heed the principle 'caveat emptor' (let the buyer beware) before they consider 'buying' the kind of permissiveness that tears at the moral fabric of their community.

George P. Tielsch"

In spite of the chief's firm stand on the issue, Eggers and I were eventually pulled off the undercover vice detail.

23

Jip Joint

In the early 70s there were all these places that straddled a fine line between legal business and prostitution. They were called modeling studios, body-painting shops, sensitivity awareness studios, or whatever. Collectively they were usually referred to as "body shops" or "body studios."

One of these joints, called the Soft Touch Studio, was located on our beat down on Pike Street. Eggers and I went in one day and started checking the small cubicles in which the gals worked. All the cubicle doors had a tiny window so that the managers could look inside and see what was going on. Of course, it was handy for us cops too, when we wanted to see if there was any illegal hanky-panky.

Looking into one cubicle, I saw a guy lying on top of a gal, and his naked butt was rapidly pumping up and down. Being that I needed to make certain that they were in fact having sex, I stood there watching for several minutes. Finally, I opened the cubical door and informed the couple that they were both under arrest.

Upon seeing me, the gal immediately started talking to the guy in French, telling him to say that they were only "simulating sex" and not having real sex. I stood there a while listening to them talk; then I informed them, in French, that I had observed them having sex.

Yes, they were both very surprised when I spoke to them in French. It was really funny, at least to me.

How is it that two French people were found engaged in illegal sex in a body shop on Pike Street in Seattle? Turned out the guy was a sailor off a French naval vessel that had put into Seattle. The gal claimed that she was just a student trying to make money in order to pay her tuition.

The French sailor, upon learning that I was born in France, tried to talk me into not arresting him.

"After all," he asked, "Why should it be against the law to have sex?"

Good point, but I arrested them anyway.

In 1975 the City of Seattle passed the "Body Studio Ordinance," banning body studios. A "body studio" was defined as any premises where the customer was allowed to "paint, massage, feel, handle, or touch the unclothed body or an unclothed portion of the body of another person, or to be so painted, massaged, felt, handled or touched by another person, or to observe, view or photograph any such activity."

The Soft Touch Studio was one example of a body shop that made the change from the "hippy" era to the "drugs and violence" era. The business was re-named "Exotica," and instead of body painting, they now offered "interpretative dancing." The way the scam worked was that there were these gals with almost no clothes on dancing behind these big picture windows. You could see them from blocks away—impossible to miss. Guys would come in, go to a small room, get promised sex, pay their money up-front, and then usually get thrown out the back door or beaten up. Sometimes they'd come back later and throw a brick through one of the big plate-glass windows for revenge. Didn't matter; the owners were making money hand over fist.

The guys weren't the only ones being scammed. The dancers, hooked by the promise of $300 a week in earnings (a lot of money then), were subject to fines that kept their salaries much lower. They could be fined for chewing gum, forgetting to close a curtain, speaking out of turn ... There were over 50 of these bullshit rules. In some cases, girls were beaten, tortured, and raped.

It was on account of a charge of extorting money out of employees that the first police raid was carried out in April, 1976. At that time, three of the managers, Tony Foster, Catherine Brown and Roger Pomarleau, were arrested. Pomarleau was also charged with 2nd degree rape of an Exotica dancer. The dancer accused him of sexual abuse and torturing her with a hot curling iron. Oddly enough, he was able to sweet-talk her into marrying him, and the charges were dropped.

Yep, business at the Exotica was as good as ever, and the complaints kept coming. Vice decided to do something about it. First thing was, they needed a volunteer. As usual the name that came to mind was "Bernie Lau." A sergeant from vice pulled me aside and asked, "Hey, Bernie—how'd you like to get 'beat up' tonight?" Hell, I didn't have anything better to do, so I answered "Sounds like fun, Sarge. Let's do it!"

I was briefed and given a beeper and $140 in Canadian money. The money was in small bills and dusted with ultraviolet powder. On my way down to the Exotica, I stopped in a tavern and had a few beers to make it seem like I was an easy mark.

After a while I went down to the club. Upon entering, I was immediately met by a cute, petite female. This sweet young thing took me to one of the many private cubicles that had doors. Inside, we talked for a while. She asked me what I was looking for, and I said, "I'd like a blow job, eh?" She said it would cost $100. So I took the large roll of money out of my pocket and peeled off $100. I acted sort of drunk, making sure she saw my wad of bills. Then I took off my clothes, except for my shorts. I laid down on the mattress, and we talked back and forth.

After she'd talked me out of all my money, I asked angrily, "Where's my blow job?" She lowered her head near my crotch and exhaled strongly.

"There you go," she said, "Now get dressed and get out."

"Fuck you!" I said; "I paid for a blow job, and that's what I want, eh?"

"Get out, or I'll have the bouncers come in and kick you out."

"Ooh, I'm so scared. What are they going to do? Beat me up?"

She left the room. I got dressed, but stayed where I was. Two big dudes came in and ordered me out.

"Fuck you!" I said, "I'm not leaving till I get my money back, eh?"

I had the beeper in my left pants pocket, so when the two approached me, I immediately stuffed both my hands in my pockets. They hesitated for a second, then grabbed me by the arms and pulled and pushed me down the hallway towards the rear of the establishment. One of them started punching me in the face. At this point I activated the beeper. They dragged and pushed me towards the rear door.

As we got to the door, I kicked it and it slammed open. All was dark outside in the parking lot. I continued to resist, and they dragged me out of the building. I was bleeding from my mouth. Suddenly, car lights came on and seven leather-jacketed vice and narcotics detectives swarmed into the circle of headlights. They saw that I was bleeding and went ballistic. I still had my hands in my pockets. The two bad guys had looks of utter panic and confusion on their faces. In a flash, they were roughed up, thrown to the ground, and handcuffed.

Meanwhile, vice detectives were attempting to gain entry via the front door, which had been locked just after I entered the establishment. However, it was made of unbreakable glass, so the detectives finally broke out one of the large front windows and swarmed through.

While the suspects were lying handcuffed and face down in the parking lot, one of the vice detectives came over to me and asked if I had anything to say to the two guys who'd assaulted me. I got the message. "Sure," I said. I went over and gave each of them a good football kick to the balls.

Several months later in court, their attorney, Tony Savage, asked me on the stand; "Detective Lau, did you lay a hand on either of these defendants?" I could truthfully answer, "No, sir, I did not lay a hand on either of them."

The money, which had been hidden in the attic, was recovered. All the suspects (the gal and both guys) had ultraviolet blue powder on their hands.

By the way, it was reported at the time that one of the guys was Roger Pomarleau himself, but that wasn't correct. Pomarleau knew me personally and would've recognized me.

In the summer of 1978, a petite, blonde 19-year-old girl named Lynn Avritt read a newspaper ad for dancers at the Exotica. She was interviewed by Pomarleau, who promised her she could make $100 a week plus tips, but she'd have to move into his condo for a week while she was "in training."

Pomarleau was a white asshole whose goal in life was to be a black pimp. He'd just gotten married to his 2nd wife, a 16-year-old black girl named "Star." He was around 6', 170 lbs., reddish hair, not bad looking. He supposedly had a reputation as a ladies' man. He wore expensive clothes and, often, a white, furry hat with a wide brim. His gold Cadillac was always parked outside the Exotica.

According to her testimony at the trial, during the time Lynn stayed at Pomarleau's condo and danced at the Exotica, he never let her out of his sight. She was forced to sleep between Pomarleau and his wife in a king-size bed. She told Star that she wanted to get away, but Pomarleau found out and beat her up. She was afraid that he was going to "eliminate" her, so one night, she tried to slip out of bed unnoticed. Pomarleau woke up. Avritt pretended she was hungry and went to the kitchen, where she got some cheese and a butcher knife. With the butcher knife hidden by her side, she went back to bed and waited. When she thought the others were asleep, she began to slide slowly out of bed. Pomarleau woke up suddenly and jumped on her. She stabbed him in the neck with the butcher knife, but he kept on coming. In all, she stabbed him ten times.

I was present at Pomarleau's autopsy. It was strange looking down at a guy I once knew, now lying on a stainless steel table in front of me, totally naked, with his chest cut open and the medical examiner removing organs from the cavity. I remember thinking to myself, "Well, Mr. Pomarleau, you don't look so tough now, do you? Looks like you finally got yourself 'rehabilitated!'"

24

Precognition

There were things you could do and things you couldn't. Like one night, when I was walking the beat in uniform on Pike Street, and I saw a hooker pick up a trick. She hailed a cab, the cab pulled up, I walked over, opened the door of the cab, and the hooker and trick got in. I shut the door and the cab drove off. "To Serve and Protect," right? Wrong! My sergeant just happened to be in the immediate area, saw the incident, and didn't have much of a sense of humor about it. I got my ass chewed out!

Every so often at roll call, I'd be assigned "plain clothes." That's where you're not in uniform and you get to drive an unmarked city vehicle. I always looked forward to that assignment. Just drive around Seattle all night, looking for trouble. Sometimes I had a partner, and sometimes I was by myself. Sometimes vice would have me working prostitution detail, so I'd drive around trying to pick up hookers. Damn, I loved that job.

You had to be careful with hookers, though. One evening, radio got a call that some guy was standing out on a fire escape, holding a switchblade and threatening two females. Turned out the guy was an officer named "Stevie," working an undercover vice detail. Somehow Stevie had gotten two black prostitutes to go up to a hotel room with him on the pretext of having a threesome. Once in the room, however, the prostitutes turned on him and attempted to rob him. Being that Stevie was working undercover, he didn't have his police identification, badge, or gun with him. All he had was a switchblade. As the two prostitutes backed him all the way out onto the fire escape, Stevie pulled out the switchblade in an attempt to protect himself.

Soon a call came over police radio, "All units, respond to: man with a switchblade threatening two females on a hotel fire escape." Sirens wailed in the Seattle night as police officers responded to the dispatch call. A multitude of officers rushed to the scene with guns drawn and kicked in the door to the room. When they realized that it was just little ol' Stevie, working a vice detail, they arrested the prostitutes and booked them for "attempted robbery." Stevie never lived that one down.

Next to working plain clothes, walking the beat was my favorite shift assignment. Walking around 1st and Pike for eight hours, going in and out of taverns and go-go joints that featured scantily-clad female dancers, all bumping and grinding to the beat of the latest sounds ... Then when my partner and I got hungry, we'd dine either at Ivar's Fish Bar or the "Eight Bells" where Eddie Sawabini, the owner, would throw together one of the finest burgers I've ever tasted, all greasy and smothered with as much thousand island, blue cheese, ranch or whatever other dressing my heart desired, free of charge, of course.

The Eight Bells was part-go-go joint, part-restaurant and bar. Eddie had come over from the Middle East and done good for himself in business, living the "American Dream." Whenever we walked the beat downtown, we'd always hit the Eight Bells three or four times a night to check and see if all was well in his nightclub.

Once, Eggers and I were working the night shift (8:00 P.M.– 4:00 A.M.) in a marked police vehicle and were assigned the Central District. Several hours into our shift, radio dispatch gave us a call, "Three Charlie Two. Respond to a disturbance at 1510 Yesler Way, Terrace Apartments (low-income housing). Man causing a disturbance and threatening suicide. (Nothing was mentioned about a gun being involved.) Eggers picked up the mike and answered the dispatcher; "Three Charlie Two—1510 Yesler Way, man causing disturbance, threatening suicide, received."

As I entered apartment 1510, I saw an Indian female and several young children huddled together in the kitchen. The female pointed towards the living room, where I observed an Indian male, approximately 50 years old, lying on his stomach with hands tucked underneath him.

As Eggers and I approached him, he suddenly turned onto his left side and pointed a .357 Colt Python revolver directly at us. Eggers was standing to my right and quickly jumped out of the way, exiting the living room area. I, however, was only a few feet away from the guy, directly in the line of fire. I knew that there wasn't enough time for me to get out of the living room without being shot, so I jumped on top of him, grabbed hold of the revolver, and pushed it away from my body, at the same time placing my left hand around the cylinder, thus preventing the gun from being fired as he attempted to pull the trigger. He didn't struggle, but simply said, "OK, Officer. You got me." I yelled out to Eggers, "I got the gun, Dale, I got the gun. Come and give me a hand!" Eggers immediately returned and assisted me in putting the guy in handcuffs.

As we helped him get into a sitting position, I noticed that his stomach was bandaged over and that part of his intestines were hanging out from under the bandages. Turns out this individual was suffering from inoperable stomach cancer and wanted to die. He wanted us to shoot and kill him.

It's called "suicide by cop." Somebody wants to end his life, but doesn't have the courage to kill him- or herself. Just point a gun at a police officer, and there's a good chance that you're going to get shot and killed. An aid unit was called and the individual was transported to Harborview Medical Emergency.

I took possession of the .357 Colt Python and placed it into evidence, but not until I'd first filed down the firing pin, thus making it impossible for the revolver to fire in the unlikely event that it would somehow be returned to the suspect or released to his attorney. But several weeks later, the Colt Python revolver was turned over to the guy's attorney. I hope the attorney never had to use it in a self-defense situation.

One night I remember having a vivid dream in which Eggers and I were involved in a shootout. That evening at roll call, I mentioned my dream to him.

"Dale, I had a dream last night where you and me were in a shootout on some street corner in Chinatown and one of us got shot and ended up at Harborview." Dale looked at me, somewhat puzzled. "Strange dream, Bernie!"

We were assigned a King Sector district car which included Chinatown. We gathered up our gear, walked out to G Deck, where our patrol vehicles were parked, checked in with radio dispatch, and headed out to start our evening shift. Exiting the garage, I drove a few blocks up James Street, turned right onto 6th Avenue, then headed down towards Chinatown.

Suddenly, our police radio started going; "Beep-beep-beep-beep-beep-beep," a signal indicating that something important was happening. Dispatch came on the air and announced: "All units: we have a sniper at the Bush Hotel! We have a sniper at the Bush Hotel firing down at officers."[1] We were two blocks away from the Bush Hotel.

I tore down 6th Avenue and skidded to a stop at the intersection of 6th and Jackson, close to where the hotel was located. BAM! Our patrol car was immediately hit by gunfire. Dale hurriedly unlocked the shotgun from the dash and exited our vehicle via the passenger

---

[1] The sniper had shot at two police officers who were walking the beat in Chinatown.

side. I grabbed my briefcase, exited from the driver's side, and took cover behind our patrol vehicle. BAM! BAM! More shots were fired in our direction. Our vehicle was getting hit. Keeping my head down, I looked over at Dale and saw him crouched behind a telephone pole just several yards from the hotel. As I watched, he fired off four shotgun blasts towards the sniper's position, a west-facing window on the 5th Floor of the hotel. Sirens wailed as more police units arrived. Streets bordering the hotel were blocked off. Soon all intersections leading into Seattle's Chinatown were closed down, causing vehicle traffic going in or out to come to a halt.

The sniper fired off another shotgun blast, then another, then he ducked his head back inside. It would later be discovered that he was only armed with a single-barrel, single-load shotgun. This meant that every time he fired off a round, he had to reload his shotgun for the next shot. He was reloading so fast that it seemed like he was using a pump-action shotgun.

Dale, still crouched behind the safety of the telephone pole, yelled out that he was out of ammo and for me to toss him more shotgun rounds. While still ducked behind our patrol vehicle, I opened my briefcase and picked out a bundle of ten shotgun shells which had been rubber-banded together. I tossed the bundle to Dale. Moments later, I took out my service revolver, aimed, and fired off five rounds towards the sniper's window as he came into view. Didn't hit him; just managed to put more bullet holes around the window, which by now was peppered with a multitude of bullet holes. Dale reloaded his shotgun and fired off four more rounds towards the sniper's position.

When Dale and I'd put together the bundle of spare shotgun shells, we'd included a few shotgun "slugs" along with the normal rounds. A shotgun slug is one ounce of lead designed to go through a cement block. Officers don't usually carry extra ammo and never use shotgun slugs, but Dale was the type of guy who planned ahead and always wanted to be prepared. "Just in case," he used to say.

Dale reloaded, this time with the slug rounds, and fired off three rounds towards the sniper's position, which only ended up blowing three 6-inch holes in the ceiling of the sniper's room. Luckily he missed hitting the sniper because, had the sniper been hit with one of those slugs, his entire head would have exploded and disappeared.

By now, other patrol officers had arrived and had also begun firing at the sniper's position. After the gun battle had been going on for nearly a half hour and the sniper still hadn't been hit, a decision was made by the officer in charge at the scene to go ahead and fire through the door into the room where the sniper was holed up. With guns drawn, several officers cautiously made their way up the Bush Hotel's stairwell, up to the 5th Floor, where the sniper's room was located.

Meanwhile, the sniper had yelled out, "I give up!" Upon hearing this, Dale came out from the protection of the telephone pole. Seeing him out in the open, the sniper leaned out and fired off one final shogun blast. "Bam!" Dale took a direct hit and went down. I ran over to him, pulled him behind the protection of the telephone pole, and yelled out for medical assistance. Dale, lying there wounded, looked up at me and said, "Bernie, the motherfucker shot me. Dammit; he shot me."

Meanwhile, one of the officers had taken up position in front of the sniper's door and shot four shotgun rounds through the door into the room. He then stepped aside as a second officer took position and fired off three more rounds. Then came total silence. Everyone waited. The air was thick with the smell of gunpowder. Minutes passed; still no sound came from the sniper's room. Several officers then attempted to break down the door, but found that it had somehow been barricaded from the inside.

It took them several more minutes to finally break through and gain entry. Once in, they found the sniper lying on the floor, dead. His body was riddled with a multitude of shotgun rounds, but he still held his single-load shotgun tightly in his hands.

The Bush Hotel shootout had lasted close to thirty minutes. 150 rounds had been fired at the sniper's position by the police. Five officers had been hit, but all lived. Eggers and the four other wounded officers were rushed to Harborview Hospital, located about a mile from the Hotel.

I got into my bullet-riddled patrol vehicle, drove to Harborview, and located Eggers in the Emergency Room, where he was being attended to.

"How you doing, Dale?" I asked.

He looked up at me and whispered painfully, "How'd you know, Bernie? How'd you know this was going to happen?"

I just shook my head, shrugged my shoulders, and answered, "I really don't know, Dale. I can't explain it. It was just a dream I had. That's all I can tell you."

The dream I experienced is what's known as "precognition." Many people throughout the world have had similar experiences. Why and how this happens, no one knows, but ever since I had that dream and it came true, I've believed that there is in fact some unknown higher power out there watching over us.

Officer Dale Eggers and the other four officers shot that evening at the Bush Hotel were lucky: the sniper had used "duck loads" in his shotgun. Duck loads contain thousands of minute lead pellets, whereas the standard shotgun load normally contains nine double aught lead pellets, and that type of load would certainly have killed them. But from that day on, Dale carried hundreds of tiny shotgun pellets under his skin. There were just too many for the doctor to remove.

Following a months-long investigation into the Bush Hotel shootout and into the background of the sniper, it was learned that he was mentally challenged, and that a year earlier, he'd been beaten up by Seattle police officers. The shooting had been an act of revenge.

The Bush Hotel as it appears today

25

Mayhem

Drugs, prostitution, vice, high-speed chases, shootouts, protecting the innocents from the "bad guys"... That's what I was looking for. I was 31 years old, and I needed action every day. Otherwise, life was too boring. I'd been a Seattle police officer for almost two years. I was still considered a rookie, but I had a reputation in the department as a martial artist, and that made me special in the eyes of the other officers.

Now, police officers don't fight hand-to-hand with suspects; we use guns and nightsticks. But there was (and still is) a professional interest in what's called "arrest techniques." An arrest technique is a way of controlling an unruly suspect after he's arrested and is being taken to jail. Traditionally a belligerent suspect was bludgeoned with a nightstick until he stopped resisting, but as time went on, it became considered more desirable to use arrest techniques that didn't harm the suspect.

At the time I'd done some undercover work, but sometimes I was sent out on patrol, driving around in a police unit alone or with a partner. I'd drive around, looking for trouble and answering dispatch. Most of the time dispatch calls were for investigating minor incidents and filling out reports for offenses such as domestic assaults, burglaries, auto thefts, barking dogs, loud music, and picking up drunks. Also there was a "one-ticket-per-shift" policy.

Every so often, I'd see action. A disturbance call would come in, one that involved violence, such as a husband or wife beating up on each other, or a drunk that didn't want to go to jail. I enjoyed these types of calls because I got to use aikido. If some guy or gal wanted to fight, I'd simply apply an aikido wrist lock and take the individual down to the ground. Flip him on his stomach and put on the cuffs. No problem; usually everything worked out fine.

However, there were some situations where the aikido techniques that I'd been taught didn't work. That bothered me. Aikido was supposed to work on everyone. In the *dojo*, your training partner grabs or punches you, and you automatically react with a technique appropriate to the attack. For example, we were taught that when someone tries to punch you, you just get out of the way, blend with the oncoming punch, redirect the attacker's energy, apply a wrist turn-out, and take him down. Then you quickly apply some sort of arm lock to pin him. No problem; the techniques work every time. In the *dojo*, at least. So when you're attacked in the *dojo*, the defensive technique is always predetermined.

Another thing is, your training partner is taught never to resist. It's a total blending of you with your opponent. It's almost like a dance and can be very beautiful to watch.

One evening in April of 1972, I was working a plain clothes detail out of the Patrol Division. My partner was Officer Bob Hawk. The time was around midnight. We'd cruised 1st Avenue and Pike Street in search of assholes, trouble, and excitement. We hadn't found anything yet, but the night was young, the bars were still open, and their patrons were getting drunk.

We decided to take our dinner break at Ivar's located on Seattle's waterfront, so we headed down Alaskan Way and parked our unmarked city vehicle just north of the Fish Bar. I ordered my usual scallops and chips, and Bob ordered prawns and chips. We were walking back to our city vehicle with our warm orders in hand, when we passed a heavy-set male (who I'll call "Charlie Ellis") standing by himself next to a pier.

Ellis said something disrespectful, like "What the fuck you looking at?" I stopped, faced him and asked, "What did you just say?" Ellis looked at me and said, "You fuckers stop staring at my wife!" I looked towards the pier and observed a heavy-set white female squatting and in the process of urinating. Being a young, naive rookie cop, I looked at Ellis and said, "Police officer. You're under arrest for being drunk in public, and your wife's under arrest for urinating in public."

I placed my order of scallops and chips on the roof of our vehicle, walked up to Ellis, and taking a hold of his left arm and wrist, proceeded to apply an aikido wrist lock on him. Well, Mr. Ellis wasn't having any of that. He lifted his left arm up and in the process lifted me off the ground a few inches. I again attempted to apply one of those aikido wrist locks on him, but he wasn't about to "allow" me to do that. Damn it, the guy was "resisting" me, and even though I was a ranking black belt in aikido, I couldn't for the life of me put a lock on him. I even instructed him to stop resisting me. To this he replied, "Fuck you, Cop!"

So I thought to myself, "OK, this guy wants to play rough, does he?" I took a karate stance in front of him and kicked him square in his nuts. Nothing happened, so I snapped kicked him again, twice. All I'd managed to do so far was to piss the guy off.

Ellis's friends pulled up to where we were, opened up the passenger and rear doors, and yelled, "Get in, Charlie!" The heavy-set gal ran up from the pier, got in the rear seat, and Ellis got in the passenger seat. The doors were slammed shut and the driver started to pull away. I yelled out, "Stop, police officer!" The driver disregarded me and started to drive off.

Being now pissed off, I reached over and broke off the vehicle radio antenna located on the passenger side of the vehicle. I guess this made the driver mad as hell, and he immediately stopped the vehicle. Officer Bob opened the passenger door and attempted to pull Ellis out. Ellis leaned back and kicked at Bob, landing a blow to Bob's right eye. Bob's face started to bleed.

Ellis, his wife, his brother, and his brother's wife were now all out of the vehicle and coming towards Bob and me. I grabbed my portable radio and put out a "Help the Officer" call over the air. Soon the City of Seattle was engulfed by the sound of police sirens coming to our rescue. Patrol vehicles arrived; a half-dozen uniformed cops came to our rescue.

Seeing that Officer Hawk was severely injured and bleeding about his face area, the responding officers went ballistic. One of "their own" had been injured, so the gloves came off. Several of the officers grabbed Ellis, threw him to the ground, and handcuffed him face down. One young uniformed officer focused, stepped back, paused, then rushed forward as if he were on a football field about to kick a field goal and kicked Ellis square in the head. I heard the "thud" of shoe hitting skull and looked away; I couldn't watch. I suddenly felt sick to my stomach. Turning, I walked away from the mayhem.

I was a black belt in aikido. All my fellow officers knew this. They looked up to me because of it, and now, here I was with my partner severely injured due to the fact that I'd been unable to protect him in the process of arresting a drunk. Because of me, he now stood a chance of losing the sight in his injured left eye. I felt shame.

Furthermore, after hearing Ellis verbally insult us, I'd responded like a rookie cop with a chip on his shoulder, a young cop with something to prove, and because of that, my partner and Ellis had both been severely injured. The responsibility for what had happened was mine and mine alone.

Why hadn't I just ignored the verbal insult? Mr. Ellis, after all, was just protecting his wife.

To top it all off, my scallops and chips were now cold.

Ellis was booked for resisting arrest and assaulting a police officer. For some reason, instead of putting the almost empty bottle of vodka that I'd recovered from the suspects' vehicle in evidence, I threw the bottle in the rubbish can. Being upset and perhaps not thinking properly, I threw away a critical piece of evidence.

Months later, Buddy Ellis went to trial for "resisting arrest and assaulting a police officer." When I was called to testify, the city prosecutor asked me who'd thrown the first punch. I answered that I couldn't recall.

During the months prior to and leading up to the trial, I'd felt guilty about the injuries sustained by both Ellis and my partner. I was responsible for letting what should have been a simple situation get completely out of control.

Ellis was found "not guilty." A lawsuit was later filed against the City of Seattle, and Mr. Ellis was awarded a $65,000 settlement.

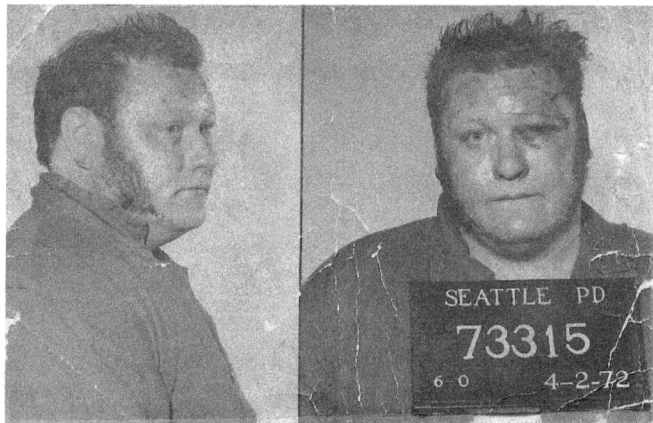

"Buddy Ellis" mugshot

Looking back, I should have just ignored Ellis's insult, gotten into my city vehicle, driven back to the station, and enjoyed my still-warm dinner of Ivar's scallops and chips.

Following this incident, I wrote letters to several of my past high-ranking aikido instructors in Hawaii, asking them to explain what it was that I was doing wrong. How should I use aikido when arresting a suspect who resisted violently? The instructors in Hawaii all answered that they didn't know. They had no idea because they'd never had to fight anyone or control a resisting individual. I was on my own!

Aikido training = no resisting. If you do resist while practicing aikido, they tell you that you have a "fighting mind." OK, so these individuals that I, as a police officer, must arrest, they are resisting, so yeah, they have "fighting minds." No argument there, but what do I do about it? How do I subdue them and handcuff them using aikido techniques?

From the very beginning of my aikido training in 1955, Tohei *sensei* would always at some point during the class go up to the biggest guy in the *dojo* and put on a wrist lock. Then when he had the guy completely locked up, he'd smile at us as if to say, "See? I have this guy completely under control. He can't punch me, he can't get away from me." All very impressive and highly convincing.

Soon after Tohei arrived in Hawaii, he published the first book on aikido in English. In the book there's a picture of him putting a wrist lock on a very large Hawaiian guy. The guy in the photo was none other than Mr. Larry Mehau, a lieutenant in the Honolulu Police Department vice unit at the time the photo was taken. Very impressive, but Larry Mehau had actually "allowed" Tohei to put the lock on him.

Tohei would do the same thing at different aikido events. He'd go up to the biggest guy in the room and apply the wrist lock. Very impressive. Very bullshit! Why bullshit, you ask? Because those guys "allowed" Tohei to apply the wrist lock. I'd be really impressed if Tohei could successfully apply that same wrist lock to someone who didn't want him to do it. It's not going to happen!

I was guilty of doing the exact same thing. Whenever I taught an aikido class, I'd go up to the biggest guy in the class and apply the same wrist lock that Tohei used to use back in the old days. Boy, look at Bernie *sensei*. Wow, he's able to control that big guy with a simple wrist lock. We're impressed.

Tohei *sensei* with Lt. Larry Mehau

No, my friend, don't be impressed. You've been duped! The guy "allowed" me to do it. Why? Out of respect since I was the teacher. If he'd resisted me, I most likely would not have been able to apply the wrist lock. That's the truth, pure and simple.

Over the years, I've gotten wiser. I now know what can be done using the techniques and teachings of aikido. More important, I now know what can't be done using aikido. Yes, aikido techniques can be highly effective in immobilizing an individual if he or she, for whatever reason, allows you to apply a lock. But if someone is fighting and resisting arrest, as was often the case when I was a police officer, you first have to stun the resister or have the assistance of other officers to render the resister incapable of fighting. Once tha's accomplished, you should then be able to apply a restraining lock on that person.

This realization didn't come to me as a flash of insight out of the void. It took years and years of trial and error, research and working with other high-ranking martial arts instructors, such as Prof. Wally Jay, Don Angier, and Frederick Lovret.

For the purpose of developing police arrest techniques, I built a *dojo* in my backyard, which we called the "Washington Budokan." Approximately ten police officers and other selected individuals would get together three times a week for training, research, and development of police arrest techniques. At the beginning of each class, I'd say, "OK, guys: what arrests were made these past few days, what techniques were used to apprehend and subdue the suspect, and which techniques worked? (And which didn't work?)" From all of us working together, we developed a handful of arrest techniques that we could rely on most of the time. But we realized as well that there were some people out there that, no matter how skilled you were or what technique you used, were going to be too strong, too drunk, too drugged out, or just too plain mean for a single officer or maybe even several officers to control without using mace or a taser.

The real world is very unforgiving. Having years of training and maybe a black belt in some martial art is no guarantee that you'll be able to single-handedly subdue someone.

So what about aikido? Well, it's a good way of keeping fit, for developing your center, for self-discipline, that sort of thing. But as far as using aikido for self-defense, I personally would recommend cross-training. Continue your training in aikido, but also train in some other martial art. Myself, I cross-train in Muay Thai Boxing.

Otherwise, you're fooling yourself and developing a false sense of security. You think pure aikido is going to work in a real fight? Good luck! How many aikido instructors have actually been in a real fight or had to subdue a resisting individual? None that I know of! For those arguing the effectiveness of aikido, simply google, "Koichi Tohei grappling," and decide for yourself!

Officer Lau frisking a student posing as a suspect (1971)

26

The War on Drugs

Ever since the age of 16, I'd wanted to be a narc. So I put in a transfer request to my patrol sergeant. A month or so later, at roll call, the sarge announced that I'd be reassigned to narcotics. Wow, here I was, finally, an undercover police officer, a "narc."

It all started out being fun and exciting. Working undercover was thrilling, though sometimes dangerous. But I didn't mind danger. Actually, I looked forward to it. Danger always made me feel alive and energized. I loved that uneasy feeling of suspense, the feeling of not knowing who I might meet next or what might happen. Wondering if today was the day I might get shot or killed.

Undercover started out as a big game for me. I had to play the role of a drug addict, and that was exciting. I got to meet and hang out with what I can only describe as "interesting undesirable individuals." Not everyone got to rub elbows with drug dealers, prostitutes, and perverts. It was something normal folks only read about in the paper or saw on the evening news. Here I was, actually associating first-hand with the underbelly of society. The bad guys, the criminals, the drug addicts. It was real. Those individuals I got to meet, know personally, and hang out with—those folks were the real thing. Instead of reading some cheap crime novel, I was actually part of one. What more could a boy from Hilo ask for?

I could picture it in my mind: making undercover buys, serving search warrants, kicking in doors, finding major drug caches, arresting the bad guys... Later, I'd write up the report, and all the guys in the office would pat me on the back and say, "Bernie, you did good. We're proud of you!"

The following week, I reported at 4:00 P.M. to the 7th Floor of the Arctic Building, Room 710, located directly north of the Public Safety Building. I didn't have to report to the police station any more, and I didn't have to wear a uniform. Just old jeans, a tee shirt, or whatever I wanted to wear.

Entering the Narcotics Section office, I was immediately greeted by several narcotics detectives wearing casual clothing and black leather jackets. Boy, those black leather jackets made them look impressive; like you didn't want to mess with them. This office was their own private world, and they answered to no one but themselves. The detectives all carried their guns tucked into their belts at the small of their back, just like the crooks on TV. And the guns weren't standard-issue police six-shot revolvers; no, they were all automatics.

One of the taller guys, a Detective Ingertilla, shook my hand, welcomed me to the unit, and told me to have a seat and relax. "Read the paper or something," were his words. I found myself a seat, picked up the paper, and started to read. 30 minutes passed. It was hard to focus, and I became restless. I got up, went over to a file cabinet, and started looking through the hundreds of mug shots of known drug dealers that had previously been arrested on narcotics violations. I wasn't comfortable just sitting around reading the paper. I was, after all, on duty and getting paid to do a job, not just sit around. After about ten minutes or so, Ingertilla looked over at me and said, "Look, kid, will you just relax? We don't do anything around here till it gets dark. So sit your ass down and quit trying to look busy. You're in narcotics now, not patrol."

So began my first night as a narc.

Over the next few hours, other detectives filtered in and welcomed me to the unit. They were all dressed casually, all had that aura of being tough narcotics detectives, and all looked very impressive to me, still a rookie cop, really, who just a few days ago had been a uniformed Seattle cop assigned to the Patrol Division. Later that evening, Sgt. Joe Sanford and several other agents sat me down and instructed me as to what the next steps were in becoming a narc. Here's what I had to do:

1. Let my hair grow.

2. Don't shave.

3. Don't wash my clothes.

4. Don't tell anyone, friends or family, that I was working under cover.

Later, I was instructed by Sgt. Joe to pick a name that matched one from the area where I was raised in order to make my cover seem all the more authentic should anyone later check me out. I made up a name that was a combination of the names of two friends in Hawaii: John and Abel Medeiros. I became "John Abel Medeiros"—Johnny Medeiros, drug dealer. I loved it!

The next step in getting us fresh new narcs to become pretend assholes and drug addicts was to teach us how to act and behave like addicts. Two other new undercover narcotics agents and I were ushered into a small room with one of the senior detectives. The detective removed a bit of marijuana from a large plastic bag, took out some Zig-Zag papers, and demonstrated to us how to properly roll a marijuana joint. I'd never seen that much marijuana before, let alone rolled a joint. Each of us was given some Zig-Zag papers along with a bit of marijuana and told to practice rolling a joint.

"Johnny Medeiros"

About an hour later, when it seemed that we'd all gotten Joint-Rolling 101 down pat, it was time for us rookie narcs to learn how to "simulate" smoking a joint. Cops aren't allowed to actually smoke marijuana because, as we all know, smoking marijuana is against the law. Now, we can pretend to smoke marijuana, but we're not allowed to actually inhale (or was that exhale? I can't remember!). So we were taught how to simulate inhaling, holding, and then exhaling the smoke. (Hey, dude, where's the smoke?)

We were also taught the proper facial expressions, body language, and verbal responses for smoking marijuana because when you're in the company of real dope-smoking addicts, you'd better well know how to "pretend" you're smoking.

I still couldn't figure out how to get around the fact that if we didn't inhale, there would be no smoke to exhale. I guess our instructors thought those dope-smoking addicts wouldn't notice. Yeah, right.

Finally, when Joint-Rolling 101 and "Simulated" Smoking 102 were over with, we all headed out to McDonald's for a meal, make that several meals. For some odd reason this course in how to interact with marijuana addicts had made us all extremely hungry. When we got to McDonald's, I ordered three burgers, fries and a soda. Boy, they sure tasted good! It must have been a new McDonald's recipe.

Months later, several other agents and I, plus a new detective sergeant (Sgt. Shoefly), drove down to Monmouth, Oregon to attend a week-long course given by the DEA guys. We were informed by the personnel instructing the course that when we narcs were out there buying drugs, we weren't allowed to actually use drugs. We were told that when drug dealers offered us a sample, we were to make excuses, like "Sorry, but I'd rather wait till I get home and I'm with my old lady," "I have to drive," etc. Yes, that's what we were actually instructed to say. We were supposed to bullshit our way out of using drugs ourselves.

Following the week-long DEA course, we returned to Seattle and went back to the Narcotics office. We were now ready for the next step in becoming narcs. Sgt. Joe took us to a large safe located at the rear of the office, unlocked it, and opened the heavy door. Lying there on a shelf were a dozen or so old-looking automatic pistols. We were instructed to go ahead and pick out a gun that we liked. However, we were given no holsters for carrying the firearm, but instead, shown how to wrap several rubber bands around the grips of the weapon and tuck it into our belts at the small of the back. The rubber bands were there to keep the gun from sliding down our pants, which might prove embarrassing, to say the least.

We were now ready to become real undercover agents. Each of us was given $200 in cash and issued a fake Washington State Driver's License and personal identification from Olympia. I was officially "Johnny Abel Medeiros," undercover narc. We were then told to start hanging out at local taverns.

"Go ahead and shoot pool, drink beer, and get to know the local drug dealers. Try to get into the drug culture, so that eventually you'll be able to buy drugs from them and start making cases," said the sergeant. Once on the streets, we'd no longer carry any Seattle police identification or police badges. Our assignment was to go out, mingle with the slime, the perverts, the drug dealers, the addicts, and the prostitutes, all the while pretending not to be cops.

The three of us rookie narcs left the office, each of us going off in our own direction. Now, we'd be out there on our own. We carried our guns, a lot of cash, and some illegal drugs so that we'd look convincing should we ever get searched by some bad guy who thought that we might be cops.

We were further instructed to phone in a report every hour or so; not by name, but by a code number that had been assigned us. My number was "905." Wow! I was now undercover secret agent 905. This new life was getting to be more and more exciting all the time. We had to check in by way of pay phones, as there were no cell phones back in the early 1970s. The detective manning the undercover phone (which was located in a closet in the Narcotics office) would answer in a gruff voice, "Yeah?" Then we'd either check in by our code number or be relayed a message, should some drug dealer have left a message for one of our undercover identities.

So it would go. Dial that special phone number, say "905 checking in," and the voice on the other end would say "OK" and hang up or pass on any message or instructions. That was about it. We were instructed to call in three times per shift at first. Several months later, when we were more comfortable in our undercover assignments, we no longer needed to call in.

Throughout the Seattle area there were numerous taverns, strip joints, porn shops, and other establishments known for drug activity. Those were the places where we'd hang out. Drug dealers, perverts, pimps, 'ho's and assholes; these were the types of individuals we'd now be associating with on a daily basis. Hanging with them, drinking with them, and of course, "simulating" doing drugs with them when we were offered drugs.

This was an exciting new world for me. For the first time in my life, I had money in my pockets, I had the power of a police commission to make arrests, and I was free to do as I wished. My only assignment was to hang out with assholes and make drug cases. What a life!

Working undercover was fun and exciting, but hanging out every day with drug dealers and perverts had its stressful side. I had to constantly be on my guard about how I responded to questions that were often asked about my involvement with drugs, where I came from, who I knew in the drug culture, where I lived, etc. I was hoping that I wouldn't someday come face-to-face with some guy that I'd arrested when I was a patrol officer. There were hundreds of individuals out there walking the streets of Seattle that I'd either arrested personally or helped to arrest. I'd testified while in uniform in open court, where I was seen by everyone in the courtroom. Hundreds of people in Seattle knew my face. Sure, I'd grown my hair long and had also grown a beard, but there was always that chance that some asshole would recognize me from my uniform days.

Ask any police officer or detective who's worked undercover assignments: their greatest fear isn't getting shot; it's getting made. When you're undercover, there's no one around to come to your rescue. We were out there on our own in the company of the bad guys, and should things go wrong, we had no backup. We didn't even have police identification to protect us. That fear and anxiety of being made would remain with me every second of my life undercover.

As I met more and more druggies, as I hung out with them, shot pool with them, bought them drinks, and eventually got invited to their homes and partied with them, I was all the while praying that there would never come a day when my cover would be blown and I'd be discovered to be Officer Bernard Lau and not "Johnny Medeiros," the drug dealer I claimed to be.

Bottom line: all the while I was having a good time "pretending," I was scared as hell!

Once my "shift" was over, I'd transform myself back into being a normal person. (As normal as possible, that is. My hair was long and dirty, I had a full beard, and my clothing had been purchased from discount stores.) The problem was, the drug dealers I was associating with would only see "Johnny Medeiros" from Monday through Friday and for only eight hours at a time. They often asked me why I wasn't around more. That was a tricky question to answer. I was mostly working nights, but for only eight hours at a time. I had no logical explanation, except to say that I had other things to take care of.

I always had to be careful what I said and how I said it. One wrong word, one wrong facial expression, or some inappropriate body language, and my cover might get blown. And I might get killed.

Once the drug dealers and addicts got to trust and accept me, my next step was to start buying drugs from them. I started by buying a baggie or two of marijuana. Over time, I'd try to buy larger quantities in an attempt to get to the bigger dealers.

Another way of working undercover narcotics was to have a "CI." Officially we called them "confidential informants." In the street they were called "snitches," and their lives were always in danger. The way it worked was this: an individual, male or female, might want to give us information in order to get back at someone, for money (which we paid them for good information), to work off an arrest (and keep from going to jail), or just to feel important. When contact was made with a prospective informant, a meeting was set up away from the Narcotics office at someplace like a Denny's Restaurant. The potential informant would be interviewed, background checks would be made, and the individual would be questioned as to why he or she wanted to become an informant. Once the individual was cleared and approved, he or she would be taken to the Narcotics office to be fingerprinted and photographed and would then be given a CI number to go by. The individual's signature was recorded in a book, along with the CI number, because whenever an informant was paid for information, he or she was required to sign a receipt. The CI would then be assigned to work with one of the undercover officers or detectives.

My first undercover buy took place in the Fremont neighborhood of Seattle. An informant had come into the Narcotics office offering to sell information regarding a guy he knew wanted to sell a "pillow of cross tops" (5,000 amphetamine tablets) for $1,000. I'd grown my hair long and had a beard, but I hadn't yet been involved in any major narcotics purchases. I needed to get my feet wet, so I was introduced to the informant, and a plan of action was put into motion. Exiting the Narcotics office, the informant and I drove to Fremont and entered the Fremont Tavern, where we were to wait for the dealer to show up. I sat at the bar and ordered a pitcher of beer, as I'd been directed to do by my supervising detectives. The informant and I sat at the bar making small talk and drinking beer. Damn, I loved that job!

About a half hour later, a guy in his late 20s came up to the bar and spoke to the informant. Minutes later, I was told to follow him outside to the parking lot, along with the informant, where I was shown a clear plastic ziploc bag containing a large amount of what appeared to be cross top tablets. Reaching into my jacket pocket, I removed a $1,000 wad of cash and handed it to the unknown guy. He took my cash, placed the ziploc bag containing the cross tops into a paper bag, and handed it to me.

I'd just made my first major drug buy. I was ecstatic. I felt important and worthy. I looked forward to returning to the Narcotics office, where I knew I'd get patted on the back and told how proud they were of me. I'd done a good job pretending to be a drug dealer. My mannerisms and appearance had fooled the dealer into selling me drugs.

This was the way it usually worked: you'd make a hand-to-hand buy, put the dope into evidence with a lab request, write up the report, try to make at least two more buys from the dealer, trying to buy a larger amount each time or, better yet, get introduced to his supplier. You'd try to get the dealer to deliver in some sort of vehicle, so that later we could jack the guy's car when we busted him. In three to six months, you filed a case with a prosecutor, got an arrest warrant for the dealer, found the dummy, and arrested his ass. Then he either plead guilty or the case went to trial. Many times, once the dealer found out that he'd sold to a cop, he'd enter a guilty plea in hopes of getting a reduced sentence. That's how narcotics worked: simple!

My instructions for this buy were to go ahead and make the buy, hand the dealer the $1,000 cash, take possession of the suspected drugs, and then just walk back to my undercover vehicle and return to the office. Simple enough, I thought. Drugs in hand, I turned and was heading towards my vehicle, when suddenly, I was overpowered and thrown to the pavement by three narcotics detectives and roughly handcuffed. A gun was put to my head, and I was told, "Don't move, asshole, or I'll blow your fucking head off!" The detectives then searched me, found and removed the narcotics that I'd just purchased, and also removed my firearm.

I panicked for a brief moment. What the hell was going on? Why was I being arrested, roughed up, and threatened with a gun in my face? The detectives knew who I was. I'd been instructed to just buy the drugs and return to the office. What was going on?

They ordered me to stand up, and then marched me over to a marked police vehicle which had been parked out of sight around the corner from the tavern. Still in handcuffs, I was shoved into the back seat of the patrol unit. Without a word spoken, the patrol officer drove me to the police station G Deck, the parking area where all arrested individuals were brought for booking into the city jail. As I was removed from the police vehicle, two detectives from the Narcotics Section came up and informed the patrol officer that they'd take over from there. In other words, they'd take care of my booking.

The transporting patrol officer had no idea that I was in fact an undercover police officer. To him I was just another scum-bag asshole that got busted for dealing drugs. Once a police officer or a detective goes undercover, his true identity is on a need-to-know basis. Even cops can't be trusted to keep their mouths shut. A slip of the tongue, an undercover identity revealed, and it becomes that much more dangerous for the undercover cop.

The two detectives took me (still in handcuffs) up to the 6th Floor of the Public Safety Building for booking. They cautioned me to keep my mouth shut and say nothing to the booking officer, except my undercover name and phony address. The jail supervisor, however, was informed that I was an undercover officer.

I was made to strip and handed orange jail coveralls. Yeah, I had to lift my nuts, then turn around, bend over, and spread my ass cheeks. That's the normal operating procedure for checking if suspects being booked are carrying any narcotics or other contraband on their person. Next, I was fingerprinted and a mug shot was taken of me. I was then placed into a holding cell by myself. Meanwhile, the informant and the guy I'd purchased the cross tops from were also being booked and fingerprinted. The whole idea of having me arrested and booked along with those two was to keep my cover intact. I was a new narc, and my undercover status was a valuable asset that needed to be kept secret as long as possible.

Early the following morning, the two detectives showed up and "bailed me out of jail." I was then taken back to the Narcotics office, where I proceeded to write out my report on the drug buy.

"Damn, Bernie. You did real good out there last night," they told me.

"If we didn't know better, we would've made you as a real asshole drug dealer. Congratulations for a job well done! I think you're going to become a great undercover agent. You're a natural."

I felt so proud of myself. After all those years of being a second-rater, I was beginning to feel worthy. Finally, someone saw that I was more than just a screw-up and a misfit; someone saw that I had talent and realized that I had great potential in making undercover drug buys. I was going to be able to provide the SPD with those all-important "stats" in the War on Drugs. I'd found my calling.

Busted in Seattle

I loved role-playing, I loved playing the part of an asshole, I loved making believe that I was a drug dealer and a junkie, and I was getting paid to do it. I couldn't believe my good fortune. My childhood dream of being an undercover narcotics agent had finally come true.

Rather than plead guilty, the dealer I'd purchased the cross tops from decided to take the case to court. By now, he'd realized that he'd sold drugs to an undercover cop, and more than anything else, he wanted to learn my true identity. There was no way around it; I had to testify in court. The accused has the legal right to confront his accuser.

But being that I was a new undercover agent and my true identity constituted a valuable asset to the police department, the presiding judge ordered the courtroom locked down. The public was not allowed in. The only ones present were the presiding judge, myself, the two narcotics detectives who'd made the arrest, a city prosecutor, the defendant, and his public defender. That was it. As few people as possible were to be allowed to know what I looked like.

The trial took approximately 20 minutes. I testified to purchasing the pillow of cross tops and to handing the individual on trial the $1,000. The two detectives testified to surveillance of the drug transaction and to the arrest of the suspect and the seizure of the drugs. The defendant was found guilty. What could he say? He'd sold narcotics to an undercover cop, and there was absolutely no way that he could get away from being found guilty.

Once the trial was over and done with, rather than exit through the front doors of the courtroom, I was allowed to exit via a private stairwell located at the rear, an exit reserved for the judge and the officers of the court. I thanked the judge and started down the stairs. I'd gone down maybe three flights, when I suddenly heard a commotion several floors above me. I could hear three or four individuals, several male voices, and one female yelling out, "Come on, I can hear him. He's right down below us. Let's get the fucking narc. Let's get him!"

How the hell did bad guys get into the stairwell? Normally it was locked from the outside, and you could only access it with a key. I continued going down, taking three to four steps at a time. I was frightened. I didn't want my cover blown, and I didn't want to be assaulted!

The bottom of the stairwell exited into a police tunnel, which ran under James Street from the county courthouse to the Public Safety Building and was used exclusively by law enforcement personnel to transport prisoners from the city jail to the courthouse for trial and back. I reached the bottom and exited into the tunnel. Then I turned right and ran to the far end where the jail elevator was located. I unlocked the elevator (all police officers were given a key), quickly got inside, once again inserted my key, and punched in the 5th Floor, G Deck. Safe!

I found out later that the defendant in this case worked for the City of Seattle in some small department and had somehow gotten hold of the key to the private stairwell. He'd given this key to his friends, just in case I exited via the stairwell, and had instructed them to rough me up if they caught me. These folks wanted to see my face real bad and find out who I was.

That turned out to be a close call. Welcome to being a narc, Bernie!

Being as working undercover is dangerous and stressful, whenever possible, we'd do stupid things to relieve the stress. One time, I remember going along with some other detectives from our unit to serve a search warrant on a residence where cocaine was suspected to be on the premises. Once entry had been gained and the bad guys had been put in handcuffs, the remaining detectives and I started to methodically search the residence for illegal drugs. We searched room by room, looking through each and every dresser drawer and closet, under the beds, and flipping over the mattresses.

Besides narcotics, we were also looking for sex toys and photo albums containing home-shot porn photos of individuals engaged in sex. More often than not, we'd find such items when we served a search warrant where cocaine was involved. For some strange reason, folks that use cocaine also enjoy taking X-rated photos of themselves while engaged in various decadent sexual acts. We justified the seizing and placing into evidence of those photo albums because, looking through the albums later, we were often able to identify other individuals involved with using or dealing in cocaine. Yeah, it was a dirty job, but somebody had to do it. Often times the ranking lieutenant or captain of the Narcotics Section would take these coveted seized porn photo albums home with him for a few days before placing them into evidence. Rank had its privileges.

In one of the bedroom drawers I was searching, I happened upon a large white vibrator. This thing must've been 12 inches long, and of course, me being somewhat of a prankster, I decided to have some fun with it. In the living room, Sgt. Shoefly was in the process of interviewing and jotting down the personal information of the five suspects, who were sitting on a couch in front of a large, glass coffee table. There were three females and two males, all in their early 20s. The good Sgt. Shoefly, a God-fearing, church-going individual, was using the glass coffee table as a desktop for his paperwork.

I walked over to the table and, without saying a word, turned on the vibrator and placed it in the center of the table. Yeah, right there in the center of the glass coffee table, right there in front of everyone. Boy, how that vibrator chattered and echoed throughout the residence as it skittered around on the coffee table. I left it on, with the suspects sitting there handcuffed and looking just a wee bit embarrassed. Then I went back to searching the bedroom for possibly more cocaine and/or marijuana, and hopefully more porn photos. Someone finally turned off the vibrator. Must have been Sgt. Shoefly.

Another time, my partner Al and I had a CI make a heroin buy in an apartment complex of maybe a hundred units located at 17th and Yesler in the black part of town. If heroin were successfully purchased, we'd be able to get a search warrant for the suspect's apartment unit later that same day. We called this particular CI "Harry the Hype" since he used to shoot heroin.

Well anyway, Harry went into an apartment to score $60 worth of heroin. When he came back to the vehicle, we tested the suspected heroin immediately. The test proved it to be burn (phony dope). This was the second time that Harry had gotten burned at this particular apartment—not good! My partner and I looked at each other and said, "Fuck this shit; we're not letting some asshole drug dealer get away with burning us twice, no way!" We decided go knock on this dude's apartment and arrest his ass, just for the hell of it. It was, after all, the crime of fraud to sell phony dope to undercover cops. (True.) Plus, it just wasn't cool.

We decided we had to do that because that's how real addicts would've acted if they'd gotten burned. You see, heroin junkies are desperate folks. End up with bunk dope when your body starts crying out for the next fix, and pure hell starts to set in as the body begins its process of going into withdrawal. Heroin withdrawal is serious, and addicts don't take kindly to getting burned.

We went up to the dealer's apartment, which was located on the 2nd Floor. Once there we started pounding on the door, yelling for the dealer to "Open up the fucking door, asshole!" Well of course, no one opened the door, so what to do next? Al commenced to kick at the door, but, after several minutes, it still didn't look like anyone was coming to open it up. It turned out the apartment complex units had all been fitted with steel-frame doors built to keep junkie-type folks from kicking in each others' doors and trying to rip off each others' dope.

We must have been making quite a racket because three black males who most likely lived in apartment units just below the one Al and me were trying to enter came up the stairs towards us with their attitude in hand, ready to fight and kick some white honky ass.

Hearing threats and insults being directed at us, Al and I turned to face these guys. I looked at Al and smiled as we calmly took out our automatics and said, "You boys really want to get involved?" Upon seeing that the two white boys were carrying two big guns, and also that they showed no fear, these individuals quickly turned and vanished without saying another word.

This slight interruption taken care of, Al and I turned back to the task of trying to kick the door in. It took another three or four minutes of kicking, but the door finally gave. We calmly walked into the apartment and demanded to see the idiot dealer who'd ripped Harry off.

The only person there was a young black female in her early 20s. She was crouched in the corner of the living room, very frightened and unable to speak. Talk about funny; usually black folks are the ones kicking in whitie's front door during burglaries. Now here you had two armed white dudes kicking in some black guy's front door.

Come to find out, when Al and I had started kicking at the apartment door, the dealer had jumped off the balcony, two stories up! (We later heard that he immediately left Seattle and ended up hiding out in Portland, Oregon.)

We confronted the young gal and demanded our $60 back. Well of course, she didn't have any money to give us, so we decided to take her stereo equipment as "collateral," till we got our money back. We proceeded to disconnect the speakers, turntable, and other stereo components. Then we left the apartment, each of us with an armful, and walked down Yesler towards where we'd parked our van.

Meanwhile, someone had called 911 to report two "armed white boys" kicking in a door. A marked patrol unit had been dispatched to investigate the complaint. So as Al and I were walking down Yesler Street, loaded down with stereo equipment, a marked patrol unit cruised by and headed towards us. The police officer recognized us, rolled his eyes, laughed, and kept driving down Yesler.

Months later, Lieutenant Dave Grayson bumped into Al and me in the hallway of the Arctic Building. He inquired if either of us knew anything about some door being kicked in at 17th and Yesler and stereo equipment taken out of an apartment. Being we didn't think it was such a big deal, we said "Yeah, the guy ripped us off during a heroin buy, so we took his stereo as collateral." Wrong answer. Lieutenant Grayson flipped out; "You two kicked in a door and stole stereo equipment?" Grayson was now totally upset. He thought we'd taken the stereo equipment home for our own use. He started giving us our Miranda warnings. "You have the right to remain silent, you have the right to an attorney, etc."

I looked at the Lieutenant, shrugged my shoulders, and said, "Lieutenant, this guy ripped us off twice. He burned us for over 150 bucks. That was city money, you know. We can't just allow assholes like him to keep ripping us off. Al and I did exactly what a normal junkie would've done, given the same circumstances. In the streets you can't allow this ripping-off stuff to happen, no way! Ripping someone off during a heroin buy is serious shit in the streets. We had to play it out like we did. We had no choice!" Grayson, still a bit upset, then asked us where the stereo equipment was presently being kept.

"Lieutenant, it's all there in the back of the undercover van. It's been there since we confiscated it as collateral."

Turned out this particular apartment complex was owned by the City of Seattle, and the apartments were being offered to low-income families. A complaint had been filed, and an official investigation had been launched to determine which law enforcement agency was responsible. Investigating officials figured it had to be some law enforcement guys that had kicked in the door because no two white boys in their right minds would dare walk into an all-black apartment complex, kick in a door, and then proceed to rip off stereo equipment. No way. It had to be cops. The DEA was questioned and they, of course, denied any involvement. The FBI was questioned, and they too denied involvement. The county sheriff's department was questioned; they too denied any knowledge. That had narrowed down the possibilities to the SPD.

The City of Seattle ended up replacing the damaged door, and Sgt. Adams of the Narcotics Section returned the stereo equipment to the apartment, hooking it all back up and apologizing to the young lady it belonged to. After all was said and done, Al and I weren't arrested or charged with "home invasion" and theft of the stereo equipment. As for the black heroin dealer who'd ripped us off, he's probably still hiding out somewhere in Oregon. We never did catch him or get our money back. Bummer!

Another time, I met this fancy dressed-up-pimp-wannabe-"Super Fly"-type, purple hat and all with a feather sticking in it hanging around 1st and Pike. He approached me and asked if I wanted to cop (purchase) some good speed (methamphetamine). Since purchasing illegal drugs was in fact my "job description," I answered that, yes, I was interested and followed him to his apartment, located a block away. Once in the apartment, he showed me what he said was high-quality speed and offered to sell me a gram for $100. I removed 100 bucks' worth of buy money from my pocket and handed it to him. In return, he handed me a paper bindle he said contained a gram of speed.

Later on, back in the Narc office, I did a "field test" on the suspected gram of speed. Well, damn it again, the "speed" wasn't speed; it was in fact ephedrine, an ingredient used in cold medications. I was pissed and not about to let this jive-ass pimp wannabe motherfucker get away with ripping me off. Fuck, no; I had my pride!

Every so often, patrol has one or two of its officers spend a month working with us narcs on the street. One particular month, we got this "Hulk"-like officer assigned to our unit. The officer's nickname was "Crusher" because he could pick your ass up off the ground, crunch you like a pretzel, choke you out, and put you to sleep. He was a power lifter and a champion wrestler. Crusher was, however, a super-nice guy, easy to get along with, and always ready for some off-beat, fun-type adventure. My kind of guy.

So I formulated a plan of revenge. I had Crusher hang with me around 1st and Pike. When I finally spotted the pimp, I arranged for another buy from him. Then I had Crusher tail the pimp and me as we went back to the pimp's apartment to make the buy. My plan was to purchase another gram of speed. The pimp, I noticed, was limping and walking with the aid of a cane. I asked him what happened, and he explained that some guy shot him in the leg a few weeks ago. I thought to myself, "No shit, dude; that's what you get for ripping people off. You're lucky you didn't get your pimp ass killed!"

We went up to his apartment (same place as before), and again, he sold me what he claimed was "top-quality" speed. I went ahead and paid him another 100 bucks. This time, however, I had a narcotics field tester with me. I put a small amount of the alleged speed into the tester, snapped the glass chemical ampule, and the liquid mixed with the supposed speed. Nothing. Once again, it was burn.

Without a word, I started to leave the apartment. When I reached the door, I opened it and told Crusher, who was waiting just outside, "Yep, asshole ripped me off again. Let's get our money back!" Crusher entered the apartment. As soon as the pimp spotted Crusher, he got a panicky, "What the fuck!"-look on his face. He started to say something, but it was too late. Crusher moved quickly, got behind the pimp, and put a choke hold on him, lifting him right off his feet. The pimp's arms and legs were thrashing wildly, and his face was turning from black to purple due to lack of oxygen. I walked up to him, reached into the pimp's right front pocket, and removed a handful of cash. I counted out $200, put the money in my pocket, and threw the rest of the money on the floor. All I wanted was the money he ripped off; I wasn't there to rob the guy. It wasn't a "robbery;" it was simply a recovery of city funds!

I looked up. Pimp dude was no longer moving. His feet were dangling, his arms limp at his side; the guy was out cold. I told Crusher, "OK, you can let him go now." Crusher released the choke hold, and pimp dude flopped to the floor like a sack of flour. Crusher and I left the apartment and closed the door behind us. What about the sleeping pimp? Well, he'd wake up in a few minutes, wondering what the hell happened.

Recovery mission accomplished, we returned to the Narcotics office. I went up to Sgt. Shoefly, the shift duty supervisor, and handed him the $200 to be put back into the "drug buy fund." Sgt. Shoefly looked at me and asked, "What's this money for Bernie?" I explained to the good sergeant how I'd gotten ripped off twice by this pimp dealer, how Crusher and I'd gone and retrieved the city money by way of choking the guy out, and how I'd simply reached into the pimp's pocket and retrieved the $200. All rather simple, I thought.

Well, upon hearing my explanation of our funds recovery escapade, Sgt. Shoefly leaped out of his chair, threw his arms up, and in a gasping voice said, "You guys just committed strong-armed robbery. Get this money out of here! I don't want anything to do with it." Sgt. Shoefly was in panic mode.

Crusher and I just shrugged our shoulders, and without saying another word, I picked up and pocketed the $200, walked slowly out of the office, and returned to the streets of Seattle looking to make more drug buys. Some folks get excited over nothing.

Crusher and I were just acting like real drug dealers would have acted under the same circumstances. And like I said, we couldn't just allow drug-dealing, pimp-ass wannabes to go around ripping off the City of Seattle and get away with it. Certainly not!

A few weeks later, I spotted the same pimp in the area of 1st and Pike. He wasn't dead! He saw me and quickly walked off in another direction.

Another crazy incident. One sunny Friday afternoon, Sgt. Joe came up to me and said: "Bernie, I just got a call from one of my CIs stating that this gal Betty is holding heroin. She's sitting in a tavern at 14th and Yesler right now. How about you go in there and bring her out? Capt. Elster and me'll be sitting a block up on Yesler, and when we see you come out with her, we'll drive down quick and pick you and her up."

"Sure, Sarge. Not a problem!"

So Sgt. Joe and Capt. Elster parked a little ways away from the tavern and let me out. I was looking my usual grungy self: long, dirty hair, unkempt beard, dirty clothes. I looked like a burned-out tramp on 1st Avenue.

So I walked down a few blocks, went into the tavern, and saw that there was only one black gal sitting at the bar. Figuring it had to be her, I sat at the bar next to her and ordered a beer. I took a few sips, put the glass down, stood up, took hold of the gal's right arm with my left hand, and said, "Hey, girl; you're coming with me!" I didn't identify myself as a police officer.

The gal didn't say a word or try to resist. I guessed she was probably too confused or frightened. It's not often that some funky-looking white dude comes into an all-black tavern and yanks out some gal. In fact, it had never happened before.

I was halfway out of the tavern, still holding onto the gal's arm, when this very tall dude came towards me. I looked up at him and smiled. I wasn't scared one bit. Hell, no, I lived for that shit! The big dude mumbled out; "You ain't takin' her nowhere!" To which I replied: "Oh, yes I am!" as I reached behind me to get the S&W automatic that was tucked into my belt at the small of my back. I brought the gun up and put it right in his face. Pimp dude came to all stop, raised both arms, and quickly backed away. I didn't say another word. Didn't need to; my big silver automatic spoke loud and clear.

I took this gal outside and stood in the middle of the street, looking up to where Sgt. Joe and Capt. Elster said they'd be. Yep, they were up there all right, parked several blocks up Yesler and reading the paper. But they didn't notice me!

So there I was, a white boy standing in the middle of the street in a totally black neighborhood. I had a gun and I was holding on to this black gal. A crowd was starting to gather on the sidewalk. They weren't happy, not one bit.

Suddenly, I heard police sirens, lots of sirens, coming towards us. By now, Sgt. Joe and Capt. Elster had also heard the sirens. They looked up from their newspaper and saw me standing there two blocks away in the middle of 14th and Yesler Street hanging on to this black gal with my gun out. Sgt. Joe quickly drove down and snatched me up along with the gal just as the first patrol units arrived, red lights flashing and tires squealing to a halt.

Come to find out, someone had placed a 911 call to report that a crazy white guy with a gun was holding a black gal hostage in the middle of the street. Just what I needed: to have my ass blown away by one of my fellow officers, thinking I was a hostage-taker. Boy, what a rush that was!

Later, we found out that when the gal saw me walk in the tavern door, she threw the tissue holding the heroin to the bar girl, who threw it into the garbage. White boy? Black tavern? Black folks aren't that stupid!

So Sgt. Joe didn't get his heroin bust that afternoon, after all. But I did manage to get my daily adrenalin rush.

Harry the Hype finally introduced me to a decent coke dealer. This was new because, usually, Harry had only been able to set up small-time, chippie buys for me. Anyway, this rich kid in West Seattle had a large quantity of cocaine for sale, a couple ounces, and wanted $3,000 for the deal. Harry introduced me to the kid, but being this kid didn't know me, he was hinky. But he was willing to meet me anyway, so I had his $3,000 in twenties. (150 twenty-dollar bills looks like a lot of money.) The kid and me, along with some of his friends, sat outside his house bullshitting back and forth. He was trying to decide whether to sell to me or not.

Time went by. Detective Rudy and Sgt. Joe were doing surveillance from a camper parked one house up. Occasionally the kid went in the house to get a drink or whatever; most likely to talk to his friends about whether he should sell me the dope or not. He was really uncomfortable with me. Hey, I looked like a puke biker, so I don't know what his problem was. Maybe he was afraid of me ripping him off.

Under my tee shirt and jean jacket I wore an "agent protection device" (a transmitter), so the back-up guys in the camper could hear every word I said. When no one else was listening, I enjoyed giving Rudy a bad time. I'd lower my head and whisper something like, "Hey, Rudy, fuck you!" or "Hey, Rudy; the little dog here says he wants you to suck his tiny red dick!"—you know; that kind of harmless bullshit to make the caper sort of fun. Anything to help the time pass.

An hour and a half went by and I was getting tired of the waiting game the kid was playing. Finally, I stood up and said, "Look, dude, I ain't got time for this shit. I got $3,000 here in my boot." I took the money out and started counting it right in front of the kid. Like I said, 150 twenty-dollar bills looks like a ton of money. The kid eyeballed the large wad of cash. I handed the $3,000 to him.

"You gonna sell me the dope or what?"

"OK," he said.

He went over and told one of his buddies to give me the dope. I was told to get in one of their vehicles, which I did, and then the kid's buddy drove us away, with me riding in the passenger seat. A few blocks away from the house, he looked over at me and said, "It's under the towel at your feet." I reached down next to the floor mat and pulled away the towel. Yep, I saw a large plastic bag containing what appeared to be several ounces of cocaine. I picked up the bag, placed it in my lap, opened the seal, and took a pinch for tasting. Sure enough, it was cocaine. Good quality, too. My tongue and mouth went numb.

I reached back with my right hand, brought out my very large, shiny S&W automatic pistol, and ordered the kid to "shut the fuck up and keep driving." The kid looked scared. Keeping my gun pointed at his head, I told him how I was going to cut off his balls, shove them into his mouth, and make him chew on them. Like I said, I tried to make work fun.

"Hey, kid," I continued, "after you chew on your own nuts, then I'll put two in your head." The poor kid started to cry and plead with me. Again I told him to shut the fuck up and keep driving towards the wooded area in Lincoln Park. This improvised scenario also had great entertainment value for the surveillance team that was following us. I glanced back and saw that Detective Rudy and Sgt. Joe were laughing hysterically.

Five minutes later, we arrived at the wooded area in the park, and I told the kid, "Relax, asshole. I'm a cop." The kid let out a sigh of relief and exclaimed, "Oh, Thank God! I thought you were going to kill me." I replied; "Nah, I was just fucking with you." Sgt. Joe and Detective Rudy were still laughing hysterically.

The driver ended up with a year in county jail, and the other kid got three years in the Washington State Penitentiary for distribution of cocaine. The kid had offered his "friend" $200 to do the deal with me. Some friend! By the way, the friend also lost his car to us.

Me, I got a pat on the back for another job well done.

I was good at my role-playing job and I seldom got made. But once in a while, accidents did happen. There was a cocaine dealer named "Doctor Dan" who'd been studying to be a doctor, when his right hand got crushed in a freak accident. My informant got me close to Doctor Dan, even into a house where we were all partying one night. I offered to buy some coke (beautiful 99.9% pharmaceutical grade stuff) from Doctor Dan, but he refused. Right in front of me, he sold a couple grams of coke to a gal, and then said that if I wanted to buy any, I could buy it off her. Smart guy, the Doctor.

One evening I went to a night club with two of Doctor Dan's gal friends. I was dancing with one of them, named "Cerise," when all of a sudden, some guy came up to me and said, real loud, so he could be heard over the music, "Hey, Bernie, how you doing?"

"Bernie?!" Fuck, I knew the guy. He was an off-duty Seattle police officer who just happened to be in that night club. I tried to look confused, like I'd never seen him before. Cerise looked at me suspiciously.

"'Bernie?' I thought your name was 'Johnny.'"

I told her that my name was "Johnny" and I didn't know who the fuck the guy was. I went over and got right in his face,

"What'd you call me 'Bernie' for? I ain't 'Bernie!' And who the fuck are you, anyway? Get the fuck outta my face! Get the fuck away from me before I kick your skinny ass, motherfucker!"

In a very low voice, I said, "I'm undercover. Get outta here." He heard me and apologized, "Sorry, guy; my mistake! I thought you were an old army buddy of mine. Sorry!" And he turned away and left.

In undercover work, small incidents, such as someone calling you by your real name, can get you hurt or a case blown, as ended up happening to me with Doctor Dan. Of course, the off-duty officer had no idea I was working on a drug case and that the folks I was keeping company with were the bad guys. I can't really blame him, but patrol officers are usually told that if they spot an undercover in public, they should say nothing to him unless the undercover acknowledges him first.

Anyway, after that evening, Doctor Dan wouldn't have anything to do with me. He was no dummy, and that's why he'd been around so long. But I'd been close, so close. I know he would've sold to me sooner or later. All my work gone for nothing.

Working undercover narcotics, I got to buy just about every illegal drug that was available on the streets of Seattle. Marijuana, speed, methamphetamine, cocaine, heroin, pharmaceuticals, and oh yes, "acid!"

Acid is one of the most powerful hallucinatory drugs in existence. You take a hit of acid, and what follows is that reality ceases to exist. Your brain sort of short-circuits. You hear things, see things that just aren't there. Often times folks on acid freak out. They see colors, they see the walls melt. One moment they're mellow; the next minute, they can change into some vile, evil, decadent monster. I may have been a bit crazy during my undercover years, but I was never crazy enough to drop acid; no way!

Through one of our informants, we learned that there was some old hippie guy living just off Broadway who was selling a lot of blotter acid.

"Hey, Bernie, wanna try cold-copping from this dude selling acid?" Sure.

Cold copping—that's when you just walk up to a house where you suspect or have information that the individual or individuals living there are selling drugs. You don't know them and they don't know you. You try to bluff your way into getting them to sell you drugs. Sometimes it works, sometimes you come close to getting your head blown off.

It was always fun to just show up at someone's house, make up a name, and say, "Joe said I could cop some (name the drug) from you." A good part of the fun was playing roles, like an actor.

This time, I decided for whatever reason to dress up like a businessman, a "Mister Big" in the drug world, with lots of money to spend. It would be a new role for me. My long hair would be no problem: I washed and blow-dried it. I put on the one and only suit I owned (which I usually used for testifying in court). Hair blown dry, I sprayed on Aqua Net, so it would stay in place. I looked sharp, I felt clean for a change.

I drove to the Narc office and walked in. Everyone whistled and made fun of how I looked. "Damn, Bernie, you getting married or something?"

"OK, guys, it's just for today, so get a good look!"

I met with Detective Sergeant Joe and got the address of the house where this acid dealer lived. I was given $300 in cash to, hopefully, purchase whatever amount of the drug I could. I picked up my briefcase and off I went to try and cold-cop some acid from this hippie freak.

Being this dealer was an unknown, I was wired with an "agent protection device," which required me to be equipped with a battery pack that fit around my waist under my shorts. The battery pack powered a transmitter, so that surveillance detectives sitting a block or two away could listen in and hear the conversation between me and the suspect. In case anything went wrong, the detectives would rush in and hopefully save me from whatever danger I might be facing. Once the transmitter and battery pack were strapped on me, a test was conducted. "OK, Bernie; say something." I said, "Something, something. Can you hear me?" It tested OK.

Sgt. Joe, myself, and a second detective drove out near where the address was and parked a block away. I grabbed my briefcase and tested the transmitter again. It worked fine. Standing straight and looking like some vacuum cleaner salesman, I walked north one block and located the address. I went up the stairs and knocked on the door, which was partly open. No one answered. Several minutes went by. I knocked again, harder this time. Still no answer, so, slowly, I entered the house.

Almost immediately, I was confronted by an aging, bearded individual wearing thick bifocal glasses and a pair of dirty, ragged overalls. He moved towards me, pointing a double-barrel shotgun directly at my face. Without thinking, I dropped the briefcase, moved sideways to my left, and deflected the shotgun with my right hand. Grabbing the barrel with both hands and holding it tightly, I moved it away from my body. The shotgun went off, "K- BOOM," both barrels at once. I then commenced to pound on the suspect's face repeatedly with hammer-fist blows. The suspect released the shotgun and crumpled to his knees as he brought his hands up to his smashed, bleeding nose.

"You broke my nose, you fucker, you broke my nose," he screamed at me. I dropped the shotgun and forced the individual onto his stomach, stepping on the gun to keep control of it. Time stopped. Sgt. Joe and his partner were suddenly at my side, handcuffing the suspect.

"You OK, Bernie?" I couldn't think. I didn't answer. I blinked a few times, took several deep breaths, and walked out of the house for some much-needed fresh air. I sat on the concrete steps shaking uncontrollably, taking in more deep breaths, all the while blinking and looking around. My ears were ringing big time.

I suddenly realized that there was a burning pain around my waist. I knew I hadn't been shot. I reached down and yanked off the battery pack. It had shorted out. I ended up with second-degree burns where it had been in contact with my skin. Well, getting burned, even though it hurt a lot and took several weeks to heal, was better than getting my head blown off by some old-time hippie freak high on acid.

The suspect was arrested for attempted murder of a police officer. A search warrant on the residence later turned up a large quantity of blotter acid. It turned out that the suspect had dropped acid earlier that morning and was hallucinating, all the while thinking that the police were out to get him.

Wearing the same suit, I later testified against the suspect in open court. When the defendant saw me take the witness stand, he jumped up and screamed, "You fucking pig, I wish I'd blown your fucking head off. I will next time, I will!" I just looked at him, smiled, and said, "Sorry, sir; you missed your chance."

27

Making Detective

I was a loyal and devoted customer of Ivar's. I often bought scallops and chips and took them back to the office to eat. One day as I was waiting patiently at the back of the line in front of the Fish Bar, there was a drunk, homeless panhandler trying to shake down the people at the head of the line. When they didn't give him any money, he flipped out and started yelling, cussing, and threatening everyone there. He started to throw stuff at them—straws, cups, napkins.

Well, I wasn't about to let this disturbance get between me and my meal. I walked up to him, grabbed his left elbow with my right hand, and applied an aikido wrist lock. I took the slack out of his wrist, increased the torque, and soon had him totally under control. Within seconds he was in such pain that he was sobbing and pleading with me to let him go. The people standing in line all clapped and shouted "thank you."

I radioed for a patrol car and had the guy booked for creating a disturbance, and after some time, I was finally able to place my order. When I tried to pay, Bob, the manager, refused my money. I explained that as a police officer, I couldn't accept free meals. Bob took my five-dollar bill and gave me $5.00 in change. From then on, Bob always gave me back the same amount of change as what I'd pay for my food. What could I do? I wasn't about to stop eating at Ivar's Fish Bar.

It was a warm Seattle evening, and I was working undercover vice. I was dressed in plain clothes and headed east on Pike Street. Walking past the Wyoming Cafe, a well-known hangout for prostitutes, I observed a young mulatto female standing in the doorway, maybe 18 years of age. As I walked by she made eye contact and smiled. I smiled back and kept walking. The attractive young gal quickly hurried to my side and started walking with me. She began by saying, "Hi, what's your name?"

"Johnny," I responded, "My name's Johnny."

"Well, Johnny, you looking for a date?"

"No, not really. I'm headed up the street for a beer."

"Where you from, Johnny? Sounds like you got some kind of a foreign accent."

"Me, well, it's probably cause I grew up in Hawaii with Chinese folks, but I've been out here a couple of years, now. I live out towards Lynnwood."

"What you do for a living, Johnny?"

"Right now, I'm doing landscaping work. Actually I mow lawns and trim hedges. Not really a glamorous job, but it pays the rent." (At the time I was building a Japanese Zen Garden in my yard, so my hands were rough, like those of a real landscaper.)

"Johnny, mind if I join you for a beer?"

"Aah, well … I guess it's OK. Sure, why not? What's your name, by the way?"

"I'm 'Esteen,' 'Esteen Richards,' but everyone calls me 'Susan.' That's my birth name, 'Susan Johnson.'"

We continued walking and entered a non-decrepit tavern located mid-block. We sat at the bar, and I ordered a Budweiser. Susan asked if she could have a rum and coke.

"Sure. Have whatever you want," I said. Drinks arrived and we sat and chatted for a half hour or so. Finally, it was time to go.

"Well, Susan, nice talking to ya, but I gotta go. Gotta get up early; got five lawns to mow tomorrow."

"Johnny, you got a wife or girlfriend?"

"Me? Well, no. Not exactly. I just got divorced. No girlfriend—too soon. It was a difficult divorce. My ex took my kid. Real bummer."

"Oh, I'm so sorry, Johnny. Must be difficult on you."

"Yeah. I'd rather not talk about it right now."

"Johnny, I know we just met, but could I, maybe, come home with you? It's getting late, and I don't really have a place to stay tonight."

"Aah, I don't know Susan. I mean, you seem OK, but I don't really know you. You could be some sort of 'Mad Gal Serial Killer' for all I know. Ha-ha."

"No, Johnny, I'm not!"

"Yeah, I know. Just joking. Well … I guess it'd be OK. But just for tonight. You gotta leave first thing tomorrow morning when I go to work."

"Oh, thank you, Johnny. Thank you so much!"

We walked to my undercover GTO, parked a block north on Pine Street. I opened the passenger door to let Susan in the car and got in. We drove off onto an on-ramp and headed north on I-5. As we approached the Ship Canal Bridge, Susan asked me, "Johnny, you're not a cop, are you?"

I looked at her and chuckled, "Yeah, right! I'm a cop. Ha-ha. And you're busted for being cute!"

"Really, you're not, are you?"

"No, I'm not. But you're still cute."

"Uh, Johnny, I'll spend the night with you, but I need to ask you for some cash. $30, maybe?"

"$30! I thought you said you needed a place to stay! You mean to tell me that I'm supposed to be giving you a place to stay for the night, and you're going to charge me 30 bucks? What kind of a deal is that? That's fucked up, girl!"

"Well, Johnny, you mow lawns for money. I fuck for money. I got rent to pay too, you know, just like you! You know what, Johnny? I'll give you the best damn blow job you've ever had! C'mon, Johnny, please? I promise you won't be disappointed."

I kept driving without saying a word, thinking, "Bingo! I gotcha!" We passed Northgate Mall, still heading north on I-5. I was halfway to Lynnwood. Looking straight ahead, I kept driving.

"Susan …"

"What, Johnny?"

"I'm really sorry, Susan, I truly am, but I can't have sex with you tonight."

"Why not, Johnny?"

"Well, because, well … because … I'm a cop! And by the way, you're still cute, but you're also under arrest for offering and agreeing to an act of prostitution."

Several weeks later, Susan appeared in municipal court on the prostitution charge. However, she lucked out and got off with just a small fine, a warning from the judge, and no jail time.

So that was basically how Susan Johnson, AKA Esteen Richards, the cute, friendly Pike Street 'ho,' and I met on that warm Seattle evening. Over time Susan and I became good friends.

Being Susan spent most of her waking hours working the downtown area of Seattle, she had personal knowledge of the criminal activity that was going on there. Any time I needed information on vice or narcotics activity—or whenever I needed someone to chat with over a cup of coffee—Susan was always there for me. She continued working as a prostitute, and I overlooked that. I didn't really care. She wasn't such a bad kid and never had that bitch-type attitude, like some of the other 'ho's that worked Pike Street.

I hated it when I'd arrest some gal for O&A ("Offering and Agreeing"), and she'd start getting ugly, getting in my face, calling me a "fucking pig" and what have you. Every so often, some prostitute I'd just busted would want to fight me. I had a simple way of dealing with gals like that. I'd just grab hold of their hair, pull off their wigs, then grab hold of their real hair, pull them to the ground, and slap the cuffs on 'em. Oh, boy. Those gals did not like someone pulling their wigs off, no sir! A lot of them were real ugly-looking once the wig came off.

My way of thinking was if some gal I just busted acted like a lady, I treated her like a lady. But if she decided to cop an attitude, called me names, fought with me, acted like a low-life bitch... well then that's how I'd treat her.

When I busted Susan that first night, she took it in stride. She didn't get pissed off, yell at me, or cop an attitude. We even laughed and talked as I drove her to jail. Hey, getting arrested for prostitution isn't that big of a deal unless, of course, if it's the gal's umpteenth time. Then she might end up doing some jail time.

I informed the vice detectives that Susan was from time to time giving me information on narcotics activity in the downtown area. "Sonny," the vice sergeant, responded; "Not a problem, Bernie. Just let us know if something major's happening, so vice can get involved."

A lot of the guys working vice either had a prostitute passing down information, or from time to time, would simply, like myself, enjoy their company over a cup of coffee. Cops need to talk. We keep a lot of things bottled up inside. Most wives didn't want to be hearing all that job talk once the husband got home, especially not vice stuff. In return, vice guys would occasionally cut the gals some slack, sometimes protect them when some pimp or other low-life street asshole was giving her a bad time or hamming up on them.

Back in the early 1970s (in the good old days), if you were an asshole, you didn't want some vice detective on your ass. Today Seattle's a clean, safe, modern city and police officers are held accountable for their actions. There is more command supervision now than there was in the "good old days." In those days the streets of Seattle, especially around 1st and Pike, Belltown, Pioneer Square, and along the Waterfront, were a lot tougher than they are now.

Back then, there were a lot of good cops, like John Sullivan, who walked the beat in Pioneer Square, Sgt. Bernie Miller, who wore black leather gloves and wielded his infamous night stick, Ed Firstead, with his martial arts background, and Sam Buckley, who kept the Pike Place Market free of drunks and safe from the local 1st Avenue "scum." And there were many other fine, outstanding police officers who gave a damn and actually did productive police work to keep the streets of Seattle safe for its law-abiding citizens.

Law enforcement was very different back then. Cops in the late 60s and early 70s could run assholes out of town and "advise" them to never return, "or else!" Cops could actually do real police work, and the bad guys hardly ever turned in a complaint. I believe that the general public and even the street assholes had more respect for cops than they do now. Mess with a cop, mouth off, get an attitude... well, what usually followed was you got your ass dragged into the nearest alley and got the shit beat out of you. Then you got thrown in the slammer. Yeah, those were fun days back then, when cops could actually "Serve and Protect."

I once mentioned to Susan that the annual written test for detective was coming up. I wanted that coveted detective's badge more than anything else. Being a patrol officer was OK, don't get me wrong, but being a "detective"... well, that was special. As a detective, you got a lot of respect and you usually got assigned to some pretty interesting units: homicide, robbery, vice, narcotics, fugitive, etc.

As I said, I'd mentioned to Susan that the yearly detective's exam was soon coming up. I explained to her how badly I wanted to be a detective, but that I'd always had problems passing written exams. Come test time, I had trouble remembering what I'd recently studied. I'd draw a blank. Well, Susan offered to help me; she offered to be my tutor.

I'd gotten a study guide to help applicants prepare for the detective's written exam. The booklet contained 100 police-related questions, each followed by four multiple-choice answers. Located in the back section of the booklet was an answer sheet listing the correct answers to each of the 100 questions. Wow. Maybe, just maybe, if I studied diligently, if I studied hard, I might pass the detective's exam on the first try.

Wouldn't that be something? Me, "Detective Bernie Lau."

Susan and I started meeting several times a week, burning the midnight oil up in my narcotics undercover apartment on Beacon Hill. I'd study the booklet, read all the questions, and memorize the correct answers. She quizzed me, night after night, until the very morning of the detective's exam.

I was ready and I showed up bright and early. The written exam was held in the Seattle Municipal Building in one of the large conference rooms. Damn! There must have been at least 200 other police officers present, all wanting to take the exam, all wanting to become detectives. I was worried. What were my chances? Some of those officers had been in the department for 15 years or more. What chance did I have against those old-timers? You had to have been a cop in patrol for three years in order to qualify to take the detective's exam. I'd been a police officer for a little over three and a half years. I was still considered a "rookie cop."

I sat in my assigned seat, feeling a bit uneasy. We were each handed test booklets and instructed to write out our full names and serial numbers and to sign the first page. Having done that, we were then required to affix our right thumb prints next to our signature. No getting someone else to take the exam for you. The test was to be timed: one hour to read and answer 100 questions. That meant you had just a little over 30 seconds to read and correctly answer each question, then go on to the next question. Not much time.

Instructions were given: "Answer as many questions as you possibly can in the allotted time of one hour. There are 100 questions in your test booklet. Don't spend too much time on any one question. If you aren't certain about the answer to any given question, go on to the next question. Begin!"

I took a deep breath and opened my booklet to the first page. Well, I'll be damned, I thought. The test contained the same exact 100 questions that I'd been studying nightly with Susan's help! I quickly went down the list of questions in the test booklet, not taking more than five seconds or so on any single one. Some questions I didn't even have to read; I just glanced at the answers and picked out the correct one. I knew the 100 questions and answers by heart.

My many nights of studying, with Susan's help, had paid off, and I breathed a sigh of relief. Never before had I felt so confident when taking a written test. I finished checking the answers to all 100 questions within ten minutes. Quickly, I scanned through the test booklet to double-check. Satisfied, I closed it, got up, and walked to the front of the room. I turned in my booklet and exited the Municipal Building, the first one to complete the test.

It would be several weeks before the results of the detective's written exam would be published. I could hardly wait. Finally, on April 9, 1974, Seattle Police General Information Bulletin Notice 74-143 listed, in the order of the individual passing scores, the names of the top 50 scorers out of those who'd passed and would thus be placed on a waiting list for the next openings in various detective units.

I held my breath as I glanced down the column at the 50 names listed. Was my name on the list? There it was! "Position 10. Name—Lau, Bernard M. Serial No. 3354." I came out listed as number 10.

Next came the oral interview, which I also needed to pass. Passing the written portion didn't automatically guarantee that you'd be promoted to detective status. We were to be called in one-by-one to be interviewed by one of the department's lieutenants or captains. The interviewer would be able to ask any questions he wanted to.

I wanted to look sharp and professional. Being as I was presently working undercover as a "police vice agent," my hair was shoulder length. I went to a local barber and had my long hair trimmed just hours before my scheduled time to be interviewed. I put on a suit and carried a briefcase with me to the interview, a briefcase that contained absolutely nothing. It was just a prop to make me look more "professional." (I was hoping the interviewer wouldn't ask me what was inside!)

I entered the interview room, and standing at attention, greeted the interviewing lieutenant. He looked at me, smiled, and said: "How you doing, Bernie? I see you came out number ten on the written. Good job! Have a seat."

The interviewing lieutenant was Dean Olson, a down-to-earth police officer who I greatly respected and got along with very well.

"So, Bernie, I understand you're doing a great job working vice. How d'ya like it so far?"

"I like it a lot, Lieutenant. I really enjoy working the streets."

"I understand you got roughed up a bit at the Exotica a few weeks ago." We chatted for another ten minutes or so. Finally, the interview over with, I stood up to leave and Lt. Olson reached over and shook my hand.

"Good luck, Detective Lau. Looks like you'll soon be back working narcotics!" So I'd passed.

As a detective I'd now be running my own confidential informants. We had a steady stream of people who wanted to become informants for us. But I'd also run capers myself. This was somewhat unusual; detectives don't usually put themselves in harm's way and do actual buys.

Shortly before Susan started tutoring me in preparation for the detective's written exam, she'd had all her teeth pulled. We're talking the entire upper and lower rows of teeth; every one got pulled. Well, me being cursed with often feeling a need to seek out damsels in distress and come to their rescue, I offered to take Susan to the dentist and waited there for her until the complete extraction had been performed. That done, I drove her to the undercover apartment and took care of her for several days until her mouth healed.

A week later, Susan returned to the dental clinic and was fitted with a set of dentures. They seemed to fit well, and Susan looked good in them. Later that day, when I returned to the apartment, Susan was in the bedroom taking a nap, so I sat in the living room, watched TV, and drank a beer. After a while, I heard her get up and call me into the bedroom,

"Bernie, come here a minute." (She called me "Bernie" in private and "Johnny" on the street.) I walked in and saw both upper and lower dentures lying on the bed. Susan smiled a great big toothless smile and invited me to come closer.

"Bernie, I just got these new dentures put in. They seem to fit OK, but I don't know if they're going to stay in my mouth or come loose and fall out when I'm sucking some guy's dick! I need to practice before I go out and give some trick a blow job. Mind if I practice on you? How about I suck your dick, first without my dentures out, then with them in? I need for you to tell me which way you think feels best, and I also need to see if they'll stay in. I can't be out there sucking on some guy's dick and have my teeth fall out. Damn, that would be totally embarrassing!"

So here I was, a young rookie cop, standing in the bedroom of our undercover apartment in front of a now-toothless prostitute who was wanting to practice the fine art of giving head on me, with and without her new dentures. I looked at Susan, and again, she smiled that big, toothless smile. I looked down at the bed, at her new set of dentures. There was something hellish about her toothless grin and the set of dentures staring up at me from the bed. Thanks, but "Oh, hell, no!" In the nicest way that I could muster up at that moment I respectfully declined her offer.

28

Dance With the Devil

"Pretend"—that's an interesting concept. Pretend to be a drug addict. Pretend to be what you're not. In the beginning, at least. Go ahead, dance with the Devil, have a good time, have yourself some fun! But over time, you'll learn a sad but true lesson. Like they say; "You don't change the Devil; the Devil ends up changing you."

Pretend to smoke dope, pretend to use cocaine and methamphetamine. Pretend that you're a drug addict as you try to make those addicts that you hang around with believe that you, like they, are really a drug addict. Why else would you be buying drugs if you weren't a drug addict? Hang around drug addicts, but never do drugs? It's not possible. You'll get made for a cop in no time. So go ahead, Officer Bernie Lau; "just pretend" and be as convincing as you can be. If not, you could get your head blown off.

"Jeff" and "Doug" had been fellow recruits in Class 64 at the academy. We were into our 3rd or 4th week of training when suddenly they were both gone, just like that. Gone! Not one word of explanation was ever given to us. Their names were never mentioned. We thought maybe they'd washed out, except that both of them had been doing well, both in the classroom and in daily physical training. Later, I found out that they'd been pulled out of the academy to work as narcs. Jeff and Doug skipped academy training all together, the idea being that they could catch up on police procedures and all that later on, when they were reassigned to patrol, perhaps in a year or so.

A brand-new police recruit who'd never done a day's work as a police officer was a valuable asset in various undercover roles. Jeff and Doug had never arrested anyone, and they'd never testified in open court. Both were totally unknown to Seattle's criminal element. No one could make them as cops because they'd never been cops, and so they were valuable.

Jeff was tall, maybe six feet, muscular, and sprouting fiery red hair. That red hair made him look like anything but a police officer. How many red-headed cops have you ever seen? Doug, on the other hand, was short and skinny, and he didn't look anything like a cop either. Though in perfectly good health, Doug gave the impression of being sickly. He had an undernourished look and sunken eyes that would be good assets for working the streets.

It would be four years before I got wind of what had actually happened to Jeff and Doug. Though they were both assigned to undercover, their individual stories turned out totally different. Jeff was primarily tasked with investigating heroin activity in and around Seattle. Within the span of a few short weeks, he began making street-level heroin connections in the Broadway District up on Capitol Hill, where lots of street kids hung out. These young runaways, both male and female, were mostly strung out on heroin. Jeff's assignment was to try and infiltrate the heroin addicts and street-level dealers and work his way up to the bigger ones.

Arresting street-level heroin dealers, most of them just strung-out junkies trying to make it from fix to fix, served no valid purpose. It was a waste of time and money. Arrest a street junkie and so what? What good did that actually do in the fight against drug dealing and heroin trafficking? There were hundreds of strung-out addicts in the streets of Seattle. They were dope sick, they were desperate, and their only purpose in life was to somehow get their next fix so they wouldn't get any sicker than they already were.

Arrest the dealers, and you maybe make a little progress for a day or two, maybe even for a week, but that was it. You weren't going to curb the endless flow of heroin coming into Seattle no matter how many dealers you arrested. Still, Jeff had his assignment: try to get in with major heroin dealers. Eventually, he'd work his way up and hopefully be introduced to a mid-level dealer.

Jeff had "befriended" a small-time, street-level dealer-addict named Tony, who was willing to introduce Jeff to his man, "Stinky," a dealer who was said to sell quarter ounces of heroin. For a "finder's fee" of $50, Tony agreed to do the introduction. Late one evening Tony had Jeff drive him to a specific house located in upper Capitol Hill, an area that was known for drug activity. Jeff parked on Madison Street near 34th Avenue and followed Tony to a house located two blocks further up. You weren't supposed to park directly in front of a dope house because that would eventually bring unwanted heat from the police. Sometimes neighbors would report suspected narcotics activity if too many vehicles came and went.

Tony walked up the stairs to the dealer's house and knocked lightly. Several minutes passed, but no answer. Tony knocked once more, a bit harder this time. Almost immediately, a deep, unfriendly voice from inside the residence spoke out, "Yeah, who that? What the fuck you want?" Tony spoke, "Hey, Stinky, it's me, Tony!"

The front door opened just a crack and a face peered out.

"Tony; what the fuck you want, boy? I told you never to come by unless you call first. Didn't I tell you that?"

Tony answered, "Yeah, Stinky, I know. I tried calling, but your phone was busy."

"Tony, who the fuck's that white boy with you? What the fuck you bringing folks to my place for, anyway?"

"Aw, it's just some guy I know. He wants to score, and he got money. You see, Stinky, right now I ain't got nothing on me, so I thought maybe you might be able to help him out, just this one time?"

"Tony, get your damn junkie ass up in this here house right now. You too, white boy. C'mon, hurry it up before I change my mind!"

Tony and Jeff entered the house. Jeff hunched over, not saying a word, and took a seat on a worn-out couch in the living room.

"Stinky" was a very large black man, weighing well over 300 pounds, and true to his name, Stinky smelled rancid! Disgusting or sickening might be a better word. Some heroin addicts chose to not shower or bathe for weeks on end because they believed not bathing produces a more intense and lasting high. Supposedly the plugged-up skin pores kept the heroin in the system longer.

Tony followed Stinky into the kitchen. Minutes later, Stinky came out of the kitchen and walked up to Jeff.

"Boy, what you want? Why you here?"

Jeff looked up at Stinky and replied in a low, somewhat frightened voice; "I just need to score some stuff. Tony wasn't holding, so he thought you might be able to help me out."

"Boy, I don't know what the fuck story Tony told you, but I sure as hell don't know what the fuck you talking about! Truth be, I think you the God damn police; a fucking narc or something. You don't look like no damn junkie to me."

That said, Stinky brought out a large chrome-plated automatic that he'd kept hidden at his side. He slowly placed the barrel against Jeff's right temple. Jeff was scared shitless. He raised both hands and pleaded with Stinky not to shoot him.

"Look, man, I ain't no police, like you be thinking. Honest. I ain't no damn cop. I do shoot up from time to time. All I wanted was just a little pinch for myself. Tony didn't have any, so he brought me here, told me you might be able to help me out this one time, that's all! Honest!"

"Well, Tony wrong, telling you that kind of bullshit. Asshole don't know what the fuck he talking about. I oughta blow your fucking head off, just in case you are the police. One thing I know for sure, you ain't no fuckin' junkie. You too clean and proper to be on that shit! All big and muscular. Hell, you ain' no junkie!"

Jeff looked up at Stinky, "Sir, I can prove it. Let me prove it to you, please!"

"Now, just how the fuck you gonna do that, white boy? You tell me how!"

Jeff lowered his hands and slowly rolled up the shirt sleeve of his left arm. Then he extended the arm so that Stinky could have a better look.

"Well, I'll be damn. Peckerwood, here, he a fuckin' junkie. Look at them ugly tracks! God damn, boy, you sure had me fooled! But it don't make no never mind; somethin' 'bout you jus' ain' right. Maybe you do hit junk, like you say, but you ain' gettin' no dope from me cause I don' be involved with that shit. Hell, no! Tell you what, white boy; I ain' gonna shoot ya. Not today at least. Now get your white honky ass out of my house, like right now, and don't you ever be coming back. You understan' me? I ain' gonna tell you twice; so get the fuck out right now, 'fore I change my mind!"

Jeff got up and darted out the front door.

"Tony, you stay put! I ain' through with you yet, boy, not by a long shot. Why you bring this here white boy I don' know into my house without callin' first, and on top of that, tell him a bunch of bullshit—what the fuck wrong with you, boy? You one dumb motherfucker, ain' you?"

Jeff hurried down Madison Street back to his vehicle and sped off. It wasn't long before he was out of the CD and headed back downtown. That was a close call for Jeff. If it hadn't been for those "tracks" (needle mark scars from intravenous injections), he might very well have gotten his brains blown out.

So how was it that Jeff, a police recruit attending classes at the police academy, now had needle tracks on his arm? It turned out that Jeff's wife worked as a registered nurse at Harborview Hospital in Seattle. Every evening, when she returned home from work, she'd inject him with a sterile saline solution. Following a few weeks of nightly intravenous injections, Jeff's arm started to develop track marks and looked like he really was shooting heroin.

Some might say that he went to extreme lengths in his quest to appear to be a junkie. All I can say in Jeff's defense is that getting your brains blown out by someone like Stinky could also be looked at as "extreme."

It's very likely that Jeff had many more exciting, unusual, and interesting tales to tell, but I never got a chance to sit and chat with him. He either retired or quit the department a few years later. Word around the Narcotics office was that he'd moved to Canada and was eventually arrested for cultivating marijuana. I can't say for certain if that tidbit of gossip was true or not, but that was the story I heard. The short time I knew Jeff at the start of our police academy training, I thought he was a pretty decent guy. He had to be or he would never have made it through the intense screening process for becoming a police recruit. Jeff, wherever you might be, I wish you well!

"Doug," was the second police recruit pulled out of Seattle Police Academy Class 64. Doug was short, 5' 8" at the most, 140 lbs. He looked like your average Joe Q. Citizen. Not good-looking, not bad-looking; just plain-looking. Someone you wouldn't think of looking at twice on the street. The kind of guy who probably has a hard time finding a date. Definitely not the kind of guy you'd make for a cop. He was quiet, never had much to say about anything. But he was an OK guy as far as I was concerned.

Word was that Doug got in with a bunch of pharmaceuticals freaks—"pill-poppers." While working undercover and "pretending" to be one of them, for whatever reason Doug eventually started to use illegal prescription drugs and, over time, became addicted to pain pills and barbiturates—both highly addictive drugs. A normal person taking a prescription medication will take one or two pills or tablets every four to six hours. But just a couple of pills every four to six hours doesn't do the job for a pill freak. Those guys want to get whacked out of their minds. That's why they take the pills in the first place, and that's why they rip off pharmacies at gunpoint.

A bad side effect of taking pharmaceuticals for any length of time is that you get addicted. A few weeks on pain killers, mood elevators, amphetamines ... whatever type of controlled substance you're taking, you'll get addicted. It happens quickly and tolerance builds even quicker. Withdrawal is a bitch. Symptoms are paranoia, crying spells, deep depression, mood swings, and violent behavior. When the pills run out, and they always do, you'll do anything to get more. That's when the nice college kid or the friendly neighbor you thought you knew so well gives not a second thought to getting a gun and sticking up some pharmacy, or ends up shooting and killing someone for more drugs or money.

It happened years ago in north Seattle just off Lake City Way. Some desperate pill addict going through withdrawal stuck up the pharmacy. Something went wrong, and the kid shot and killed the pharmacist, just like that. One shot to the chest was all it took to end the guy's life and all for a bunch of pills.

So Doug was hanging around with these pill freaks and started taking pills, maybe because he didn't want to get made as a narc. Or maybe he just liked the way the pills made him feel, who knows? I can tell you from personal experience, pain pills do make you feel good. Anyway, Doug was taking more and more pills to try and reach that same high. He was addicted.

One afternoon, he came into the Narcotics office, higher than a kite. The sergeant took one look at him and said; "Hey, Doug, what's wrong with you? Come here and let me look at you. Doug, you're fucking high! You doin' drugs?"

"No, Sarge, I'm just tired. Stayed up late last night, drank too much, then I took too much NyQuil." On he went with the improbable explanations, but the sergeant wasn't buying. Shortly thereafter, Doug got retired on a medical disability.

Much later, there was a rumor that Doug had tried to kill himself. The way I heard it, he'd gotten hold of a shotgun and put the barrel either to his face or maybe in his mouth. But just before pulling the trigger, he either flinched or moved his head slightly. Doug didn't die, but he did manage to blow part of his face off.

After hearing about Ronnie's tracks and how they'd once saved his life, I decided to do the same thing myself. I planned to shoot up several times daily, with water, of course, until my own tracks started to develop. When first attempting to purchase heroin after going undercover, I'd often been told by the dealers to let them see my track marks. Heroin dealers (who are usually also addicts themselves) are extremely paranoid and much more cautious than other types of drug dealers. Addicts do not want to get busted! Being arrested would more often than not mean spending long hours or days locked up, and without his daily dose of heroin, the addict goes through the unspeakably long and painful nightmare of heroin withdrawal.

When I first started working undercover, I'd made maybe three or four futile attempts to purchase heroin. It was always the same; "Let's see your tracks!" In response, I'd just say, "Fuck you, asshole," then turn and walk away. I once tried arguing with a dealer, saying that I didn't want to show him my tracks. The dealer simply said, "Fuck you, you're a fucking cop!" and quickly ran off. It was no use; no tracks, no buying heroin! So when I heard of Ronnie and his tracks, I thought that might work for me too.

But I had no wife, let alone one that was a registered nurse, to assist me, so I'd have to learn to do it all by myself. First thing I needed were syringes. So one afternoon, I walked into Sally's Pharmacy in Mountlake Terrace, near where I lived, to purchase syringes. Being I was working undercover at the time, I looked seedy. OK, I looked like an asshole off the street; pretty bad.

I entered the pharmacy and walked up to the counter, which was located towards the rear of the store. Behind the counter was this gal in her mid-30s. Her official-looking name tag read "Sally," so detective that I was, I immediately concluded that she was the owner. I began my quest for syringes by saying, "Ma'am, I'd like to buy some syringes."

"Sally" looked down at me from behind her slightly raised counter. She didn't seem at all friendly.

"Syringes. How many ccs. and what gauge needle do you normally use?"

Damn, I wasn't ready for her "20 questions." What's a "cc?" Hell, I didn't know a "cc" from my own "pp." And that question about some sort of "gauge?" I didn't have the slightest idea what Sally was talking about.

For the next several minutes, I tried to bullshit my way into getting her to sell me those much-desired syringes. Hell, it wasn't like I was trying to buy morphine or something. Sally quickly got tired of my shenanigans and said, "Get out of my pharmacy right now, or I'm calling the police!"

Sheepishly I took out my badge and police ID and explained to her that I was in fact the police, an undercover detective at that, and I was just pretending to be a heroin addict. I told her that I needed to purchase syringes to carry on my person as a prop since at times I hung out with heroin dealers.

"Detective, what you'd most likely be looking for would be a 1 cc. syringe with a micro-gauge needle."

Wow. I learned something new every day. Sally sold me two packs of syringes, which came ten to a pack. Four bucks total. From that time on I could purchase all the syringes I wanted; it was no longer a problem.

Over time Sally and I became good friends. And no, I never boinked her.

With two packs of syringes in hand, I hurried home. Once there, I headed to the bathroom to begin what would become my daily ritual for months to come: sitting on the toilet and shooting myself up with tap water so that eventually my left arm would develop those track marks. The mark of the junkie!

Yeah, looking back, I must have been fucking nuts. What cop in his right mind would shoot up daily just to make those ugly-looking tracks on his arms? Well, that was me back then; I was as nuts as they came. I was willing to do whatever I had to do to be the best damn undercover narc in the history of the SPD, even if it meant shooting up with water several times a day and making tracks on my arm.

I didn't know the first thing about shooting up, so it was one of those trial-and-error-type learning experiences. Rather quickly, over a week's time, tracks did start to form on my upper left arm, but there was also swelling and bruising of various colors. Dark blue with a hint of green and yellow and lots of pain. My arm hurt like hell, but I was proud of my new tracks and willingly displayed them to those heroin dealers and junkies who asked to see. I was lucky that I didn't lose my arm to infection, or worse, die from some sort of staph bacteria. Tap water isn't sterile!

There were some black dealers who wanted to actually see me shoot up as I attempted to buy heroin from them. Black dealers do not trust white boys wanting to buy dope, tracks or no tracks! In such cases I'd very quickly get the hell out of wherever I was at, and in time, I learned to just stay the hell away from black heroin dealers. Way too dangerous. Not worth getting killed over some heroin buy gone bad!

Of course, I never mentioned or showed my tracks to any of the detectives I was working with or to any of the shift sergeants. They definitely would not have understood.

One afternoon, I'd gone to the CD and given a young addict $80 to go cop me a spoon (gram) of heroin. He took the money and told me to wait. That happened a lot when I was buying heroin; the dealer didn't want anybody coming over to his place, and I knew that the addict I gave my money to was going to take some off the top for himself. That's just how it worked.

So there I was, a white boy pretend-junkie, waiting for my fix. Well, me being the only white guy for miles around, I couldn't just stand there with my arms crossed waiting for the addict to return with my dope. I had to somehow look like I fit in. So I went into my pretend-addict mode. I hunched over a bit, making it look as if I was dope sick and cramping. I crossed my arms over my chest, held my head down, sort of shook as if I was freezing, all the while sucking in my breath every few seconds, like I had a bad case of the flu. I shifted around in small circles and in time, propped myself against a building. I pretended severe impatience and anxiety. I was acting like how a junkie needing his next fix would actually act.

About five minutes had passed, when two older, well-dressed black gentlemen happened to walk by. They looked over at me, paused several feet from where I was leaning, and I heard one say to the other, "Now, ain't that pathetic; a white boy junkie. That's a God damn shame!" They shook their heads in disgust and went on their way. Staying in my pretend-junkie mode, I smiled inwardly and said, "Yes!" for I'd just passed the test. Those two black gentlemen thought I was really a junkie, a heroin addict in need of a fix. What a great moment that was for me—to be good enough in my craft of "pretending" that I could, in the center of a totally black neighborhood, pass for a heroin junkie. I was so proud of myself!

I can't recall exactly how I got to drive up to "Lilah"'s house all by myself and be welcomed in. Lilah lived on Madison Street near 30th, as did a lot of heroin dealers back in the mid-70s and early 80s. Lilah was in fact a heroin addict. I must have met her somewhere weeks or maybe months earlier because it wasn't often that a white boy could just drive up to some black dealer's place all by himself and be welcomed in.

Lilah was the only female I ever purchased heroin from in Seattle. She was heavy-set, in her late 30s, soft-spoken, and trusting.

I knocked on Lilah's door and acted as if I needed a fix real bad, and she let me in. I was looking real messed-up, like I was "jonesing" (dope sick) real bad. I had snorted water up my nose before I drove to her house. Snorting water hurt like hell and shot sharp pains up to my brain. But the water going up my nose made my eyes and nose water, and also made my nose itch. Made me look like a junkie in need of a fix. I sat down on Lilah's ratty old couch, half-way crouched over with my arms folded tightly over my stomach, and rocked back and forth as if in pain. I mumbled, "Damn, I'm sick! I need something right now. How long's it gonna be?" Lilah looked at me and said, "Hold on there, boy. Won't be much longer."

Time slowly drifted by. About ten minutes later, there was a knock on the front door. Lilah got up to answer. I looked up to see who it was, and to my amazement (and fear), in walked Irving Paul, the head of the Public Defender's Office! The same office from which the District Court for the City of Seattle assigned counsel for defendants who couldn't afford their own lawyers. Irving Paul, all 6'3"of him, was standing just a few feet from me.

It had been a little over a year since I'd been in Seattle District Court, in uniform, as the arresting officer testifying in a case where Paul had been counsel for the defense. He had cross-examined me as I sat in the witness stand, testifying against his client. We'd often spoken to each other in the hallway of the courthouse and had gotten along with each other pretty well.

My mind started racing. I thought to myself, "Shit, my cover is about to get blown! Irving knows I'm a cop. I'm gonna get made!" All I could do was to continue pretending to be a sick junkie. I stayed hunched over and rocked back and forth. When working undercover, I often wore a leather cap, and this cap now partly shielded my face and helped disguise my identity.

Paul gave me a quick glance, then looked back at Lilah, and they continued their conversation. I'd already given Lilah $60 for the buy. She came over and asked if I had a car. I answered "yes," stating that it was parked out in front. Paul had bummed a ride to Lilah's house. Lilah, of course, didn't have a vehicle at all; few drug addicts do. She asked if she could borrow my car in order to go get the heroin.

Now if I said no, I wouldn't be getting any heroin. I really wanted this buy. It wasn't every day that you had the chief of the Public Defender's Office right there in front of you asking to borrow a Seattle police undercover vehicle to go purchase heroin. But the undercover car had a police radio tucked under the driver's seat. It wasn't turned on, but it was portable and could have slid out from under the seat during a quick stop.

I decided to take a chance and handed Lilah the keys. She and Mr. Paul left the house, saying they'd be back in 15 minutes.

Alone in the house, I immediately went to the bathroom and, using a pen, wrote my initials, my police serial number, and the date on the wall, behind the toilet. The writing wouldn't be visible unless you scooted down on your knees and looked behind the toilet. This was something I did whenever possible. That way, if in court the defendant claimed that I'd never been in his or her house, I'd just smile and advise them to go check behind their toilet where they'd find my initials, police ID number, and the date I was there. Worked every time. I surprised many a drug dealer with my method of leaving my mark in their bathroom—"the mark of the narc."

Back in the living room and sitting on that old couch, I started writing down notes on the layout of the house as well as other observations. "Cracks in the ceiling, running north to south; beat-up gray couch, chicken being baked in the oven," etc. I observed everything and jotted it down for my pending report. Judges and juries liked that stuff. Defense counsels and defendants didn't.

It was turning out to be a very interesting case, and I was looking forward to testifying in open court that Mr. Irving Paul himself went and got me heroin and used a seized undercover vehicle with a police radio tucked under the driver's seat. Fun!

A lengthy 40 minutes went by. Lilah and Mr. Paul finally returned. I held my breath, wondering if they'd somehow discovered the police radio hidden under the seat. I sat there on the couch, half hunched-over. Lilah came over and handed me a small balloon that she said contained heroin along with the keys to my vehicle.

I immediately asked to use the bathroom, and Lilah said OK. Getting up off the couch, I stumbled towards the bathroom. On purpose, I left the door partly open. I wanted Lilah to hear me in there. I turned on the faucet, sat on the toilet, took a spoon out of my jacket, and put a small amount of water in it. Then I struck several matches and held them under the spoon as if I was cooking up the heroin. The purpose of the heat was to dissolve the heroin and whatever it was cut with in the water. I, of course, didn't put any heroin in the spoon, just water.

Next, I placed a small piece of cotton into the spoon to act as a filter for when I drew the mixture up from the spoon into the syringe. That done, I rolled up my sleeve jacket and tied off my left upper arm so that a vein would pop up, thus making it easier to insert the needle into my vein. By tying oneself off, it also keeps the drug on hold till you release the tie. That way, the drug hits the body all at once, resulting in a hard-hitting rush—the rush that all addicts crave. I carefully inserted the needle into my vein and slowly pulled back on the plunger, drawing up a bit of blood into the syringe, making certain that the needle was in fact in a vein. If I missed a vein and pushed down on the plunger, I'd end up with a lump in my arm that would result in a black and blue bruise and the possibility of infection.

I slowly pushed down on the syringe's plunger, forcing the mixture of water and blood into my vein. Then I withdrew the needle, put the red cap back on, thus keeping myself from getting poked, and put the syringe back into my jacket pocket.

Next, I hunched over the sink and shoved the index finger of my left hand down my throat. I gagged and started making heaving sounds, like I was throwing up, I wanted Lilah and Paul to hear me "throwing up." Throwing up is a normal body reaction to the opiate being introduced into the body. There's a saying among heroin addicts: "Shoot up, throw up, nod out."

Then I cupped some water into my right hand, held it to my nose, and inhaled sharply. The water stung as it entered my nose and made my eyes water, so that I resembled a heroin addict that had just shot up. I left a few drops of tell-tale blood in the bathroom sink and a small piece of bathroom tissue with my blood on it, further proof that I'd shot up. This would help preserve my cover as a junkie.

I shuffled back into the living room, where I found Lilah on the couch, slumped over, nodding out, her syringe lying by her side. Irving Paul was nowhere to be seen. I suppose he'd left shortly after returning with Lilah and the heroin. In all honesty I wouldn't be able to testify that Mr. Paul had given me any heroin or that I'd witnessed him using heroin. As far as I was concerned, all Paul did was drive Lilah to pick up the heroin and drive back, nothing more.

I exited Lilah's house, got into my vehicle, and once again drove off into the darkness of the Seattle night. This was going to be one interesting report to write up!

Several months later, Lilah was arrested on one count of sale of a controlled substance to an undercover police officer (me). She pleaded guilty to the charge and received a sentence of six months in the county jail. I hope she eventually got herself off heroin and on the methadone program; she wasn't that bad a gal. The only mistake she made was letting some white boy into her house and selling him dope. "Never trust whitie!"

A year or so later, I bumped into Irving Paul in the hallway of the county courthouse. We stopped to chat and he asked, "Detective Lau, was that really you all crumpled up on the couch that day?" I smiled and proudly replied, "Yes, sir, Mr. Paul, it certainly was. Ha-ha! Fooled you, didn't I?" Paul looked at me, smiled, shook his head, and said, "Yeah, Detective, you sure had me fooled!" He then turned and slowly walked off to defend another one of his many court-appointed clients.

I'd heard that Paul, who looked like a tall Rip Van Winkle, had been a heroin addict for many years and was on methadone, a state-funded program designed to help heroin addicts to be able to function in society.

Several years ago, he passed on. It was sad, in a way, as I'd always liked the old guy. He was a pretty good attorney and got many of his clients found "Not Guilty." He was never an asshole in court. He was just another recovering addict trying to live one day at a time and help out other addicts who couldn't afford counsel. May he rest in peace!

29

Busted

"Hey, Bernie, you feel like getting arrested and locked up in the Pierce County Jail?"

"Aw, hell, Sergeant, why not? I ain't got nothing better to do today. May as well go to jail."

So my partner Al and I got "volunteered" to get busted and thrown into the Pierce County Jail, which was located near Tacoma, Washington, some 50 miles south of Seattle.

Word was that one of the jail booking sergeants was recommending attorneys to people as they were being booked. This jail sergeant would get a kickback for every defendant that hired an attorney that he recommended.

Sgt. Bert and another detective from our unit drove us out to Tacoma and suggested we get drunk before being arrested and booked. That would make us look more convincing.

We got dropped off at some low-life tavern on Tacoma's skid row. Sgt. Bert told us they'd come by in an hour or so, arrest both our asses, and throw us in jail. Yeah, OK, so we had an hour to get drunk before we went to jail; I guessed we could accomplish that.

We grabbed a table, bought ourselves a pitcher of Budweiser, and proceeded to get drunk. I sat back thinking, this job is fun; another adventure in the making! I'm about to be arrested, handcuffed, transported to the Pierce County Jail, and booked like some common, low-life criminal. I loved that job. Imagine the sergeant telling Al and me to get plastered on company time and money. But then again, drinking while undercover is usually allowed anyway. Hell, I could go to work every day, check in, and then go get myself a beer to start my day off right. Such a deal!

Since drug dealers and assholes hang out in taverns, drinking beer is a necessary part of undercover work. And slightly drunk, I didn't have to work so hard at trying to look or act like an asshole. After a couple of beers, an attitude kicked in automatically.

Al and I drank beer, shot some pool, sat, and bullshitted. A while later, we got up to shoot pool, when suddenly Sgt. Bert, the other detective, and two uniformed Pierce County police officers burst into the tavern. Before we knew it, Al and I were face down, getting handcuffed and read our rights. The two uniformed officers had no idea that Al and I were in fact Seattle police officers. To them, we were just two asshole drug dealers.

They drove us down to the Pierce County Jail, where we were booked and charged with "suspicion of trafficking in heroin." Bail was set at $10,000 for each of us. It wasn't "pretending" anymore; this arrest was for real!

None of the jail officers knew about our true police identities, and so we were treated like real criminals. We were fingerprinted, our mugshots were taken, and we were told to strip. Next came, "OK, guys, lift your nut sacks, turn around, bend over, and spread your butt cheeks," so that the booking officer could observe our assholes to make certain we weren't hiding any contraband or drugs up there. Bending over in front of some booking officer and spreading your ass cheeks isn't exactly fun. It's degrading, but it's a necessary part of the booking process. Lots of suspects do in fact try to smuggle contraband and illegal drugs into jail via their rectums.

Al and I were then each given a pair of red overalls and plastic slippers to put on. The booking process over and done with, we were placed in separate holding tanks (each holding tank can accommodate 15 or so individuals). I'd thought, or rather hoped, that we'd be housed together in the same holding tank. That way we could watch each other's back. But no, we were immediately separated. Not good!

The "Tank" was a concrete cell block with no windows and had one solid metal door for entry and exit. Once that door was slammed shut, no one could see or hear what was going on inside. Back in the mid-70s, jails didn't have surveillance cameras monitoring each cell block.

Suddenly, my situation was no longer fun. This was getting to be serious shit. I'd been a police officer for five years or so prior to this "arrest," and during that period of time, I'd arrested some 50 or so individuals. Some arrests were made while I was working uniform patrol, others while working narcotics. All I needed now was for some asshole that I'd arrested in the past to be in the same cell block and recognize me.

I wasn't scared at first, but I didn't feel quite at ease either. If I somehow got made as a cop, or worse, made as a narc, the 15 or so individuals in the Tank would proceed to kick my ass. They wouldn't hesitate a minute to mess up a cop, and the jailers on the other side of that metal door wouldn't be able to hear a damn thing. No, this pretend shit was no longer fun.

When I was placed in the Tank, there was only one bunk left, and that bunk was located right next to the single toilet. Last man into the Tank always gets the bunk next to the shitter. I lay on my bare mattress, not saying a word to anyone. Some of the guys were playing cards, others were just sitting around smoking and talking.

It was now around 5:30 P.M. Sgt. Bert was supposed to have posted my bail and gotten us out by now. He'd said it would just take a "couple of hours," and they'd have us out. Being that this Pierce County arrest was for real, he couldn't just walk into the jail and have me released. This arrest and booking were the real thing. For all practical purposes, I, "John Abel Medeiros" was, in the eyes of the law, an actual criminal arrested on heroin charges. A cash bail would have to be posted in order get me released.

Come around 6:00 P.M., "dinner" was brought into the Tank. Each of us were given two slices of white bread, one slice of bologna, and a small carton of milk. That was it.

Dinner sucked; my bunk next to the shitter sucked. Each time one of my fellow inmates had to take a pee or "whatever," that individual would be doing his business just two feet away from me. It was nasty. Welcome to the harsh reality of the real world, "Johnny Medeiros!"

At 8:00 P.M. all lights in the Tank, except for several dim ones, went out. I couldn't sleep, nor did I dare. It was too dangerous. Everyone in the Tank was either talking or cussing. Names were being tossed around, guys asking each other if they knew "so-and-so," etc.

Suddenly, I heard the name "Ronnie Hanson." Someone was asking if anyone had ever had bought dope from Ronnie Hanson. Yeah, lots of these guys had bought drugs from Ronnie, and yeah, they all knew him. I too knew Ronnie Hanson because I'd personally arrested him on drug charges less than a year before in the parking lot of Dick's Drive-in up on 45th in the University District. If Ronnie Hanson were presently in the Tank, or if he were booked while I was still there, I'd be in serious trouble.

Ronnie was the one that got away. After I arrested him, he said that he had to pee real bad, so I uncuffed him and allowed him to use the restroom in a nearby restaurant as I stood guard outside the bathroom door. Big mistake! While I was standing guard, he somehow managed to escape by climbing up through the ceiling panels, making his way up onto the roof, and shimmying down the side of the building. I really don't know how he managed that without breaking a leg, but somehow he did.

I knew Ronnie Hanson all right, and I was still looking for him. But I was praying that I didn't finally locate him right here in the Tank with me.

"Hi, Ronnie, remember me? Detective Bernie Lau. I arrested you several months ago, and you escaped from my custody. By the way, I'm arresting you again, but you'll have to wait till I get bailed out before I can formally arrest you."

Yeah, that would be funny, but not.

Some ten hours later, I finally did get bailed out. I guess it took Sgt. Bert a bit longer than expected to get hold of the $10,000 required for my bail. I'm glad it was only $10,000 cash. Next time, Sergeant, book me for "urinating in public" or some lesser charge, so my bail won't be so high.

All of the formal paperwork—arrest record, fingerprints and mugshots—pertaining to my undercover Pierce County arrest in the name of "Johnny Abel Medeiros" was supposed to have been squashed immediately and not forwarded to the FBI lab for fingerprint identification, formal recording, and entry into the NCIC (Nation Crime Information Center) database. Remember that, in the eyes of the law, this had been an actual arrest at the time of my booking, and all arrest records are automatically forwarded to the FBI for filing.

Several years later, I was on the 4th Floor of the Public Safety Building flirting with Rosie, one of the many cute gals working in the Records Section. I was looking pretty disgusting even for an undercover cop. (I'd worked hard at it.) Rosie looked at me and said, "Bernie, I can't believe you can look this bad and not have some sort of a police record!" So for fun, she entered my name and date of birth into the NCIC database, and guess what: she got a hit! The FBI files came up showing "Bernard Lau," arrested on such and such a date in Pierce County, Washington, for "Sales of Heroin." Record showing "Arrest with no conviction."

The Pierce County Police Department had never been informed that at the time of my arrest and booking, I was in fact a Seattle police officer working undercover. They had forwarded my arrest record, fingerprints, and mug shots to the FBI Lab in Virginia for processing. Surprise, surprise! It seemed that no one in our Narcotics Section had bothered to stop the paperwork from going through after I got bailed out, like they said they would. My real name and arrest information were now in the NCIC database. And though I was booked under my alias of "Johnny Medeiros," my fingerprints, when checked in the FBI Lab, came back belonging to "Bernard Lau." Detective Bernard Lau now had a police record, and for a felony arrest at that. Not good!

It took the Seattle Police Department over six months to finally get my name, arrest information, and mug shot removed from both the NCIC database and the FBI files. You just can't call up the FBI and say, "Hey guys; Bernie wasn't really a heroin dealer. The arrest was only a 'pretend' arrest!" No way!

By the way, that Pierce County jail booking sergeant who was recommending attorneys' names to the bad guys—he got busted, but was allowed to resign. I never did find Ronnie Hanson, and to this day, I can't watch any movies with jail scenes. Though I spent only ten hours locked up in that tank, the memories still haunt me.

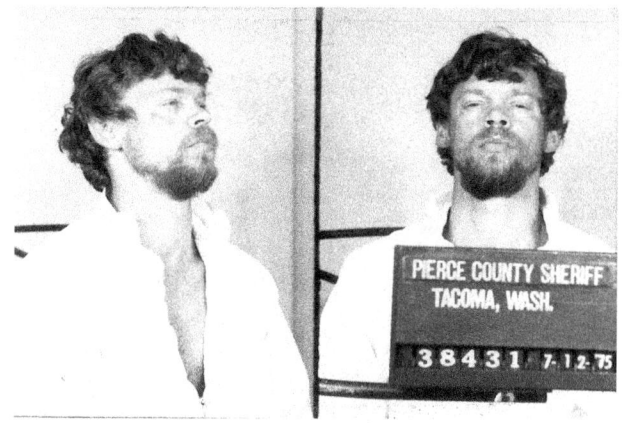

Busted in Tacoma

30

Johnny Medeiros

"Arnold De Breuil" had been arrested on drug possession charges and quickly decided to cooperate with SPD narcotics detectives rather than face jail time. De Breuil said that he knew this UW Chem student who was interested in producing large batches of methamphetamine. De Breuil was willing to introduce an undercover agent to this guy in exchange for having his own charges dropped. The undercover was, of course, to be me.

I was excited, as no one in the SPD had yet been able to infiltrate an actual meth lab. If I could manage this, it would be quite a feather in my cap. I'd certainly receive several commendations from the Chief and other top brass in the department. I was ready and willing to start.

Late one afternoon, Detective Paul introduced me to the snitch, De Breuil. I disliked him immediately, which, for me, was rather unusual, as I normally got along with just about anyone. But this De Breuil guy looked like a rodent. He was skinny, had beady eyes, stood sort of hunched-over, and had himself an attitude. He'd been busted while living on a houseboat in Lake Washington, where he'd gotten caught with an ounce of cocaine, and now all of a sudden, he was acting like he was all-important. And he was ready to rat out some UW student, who he claimed, was "interested in," maybe, manufacturing methamphetamine.

Like I said, I couldn't stand the guy or his attitude, but each time I heard him say the words, "possible meth lab," well, I decided to put up with his bullshit and see where it might go. I really wanted to take down a meth lab, and I wanted to be inside the meth lab when the "cook" (chemist) was manufacturing the meth and the bust went down.

Meanwhile, I'd rented myself a small 2nd-story furnished studio apartment in the Fremont District, located at 3517 ½ Fremont N. Having an undercover apartment, I could invite drug dealers over to "my place," share a few beers, and set up drug buys while the TV was on in the background with no one watching. (Typical for addicts and assholes.) The apartment was great for my cover. I had an old black-and-white TV, a fridge stocked with cold Budweiser and red wine, a cupboard with canned tuna, a loaf of white bread, peanut butter, various kinds of chips, and lots of Nestle's Crunch.[1] What else could a guy want? The apartment was costing me (well, OK, costing the city) $85 per month—a great deal.

Several days following my meeting with De Breuil, it was decided that he'd bring this UW student up to my apartment for an introduction. So the day came. It was late afternoon by the time De Breuil showed up with your average-looking college student. The guy's name was Seth. We were introduced, but didn't shake hands (assholes and druggies don't normally shake hands),

---

[1] Drug addicts, especially heroin addicts, crave sugar.

and I got Seth and myself a Bud. (I didn't offer one to De Breuil. Fuck him.)

We started to shoot the shit, talking about totally unimportant and useless stuff. I started on my second beer, giving Seth another one too. Finally, the conversation started to turn to drugs. Funny what a few beers will do.

Seth went on to explain that "Me and my two buddies want to make a million dollars, and then we're going to retire." I was thinking, "Don't we all!" By the third beer, Seth had informed me that one of his buddies, a Chemistry student, had recently gotten hold of a formula for cooking up meth. Chemistry guy said it was an easy formula to follow, and that the entire process would only take five hours or so. All they needed was the glassware to cook it up with and some liquid P2P.

I listened, but didn't believe what I was hearing. These guys wanted to make a million bucks, and all they had was this piece of paper with some kind of formula written on it. All they had was a damn piece of paper. That was all.

I'd had three beers, and now my creative thinking had been activated. (I think better after I've had a few cold ones. Or at least, I think I do.) I kept flashing those two words in my head, "meth lab." Then I pictured myself on the front page of the Seattle Times, standing tall next to the chief of police, displaying several pounds of pure methamphetamine to the news media and viewing public. "Detective Bernie Lau of the Seattle Police Drug Task Force, following months of dangerous undercover work, successfully, single-handedly infiltrated a hazardous methamphetamine lab," etc., etc. We'd also have to display some money and firearms (obtained from the police Property Room) along with the dope. You never see a drug bust on TV that doesn't show lots of drug money and some guns along with the dope. Gotta make it look good for the chief.

I focused back to the present. "OK, Seth, bottom line; what you need from me?"

He answered, "Well, just about everything. All the glassware, beakers, glass tubes, Bunsen burners, filters, and high-wattage lamps for drying the stuff, once you got it in crystal form."

"Seth, you didn't mention P2P!"

"Yeah, we need that too. Can you get some P2P?"

"Seth, I can get anything you want. Want some guns with silencers, some automatics . . . ?"

"Aah, no. We don't mess with guns. All we want to do is make this batch and retire." (There he went again; his buddy had a piece of paper with a bunch of writing on it, and Seth was talking about retiring!)

I said to Seth; "OK, guy, come back in a week. And meanwhile, I'll start gathering up what you need. You got a van or something?"

"Yeah, my buddy's got a van."

"Good. I'll have De Breuil here let you know as soon as I have the stuff."

Seth got up and walked out the door. De Breuil got up and started to say something. I looked up at him and waved him off. Bye. Nothing to talk about.

Finally. Alone once more in my apartment. Felt good. I got up, walked over, and turned the damn TV off. Can't stand it when folks leave the TV blaring in the background with nobody watching.

P2P is actually an industrial cleaning solvent, and at the time it sold for around $20 a gallon. Bikers used to buy P2P by the 50-gallon drum until the feds caught on and added it to their list of "controlled products." The average citizen could no longer purchase it, and if you did somehow manage to locate a supply, just an ounce of it could cost you $1,000. But there was absolutely no better product for the manufacturing of Methamphetamine than P2P.

So anyway, Seth and his two nameless buddies, who I thought of as "Larry & Moe," were willing and ready to get started with their meth lab caper. All they needed was for the Seattle Police Department's Narcotics Section, in the person of "Johnny Medeiros," to provide them with everything they needed to actually begin production. And undercover police officer Johnny Medeiros was willing do whatever he possibly could to grant them their wish.

Seth had mentioned to Johnny that he had a secret location where this meth could be "cooked." No one around for miles, so no one to smell the tell-tale odors of meth lab chemicals. That meant that now we had the following setup: Seth would provide the secret location. Moe, the Chem major, had the all-important secret formula, written on a piece of paper. And Larry ... well, I had absolutely no idea what Larry had to contribute, but he too wanted to be a millionaire.

The law says that when two or more individuals plan to commit a crime, it's called a "conspiracy," and that's a crime in itself. So we of the Seattle Police Narcotics Section found ourselves dealing with a conspiracy to illegally manufacture the drug known as methamphetamine. Worked for me.

Now, we just had to figure out what the SPD could do to assist the conspirators in hatching their plot. First, we needed to provide them with the necessary chemicals and glassware because without our help in that regard, they would never have been able to commit the crime of illegal methamphetamine production.

I'd informed Seth that through my biker connections I'd be able to provide the P2P and the required glassware, but no way was I going to just hand over a gallon of P2P. I was willing to "front" (give up something in hope of getting something back in return) him a couple of ounces of P2P, but in return, I wanted an ounce of the finished product: pure, 99.9% unadulterated methamphetamine. That was the deal. Otherwise, no deal.

Seth needed to talk that over with his partners. Now Seth was beginning to refer to his friends as his "partners." Yes, we did indeed have a conspiracy in the making. "Partners" was noted in my follow-up report: "Suspect Seth now refers to his friends as 'partners,' partners who are actively conspiring to commit a crime, by definition a 'conspiracy.'"

I wondered if those dummies realized that a million bucks divided three ways comes to only $333,000, and that wasn't enough money to retire on for the rest of your life. Not unless they planned on retiring somewhere in the Third World.

Next afternoon, I checked into the Narc office and found Detective Jerry sitting at his desk.

"Hey, Jerry, I met that kid De Breuil was talking about. You know, the guy who wants to be a millionaire by cooking up a load of meth. He and two of his buddies 'have a dream.' Only problem is, all they got right now is a piece of paper with a meth formula written on it. They ain't got no P2P, they ain't got the necessary glassware. They do, however, have a secret location where they can cook up this shit, where no one will smell the chemicals. What do you think, Jerry? Should we help them make their dream come true?"

Jerry chuckled, "Sure, Bernie, why not? A meth lab would be a hell of a bust. I'll call my warehouse guy and pick up a gallon of P2P tomorrow. All he usually wants in return is a bottle of good booze. I think a gallon of P2P runs about 20 bucks, but of course, no one can buy that stuff without the proper paperwork. DEA controls all P2P distribution now."

"Jerry, Seth said they'd also be needing beakers, glass tubes, and so on. Think we can come up with that?"

"Like I said, Bernie, my guy who runs the warehouse handles just about anything you can think of. You name it, he either got it on hand or he can get it. Tell you what; have Seth give you a shopping list of exactly what glassware they'll be needing, and I'll give the list to my guy. It may take a few days to fill the order, but I'm sure my guy can get the stuff. Bernie, are these guys really that dumb?"

"Looks that way, Jerry."

"Oh yeah, one more thing. I just got a call a few minutes ago from some gal that wants to be an informant; name's Christina or something like that. Wanna be here when I interview her?"

"Hell, yeah, Jerry, you know me. I'm always ready to have some gal informant working under the covers with me! Ha-ha!"

"Bernie, you're a dog; you know that?"

"Well, Jerry, I'm good looking, charming, and single. What can I say?"

"I'm not so sure about the 'good-looking' part, Bernie. You're getting to look like those druggies you hang out with. Seems like every week you look worse and worse."

"Jerry, you know I gotta be convincing. That's the only way I can get in with those assholes and buy dope. I gotta look, smell, and talk like 'em."

"What do you do when they offer you drugs, Bernie?"

"Hey, you know me! Remember during that 'Joint Rolling 101' session you and Sgt. Bert had us go through, and you showed us how to simulate taking drugs? You had us practice for over an hour. Remember how convincing I got to be?"

"Yeah, OK, Bernie. Just watch yourself. I'd hate to see you get fucked up and using drugs. That street lifestyle can creep up on you, and, before you know it, you cross the line, and you got problems."

"Hey, Jerry, I'm the last person you need to worry about. When it comes to pretending to take drugs, I'm a simulating specialist. I can fool the best of 'em. Oh yeah, Jerry, another thing. Next time you see your pet rodent, De Breuil, tell that motherfucker to tell Seth to make up the list of what they need as far as the glassware goes. I want to have the list next time I meet with Seth. Let's get this thing moving!"

"Yeah, OK. I'll have him give Seth the message."

So it looked like the caper was on its way. I'd get me a meth lab to take down after all.

Next morning Jerry and I met over breakfast. He'd already made a call to his P2P man. We could pick up the gallon as soon as Jerry picked up the bottle of booze for the trade. We finished breakfast, then walked to the roof of the police garage, where a half-dozen undercover vehicles were parked. The vehicles had been seized during various drug arrests. Deliver drugs to an undercover in a vehicle and it becomes ours when the bust goes down. What a deal!

Jerry picked out a metallic gold Porsche. Nice ride. Some dummy sold dope out of it a while back, so it became ours. Sorry about that, dummy!

Jerry stopped at the liquor store located next to the Smith Tower, near 2nd and Madison. Booze purchased, Jerry continued a mile or so down Airport Way and pulled up at a warehouse. I stayed in the car while Jerry went in. This way, I don't know Jerry's guy, the guy doesn't know me. Best to keep it that way. Ten minutes later, Jerry returned with a gallon of P2P, got in the Porsche, and away we drove.

"Well, here it is, Bernie; a gallon of P2P."

Looked like any other gallon of liquid to me. But it wasn't any other gallon; it was a gallon of fucking P2P, worth thousands of dollars on the streets.

Now that we had the most important item necessary for making meth, the P2P, I was getting excited. The caper was starting to come together. All we needed was the glassware for cooking up this P2P and turning it into fucking pure methamphetamine.

Saturday morning: delivery day and time to get the show on the road. I loaded up the undercover van with the glassware and two ounces of P2P liquid that I poured into an empty jar. I kept the rest of the gallon in the Narc office under lock and key. I loaded a half-dozen firearms into the van for visual affect. Most bikers deal in firearms and always have guns on their person or available nearby, so it made my cover more convincing. I'd enjoy scaring the fuck out of this dummy wannabe millionaire. I loaded up a few sawed-off shotguns, several rifles, and some hand guns, all of which had to be signed out from the police Property Room. All that was required was a list of what was checked out and our signature. Simple as that.

The plan was for Seth to meet me in the parking lot of the Museum of Natural History around 11:00 A.M. Another undercover from our unit would be somewhere in the distance, taking photographs of the delivery. Photographic evidence is seldom challenged in court.

I drove off, my mind going a gazillion miles an hour. I was excited beyond words; I was getting me a meth lab! As I drove, I felt the rush coming on. Live on the razor's edge and then jump off! That's how I liked living life. "Show time!" I said to myself, as I drove into the parking area of the museum. "Let's do this!"

I spotted Seth in a dark van at the far end of the lot and drove up. I saw that he had another white male with him. I started in, "What the fuck's this shit; who the fuck said you could bring someone? Who the fuck is this guy?" Seth introduced the other guy. "This is Larry, one of my partners." (There he went again, using the word "partners.") I glanced at Larry, but didn't say anything. I acted pissed. I said to Seth, "Hey, asshole, don't you ever bring someone around without first asking me, you understand?" Seth wimped out some lame response. Larry just looked at me. I could already tell that Larry had an attitude; his body language spoke for him. I was thinking, "OK, asshole, act tough now! We'll see how tough you are when this shit goes down and they slap the cuffs on you and throw your ass in jail. Go ahead and act tough now while you still got your freedom!"

I opened up the side doors of the van and showed them the several large boxes of glassware.

"Hurry up and unload the shit, and be fucking careful. You break anything, and I'll kick both your asses."

As Seth and Larry unloaded the boxes, they spotted the guns. I smiled to myself as I saw the blood drain from their faces. They looked at each other and then back at me, but no words came out of their mouths.

"What the fuck's your problem? Never seen guns before? Hey, you guys wanna buy any guns? Give me a fair price and we'll talk."

All Seth and Larry can do is shake their heads and hunch their shoulders (not so tough now, are you?). Boxes unloaded, I said "OK, now for the P2P." I reached into the glove box and carefully took out the jar of P2P. Their eyes lit up. I had their attention now; I could see their minds reeling with thoughts of making that meth and a million bucks. I handed over the jar. Seth now had that all-important ingredient, the precious P2P.

I looked at Seth and said, "Remember, I want an ounce of pure meth in exchange for these two ounces of P2P. Do not fuck this up!"

For the next few days, detectives in our unit were busy setting up surveillance around Seth's place of residence. An undercover camper was parked a half block away. Detectives ran eight-hour shifts out of the camper, watching who came and went. Surveillance isn't fun, but it's necessary if you want to catch crooks and in this case find out where their lab was located.

Thursday, around noon, rat De Breuil strolled into the Narcotics office and informed Detective Jerry that Seth had just called him and wanted a meeting with "Johnny" at a tavern up on Nickerson, just south of the Fremont Bridge. I made a note that the tavern was just two blocks west of Seth's house. Dumb kid, setting up a meeting right in his own back yard. The meeting was set up for the following day at 7:00 P.M.

Next day I showed up at the tavern. I heard someone call out "Johnny; up here." I looked up with a pissed-off expression on my face, went up the stairs, and took a seat at their table. This time there were three white males, including Larry and Seth. Damn it! (Actually it was good because now I'd get to find out who the chemist guy was.)

I started in on Seth about bringing someone else, but then decided, fuck it, I need a beer. I ordered two Buds for myself, but the waitress said she could only serve me one beer at a time. I looked at her for a moment, then I said, "OK, bring me a fucking pitcher with two glasses." She gave me a dirty look, turned, and stomped off. Soon she returned with a pitcher of beer, but only one glass.

I chugged down a quick glass, filled my glass again, and chugged down a second. I was supposed to be a biker, and bikers drink a lot, so I had to act the part. That meant I couldn't ask the waitress for a receipt. What's a biker need a receipt for?

But a narc needs a receipt. We're supposed to report our expenses. If I didn't get a receipt, I couldn't get reimbursed by the city. My usual solution was to get one of my snitches to sign a few blank receipts and at the end of the month, I'd just fill in the amount that I was short. It was a bitch keeping track of money when working undercover. You got federal funds in one pocket, city funds in another, and your own money in your wallet ... or is that my own money in my jacket?

Example: I pay to shoot pool. I take a ten-dollar bill out of my city pocket. I get change. I'm not thinking, so I put that change in my wallet or the left side pocket, which is for federal. I'm drinking beer, I'm shooting pool, I'm trying to be an asshole, I'm looking to buy drugs ... I can't keep track of what goes where!

I started my third glass of beer, then decided to get down to business. "OK, Seth, got what you owe me?"

"No, not yet."

In a calm voice, I leaned over to him and asked, "What's the problem? You got my jar, so now where's the fucking powder?"

"Well, we were talking, and you know, we don't really know you, we just met, and we wanna be careful ..."

"Seth, you and your little boyfriends here have only two choices: one, you give me back my P2P right now, or two, I give you till this Sunday to deliver as promised. Anything else isn't an option. I got people waiting for this stuff. People you don't wanna piss off. Remember: you came to me. I didn't come to you. I took care of my end of the deal. Now, it's your call. And let's not forget all that glassware. You think I can just return that shit and say 'Well, guys, those boys got cold feet all of a sudden, and now they just wanna return all this stuff?' Seth, that's not how the real world works. I'm being real calm right now because you guys are just a bunch of dummies who wanna make a million dollars. Don't make me show you my other side. I'm a Gemini, and I got two extreme personalities. Believe me, you don't wanna meet my other side. Now, tell me what it's gonna be." I opened my vest a little so Seth could see my automatic. Upon seeing the gun, Seth and his two buddies' faces went pale and their eyes got big. They were scared shitless. I knocked back another glass of Bud, sat back, and enjoyed the moment. Finally, Seth spoke.

"Johnny Medeiros"

"Johnny, you're a Gemini?"

"Yep. June 8, 1941." I took out my driver's license and showed him.

He went from scared to astonished. He reached into his back pocket, took out his driver's license, and handed it to me. Seth Donaldson, date of birth, June 8, 1951. Ten years apart to the day. What a coincidence! I nodded my head in amusement. I looked at Seth and said, "Now I know where you live, you dummy." I tossed the license back to him.

His pals both had a sick look. Poor Seth looked ill too.

"Don't worry, bro'," I told him. "Just be here at the tavern next Sunday at 3:00 P.M. without fail. Do that, and you and your friends have absolutely nothing to worry about."

Sunday at 1:00 P.M. a trio of detectives went to the tavern to shoot pool and drink beer. (Two hours before delivery is standard surveillance.) They all had wives or girlfriends with them as part of their surveillance team. At 2:50 P.M. I walked in and took a seat upstairs, where we'd sat on Friday. I ordered a pitcher of Bud along with a basket of fries, sat back, and relaxed.

At 3:21 P.M. Seth walked in by himself. He looked up, saw me, came up the stairs, and took a seat at my table. He started making excuses for being late, and I cut him off.

"Do you have it or not?"

"Yes, but it's in my truck, parked around the corner."

I exhaled loudly. "Damn you, Seth, what the fuck's wrong with you? It's not that big a deal."

Seth blabbered, "I've never done this kind of thing before ... I'm new at this ..."

Again, I cut him off. "Seth, you and me are gonna walk over to your truck, and you're gonna hand me what you owe me, or I'm gonna kick your damn ass right here in front of whoever wants to watch."

So we started to leave the tavern, and I told the bar girl I'd be right back and to leave my beer alone. We went to his camper and he unlocked the door. We climbed in and I shut the door as Seth reached under the carpet and brought out a baggie of white powder. I opened the baggie and asked him if the weight was on (an ounce of meth should weigh 28 grams). I warned him the weight better be on or else! He assured me that it was. I took a pinch of meth from the baggie, held it under my nose, and inhaled sharply. Yeah, it fucking burned.

"OK, Seth, you did good. Give me a call next week, when you're ready to do the final batch, so we can wrap this thing up." I handed him the number to our undercover phone at the Narc office.

"Yeah, OK, Johnny. I'll let you know." Back to the tavern to finish my beer.

The surveillance team had already left. I smiled to myself. I'd just got me an ounce of pure methamphetamine, I'd got Seth on a delivery charge, and I now owned his van. All done in one day. What a dumb fuck! Now, I could relax a little.

Pretending to be an asshole isn't really all that easy, at least not for me. Most of the time I had to work at it. Undercover is fun, though. It's a game. The only thing is, you can never forget and fuck up at the wrong time in the company of the wrong folks. You do, and you'll probably never see who hits you.

Language, facial expressions, tone of voice, the way you smell, what you wear ... especially what you wear. Even the condition of your shoes and your socks could be important. Are they the type of socks a biker would be wearing and are they in the condition that a biker's socks would be in? Do your socks stink, really stink? Or do they have that downy, fresh-washed smell?

What kinds of stuff do you carry on your person? Do you have a piece of paper in your pocket with a City of Seattle letterhead on it? Sometimes the bad guys make you empty your pockets, or they go through your wallet. Do you have a business card in your wallet that reads, "Bernie Lau, Seattle police officer?" If you do, and the bad guys find it, it's bye-bye. What you say and how you say it—you've got to be constantly aware of everything around you while appearing to be relaxed. Some game, huh?

I left the tavern, got in my GTO, and drove back to the office. I was happy. The Meth Lab Caper had begun. Alone in the Narcotics office, I put a small amount of meth into a field tester, pinched the packet, thus breaking a small glass vile in the packet, and ... zap! Instant amber. The shit was real!

I phoned radio and got a case number for filing the evidence. For the name of the suspect on the form I entered "John Doe." I put the ounce of meth into the evidence envelope, sealed the envelope with red evidence tape, initialed all the seals, and filled out a lab request. Only thing left to do was take the envelope over to the Property Room for filing. I could write up my report tomorrow. In a week or so, I'd receive a form from the State Patrol lab in Olympia indicating if the powder was in fact methamphetamine. Also listed, would be the exact weight and purity of the suspected meth.

After placing the evidence into the Property Room, I walked back up James Street to my GTO. I passed a Seattle cop in uniform walking down towards the police station and as we passed each other, he gave me that "cop look." You know, the one that says "I don't know you, but I know you're a fucking asshole. I don't like your type, and I'd sure like to bust you!"

Feeling this officer's vibes, seeing the way he looked at me, his body language—I got pissed. Without thinking, I instantly reverted to Johnny Medeiros, anti-social biker asshole. My demeanor, my attitude, my entire thinking process did a 180 on me. Now I was no longer playing Johnny Medeiros; I was Johnny Medeiros.

Cops in uniform were starting to bug me. I was beginning to think that most of them were power-tripping assholes. They always looked at me like I was a piece of shit, like I was some sort of low-life, asshole scum. As I continued down James, I was thinking to myself, "Fuck you, asshole, you think you're hot shit just because you got on a uniform, carry a gun, and wear a badge? Well, you ain't shit motherfucker. You have absolutely no idea who I really am and what I'm capable of doing to you. Yeah, you're a cop in uniform, but you know what, 'Officer Fuckhead?' You ain't shit, so fuck off. I could be anybody, and you're passing judgment on me just because you don't like the way I look. Fuck you!"

My personality was changing. It was getting easier and easier for me to get into "Johnny Medeiros" mode.

Det. Bernie Lau loses his personal identity to "Johnny Medeiros" (1976)

31

Bird Dog

"What's a 'bird dog?'" I asked.

"A bird dog," answered Detective Jerry, "is a vehicle tracking device. Actually it's a transmitter that sends out a signal on the location of the vehicle it's attached to by way of a powerful magnet. The main unit's shaped like a tube and looks like one of those emergency flares at accident scenes. You just slip it under the vehicle, say in a wheel well or some place where you got metal, and bam! The magnet clamps down, holding the transmitter unit. The 'bird dog' will send out a signal for months. With a small portable monitor in your own vehicle, you can then track the vehicle's movement while you stay several blocks behind it. The nice thing is that you don't have to maintain visual contact. Bernie, I also got a hold of my contact at the phone company. He told me that as soon as I get a warrant signed by the judge, he'll be able to set up a pen reg in our office."

Jerry continued to explain. "The pen register is a telephone unit that prints out the phone numbers of all incoming and outgoing calls from the residence of interest. Once the numbers are printed, we use the reverse directory to look them up. The reverse directory should list the name and address that goes with the phone number in question. If the phone number comes back unlisted, then my guy at the phone company will look it up for us. Remember, I told you that here in narcotics we can get just about anything we need. You just got to know who to go to."

The following day Detective Jerry obtained the tracking unit from his source at the DEA, and with the required signed authorization in hand from the judge, the pen reg was set to be installed the following Monday.

"You know what, Bernie? I think we'll put the bird dog on Seth's GTO to start with. I don't think he'll be driving that van all over the place. Tell you what; take tomorrow (Friday) off, and early Sunday morning, say around 3:00 A.M., meet me here at the office, and we'll go over and put the bird on his GTO."

Early Sunday morning Jerry and I drove out to Seth's neighborhood, where we spotted his red GTO parked in front of his house. I stayed in the Porsche as Jerry positioned the bird dog inside the left front wheel well. There was a muffled thump as the powerful magnet attached itself to the metal.

Monday morning I walked into the Narcotics office and Jerry told me that the guy from the phone company would be in around 10:30 to install the pen reg. The guy arrived, but no introductions were made. He was there to install a pen reg, not to shoot the shit. Better not to know who he was.

20 minutes later, the phone guy announced that the pen reg was installed. He ran Detective Jerry and me through the basic workings of the monitor, which was a rather simple operation. It printed out incoming and outgoing calls. If the phone was busy, the red light came on. When the line was not in use, the green light came on. After his explanation, the phone guy shook

hands with Jerry and left the office. Jerry walked over to the closet housing the pen reg and shut and locked the door.

"OK," Jerry said, "Let's get some breakfast."

At the cafe downstairs, we were having breakfast, and I started talking to myself. Jerry looked up at me and asked, "Who're you talking to?"

"Nobody. Just myself," I answered.

"Do you always do that?"

"All the time. Sometimes I even answer myself. I've always done it and probably always will, and please, Jerry, it's a private conversation, so don't butt in."

"Sorry, didn't mean to be rude."

"Truth is, I've been talking to this guy in my head ever since I was two or three years old. I don't know who he is, but sometimes he gets really mad. It's scary."

"Bernie, I really don't know about you. Ever seen a shrink?"

"Jerry, please call me 'Johnny' in public. Remember what I told you happened with the Doctor Dan case?"

"OK, 'Johnny.' By the way, tomorrow we got this gal Tina coming in. She wants to be an informant. She used to do speed and lost her two kids over it, so now she wants to work for us so maybe she can get her kids back. I thought you might wanna meet her tomorrow when I interview her. Girl informants can get you into a lot of places you can't go by yourself. Interested?"

"Hey, Jerry. I got no objections to having a female CI working under me."

"Like I've said before Bernie, you're a dog."

"Don't call me 'Bernie!'"

Breakfast was finished, so we went back up to the Narc office. Detective Jerry unlocked the door to the closet housing the pen reg. We went in and he locked the door from the inside. I gave him a funny look.

"Relax, Bernie. I need to explain a few things to you. As you know, we needed a signed court order for this pen reg. Now, that signed piece of paper allows us to wire into Seth's home phone and obtain the phone numbers for those incoming and outgoing calls. However, it doesn't allow us to listen in on any conversations. You understand what I'm getting at?"

I nodded.

"Now," Jerry continued, "here's the tricky part. My guy at the phone company wired this monitor in such a way that we can in fact listen in on any incoming or outgoing calls."

"Yeah, I understand."

"So what's your view on all this? You know this is highly illegal, listening in on phone conversations without the proper authorization. If we get caught, we're fucked. I mean really fucked. We go to federal penetentiary. If you're not comfortable with this, just say the word, no problem, and this conversation won't ever have taken place. If you need time to think about it, let me know."

"Hey, no problem here. Who all knows about this?"

Jerry answered, "Just you, me, and my guy at the phone company. No one else."

"What about the other guys in the unit?" I asked.

"Nope, no one. Just us three. That's why the lock is on the inside here. I explained to the sergeant that the inside lock is to maintain the chain of evidence with the printed phone numbers we obtain from this pen reg, just like with any other court case. This meth lab is our case, so we're responsible for that chain of evidence. One more thing; this small tool box under the desk and what's inside doesn't exist, understand? I got a good combination lock on the toolbox. I don't like keys. Too easy for them to fall into the wrong hands. If you're ever questioned about the tool box, if someone wants the combination, or if they ask you what's inside, just play dumb. Just say you don't know and that Detective Jerry is the only one with the combination. There's no reason for anyone to ever ask about the box, but we gotta cover all the bases just in case."

Jerry lined up the five numbers at the base of the combination lock in the proper sequence, pulled on it gently, opened it, and removed it. He then opened the toolbox, reached in, and pulled out a set of small ear phones.

"My phone guy re-wired the pen reg so that all you have to do is plug the earphone jack into that socket. He put a frequency filter in the line so that someone on the other end will never hear momentary static or any clicks when you plug in your earphone." Jerry locked up and we left.

Late Friday afternoon, a young Chinese-Eskimo gal showed up at the Narcotics office.

"Hi. I'm Tina. I'm supposed to meet with Detective Jerry."

I walked up and introduced myself; "Hi. I'm Detective Bernie Lau."

I escorted her to a small conference room. She was cute: petite build, dark hair, pretty smile, aah, yes—small titties too! I hoped we'd end up signing her on as an informant.

I yelled over at Detective Jerry, "Hey, Jerry! Our gal's here for the interview." The interview began with the usual questions: date of birth, present address, etc. Some background information was also asked of her, such as "Have you ever been arrested?" "Do you do drugs, and if so, what kinds?" and so forth.

"Ok, Tina, tell us why you want to be an informant," Jerry asked.

Tina sat nervously clasping and rubbing her hands together; she was holding back tears as she started to tell us about her childhood growing up on the reservation in Alaska. She told us about giving birth to two beautiful daughters, who she loved very much. But there was no father around to help with the financial support needed to pay for food, clothing, or medical expenses.

She'd done the best she could to provide for her children, and wanting them to have a better life, she'd left Alaska and moved to Seattle, to the big city, where, people said, good jobs and reliable health care were available. But finding work when you're part Eskimo isn't easy. She took whatever work she could find; low-paying, entry-level jobs. The State of Alaska did send Tina a quarterly check because of the oil pipeline, but those checks didn't last long when they had to provide for three people.

A year or so after arriving in Seattle, she started drinking. Before long, the drinking got out of control. Next came drugs, speed mostly, which helped her work long hours at menial jobs. Drug tolerance eventually built up. She needed more drugs. Buying more drugs meant that she had less money for her daughters. It was starting to destroy all their lives.

Eventually, DSHS took away her children. Luckily custody of the girls was awarded to Tina's mother, Mary Owl, who lived in Yakima, Washington (several hundred miles east of Seattle). At least now Tina's daughters would be well taken care of, and Tina would be able to spend time with them whenever she wanted to. They were in a safe and loving environment.

However, depressed at being apart from her girls, she once again returned to drinking and drugging. More often than not she found herself sleeping in homeless shelters and standing in food lines. As Tina kept talking, her face grew sadder; she was on the verge of tears. I took hold of both of her hands, looked into her eyes, and in a soft, gentle voice said, "Tina, that was yesterday. You don't have to sleep in shelters any more or wait in food lines. Things are going to be OK; don't worry. We'll work all this out."

She looked up at me, tears running down both cheek, her lips trembling. She couldn't say anything; she just squeezed my hands, lowered her head, and wept uncontrollably. Still holding Tina's hands in mine, I looked over at Detective Jerry.

"What do you think—coffee time?" I took Tina down to the Arctic Building Cafe while Jerry did a criminal background check on her. A half hour later, we went back up to the office. Tina's story had been verified. She'd been completely truthful; no arrests or criminal history of any kind.

Jerry then took three Polaroid photos of Tina. One was placed into the unit's confidential informant file, one photo went into my personal informant file, and Tina was given the third photo to keep. She was then assigned her own confidential informant number: No.

43. Now, whenever she called in, she'd identify herself only as "No. 43."

Being she was presently homeless and had been living on the streets of Seattle for some time, Jerry and I decided to rent her a room. Jerry filled out the required paperwork requesting money from a fund that was set aside for new informants. Sgt. Bert looked over the request form, smiled, and signed it. Tina was then handed $150 cash, which she signed for.

I left the Narcotics office with Tina in tow and took her to rent a room in a low-rent hotel located a block northeast of the Pike Place Market. The room wasn't much to look at, but at least Tina would be safe and have a dry, warm bed to sleep in. Room rented, Tina and I jumped in my GTO and headed out for an evening drive along Alki Beach.

As we drove along, Tina asked me about my personal life. Was I married? Did I have a girlfriend? I answered, "No and no."

I explained to Tina that my job kept me rather busy and that working undercover, well, I kind of had to look like a dirt-bag, junkie asshole most of the time. I never knew who I'd bump into when I was off-duty. It would be difficult to explain to the scum who knew me from the streets why I was suddenly all cleaned up and wearing good clothes, when they normally saw me dressed like a bum.

"That's one of the drawbacks of working undercover, Tina. I get into a certain character role, an asshole junkie dirt-bag. I need to stay in that role till whatever cases I'm working on are over with. Sometimes for several months, sometimes years. And that's my job; hanging out with assholes and junkies, buying drugs, and acting the part of an asshole. Most gals aren't interested in going out with a guy that usually smells bad and looks like an asshole. If some gal did decide to go out with me, and I told her who I really was, she'd most likely blab to her friends about her new boyfriend being a narc. Not good! That could put me in a bind. I could get my head blown off if the wrong people found out that I was really a cop. So again, to answer your questions: no, I'm not married, and nope, I don't got me no girlfriend, but I do have my own home!"

I glanced over at Tina and grinned, "Hey girl, wanna see my place?" Tina smiled at me, "Anytime you're ready, Mr. Johnny Medeiros. I guess it's your place or mine!"

The following morning I made breakfast for Tina and explained that it would be a good idea if for the next few weeks she hung around the Pike Place Market and got to know some of the assholes and drug dealers. I explained to her that she needed to call in once or twice a day and keep me updated. Other than that, she was free to shoot pool, have a beer or two, and find out what was going on in the area, drug-wise.

Tina asked "Will you guys pay for my weed?"

"Well, being you're now officially working undercover for SPD Narcotics, we'll be giving you a weekly allowance. Now, what you spend that money on is entirely up to you. However, you can't officially say you're buying weed with that money, or that we're OK with you smoking dope."

(Once, a new undercover police agent had listed the following on his monthly expense account "$300 spent for beer and shooting pool." That was it. No other explanation, such as surveillance or whatever, just "$300 for beer and shooting pool." Good thing the sergeant caught it before it went to our captain for the monthly financial review. That agent learned "Creative Report Writing 101" real quick.)

"Tina, you got a good thing going for yourself now; a safe place to live, money for food and clothing, and whatever else you may need. You also got protection provided by the entire Seattle Police Department. Try to remember that what you're doing now is really a job. You're getting paid good money to do a job, so don't fuck it up."

Tina, sitting on the couch, turned towards me, took my hands, looked up at me, and said; "Bernie, I promise I'll do good. I won't mess it up; you'll see. You won't be sorry. I'll make some good narcotics buy cases for you. I already know a pretty big marijuana and hash oil dealer in the Market. I'll introduce you to him in a few weeks, once he gets to know me better and starts to trust me. His name is 'Bobby.' He hangs around the El Bistro Tavern in Post Alley. He's usually there every day, shooting pool and selling hash oil."

Tina leaned over and kissed me lightly on the lips. She stood and took me by the hand and led me into the bedroom. Time to "de-brief" my new informant. I loved that job!

Back in my days of undercover work, many of our narcotics cases and search warrants were developed with the help and assistance of female informants. Bring a good-looking gal into any drug equation and guys automatically clicked over to stupid mode. Face it; guys dig chicks and dopers dig chicks more because cocaine or meth make guys (and gals) horny. But even before the fucking mode comes into play, "pussy power" is what distracts. Say you got some gal who wants to become an informant for whatever reason. She comes to the Narcotics office, gets registered, and is then "assigned" to work with one of the four or five undercover agents assigned to narcotics. She goes to some dealer she knows with the undercover officer in tow, she knocks on the door, and, nine times out of ten, the dealer will let her and the unknown agent inside.

"Hi, Tommy. This here is my boyfriend, Johnny, and he's looking to cop some meth ..." The dealer will most likely sell drugs to the undercover without any questions.

One of the many perks of working undercover was that we sometimes got to partner up with some hot chick that wanted to become a snitch. You had to be quick, though. As soon as a new face showed up and had her interview, that was the moment to step in and claim her for yourself. If several narcs were present when the gal walked in, we'd flip a coin. Once a female snitch was assigned to one of us agents, it was only a matter of time before the agent had sex with her. Sometimes it took a few days to "de-brief" an informant, sometimes it was just a freeway ride away.

(I personally witnessed one fellow agent get assigned to a cute, skinny blond chick who'd just been registered as a CI. The three of us drove off in our undercover VW van heading south on I-5 to check out some dealer that she knew. My fellow narc was driving and the new gal was sitting between us. About five minutes into the ride, the gal reached over, unbuttoned my partner's fly, and took his dick out. She then proceeded to suck him off, just like that, no warning, no requesting permission to go down on him, she just took matters into her own hands. Yeah, there we were, two of Seattle's Finest, driving down the highway to fight the War on Drugs as my partner was getting head from a cute new CI.)

Later that afternoon, I dropped Tina off in the Pike Place Market and headed to the Narc office. Detective Jerry informed me that De Breuil had disappeared on us. Gone! No one had seen or talked to him for over a week. Jerry continued, "We got a drug possession charge on him still pending. It's just a matter of time before he gets picked up for something. Then we'll arrest him on the possession charge and lock his ass up for good! As for Seth, I checked the pen reg when I came in. He's only been calling two or three numbers. One belongs to some gal named 'Kathy.' You're not going to believe this, Bernie, but it so happens that this Kathy is the daughter of our Police Guild attorney. I kid you not. I double-checked her name and home address. It's her, alright. Small world isn't it?"

"So what do we do about it, Jerry?"

"Nothing, Bernie. No use blowing this whole case just because her dad's on our side. Her personal choice of people she hangs with is not our problem. No, let's just keep this between you and me for the time being. She might not even be involved."

"OK. I'll just list her as 'Jane Doe' in my 'Seth File.' Yeah, it's a small world. Jerry, later on tonight I'll give Seth a call. I'll tell him that after this next meth delivery, it's time to cook up the last batch, and I'll offer him the remainder of the P2P."

"One thing we gotta make certain of, Bernie, is that when you give Seth the remainder of the P2P, almost a gallon's worth, make sure he knows you're gonna be with them in the lab when they cook it up. With that much P2P remaining, he can manufacture several pounds of pure meth. The 'Mother Load!'"

"Not a problem, Jerry. I'm sure he knows that."

"I got some errands to run, Bernie. Why don't you hang in the closet? If I'm not back by 9:00 P.M., go ahead and take off for the rest of the evening. Come in tomorrow around noon or so."

I went into the pen reg closet and latched the inner bolt behind me. I unlocked the tool box, removed the small headset, and plugged it into the pen reg. No one was on the line. I sat back and read a copy of High Times. About a half hour later, on came the red light. I quickly put on the headset and held my breath. It was an incoming call. Seth was talking to some old lady.

"Seth, deary, how've you been?"

"Oh, just fine, Grandma, busy with school you know ... study, study, study."

"Oh, that's so good, Seth. You get that education—it's important, you know. Without a proper education, you'll never be hired anywhere for a good-paying job. You know that, don't you?"

"I know, Grandma. That's why I'm in school."

"Seth, I called to let you know that I just baked your favorite pie: banana cream."

"Thanks, Grandma. How 'bout I come by tomorrow after class?"

"That'd be good. And bring your friends with you. There's plenty of pie to go around."

"Thanks, Grandma. I'll see you tomorrow afternoon after class."

"OK, Seth, dear. I'll see you tomorrow. Bye."

"Bye, Grandma!"

Green light back on. I felt strangely excited. It was the first time I'd ever listened in on a phone conversation. Sort of surreal, but exciting. To be able to listen while the people talking had absolutely no idea that you were listening. Wow, that was thrilling. Just like being a spy.

Next afternoon, Jerry asked, "Bernie, you get anything useful last night on the pen reg?"

"Yeah, I found out that Seth's favorite pie is banana cream. His grandma made him a fresh pie and invited Seth and his pals over to her place after classes today."

I decided to try my luck once again and see if Seth would get another phone call I could listen in on. I headed to the closet with my copy of High Times, the marijuana magazine that tells its readers everything they ever wanted to know about growing and cultivating marijuana, and more.

I was sitting down reading when the red light came on. Quickly, I put on the headphones. The voice sounded like Seth talking excitedly to one of his partners.

"Fuck, man, I let Kathy use the car yesterday and she fucking gets into an accident. She rear-ended some dude, fucked up the hood. I jacked it up to check for damage, and, fuck, I found this thing in the wheel well, some fucking red thing with a huge magnet."

"You know what it is?"

"No man, I don't fucking know what it is. At first, I thought it was a bomb, but there's no wires, only a fucking red tube mounted onto a fucking huge magnet. I'm calling my attorney. I'm leaving right now, I'm taking that thing with me. I'll call you later, FUCK!"

Damn it! Seth had found the bird dog. Now what were the chances of that ever happening? Talk about bad timing! The DEA was going to love this. We lost one of their tracking devices! Shit.

Well, what was done was done. Now I had to think about how I'd respond when and if he called me. Until then I'd just have to wait. The phone number I gave Seth was for the undercover phone in the closet, and no one was allowed to answer it except me. I had to be there when Seth called; my entire meth lab case could be riding on that call.

I needed to be cool. What would a real meth dirtbag have said, what would he have done in such a situation? At least I was prepared for the fucked-up news. I needed to act surprised, real surprised. Think, Bernie, think! No, not "Bernie." "Johnny." I needed to be "Johnny" when that call came in.

Time to be an asshole. I went to my locker and took out two warm Buds that I'd stashed there. Warm beer and a Nestle's Crunch. Tasted like shit, but it would get "Johnny" in the mood. I got my two Buds, plus the candy bar, and returned to the closet, locked myself in, and waited for the phone call.

Sure enough, an hour later the phone rang and, with two warm beers drunk, Johnny'd got himself a bit of an attitude. He answered the phone.

"Yeah, what?"

"Johnny, it's Seth."

"Yeah, Seth, what the fuck you want?"

"Johnny, we may have some real problems."

"Problems? What the fuck you talking about, dude?"

"Johnny, I found this device under my car. My girlfriend was driving my car, and she got into an accident. I found some sort of red device under my car, so I took it to my attorney, and he said it was some kind of a tracking device."

"Fuck man, that's federal stuff! Fuck, if you got fucking feds on your ass, I ain't wanting nothing to do with you. Fuck man, that's heavy shit. What the fuck you involved in, anyway? You rob a bank or something?"

"Nothing, Johnny, really nothing. Just what we've done so far. You know, the P2P stuff."

"'We?' Fuck you, man, I didn't do nothing. Fuck that. You're not dragging me into your bullshit, whatever it is. And what the fuck you talking to me on the phone for, anyway? You stupid shit. Just stay the fuck away from me. Call me in a month or two if everything's cool. Other than that, don't be calling me. Fuck that!" Johnny hung up.

I called Detective Jerry at his home. "Jerry, you're not going to believe this; Seth found the damn bird dog. I guess Kathy was using his car and rear-ended some guy. Seth put the car up on jacks to check for damage and found the damn unit."

"So Seth called you?"

"Yeah, just a few minutes ago. He called in a panic. I quickly turned it around on him. I told him that it sounded like federal shit and not to be calling me. I told him to call me in a month or two if all was cool. Damn it. Fuck!"

"OK, Bernie, I guess we just sit tight and wait for a month or so. I'm sure he'll be calling back. Meanwhile, hook up with Tina and see if she can start introducing you to that hash oil guy. As far as Seth goes, we already got a hand-to-hand delivery to you with that meth sample, so either way, he's going down. We'll get the bird dog back from his attorney when we bust him."

I headed home, showered, and cooked myself rare liver and onions. I washed down my meal with a couple of ice-cold Buds. I needed to get me a good night's sleep. I wished Tina were there.

32

The Great Meth Lab Bust

Since I was pretending to be an asshole biker, I'd gone out and bought myself a real fucking Harley-Davidson chopper, a "Pan Head" at that. I pictured myself driving into the police garage on my chopper, looking like a puke biker. Now, that would be funny. I could hardly wait. Bike ran real good, but she wouldn't stop leaking oil. Typical Harley!

"Johnny's" chopper

So I decided to ride my chopper to work for the very first time. I'd never ridden a chopper in my life, but how hard could it be? I figured, if I could ride a bicycle, I should be able to ride a Harley-Davidson chopper, right? It was starting to sprinkle, but I figured, what the hell, bikers ride in the rain all the time.

I got on, kicked it over a few times, and she started up. Damn, I loved the sound of a Harley! No other like it. As I headed out my gravel driveway, I gunned the engine. Big mistake! The chopper came up from under me, flipped me off, and landed on my left leg.

I heard a loud crack. Fuck! The damn engine was racing like hell. I tried to stand, but couldn't. I somehow finally managed to turn the bike off. Again I tried to stand, but the damn pain was too much. Damn fucking pain! I yelled out. I lay on my back, rain hitting me in the face. I realized that my lower left leg was broken. Fuck! I'd just broken my fucking leg, and I hadn't even gotten out of my fucking driveway! Shit!

The doctor told me I'd be in a cast for six weeks. I could've taken a total of six months off with full pay because the accident happened while I was on my way to work, so that made it "job related." I could've just kicked back at home, making about 600 bucks more a month because taxes wouldn't be taken out. A very sweet deal; stay home for six months at full pay, tax-free, drink beer, and watch TV. It doesn't get better than that!

But no, no way. Not me. Not Johnny Medeiros. I'd gotten Tina starting to work with me, and I wasn't about to let some other undercover work with her, no fucking way. Tina was Johnny's informant; no one else would get her! Tina and I'd hooked up; she was depending on me, and I wasn't about to let her down. Yeah, my leg was busted, so what? Isn't that what they make crutches for? And what better cover? What cop in his right mind would go to work every day with a busted leg, when he could take six months off while still drawing his full pay, tax free?

Well, Johnny would, that's who. Johnny would rather hang out in the Pike Place Market than stay home, drinking beer with sweet Tina and making drug cases. I took a week off, cause the pain was getting to me. I finally got the doctor to write me a prescription for 100 demerol tabs. Demerol's a great pain killer. Yeah, demerol and ice-cold beer; what a great combination! Pain? What pain? I didn't have any more pain; I felt good! I started chasing pain pills with beer every couple hours.

Street folks saw a grungy dude on crutches with a broken leg, hanging with an Eskimo chick, popping pills, and drinking beer. Well, one thing for sure, he wasn't no cop. I was playing the role to the max. In my mind I wasn't a fucking cop; I was "Johnny Medeiros," a fucked-up biker asshole with a fucking broken leg, hanging with this cool chick, drinking beer, popping pain pills, and talking shit. I loved my job!

Five days a week, sometimes six or seven days in a row, Tina and I would hang out in different taverns in the area of the Pike Place Market. One sunny afternoon, she finally introduced me to this hash oil dealer friend of hers; "Bobby." We met Bobby at his usual hangout, the El Bistro Tavern. Tina called him over to our table and told him that I was looking to buy some hash oil.

I didn't know a damn thing about hash oil, but I'd heard it would turn a normal marijuana joint into some out-of-this-world, super fucking smoke. Bobby took out a gram bottle from his jacket pocket and sold it to me for $60. Fucking great! I now had a hand-to-hand drug buy from a hash oil dealer, who Tina said was also a major marijuana dealer.

Making that first hand-to-hand buy from any new drug dealer is always exciting. Once Johnny made the buy, the guy now belonged to Johnny and the SPD. It was only a matter of time before the asshole got busted! The guy had no way out; it was a done deal. He was living on borrowed time.

I had a week left to go in my leg cast, when I got a call from Seth. A month and a half had gone by, and finally Seth was calling.

"Hey, Seth, what's up? Everything cool on your end? Whatever happened with that bomb someone put under your car? Ha, ha!"

"Johnny, I told you it wasn't a bomb, it was some kind of tracking device. My attorney checked around with some guys he knows who're feds. They looked into it, and nobody came up with anything, so my attorney thought maybe someone just wanted to pull some sort of prank on me. Probably some college kid who wanted to fuck with me."

"Well, I guess that's good news. So what you want? Why'd you call?"

"Ah. I was thinking we could meet someplace and talk about that 'investment' we had."

"Well I don't know Seth, see I'm kinda fucked-up right now. A month and a half ago, I dumped my chopper and broke my leg. Can you believe that? Broke my fucking leg. I'm in a cast now, on fucking crutches."

"Oh, well, good, I mean ... uh ... how bad is the break?"

"Hurts like a motherfucker, but I can still fuck! I got me some heavy-duty pain pills, they work good with beer. I don't feel a thing. Hey, how about I meet you somewhere around the Market? You know the El Bistro Tavern? It's on the south side of the Market."

"Yeah, I know it. When you wanna meet?"

"How about tomorrow afternoon, say, about six-thirty?"

"OK, I'll be there. OK if I bring my two friends with me?"

"Fuck, Seth, you can bring your sister, for all I care. You got any sisters I can fuck?"

"Ah, no, Johnny, just a brother."

"Too bad. See ya tomorrow, six-thirty."

Seth, you stupid shit. You want to talk about your "investment," again? Here you find some tracking device on your car, and you think maybe someone wants to play a prank on you? State-of-the-art federal tracking equipment as a practical joke? Your lawyer asks a fed? So what's the fed going to say; "Why, your client must be under some sort of federal investigation. You should let him know he'll soon be arrested?" No, all the fed is going to say is, "Uh, someone must be playing a joke on your client."

Next afternoon, Tina and I were once again drinking beer at the El Bistro Tavern. It was going on six-fifteen. We'd been there for over an hour, just kicking back, munching on boiled shrimp in the shell.

Tina had been hanging out with me for the past month and a half. Most street folks around the Pike Place Market now knew us as Johnny and his old lady, and they were comfortable with our presence.

Sitting in the El Bistro, I brought Tina up to date on Seth and the pending meth lab case. I told her to just sit by my side and not say anything. At six-forty Seth and his two pals walked in. I greeted Seth and told him to get my gal and me a couple of Buds. Seth started to say something, but on second thought, just got the beers. Seth also got himself a beer. His two "partners" just sat there at the table like a couple of dip-shits, saying nothing.

I didn't introduce Tina to Seth or his partners. It wasn't his fucking business who Tina was. She was with me—that's all Seth needed to know.

"OK, Seth; so what's the story?"

"Well, things seem to be cool. We want to finish this up as quickly as possible. You know, cook up that final batch."

"Whoa, wait a minute there. We're talking a lot of liquid here. You guys capable of handling that much? We're talking about a couple of kilos of finished product, right? How long from start to finish?"

"No problem," said Moe, the Chemist. "I can do the entire process in about 10 hours, start to finish, but I'll need a little more glassware. That way I can cut some time off by having several things going on at once."

"You got a list?" I asked.

Moe handed me a folded paper with a bunch of writing on it.

"OK, now, you guys know that I'm not letting almost a gallon of this stuff walk. In other words, the P2P and me go together or the deal stops here. It's non-negotiable."

They all looked at each other and started to mumble back and forth.

"Hey, guys, hello? Is there a problem? You either take me along, or you get the fuck out of here now. It's all very simple really. I don't give a shit if you do this or not. I got the liquid. I got guys just like you who can make this shit, but if I deal with you guys, I end up with a whole lot more dope. I get half and you get half."

Seth spoke up, sort of agitated, "Half! No way, man. There are four of us involved, so we figured each of us gets a fourth."

I looked over at Tina and said, "Hey, Babe, go get me another Bud. Turning back to Seth, I said, "Here's the deal: Moe here is the chemist, so he's important. Then you got me providing the liquid and glassware, that makes me important too. That, my friend, makes two, and two equals 50% in my book."

Tina returned with two beers. I reached into my jean jacket and took out three demerol tablets. My leg was starting to fucking hurt. I handed Tina one of the tablets and popped the remaining two into my mouth. I swallowed them with a large swig of cold, refreshing Bud. Aah; relief is but moments away. I loved fucking pain pills. I'd been on them for over a month and a half. My doctor didn't mind refilling my demerol prescription. He knew I was a cop, so it wasn't a problem.

Seth blurted out: "I provide the cabin, I mean, the house where we do all this!"

I cut Seth off. "Hey, asshole, you listen up. I can provide a half-dozen places right now, if need be. The only two important players here are Moe and me. End of story. Moe takes half of the finished product, I take the other half. Like I said, you don't like it, get the fuck out of here!"

Tina cuddled up next to me and gave me a little kiss on the cheek. I bent down and gave her a big ass kiss smack on her lips. We French-kissed for about a minute. Tina's hands found my crotch, I put my hand under her shirt and fondled one of her tiny breasts. Tina moaned. The three stooges stirred in their seats. They were very uncomfortable and tried to look away. They really didn't know what to say or do.

Tina had thrown in what's known as an "interrupter," which is something that distracts attention away from topic of conversation. It worked; they totally forgot what it was we were talking about. They lost their focus while Tina and I remained in control.

After a while, we came to an agreement; it was going to be a 50-50 split on the dope. (Thanks, Tina.)

I told Seth that it had to be Saturday, the day after tomorrow, 9:30 A.M. on the dot. I'd be in the parking lot of the Museum of Natural History with the liquid and the extra glassware. Be there, be on time!

Seth and his "partners" got up and left. Tina and I stayed behind. We didn't have any place we needed to be except right there in the El Bistro Tavern, popping pain killers and drinking Buds. Life was good!

By 8:00 A.M. Saturday morning all surveillance was in position. We had absolutely no idea where the meth lab was. I had my GTO, the P2P, and the extra glassware in the trunk. I also had a voice-activated device set up in the ashtray of the GTO, so that I could be in constant one-way communication with the surveillance team. Though I could only transmit, not receive, I'd be transmitting my location every several minutes. That way the surveillance vehicles could lay back several miles, and by doing so, not stand a chance of being spotted by Seth and his team.

About 9:30 A.M. Seth, Moe the Chemist, and Kathy arrived in one vehicle, and Larry pulled up in another. Seth was driving his GTO. Good! Now, once Seth and the others were busted, we'd have another GTO at our disposal.

I looked over at Seth. "Nice GTO you got there, dude!"

Seth answered, "Yeah, thanks. She's my baby."

I was thinking to myself, "Not after today, dude. This is the very last time you'll ever drive your baby!"

We all got out of our vehicles and gathered around. Seth wanted to see the P2P, so I opened up the trunk and showed him.

"OK, boys, where to?"

Seth answered, "Just follow us, Johnny." Larry was instructed to lay back a few miles to check for surveillance or whatever might seem unusual.

We got back into our cars, and Seth pulled out of the parking lot. I followed him.

They seemed to know a little bit about counter-surveillance. But if they'd really known what they were doing, they would have had Moe ride with me. That way, there would have been no way I could have given my position and location to my backup every few minutes.

This pending meth lab case being so important, the brass requested and got the Washington State Patrol Narcotics Task Force to work with us. WSP had had one of their surveillance planes in the air, monitoring my every move ever since I'd pulled into the museum parking lot.

Seth headed east onto SR-520, across the new floating bridge, and then south on I-405 to SR-90. Then we drove east and out of the jurisdiction of the City of Seattle.

Seth had once mentioned to me that he knew for certain that Seattle cops weren't allowed to make arrests outside of their jurisdiction. He'd told me that he knew "a little something" about the law. That's the problem with knowing "a little something" about the law; it's what you don't know that gets you in trouble. Narcs are all given special commissions, so that we did in fact have arrest powers in other jurisdictions, and in return, we did the same for them.

Following Seth's GTO, I gave my position every five minutes. A few miles before the Snoqualime Summit Exit, Seth pulled off to the right onto a gravel road. We continued on for about three miles. The area was beautiful; lots of trees and brush. No folks up there. Suddenly, a cabin came into view. Seth pulled up and parked. Coming over to my vehicle, he once again reminded me that "Cops can't touch us up here, we're safe." I didn't say anything.

Ten minutes later, the second vehicle pulled up. Seth went over and talked with Larry. I couldn't hear the entire conversation, but I did hear Seth say "Everything seems cool." Seth and his partners seemed to relax. I got the P2P and glassware out of the GTO trunk and headed into the cabin. Moe took the items from me and started setting up the equipment in the kitchen area. Kathy and Larry hung out in the living room.

For the next six hours, Seth and Moe stayed busy in the kitchen, setting up and performing the manufacturing process of turning liquid P2P into pure methamphetamine crystals. After a while, Kathy and I went in the kitchen and watched. There was no bathroom in the cabin, so when I had to piss, I just went out and pissed in the bushes.

Although I couldn't spot the surveillance team, I knew they were close by. Standing next to my GTO, I took the opportunity to talk to the ashtray. I could be several feet away and my voice was still picked up by the high-tech transmitter.

Ten hours. Damn, that was a long time with nothing to do. But the payoff would be huge. Almost a gallon of P2P, transformed into several kilos of pure, industrial-grade methamphetamine.

Almost six months' worth of undercover work was about to pay off. In just a couple of hours, the Great Meth Lab caper would be over with, and I'd be a hero!

Moe was in the final stages of the process. I was standing in the doorway of the kitchen, making small talk with Seth. Hidden in my boot was a beeper that I was to press as soon as the meth was processed from liquid into crystals.

BOOM. The front door of the cabin suddenly came crashing in! What the fuck was going on? I hadn't pressed the beeper! Plain clothes detectives and uniformed officers from various jurisdictions rushed into the cabin. They were yelling "Police; get the fuck down, get on the floor, don't fucking move!"

Seth, Moe, Kathy, Larry, and I were slammed to the ground and handcuffed. The shock on my face was real. I didn't give any signal! Why was the door kicked in? The process wasn't finished yet and the meth was still in liquid form. What the fuck was going on? Something was definitely wrong, very wrong.

Seth, still face down on the ground, looked over at me and asked, "Johnny, how did you really break your leg?" He was finally starting to suspect that I might be a cop. Still face down and handcuffed myself, I looked over at him and said, "Like I told you, Seth, I dumped my chopper." That was the last time I ever saw or spoke to Seth.

Overtime pay. That was the reason for kicking in the door early; it was because of fucking overtime pay. A dozen or so police officers on overtime pay amounts to a hell of a lot of city money. Word had come down from the brass at SPD to bring the caper to a close. The overtime pay was getting too high. "Shut it down now," had been the order. Six months of dedicated undercover work, and they decided to pull the plug just hours before it would have been over and done with. I was pissed! What a photo op that would have been! Detective Bernie Lau, wearing a huge smile, standing in front of several kilos of pure, sparkling white methamphetamine crystals on the TV Nightly News and most likely pictured in the Seattle Times. All there was now was Bernie standing in front of two buckets of methamphetamine in liquid form, no news coverage whatsoever, and certainly no smile on my face. Fuck!

One month following Seth's arrest, I happened to be standing in the lobby of the Public Safety Building. As I stepped into the elevator, I bumped into a defense attorney that I'd known for several years. I respected this attorney as he was one of the few defense attorneys who wasn't an asshole. Looking up, he said, "Hi Bernie. I got assigned the 'Meth Lab' case, the one where Seth and his buddies were arrested in some cabin. Any information you can share with me?"

I paused a minute, puckered my lips, and said, "Poor Seth; he sort of got set up. It all started when this low-life puke named De Breuil got busted on a drug possession charge. He decided to cooperate with us in return for a lesser charge and no jail time. De Breuil promised to get us a big drug bust. Said he could introduce one of SPD's undercover narcotics detectives to these guys. He said these guys were going to set up a huge meth lab. De Breuil swore that this was going to be a major drug bust."

"Truth is, De Breuil put the idea of making a million dollars in Seth's head. De Breuil knew that we could provide the P2P and all the necessary glassware. De Breuil played us all; he was the one who started this whole meth lab caper. He'd given Seth a piece of paper with a chemical formula for the manufacture of methamphetamine. He enticed Seth and his two buddies to cook up and manufacture enough methamphetamine to try to make themselves a million dollars. We, the Seattle Police Department Narcotics Section, provided the necessary P2P to manufacture the methamphetamine. We also provided all the necessary glassware to build a lab."

For a moment the attorney just stood there, dumbfounded. Finally, he asked me if I'd be willing to repeat what I'd just told him to the presiding judge. I said I would, so Seth's court-appointed attorney and I walked across the street to the King County Building, where, in the judge's chambers, I related the entire story.

In the end the case never went to trial. The charges were plead down to "attempted possession of a dangerous drug." A sentence of six months in the county jail was handed down to each of the three defendants, plus three years probation. Seth, however, did lose his prized GTO and his van to the Narcotics Section. A few months later, the GTO was transferred to the Narcotics Task Force of the Washington State Patrol in return for their having providing the "Eye in the Sky" for surveillance. The cabin was also seized.

It was the major meth lab bust that could have been, but wasn't!

Meth lab bust

33

Blown

After the Great Meth Lab caper was over and done with, Tina and I concentrated on Bobby C, who'd previously sold me a gram of hash oil for $60. While I was busy with the stooges, Tina had been able to get close to Bobby C. and make some buys. My time and trouble with the Harley had not been completely wasted; I now had an excellent cover as a biker and dealers felt comfortable talking to me. It was well known that bikers moved a lot of product, and I thought that Johnny should be able to move up the ladder.

So Tina and I went to work. That meant hanging out at the El Bistro Tavern, drinking cold Buds, and feasting on boiled shrimp in the shell, which I always purchased from one of the nearby fish stalls in the Market. I spotted Bobby C. shooting pool and invited him over for a beer.

"Thanks for the beer, Johnny. So what's up? Need any oil?"

"Man, I ain't gonna bullshit you, I haven't been around hash oil at all, and I don't know the first thing about it. How do you mix it with weed? I know oil's strong stuff, but if I don't know how to mix it in with the marijuana I got on hand, then the oil ain't of no use to me."

"Johnny, this oil I got coming in is pure hash oil from Afghanistan. I got a couple small bricks of hash that are dynamite. One brick even got a gold stamp on it as a trademark of purity. In other words, the gold seal shows that there's no better hash available anywhere in the world. None! The guy I deal with only sells the absolute very best."

"OK, Bobby, that's all well and good, but what about the oil? Like I said, I need to learn how to mix it. So if I buy another gram of oil, will you show me how to mix the damn stuff with weed?"

"No problem, Johnny. Come by my place tomorrow afternoon. I get off work at five-thirty. Give me a chance to clean up after work. So come by, say, around six. I live in the Tower 801 Apartments on Pine Street. You know, that round apartment building."

"Round building. Yeah, I know the one you're talking about. I always wanted to see what those apartments look like. Are the rooms round? That would be so fucking cool, a round apartment!"

"No, it's not round inside, but you'll get to see for yourself tomorrow. By the way, I'm on the 9th floor, Room 907."

"OK, tomorrow, 6:00 P.M., Apartment 907. Got it."

"One thing, Johnny. When you and Tina come up to my apartment, I want you to walk up from 1st and Pine and stay on the left side of Pine Street. Left, that's the north side. Don't be driving up and parking. I don't let anyone just drive up and park when they come to see me."

"Why's that?"

"Oh, nothing, really. It's just a good luck quirk I have with first-time visitors. I know it's strange, but, hey, not that big of a deal, right? Tell you what, Johnny,

I'll have a couple of ice-cold Buds waiting for you and Tina when you guys get there. Make up for that long walk."

"Sounds good to me, Bobby. Thanks."

"Thanks for the beer, Johnny."

Bobby got up and went back to shooting pool.

Work done, it was time to move on.

"Say, Tina, you hungry?"

"You kidding, Johnny? You know I'm always hungry. Johnny, how about Ivar's? Can we eat at Ivar's? At the fish bar outside? Please, please?"

"Ivar's? Sure. Ivar's it is. Tina, tell you what; how'd you like to dine inside for a change? You know, make like all them fancy folks eating dinner at a nice table with a view overlooking Elliott Bay."

"But won't that be expensive, Johnny?"

"Hush, Tina. You forget that we got city money that needs spending. If we don't spend the funds, we get that much less money next quarter. Yes, dining at Ivar's is expensive, but, hey, we deserve it. So OK, we're dining inside tonight and the city is picking up the tab."

Tina jumped around me like a little girl, "Johnny, how come you're so good to me?"

"Well, Tina, it's because you're so 'bad' in bed."

"Johnny, that's not a nice thing to say. Am I really that bad in bed? I thought you enjoyed how I fucked. You never complained before!"

"Tina, Tina. 'Bad' means 'good bad,' not 'bad bad.' You know, bad as in 'bad and nasty!'"

"Oh, OK. I understand now. So Johnny, how much more 'bad and nasty' should I be next time?"

"Well, Tina, if our dinner comes to over $50 tonight, I expect you to be very bad when we get home. Very, very bad!"

"OK then; I'll order lobster. Do you know if they serve lobster here?"

"Tina, Ivar's is a seafood restaurant, right? So of course, they serve lobster. Dumb, dumb!"

Tina and I walked down to the waterfront and went into Ivar's. Nice place! As we entered the lobby area, a hostess approached us and asked, "Can I help you?" I answered, "Yeah, hi. My girl and me'd like a table for two; a window seat, if possible."

The hostess frowned as she looked at me, then at Tina. Damn it, I knew that look. I'd seen it all too often. The look that said, "You look like a bum and that gal of yours looks like a squaw fresh off the reservation. How dare you come in here asking to sit in the dining section next to proper folks?"

The hostess looked towards the bar area and said, "There's at least an hour's wait. Why don't you and your friend just go sit at the bar? You can order food there, you know." I thought to myself, "Sit at the bar? You mean in the dark? Hell, no! I ain't sitting at no fucking bar! Tina and me came here for a nice quiet dinner. We're not sitting in no fucking bar; no way!"

I worked at keeping my cool. "OK, Bernie, just relax and take a deep breath." I released my tension slowly, relaxed and centered myself. OK, I felt better. I was OK. The hostess looked at me and inquired, "Do you folks want to sit at the bar or not?"

I smiled, looked at the hostess and said, "Hold on a minute, lady. I'll be right back."

The hostess turned and walked off, leaving us standing in the lobby area. I pulled Tina towards me and gave her a hug.

"Hon, wait here a few minutes, OK? I'll be right back. Just stay put!"

I exited the restaurant and walked over to the open-air Fish Bar that was located in front of Ivar's. I knew Bob, the person in charge.

"Hey, Bob, can I talk to you for a minute?"

Bob came over.

"Sure, guy, what's up?" (Poor Bob never knew what to call me. He knew I was a cop and worked undercover, and I had several fake identities. So he always just called me "guy.")

"Bob, I got this gal with me. She's a good gal, not some tramp. I'd really like to enjoy a quiet dinner with her in the dining area. I know I don't look my best, you understand, cause of my work. I was being polite, but this hostess inside, she's got an attitude and won't let my friend and me sit in the dining area. She said we should sit at the bar!"

Bob cut in, "Oh, her. That's Marsha. Yeah, she can be snob at times. Make that a bitch. I understand, guy. Say no more; I'll take care of it. Just go back in, and in a few minutes, I'll make sure you and your lady friend have the best window table available. And, guy, come around more often, won't you? Don't be so scarce. I always like to chat with you. And enjoy your dinner!"

"Thanks, Bob, I will. I'll come by more often, I promise. Bob, you gonna retire soon?"

"No way, guy, never. I'm here till I die. I wouldn't know what to do with myself if I retired. I've been here for over 25 years, and this Fish Bar is my life, my home. I'm happy here!"

I walked back into the restaurant. Tina was still sitting in the waiting area. I sat next to her, held her hand, and made small talk, but I didn't mention anything about my talking to Bob. Within a few minutes, a respectable-looking gentleman dressed in a dark coat and tie entered the waiting area from a back office. He went up to Marsha the hostess and spoke to her for a moment. Her expression changed suddenly. Nervously she looked over at Tina and me, then glanced down at the floor. The hostess nodded several times, but kept looking down at the floor. The gentleman looked over at Tina and me, nodded, and smiled. Then he turned and disappeared into the office. Marsha grabbed a couple of menus from the stand and walked over to us.

"Sir, your table is ready. Please follow me."

Marsha led us over to a corner table, one which offered a full, unobstructed view of Elliott Bay. Good; we'd have a view of the setting sun. She placed the menus on the table, turned, and walked off without saying a word. Tina and I took our seats. She turned and looked me in the eyes.

"Johnny, what was that all about? What did you do?"

"Well, Tina, I got a very good friend that manages the Fish Bar outside. In the past, I've done him several big favors. Tonight I was the one asking for a favor, and he was only too happy to help me out."

"Johnny, you know a lot of people, don't you?"

"Yes, I do, Tina, and in this world of ours, it's who you know that makes it possible to get things done."

Tina and I picked up our menus. Wow. Dungeness crab, King crab, clams by the bucketful, fresh live oysters on the half-shell, several selections of fresh salmon, freshwater trout, gooey duck (a clam that resembles a big dick), East Coast lobster, a selection of steaks and prime rib, Ivar's own clam nectar, freshly-made Boston and New England Clam Chowder, baked potato, garlic mashed potato, fries, several types of fresh salad . . . on and on.

OK, Seattle Police Department, here goes; tonight Tina and I feast, and you guys pick up the tab!

Our waitress came over, introduced herself, and took our orders. Tina ordered the lobster, garlic mashed potatoes, and a fresh garden salad. I ordered filet mignon, cooked "very rare," a bucket of clams, Dungeness crab, garlic mashed potatoes, and a small dinner salad. As an appetizer, I ordered a dozen fresh oysters on the half-shell, great for later that night. (I hoped!) Tina ordered a white wine, and I ordered a glass of merlot off the wine list (no house wine for me that night), and coffee with cream. The dinner would be a celebration of what was to come in the very near future: Bobby's arrest. I loved my job!

We relaxed, chatted, and enjoyed ourselves as we dined at our leisure. Working the streets of Seattle could be tough, dangerous, and highly stressful. It was refreshing to take a break from reality every so often. I'd always worked hard in undercover. Now, Tina was working just as hard and putting her life on the line every time we hit the streets. Narcotics work is no walk in the park. Cops and informants had been killed in the past. So far it had been OK for us. No problems, no one had made me. But you never knew from one moment to the next. Things could go very wrong in an instant, and you could be shot and killed.

Anyway, just then I was trying not to think about work. I just wanted to enjoy the fine meal and Tina's company. The rest of the world could wait till tomorrow.

Dinner finally over with, Tina had warm apple pie *à la mode,* and I ordered myself a shot of VSOP Napoleon Brandy. Warm snifter in hand, I sat back and enjoyed the moment. Tina reached over, took my hand in hers, and laid her head on my shoulder. It was a perfect evening.

Eventually, the waitress came over with the bill and told us to enjoy the rest of our evening and to please feel free to come again. How nice of her! The dinner bill totalled $75. Not bad, not bad ... as long as the city was paying. I handed our waitress a $100 bill and told her to keep the change.

As we were about to exit the restaurant, I walked over to the hostess, Marsha. I handed her a crisp 20-dollar bill. She started to smile as she reached out to take the bill from my hand. I looked her right in the eyes and said, "This is for Bob. Make sure he gets it." That done, Tina and I left the restaurant and headed back towards Pike Street. As we were walking along, Tina looked over at me and asked, "So Johnny, was the dinner more than $50?"

We didn't get up until late the next day.

In the afternoon, we met with Detectives Jerry and Tom and briefed them on the previous day's meeting. Tom was pleased that we were breaking into a new kind of drug.

"You should start out from 1st and Pine around 5:20 P.M. Take your time; better not to be right on time. You know how dope deals never go down on time. Me and Jerry will be doing the surveillance, but you won't see us. While you're up there with Bobby, spend some time, shoot the shit, see if you can get him talking about his connection."

"No problem. He likes to talk. Maybe he'll let something slip."

Meeting over, Tina and I went to the El Bistro. It was around 4:45 P.M., so we had a beer. It's always the same before a dope buy. You go over in your head what might go down, what might go wrong. It's normal with undercovers.

An undercover always fears getting made. Nothing scares us more. Not the guns, the sickos, the dope dealers, the strung-out addicts; none of that bothers us as much as being made. That's what keeps us up nights worrying about the next meeting with the bad guys, the next drug buy. We never get used to it.

5:13 P.M. Time to move. We took our time walking up Pine Street, looking in store windows as we went. We didn't want to seem too anxious. We wanted to make it look like we were just goofing around. No rush, no big deal. The reality was that there was always built-in stress every time a narcotics buy went down. You never knew what would happen. Going into a dealer's apartment could be very dangerous.

We worked our way up to Bobby's apartment in 20 minutes or so, and then we crossed Pine Street and went into the lobby. I pushed the elevator button, the door opened, and we got in. No one else was inside. We rode straight to the 9th Floor without a stop, exited the elevator, and located Number 907. I paused before knocking and took a deep breath. "Showtime!"

Just as I was about to knock, Bobby opened the door. "Hi, guys! Come on in. Here in the kitchen. Have a seat." We all sat around the kitchen table.

"So what's the good word, Bobby? Got those two cold Buds?"

"Boy, you don't waste any time, do you, Johnny?"

"Hell, no. Not after hiking up eight blocks. I'm tired, my fucking leg hurts like hell, and I'm ready for a cold one!"

"Tina, want one?"

"Sure." Bobby pulled two Buds out of the fridge.

"Here, enjoy!"

"Bobby, I'm curious. Why the fuck did you have us walk up from 1st and Pine on the north side of the street? What gives?"

"Well, if you must know, I watched every step you guys took, all the way from 1st and Pine to this apartment. See those binoculars? I've been watching you every step of the way for the past 20 minutes."

"Why?"

"Just to make sure you weren't being followed, or to see if you had some folks walking along with you, that's why. It's my ass. I'm already on probation on a drug beef. It's a bullshit rap, but I can't afford not to be careful. I hardly ever allow anyone to come up here, but when I do, I have them walk up here the same way you and Tina did. OK, Johnny, you got the 120 bucks? You wanted two grams of the oil, right?"

"Yeah, Bobby, two grams. Here's the money." I gave Bobby the $120. He took it and handed me two one gram-size vials which he said contained hash oil. I was happy and thinking, "Hand-to-hand buy number two. I got you, Bobby; you're mine!"

"OK, Johnny, come over here by the stove, and I'll show you how this works. It's simple, really."

Bobby put a small pan on the stove with a little water in it. He turned on the gas burner and waited a minute till the water started to boil. He then carefully placed a small glass bowl into the boiling water. There was about a quarter gram of hash oil on the bottom of the bowl—about the area of a dime. Bobby let the bowl sit in the boiling water for a few seconds till the tar-like hash oil started to melt. Next, he began to add finely-grated flakes of marijuana till the bottom of the bowl was covered. Then he took a chopstick and began to stir the flakes into the melted hash oil.

"See, Johnny? Nothing complicated, really. Just heat, stir and mix; there's nothing to it." Holding a hand towel, Bobby carefully took the glass bowl out of the pan of boiling water and placed it on a pad on the kitchen table.

"OK, Johnny, next, we let this cool down for a few minutes, then all's left to do is take out some of the flakes and roll yourself a joint."

"Damn, Bobby, I thought it'd be more complicated than that. Hell, even I can do that. Thanks!"

"One thing, Johnny. You need to experiment with how much oil to how much marijuana. You don't want to use up too much of the hash oil, but you still have to make sure you've got enough mixed in with the weed to get the high of the oil. It's trial and error. You'll catch on in time. OK, it's cooled down. Time to roll yourself a joint."

Bobby handed me a pack of Zig-Zag papers. I took the paper and put a small amount of the hash oil-coated marijuana flakes onto the paper. Then I rolled up a joint, wetting the edge with my tongue before the final quarter roll of the paper. I handed the joint to Bobby.

"No, Johnny, that's OK. You go ahead. I'm not smoking right now. I got things to do later on, but you go ahead and light up."

Sometimes you had to. It was no big deal. I took the lighter and lit up the joint. I took a hit, and held my breath: five ... ten seconds, then I slowly let the smoke out. I sat back and relaxed. Oh-oh. It hit me. Fuck! Oh, boy. The shit was potent. All of a sudden, I couldn't think. I slowly reached for my beer. With great effort, I took a swig. The beer tasted delicious; never knew beer could taste so good. I took another swig. Fuck! I looked around the room, but I couldn't focus on anything.

"Tina, you OK?"

"Yeah, Johnny, I'm right here. Don't worry; everything's fine. It's just the hash oil."

I felt Tina take hold of my hand.

"Tina, I want to get out of here. I need some fresh air. Can you help me, please? Tina, I want to leave now!"

I vaguely heard Bobby say something to Tina, but I couldn't understand what. I was no longer comfortable in that apartment. I couldn't think. I was scared.

"Tina, please help me. I want to leave now!"

It was a good thing that Tina hadn't also hit the joint. Otherwise, we'd have been at Bobby's for the rest of the evening. Bobby gave Tina the rest of what remained in the glass bowl. Slowly Tina somehow managed to get me into the elevator and down to the lobby. Everything had slowed down, but I was aware that I was with Tina and that she was helping me walk down the street. Everything was messed up. I couldn't focus, I couldn't hold a thought. Lights, colors, sounds were all blurry. I wasn't at all comfortable in that state. As stoned as I was, it would be the easiest thing in the world to slip up and blow our cover. It was scary!

Tina finally got me to 1st Avenue, then she headed us south towards the Narcotics office, figuring that was the best place to take me in my condition. I sure couldn't have driven. As we passed a Diamond parking lot near Pike Street a parked car honked at us.

"It's Jerry. Johnny, Jerry's here!"

Detective Jerry got out of his unmarked city vehicle and walked over to us.

"Tina, what the hell's happened to Johnny?"

"Bobby was showing Johnny how to mix hash oil with marijuana flakes. Then Bobby had Johnny roll a joint and made him take a hit. I'm sure it was because Bobby wanted to make sure that he wasn't a cop. I think Bobby put way too much hash oil in the mix because he wanted to get Johnny fucked up. One hit; Johnny only took one hit, that's all. That was pure hash oil; it's way too powerful. Look at him, he can't even walk or talk. Johnny's wasted!"

"It's OK, Tina, it's OK. Don't worry, I'll drive him home. You can go back to your hotel room, if you want."

"No, Jerry, I'm staying with Johnny. We work together every day now. He's my partner, and I'm not leaving him alone, no way. You know what, Jerry? I care about this guy. Johnny's a good person, a real good guy. We've been through a lot lately, working around the Market, making drug buy cases for you guys. Jerry, will you drive us home to Johnny's house? Please? Look, Jerry, I've stayed at his place a lot of times, so it's not that big a deal. I can take care of him. We can't just leave him alone in this condition."

"OK, Tina. You can stay with him. I'll drive you guys home."

"By the way, Jerry; what happened to Tom? Wasn't he supposed to be with you on surveillance?"

"Yeah, he was with me. After you guys left the apartment, Tom and I went and sat around in the lobby and waited a few minutes before leaving. Tom had things to do, so I dropped him off at his car."

"Jerry, Johnny's got the GTO parked in the garage on Western. Is it OK to leave it parked there overnight?"

"Yeah, no problem. It'll be safe. You guys can get it tomorrow."

Detective Jerry drove us to my home in Mountlake Terrace, and with Jerry's help, Tina put me to bed.

"OK, Jerry, thanks for the ride. Jerry, how about you give Johnny off tomorrow? Let him rest a bit, please?"

"Yeah, OK, Tina; no problem. I'll let Sgt. Bert know. You guys take the day off."

The following morning I woke up hungry as hell. I found myself buck-ass naked in my own bed without the slightest idea how I'd got there. Last thing I remembered was drinking a beer at Bobby's. What the fuck happened? I heard noise in the kitchen.

"Hey, who's there?"

"Johnny. You're finally alive again. Welcome back."

"Tina, what happened? How'd I get here?"

"Ha, Johnny. You got fucked up yesterday! You smoked that joint at Bobby's, the joint that had hash oil in it. You took one toke, and you were fucked up royal."

"Tina, what time is it? What about work? Don't I have to go into the office?"

"Relax, Johnny. I took care of all that. I got you the day off."

"You did? Thanks, Tina. You're OK!"

"Tina took off her clothes and jumped into bed. For some reason I was horny as hell. Damn, sex was never so good. Hash oil rules!

The following day Tina and I got a ride to the Narcotics office from Sgt. Bert, who lived only a few miles from my place. After arriving at the office, I sat at my desk and typed up my report on Bobby C and the second hand-to-hand hash oil buy. Tina helped me out with the details of what all transpired at Bobby's as I had a difficult time remembering. Report done, I got a case number from radio, placed the hash oil into an evidence envelope, and dropped it off at the Evidence Room.

Tina and I then walked down to Western Avenue, where I got my GTO out of the parking lot. The plan was to head back to the El Bistro Tavern and try to get a larger hash oil buy from Bobby. First, however, I stopped by the Market and purchased a half-pound of boiled shrimp in the shell. Going into the tavern, I took a seat while Tina went to the bar and got us a couple of cold Buds. When she came back, she handed me my beer, sat down, and said, "Hey, Johnny, Bobby's in the back, shooting pool."

I took a few swigs of beer, got up, and walked over to where Bobby was.

"Hey, Bobby. How goes it? Man, that was some potent shit you fixed for me the other day. Shit, man, did I get fucked up or what!"

Bobby didn't look at me, he just kept shooting pool.

"Hey, Bobby, what the fuck? Too proud to say hi?"

Bobby finally looked up. "Stay the fuck away from me, man. I know you're a cop!"

"What the fuck you talking about, Bobby? That's crazy shit you're sayin'. I ain't no cop!"

"Oh, yeah? The other day, when you and Tina left my place, I followed you guys down to the lobby and guess what? Sitting right there in the lobby were two detectives—the same two who arrested me a year ago. So don't be telling me that you ain't no fucking cop! Leave me the fuck alone. I ain't got nothing to say to you! You're a cop. Now get outta my face."

I went back to where Tina was sitting. My mind was starting to race. God damn it, here we go again. Fucking Jerry and Tom. How fucking stupid could they be to sit right there in the lobby area of Bobby's apartment building? All they had to do was witness Tina and me enter and leave the apartment building. They should have been surveilling us from across the street or something, not right in the fucking lobby of the apartment building!

So now my cover was blown. I'd been made as a cop. Tina too. Not good. Not good at all. Tina and I wouldn't be able to do any more undercover work around that area. There was no way of knowing who Bobby might have tipped off about me being a narc and Tina being a snitch.

"Fuck it," I thought, "I ain't leaving the tavern. Fuck Bobby!" He probably expected Tina and me to get out in a hurry. Well, fuck that! I'd sit there till I was good and ready to leave. I hoped Bobby would try to pull some shit. I'd arrest his fucking ass right there! Tina was, of course, worried.

"Johnny, what now? What do we do?"

"Nothing, Tina. We're just going to fucking sit here and drink beer. Here, have a couple of pain pills!"

I handed two to Tina and I took two myself. Soon I got a good buzz going. Pain pills helped me relax, mellowed me out. I'd been on demerol ever since I'd had the spill on my chopper. I knew I should start to taper down, but I loved the feeling I got. I could see that Tina too was feeling no pain.

"Like I said, Tina, fuck it. What's Bobby going to do? He certainly ain't gonna come over and try to assault me. I wish he would, though. I'd love to kick his ass!"

I was certain that Bobby realized that being I was a cop, I most likely had a gun on me. I'd have liked nothing better than to shove it right in his face and say "You're under arrest, motherfucker!" Nah, I'd arrest Bobby in due time, but meanwhile, I'd let him sweat it out. He knew he was going to get arrested, and being he was still on probation, that meant definite jail time. "Yeah," I thought to myself, " I'm gonna let him sweat!"

About an hour and several beers later, Tina and I got up and left the tavern. Bobby C. was still in the back shooting pool by himself. We made our way back to the Narcotics office. Detective Jerry was at his desk. Tina and I walked up to Jerry's desk and I pulled up a chair. I sat there for a moment starring at Jerry.

"So what's up, Bernie? Feeling better? You were sure messed up the other day."

"Yeah, I was, Jerry, but you know what? You and fucking Tom are both dumbshits! You got my fucking cover blown!"

"What're you talking about, Bernie? What do you mean 'we got your cover blown?'"

"Well, Jerry, me and Tina just came from the El Bistro Tavern and guess what? Bobby C. was there, shooting pool by himself. He wouldn't talk to me at first, but when he finally did, he said he saw you and Tom sitting there in the lobby of his apartment. He followed me and Tina down right after we left. Did you or Tom happen to notice him in the lobby? Well, did you?"

"No, we didn't. You sure Bobby said he spotted us?"

"Jerry, how else would Bobby know that you and Tom were sitting there smack in the middle of his damn lobby unless he spotted you? And neither of you spotted Bobby. He saw both you dummies, and you didn't see him. You had your backs to the elevator, right? Nice going, Jerry. Thanks a lot. You guys sure covered our asses, didn't you? Great way to get Tina and me killed."

I expected Jerry to say something, anything, like "Sorry, guys. Guess Tom and I fucked up." But no, Jerry didn't say a thing. He just sat there looking like the dumbshit that he was. God damn it, I was pissed! That fuck-up just shouldn't have happened, not with two experienced detectives. What were they thinking!

"C'mon, Tina. Let's get outta here." Shaking my head, I reached over, took hold of her hand, and led her out of the Narcotics office. Fuck this bullshit! We drove back to my home in Mountlake Terrace. I was still pissed.

I didn't feel safe spending the weekend at my place. Tina and I had now had our covers blown. Bobby knew that I was a cop, he knew that Tina had set him up, and he knew that he was gonna be arrested soon and, most likely, jailed for a long time. No telling what he was likely to do or have someone else do for him as payback.

"Tina, you know what? Hell with it! What do you say we take off for the weekend and get us a room up at Snoqualmie Falls. I'll use city money to pay for the room and meals. Fuck them. Jerry and Tom owe us big time! First the city fucked up my six months-worth of work on the Meth Lab Caper, and now these two dumbshit detectives fuck up and get our cover blown."

"You serious, Johnny? You mean we can spend the weekend at Snoqualmie Falls Lodge?"

"Hell, yes, hon. I'm serious!"

Tina slid over closer to me and held me tight.

"Hey, Johnny. You're OK. You're a good person and I'm happy being here with you. I feel safe when I'm with you."

Driving off into the night, I headed out on I-90 towards Snoqualmie Falls. It was an easy 30-minute drive with hardly any traffic. We listened to the music on the radio. We were both quiet.

I liked working undercover. It was fun and exciting. Undercover assignments were always about living on the edge, about walking the razor's edge and then jumping off. It was dangerous work, maybe, but I never really thought about the danger. Danger was what made life exciting. Never knowing what was going to happen next, always worried about getting made and never knowing what would happen if I did. At work, my adrenalin was usually turned up high, but eventually, there'd be a crash that sometimes lasted for days.

It was like a roller coaster ride; lots of highs, lots of lows, lots of thrills, lots of twists and turns. And then you needed to stop and get off the roller coaster or you'd be certain to crash. Now, my body, my mind, and my spirit needed some peace and quiet. As much as I loved the job, I sometimes needed to get totally away from the constant stress and danger. This was one of those times.

"Tina, you ever been to Snoqualmie Falls before?"

"No, Johnny. I've heard of it, but I've never been there."

"Good. Guess what? You're in for a treat!"

We finally pulled into the parking lot of Snoqualmie Falls Lodge.

"You know, Tina, it's too dark right now to see the falls. Let's just go check in and see if we can get ourselves one of them luxury suites."

"Johnny, won't that cost a lot?"

"Tina, not to worry. I told you the City of Seattle was treating us to a weekend of total relaxation. No Bobbie C. to worry about, no drug deals to make, no dip-shit detectives to screw us up; nothing! Just you and me relaxing in total style and comfort, far away from the bullshit of the SPD and the Narcotics Section. The hell with Detectives Jerry and Tom. From now on every time they screw us over, I'll make them pay for it one way or another. Believe me, I will. I'm tired of their fuck-ups, tired of their bullshit, tired of them putting us in danger like they did. Damn it, it could have turned out real bad for us."

Tina and I entered the lobby of the lodge and went up to the desk to check in. I realized that we weren't exactly dressed properly for such a classy establishment. I identified myself as a Seattle police officer to the young lady behind the desk and politely asked to speak with the night manager. A few minutes later, a well-dressed gentleman with a genuine smile on his face approached us and introduced himself.

"Good evening, Officer. How may I be of service?" I quietly flashed my detective's badge and informed him that we wished to apologize for not being dressed more presentably. I went on to explain that my partner Tina and I had been involved in an undercover assignment for several months, and due to the stress of undercover work, we needed to get away for a quiet weekend. I assured the manager that there would not be any danger to the lodge because of my partner and I being there.

The manager thanked me for explaining and said that he wasn't concerned about any potential problems and that he totally understood. He went on to say that he had several friends and acquaintances in the SPD, who also occasionally stayed at the lodge for the exact same reason.

"Detective Lau, I totally understand how stressful police work can be, let alone undercover work. You and Tina are both welcome to enjoy a quiet and relaxing weekend with us here at Snoqualmie Lodge."

That said, he went behind the front desk to check us in personally.

"Detective Lau, how about if I upgrade you and Tina to one of out best suites? It overlooks the falls. In fact, you'll be pretty close to the edge of the falls. It's quite a breath-taking view. I'll also give you a VIP discount on top of that."

"Thank you, sir. That's very kind of you. However, our weekend here is being paid for by the City of Seattle. Tina and I recently received a nice bonus for taking down a methamphetamine lab. I worked on that assignment for over six months."

The manager was all ears as I related to him some of the details of the undercover meth lab investigation, like how I continued working undercover while on crutches after I broke my leg in a motorcycle accident. (However, I didn't reveal the fact that the accident was due to my stupidity in not knowing how to ride a chopper.)

Check-in information filled out, I put the room charge on my personal credit card. I'd reimburse myself once I got Tina paid for introducing me to Bobby C. and being with me throughout the hash oil buy. I'd also tack on extra money for Tina and me getting burned, due to the stupidity of Detectives Jerry and Tom. I'd put in for $500 for Tina introducing me to Bobby C. and an extra $300 for Tina and me getting burned. $800 total—that sounded fair for what we'd gone through. The $300 would be more than enough to cover our weekend getaway of lust and relaxation.

Our weekend at the lodge was superb. The suite was luxury beyond words, the view of the falls was breathtaking, the food was excellent, and the sex, well, it was orgasmic!

34

Bobby C.

Late Monday afternoon, Tina and I showed up at the Narcotics office. As we walked in, the first thing Jerry said was he wanted to know where we'd been all weekend.

"Bernie, I tried to phone you all weekend. Where were you?"

"Well, Jerry, I did have the weekend off, correct?"

"Well, yeah. I was just wondering where you guys were, that's all."

"Jerry, let's just say that we were out of town. Where we actually were isn't your concern. You got us made. Our cover got blown because you and your dumb partner Tom were so damn stupid! You put both our lives in danger. So because of that, me and Tina decided to get the hell out of Seattle. End of story. Like I said, where we ended up is none of your damn concern. Now let's get down to the business of getting Tina paid for introducing me to Bobby C. And by the way, I'm putting in a request for an extra $300 for the danger you and Tom put Tina in by getting her cover blown. You realize she can't work in Seattle any longer, don't you? We could have gone on to making a hell of a lot more hand-to-hand buys from dealers around 1st and Pike. There's a lot of dope being sold out there, but on account of you and Tom fucking up, we can't be out there working any more! Damn it, Jerry, what the fuck were you guys thinking?"

Well, Tina did get paid the $500 for introducing me to Bobby C. The $500 came from city funds and the extra $300 that I demanded came from federal funds.

There was no problem getting Sgt. Bert to approve and sign off on the payment to Tina. Sgt. Bert had learned of Jerry and Tom's screw-up and wasn't too happy about it.

Being my cover was most likely blown around 1st and Pike, Tina and I decided to work the Broadway area up on Capitol Hill. Lots of college kids there, lots of gays, meaning lots of methamphetamine and heroin activity.

Tina was still living in that run-down hotel next to the Public Market near 1st and Pike. I decided to let her stay at my place till it was time for her to leave Seattle. Living in the downtown area would in time get her killed, thanks to Bobby C. No, make that thanks to the stupidity of Detectives Jerry and Tom. In the streets of Seattle, a known snitch would soon be a dead snitch.

Being as Tina didn't have any personal belongings left at the hotel, there was no reason to go back, so I drove home with her after I got off shift. Prior to leaving for work the next afternoon, I gave her a quick lesson in the firing of my 12-gauge double-barrel sawed-off shotgun.

"Tina, all you need to do is point the shotgun in the general direction of the asshole and pull both triggers. That's all you need to do. Don't wait or hesitate. Don't talk. Just point it and pull both triggers. Now, this is important, Tina. When the police show up, what you say is 'Officer, I feared for my life!' That's all you need to say. Don't say anything else! Just 'Officer, I feared for my life.' So I shot the motherfucker!"

Back in the Narcotics office, Jerry was waiting.

"So Jerry, what we gonna do about Bobby? We gonna bust him or what?"

"Yeah, that's what I wanted to talk to you about. Seems Bobby moved out of his apartment up on Pine. He's not there any more. Me and Tom went up there this morning with an arrest warrant. Had the building manager let us into his unit. Bobby's moved out. All his personal things were gone."

"How about his wife's place up on Latona, that house just east of the 45th Exit on I-5?"

"Yeah, right. I got the address somewhere in my old case file from when we busted him. I'll look it up. Sorry about the screw up, Bernie."

"Yeah, OK. But apologize to Tina too. You got her real scared over that. I had to babysit her all weekend, you know, and I'm billing the city for it. Wasn't cheap to hide her out."

"Sorry, Bernie."

"OK. So say Bobby moved back into his wife's house," I said. "There's a good chance he stashed his dope there. He'd never get rid of it. Him moving back there gives us probable cause to get a search warrant and allows us to conduct a search for dope. If he's there, we bust him. If not, we work his wife to find him. She'll give him up."

We went over to the courthouse and found a judge. I raised my right hand and swore that the information listed in the search warrant was true to the best of my knowledge. We also got a probation violation warrant on Bobby signed by his probation officer, so he wouldn't be able to make bail. We then went to the parking garage, and Jerry checked out a Dodge, your basic plain clothes police vehicle, to serve the warrant. On the way we requested a uniformed officer's presence, which eliminated any potential problems due to us not being in uniform. We drove to within a few blocks of the address on file and waited in our undercover vehicle.

Ten minutes passed. A marked police unit pulled up in back of us and a uniformed officer got out and came over. The officer greeted us, "Hi, guys. So what's up? Hey, Bernie, is that you?"

"Hi, Dale. Yeah, it's me! Your old partner."

"Damn, Bernie, you look worse every time I see you. You look like a total dirt-bag asshole, now!"

"Thanks for the compliment, Dale!" It was Officer Dale Eggers from back when I was working vice.

"OK, Dale, two blocks down, large white house on the right. We got a VUSCA (Violation of the Uniform Substance Control Act) arrest warrant for a Bobby C. I bought hash oil from him twice last month, and now we're going to arrest his ass and lock him up. That's his wife's house; I don't think she knows he's back to dealing drugs. After we arrest him, you take Bobby into custody and transport him downtown, OK?"

"My pleasure, Bernie!"

Jerry and I drove down another block and parked. Eggers pulled up behind us. The three of us got out of our vehicles and walked towards the house.

"Dale, how about you go round the back of the house, just in case Bobby decides to run. He's not going to want to go to jail. He's already on probation."

"OK, Bernie. I'll get the back."

Jerry and I approached the house. Jerry knocked. A minute went by. Jerry knocked again, harder this time. The front door opened and an attractive young female stood in the doorway and said; "Can I help you?" Jerry and I displayed our police IDs and asked if Bobby was at home.

"Ah, yes, he is, Officers. May I ask what this is all about?"

"Yes, ma'am. We have an arrest warrant for Bobby."

"Arrest for what? What did Bobby do?" She turned her head and called out, "Bobby, there's two police officers here wanting to talk to you ... Bobby, I said some officers want to talk to you!"

Bobby came to the door, saw Jerry and me and turned pale. Jerry stepped up and informed Bobby that he was under arrest on a narcotics violation warrant and also on a parole violation warrant.

Meanwhile, Eggers came around to the front of the residence. Detective Jerry addressed Eggers, "Officer, this here is Bobby C. We have an arrest warrant for him. Would you kindly cuff him and give him his Miranda rights?" Eggers approached Bobby, had him turn around, placed the cuffs on him, then patted him down for weapons or contraband.

"OK, Bernie. He's clean." Eggers then faced Bobby and read him his Miranda rights.

"Bobby C., you have the right to remain silent. Anything you say can and will be used against you in a court of law. You have the right to an attorney at this time and to have him present before making any statements or answering any questions. If you cannot afford an attorney, one will be appointed for you in a court of law. Bobby, do you fully understand your Miranda rights that I just read you?" Bobby looked away. "Yeah, I understand!"

Bobby's wife started to sob. "Bobby, what've you done now? You promised me you weren't going to deal drugs any more! Bobby, why? Why are you doing this to me? You promised!" Bobby just stood there, not saying a word.

We had Bobby's wife sit in the living room as Eggers started writing up an arrest report. Jerry and I took Bobby outside and Jerry said; "We're gonna search her house from top to bottom, and when we find your dope, and we know you've got dope stashed in there, we're gonna arrest your wife and throw her in the slammer."

"She's got nothing to do with it."

"Your call. You got exactly one minute to come up with the answer."

"What's the question?"

"Where did you stash the dope?"

"It's in the bathroom, up in the ceiling. Just move the ceiling tile over. You'll see it."

"What kind of dope and how much?"

"About an ounce of hash oil and a half-kilo of weed—good weed."

"Is that all there is, Bobby? You telling us the truth?"

"I'm telling you the truth, that's all of it. I swear that's all."

Jerry said to Eggers: "Here's the warrant number for your report. Take him down and book him. I'll radio a case number when you get there."

Without further ado, Bobby was whisked away.

Jerry and I went back into the house. "Ma'am, Bobby told us that you weren't involved and that you didn't know anything about the drugs. So you don't have to worry."

"Officer, I'm sorry about all this. I really thought Bobby had stopped dealing drugs. After his arrest, he promised me that he'd stop. I guess he lied."

"Yes, Ma'am, he's still selling drugs."

Jerry stood on a foot stool located in the bathroom. Directly over the sink he lifted one of the ceiling tiles and reached up and around.

"Here it is." He retrieved a small blue tote bag, brought it out to the living room and opened it up.

"Just like he said. Hash oil and marijuana and some money too." We counted the money. A total of $1,473.

"Funny. Bobby didn't mention this money to us. Well, no matter, it's not his any more."

"Jerry, I just got an idea. How about we turn the money over to Bobby's wife? What do you think? Have her count it out once again and then sign for it. Think that would truly piss Bobby off?"

"Bernie, I like that idea. Yeah, let's do it!" Jerry motioned to Bobby's wife to come over.

"Ma'am, we're sorry about all this, but Bobby sold hash oil to Detective Lau here, not once, but twice. He's also presently on probation from that drug bust last year. He's probably going away for three to five years. Now, we have all this cash here, almost $1,500 total. We have every legal right to confiscate the money, but Detective Lau here, suggested we have you sign a receipt and turn the money over to you. After all, you're still legally married to Bobby, so we figured you're entitled to whatever money he had."

Bobby's wife was speechless for a brief moment.

"Officers, can you do that? I mean can you really turn all that money over to me?"

I answered, "Yes, ma'am, we can do that. If we place the money into evidence, it'll just end up in some city funds. It won't do the Narcotics Section any good. I say turn the money over to you. Bobby's taken advantage of you and lied to you long enough."

Bobby's wife grinned a little, "Officers, you know what? I'm going to use that money to hire me a lawyer and divorce Bobby's lying ass, pardon my use of words!"

That said, I had Bobby's wife count out the total, $1,473, and sign a receipt.

"Thank you, Officers. I'm finished with that jerk. He's been nothing but trouble since we got married. My parents tried to warn me, but you know how it is when you're in love."

Jerry and I drove back to the Narcotics office, where we wrote up our arrest incident report, placed Bobby's confiscated drugs into evidence, and called it a night.

Usually after being booked, a subject is interviewed by a detective within hours. We decided to let Bobby stew in jail over the weekend. We knew his wife wasn't going to bail him out. We'd remind him what being locked up feels like.

It was around 6:00 P.M. when I finally got back home. Tina was happy to see me.

"So Johnny, how'd everything go? Did you find Bobby? Is he in jail?"

"Yeah, Tina. He's sitting in jail, and he's going to be sitting there for a long, long time. He ain't going nowhere! We got his dope, and we also got all his cash, almost $1,500, which we turned over to his wife. That'll really piss him off! Come Monday afternoon, Jerry and me are going to try to turn him. I want his marijuana connection. Tina, can you just imagine if I somehow ended up getting two or three kilos of Canadian weed from his main man? That'd be something wouldn't it? Say, I'm starved. How 'bout I shower and then we hop on over to Stewart Anderson's in Lynnwood and have us some prime rib?"

"Well Johnny, is the city paying again?"

"But of course. Need you ask?"

35

Tea Party

Late Monday afternoon, Detective Jerry and I made our way to the county jail to interview Bobby C. We were buzzed into a holding area, where we put our firearms in a locked box. Next, we were buzzed into the actual jail area. I filled out an inmate request slip listing Bobby's full name and booking number and handed it to the jail officer. We waited for about ten minutes before the jail officer reappeared with Bobby in tow.

Bobby wasn't really all that pleased to see us.

We took him to one of the interview rooms and shut the door. Then we all sat down.

"OK, Bobby, we found the drugs and money right where you said we would. It's all in evidence. You had quite a bit of dope and money there."

"When can I get the money back? I need it for lawyers."

"Sorry, Bobby, it's been confiscated. (We'd decided it might be better not to tell him that we'd given it to his wife.)

"So what you guys want now? You already got me. You got all my dope and the money!"

I spoke up; "Yes, Bobby, we do. But you got that Canadian connection, and we want him!"

"Fuck you guys. I ain't no damn rat. Fuck you, no way! I ain't got shit to say to you. Now, leave me the fuck alone, both of you! I ain't telling you shit!"

"Well, Bobby, that's not how it works. You're just a small fry, a nobody. We can make your next five to ten easy or a living hell. You violated the terms of your probation by going back to dealing drugs. That probation violation alone is going to get you three years. There's no way around it. You also sold hash oil to Detective Lau here. He made two hand-to-hand buys from you, and there's no way you'll be able to beat that in court. You sold dope to a cop, Bobby. You got no defense. You're screwed!"

"Yeah, I may be screwed, but I spotted you and that other dumb-ass detective partner of yours, sitting in the lobby of my apartment, didn't I? Damn, how dumb can you guys be? And you call yourselves 'Seattle's finest.' I'd sure hate to see 'Seattle's dumbest.'"

Jerry said, "Shut the fuck up, asshole. Yeah, you spotted us, but you're the one in jail, not me. So now who's the dumbshit?"

Bobby didn't respond, so I continued; "Bobby, you're going to give up your guy. Not only that, you're also going to introduce me to him, and after that I'm going to buy a few kilos from him, and then I'm going to bust him, just like I did you."

Bobby snickered, "Dream on, Detective. No fucking way; you're crazy if you think I'm going to give you the name of my connection and then introduce you so that you can bust him. There ain't no way in hell I'm doing that! No fucking way!"

I continued, "OK, Bobby, you just listen up and pay attention to what I'm about to tell you. Don't say a word, just listen. We got you on a probation violation, that's a definite three years. I got two hand-to-hand buys from you. Then we got you for possession of a dozen vials of that hash oil, plus that large baggie of marijuana. Then we got you with all that cash. All that cash and the amount of drugs you had in that blue tote bag qualifies you as a mid-level drug dealer. That's five to ten years, plus three years on that probation violation. You could end up doing close to 13 years. And another thing, Bobby, after you get sentenced and locked up in Walla Walla[1], I'm gonna put out a snitch jacket on you. You'll be killed within the first six months, Bobby, and that's after you get raped for being a snitch. You won't last a year!"

About then Bobby was looking real troubled and uneasy, "You wouldn't do that to me, would you?"

"Bobby, I want the name of your guy and an introduction. You got three minutes to make up your mind; three minutes. After that, no deal! What's left of your future is entirely up to you."

I looked at my watch, "Clock starts ticking now, Bobby!"

Poor Bobby. He was a cornered rat. He had nowhere to run to. He was trapped and he knew it. I had him! I knew he was going to give up his guy. I could see it in his face; there was no doubt in my mind.

"One minute, Bobby. You got one minute left. After that, no deal!"

"15 seconds, Bobby. Ten seconds, nine, eight, seven, six, five, four, three, two ... "

"OK, OK. His name is Juddestin. Juddestin Maya. He hangs out at the City Zoo on Eastlake."

"Now, that wasn't so difficult, was it, Bobby?"

I looked over at Detective Jerry, and we both smiled.

Thursday, 9:00 P.M. Detective Jerry, myself, and Bobby C. found ourselves at Denny's Restaurant, located several blocks north of the City Zoo tavern.

I started in: "OK, Bobby, tell me once more about this guy of yours."

"Yeah, OK. Like I said, his name is Juddestin Maya. He's part American Indian, don't know what tribe, he's about 23 years old, 5'10", maybe 150 lbs. Real nice, mellow guy, easy to get along with. You know, Johnny, I've been good friends with this guy for a long time. Do I really have to do this? I mean, sure he sells dope, but he's really a nice guy, not some asshole. He never hurt anyone. Isn't there some other way we could do this?"

"No, Bobby, there ain't no other way. You made the decision to cooperate and save your own ass, so stop wasting my time and let's get on with this."

"Well, like I told you before, he hangs out at the City Zoo. He's there every night. Usually comes in around ten."

"OK, tell me again where he gets his dope; this supposedly high-quality Canadian marijuana."

"The dope comes in from Canada. Some guy flies over the Canadian border into Washington State in a Piper Cub and drops the marijuana in some vacant field near a glider airstrip up towards Issaquah. The way it works is Judd camps out for a few days up in that area in his camper, and if everything looks cool, he makes a phone call, and the next evening the Piper Cub flies over and the weed gets thrown out in duffel bags. Slick operation. He's been doing it for two years now, and never had a problem. He gets about two loads dropped a month, usually 1-200 lbs. of weed per load."

"Where does he stash the weed?"

"That I don't know. I never asked him and he never said. Not the kind of thing you ask a dope dealer. All I know is that I can order any amount from one to 50 kilos if I got the cash. It's never been a problem. I've ordered 15 kilos in the past."

I looked over at Jerry.

"Bobby, did I hear you say up to 50 kilos? That's 110 pounds of marijuana. Are you certain about this?"

"Yeah. I ain't lying to you. Judd said he can deliver any amount as long as I got the cash."

My head was spinning. Damn! 50 kilos, 100-plus pounds of prime weed! That'd be some arrest. The "Mother Load," as we called it! But the way things had been going for me, I was doubtful. No way this kid could have 50 kilos of prime Canadian marijuana on hand ... or was my luck about to change?

---

[1] Washington State Penitentiary

Detective Jerry spoke up, "OK, Bobby, here's the deal. You and Detective Lau show up at the City Zoo tonight, say around a quarter to ten. Have a couple of beers, shoot some pool, relax, play darts, or whatever. Look at chicks' asses, for all I care. Later on, if Juddestin is in there like you say, I want you to introduce 'Johnny' to Juddestin. Mention that Johnny here is interested in getting a kilo of that Canadian weed. Tell Judd you've known Johnny for a long time, etc., etc. Tell him whatever bullshit story you need to make up to gain his confidence. Don't push too hard. Just mention that Johnny's interested, sit back, and let Johnny take it from there."

At 10:50 P.M. Bobby and I entered the City Zoo tavern. It was crowded, but we found a table. The Zoo held five pool tables, all free before 5:00 P.M. After that, 50 cents till closing time. Lots of games: shuffleboard, couple of pinball machines, three dart boards, plus a lot of cigarette smoke and chicks, lots of chicks, in tight denim jeans, showing off their asses.

I ordered two Buds and threw down a ten. The waitress came back with the beers and left the change on the table. I didn't leave a tip. Bikers and assholes don't tip!

"Johnny, there's Judd over in the corner by himself."

Bobby looked over at Juddestin and raised a hand; Judd nodded in return. Me, I didn't look at Judd; I acted uninterested. I just focused on a gal's tiny ass as she shot pool with some low-life. What a great night! I was drinking a beer, looking over at some chick's tight ass, about to be introduced to a major marijuana dealer.

"Johnny, I'm going over and talk with Judd. That OK with you?"

"Yeah, OK. No problem. Just don't you rabbit on me. Don't you dare run, or I'll chase you down and fucking shoot you! And I ain't kidding! You'd be a fleeing felon, and I could empty my gun in your back, got it?"

Bobby said nothing. He got up, took his beer, and walked over to Judd's table. They sat there chatting.

Judd looked over at me every so often. I just sat at my table, drinking my beer, and ignored them. I acted like I couldn't care less about anything. About 15 minutes went by, then Bobby returned to our table.

"Ok, Johnny. I told Judd you were interested in getting a kilo of Canadian, and he said no problem. Just asked if you were cool and if you had the money. C'mon, he wants to meet you."

I took in a deep breath, let it out slowly, and finished my beer. I didn't want to seem too anxious. I stood up, walked over to Judd's table, and nodded a greeting.

"How you doing? I'm Johnny."

"Hi, I'm Judd. Have a seat."

I sat and ordered a pitcher of beer for the three of us. Judd started the conversation; "So, Johnny, Bobby here tells me you're interested in 'Canadian.' How much you looking to get?"

"Yeah, I'm interested. That is, if it's as good as Bobby says it is. Let's say '2.2'[2] to start with. If the quality's what you say it is, who knows, I might order up 10 or 20 kilos next week."

"You won't be disappointed, Johnny; I guarantee it. Canadian's the best weed around. Trust me, there ain't anything better anywhere! So, OK, Johnny, when and where? How you want to do this?"

"Well, Judd, how bout tomorrow afternoon, say around two? That OK with you?"

"Yeah, sure, no problem. I'm available 24 hours a day, seven days a week. And I don't take weekends off!"

"One thing, though, Judd. I got this biker buddy of mine who's putting up half the cash. OK with you if he comes along with me? He won't front his bucks."

"Not a problem, Johnny. As long as you say he's cool. It's fine with me."

Bobby, Judd, and I drank our beers and made small talk for the next half hour.

"Well, Judd, I gotta run. My old lady's got some hot, wet pussy just waiting for me to munch on. (We all laughed.) So see you around two tomorrow."

---

[2] 2.2 lbs. = 1 kilogram.

"Yeah, 2 P.M. tomorrow. See ya. Thanks for the beer."

Bobby and I left the tavern and drove off to Chinatown to meet up with Detective Jerry at Sun Ya Restaurant. As we walked in, we spotted Jerry sitting in the last booth.

"So, how'd it go, guys?"

"Real good. I met Judd and everything's cool. I'm supposed to meet him again tomorrow at 2:00 P.M. to pick up a kilo of that Canadian weed."

"It went that smooth, Bernie?"

"Yeah, Jerry, not a problem. Judd's a nice kid, just like Bobby said. He didn't ask any questions about how long I'd known Bobby or anything like that. I guess he really trusts Bobby here. Jerry, I'm going to order. Bobby, order what you want."

"Yeah, thanks. Can I have a beer too?"

"Sure, Bobby, have two, for all I care."

Chinese meal over with, and Bobby finished with his beer, Jerry and Bobby headed out. Detective Jerry had Bobby to re-book.

I called out; "By the way, thanks, Bobby. I'll be in touch."

Bobby looked over his shoulder as he exited the Sun Ya. He didn't answer. Talk about "The Last Supper!" Poor guy. He'd soon be doing time in Walla Walla for at least the next four years. That's a long time to do just for selling "Johnny Medeiros" those two vials of hash oil. A very long time.

Before our Sun Ya dinner was finished, I'd asked Bobby if he'd informed anyone about me being a cop or Tina being an informant. Bobby had shook his head.

"No, Johnny, I never told nobody. Yeah, I was fucking pissed when I realized that Tina'd set me up, but I figured it was really my fault for going back to selling drugs even though I was on probation. It was my mistake. And Tina's a good kid. I didn't want to see her get hurt."

Friday afternoon, 2:10 P.M. Detective Dan and I drove up to the City Zoo. As we walked in, I spotted Juddestin sitting at the same table as the night before.

"Have a seat, Johnny. Who's your friend?"

"This here's 'Dirty Dan.' Just another biker-trash friend of mine."

Dan nodded towards Juddestin and took a seat at the table. Juddestin nodded back and said "Hi!"

I went over to the bar, bought three Buds, and returned to the table. Judd started the conversation.

"Nice day, eh, Johnny? You ready to go for a drive?"

"Sure. Where to?"

"Oh, just out of town a bit. Say, about 40 miles or so. You got enough gas in your car?"

"Yeah, at least half a tank."

"Good. That should be enough."

"Where we going, Judd?"

"You'll see. I don't like doing business here in town. I know for a fact that Seattle cops can't arrest you once you're outside of the Seattle city limits, so I do all my business out of town. I never sell drugs in Seattle. Gotta be safe, you know! Finish your beer and we'll be off."

Beers finished, Dan and I followed Judd out of the tavern. Judd pointed out a yellow Dodge Ram Truck that had a trailer hitched up to it. The truck was parked just a half block down the street. Dan and I hopped into our undercover GTO, followed Judd out of Seattle via I-5, then turned left onto I-90 and headed east towards Snoqualmie Falls.

Damn, here we were again. Months ago, Seth Donaldson made me follow him east on I-90 to his secret location during the Meth Lab Caper. Donaldson had also believed that Seattle cops couldn't make arrests outside of the Seattle city limits. Now this dummy, Juddestin, who I'd met just yesterday, was making me follow him out of town, way out of town, because he knew "for a fact" that Seattle cops couldn't make arrests outside the city limits. Where'd these guys get their information?

Prior to Dan and me meeting up with Judd, Sgt. Bert had been assigned to be our surveillance during this marijuana kilo buy. Dan, Sgt. Bert, and I'd figured that this would be just another normal drug buy. I'd expected that we'd meet Judd at the City Zoo, have a beer or two, then step outside the tavern and follow him out to his vehicle, where the buy would take place. I'd give Judd the the money, he'd hand me the kilo, then go back into the tavern. Dan and I'd drive back to the Narcotics office with the kilo and write up our report. No big deal.

But now here we were once again headed east on I-90 way out of town. I just hoped that Sgt. Bert would be able to follow us. Neither Dan nor I had a portable radio, so we had no way to communicate with the sergeant. Undercovers don't usually carry radios, not when we're meeting with the bad guys. Never know; they might have wanted to search our vehicles. It had happened in the past.

20 minutes went by. We were still headed east on I-90. Finally, we passed the Fall City limits. Judd made a right turn and exited off the interstate onto a dirt road. We followed him for a mile and a half on this dirt road that seemed to lead nowhere. Suddenly, he pulled off to the left and parked in a large clearing. He seemed to know the spot well. Getting out of his truck, he yelled over at Dan and me, "OK, guys, this is it."

I figured Judd probably had the dope hidden somewhere out there. Way out, far away from the long arm of the law. Far away from the arresting power of the SPD. Well, he got one thing right: this location was, sure enough, way out there.

Next thing Judd did was he went to the back of his trailer and started cranking it up. Surprisingly the trailer that he'd been pulling turned into a camper. Five minutes later, it was fully erect and looked very nice. Judd walked to the front right of the vehicle, opened a canvas door, and invited Dan and me inside. I entered and couldn't believe my eyes. It had walls with pine board paneling. There was a large bench to the right, and the interior was like a small room. It certainly didn't look like any camper I'd ever been in. It was totally first-class.

Judd invited Dan and me to sit on the bench and informed us that he didn't like to rush business. He went on to say that he was going to boil some water and asked Dan and me if we'd rather have tea or coffee. Dan and I looked at each other and smiled, "Tea, please."

Tea or coffee. Was this guy for real? But, yes, Judd was indeed heating up a pot of water on his small butane stove and, as the water heated up, he took fancy cups and saucers out of nearby storage cupboards. Then he brought out an unopened package of cookies.

Picture this: in our undercover roles, Dan and I were supposed to be two bad-ass biker dudes. We were dressed like bikers with boots and leather jackets. We had knives tucked in our belts, our beards were unkempt, our shoulder-length hair looked like it hadn't been washed in weeks, and we smelled! But there we were, sitting in a nice camper parked in the middle of nowhere far away from civilization with this young, dumb-ass kid drug dealer who was throwing us a tea party before getting down to the business of selling us a kilo of weed. You just can't make this shit up.

Judd served us our tea. I raised my cup by its dainty little handle to salute his sentiments. "Cheerios," said Dan, trying to get into the moment. We sat around for 15 minutes or so, drinking tea out of fine china, munching on gourmet cookies like a trio of English queens. It was really quite lovely, the fresh air, the smell of the pines, the absolute quiet.

Finally, Dan looked over at Judd, "Hey, dude, thanks for the tea and cookies, but tea time's over with. I'm here to buy dope. I ain't got all fucking day for this stupid shit! So now where's the weed?"

Judd replied, "OK, OK," then reached into a small tool box, took out a Phillips screw driver, and asked Dan and me to get off the bench. He then proceeded to unscrew the half-dozen or so screws that held down the top board. Several minutes later, Judd had removed the top board and laid it aside. He then reached into the bench and brought out a kilo of marijuana. That's right; all that time Dan and me had been sitting directly over Judd's stash of marijuana.

I took the kilo of marijuana from Judd and let Dan have a look at it. Dan leaned over and looked into the bench compartment. Then, out of the blue, he reached behind his back and pulled out his automatic pistol as he yelled at the top of his lungs:

"Police Officer. Down! Get the fuck down! Both of you! Don't move or I'll fucking shoot the both of you!"

Had I heard right? Did Dan just say "both of you?" I dropped quickly and lay face-down, as did Juddestin. We were both in shock! Juddestin because he just got his ass busted, and me because I had absolutely no idea that Dan was going to do that. The plan was for Dan and me to buy a kilo from Judd, leave, and then at some later date, try to set up a larger buy.

You see, in working undercover, a dealer who doesn't know you or just met you isn't going to sell you 10 or 20 kilos the first time. No way. I'd just met Juddestin the day before, not even 24 hours ago, and I was actually surprised that he was willing to sell me a kilo that easily.

Usually the dealer would sell you a "lid" or a baggie of marijuana to start with, but never a whole kilo. If a dealer sold a small amount of weed to someone he didn't know and somehow got busted, it wasn't that big a deal. The guy would most likely just get a small fine and maybe probation. But if a dealer got busted for selling a kilo of marijuana, well, that was a different story. That would be jail time for certain.

Judd and I were face down in the camper. Dan reached to the small of my back and removed my firearm. Just then, Sgt. Bert pulled up alongside, came over, and helped Dan put the handcuffs on us. I still didn't know why Dan decided to make the arrest instead of getting the kilo and leaving like we'd planned.

Judd was taken outside and placed face down on the ground with Sgt. Bert watching over him. Dan said, "Hey, Bernie, stand up. I want to show you something." Dan reached over and removed my cuffs.

"Look into the bench compartment." he said.

"Yeah, OK." I looked in.

Kilo brick upon kilo brick of marijuana were packed tightly together in the compartment. I couldn't believe what I was looking at. We started removing the kilo bricks one by one and laying them on the camper floor. All total there were 45 bricks of prime-grade Canadian marijuana. That and several large shopping bags of broken-up bricks of marijuana.

Looking back, I'd worked six months trying to take down a meth lab that ended up getting shut down too early due to "overtime pay concerns." Then I got made as an undercover cop because two dumb detectives screwed up their surveillance. Then yesterday evening I'd met Juddestin Maya at the City Zoo tavern, and just 17 hours later, Judd was busted, and we seized 108 pounds of high-grade marijuana. We also seized Judd's Ford Ranger pickup truck and his very nice camper-trailer along with his tea and cookies. Sometimes you get lucky!

Sgt. Bert placed Juddestin Maya, still handcuffed, in the back of his vehicle and drove back to Seattle to book him on sale and possession of marijuana. Detective Dan and I stayed behind to "process the crime scene." The 45 bricks of marijuana were logged in our police report and then placed into the trunk of the undercover GTO. Dan drove the GTO, following me, while I drove Juddestin's pickup truck and camper-trailer. He followed me to the Seattle Police Impound Lot located at Charles Street just four blocks south of the police department, where the pickup truck and camper-trailer were logged in with the duty evidence officer on site.

That done, I jumped into the GTO and Dan drove us to the 4th Floor of the Seattle Police Parking Garage, the same floor where the Police Evidence Property Room is located. Once the 45-plus bricks of marijuana were properly stored and entered into the log book of the Property Room, Dan and I took a few moments to have our pictures taken with the "Mother Load." Then we returned to the Narcotics office to finish up our paperwork.

But that would have to wait till tomorrow. Now it was time to celebrate a job well done. Sgt. Bert, having finished booking Juddestin, had returned to the office. Also present were Detectives Jerry, Tom, and three or four others. Booze was brought out of personal lockers, and it began to flow freely. A toast was proposed to Juddestin Maya for without his being an idiot, we wouldn't have been there celebrating. Next was a toast to me for talking Judd into selling me a kilo of marijuana. Next, we toasted Detective Dan. Then came a toast to Sgt. Bert for his part in the caper. And last but not least, we toasted Bobby C.

It was a great evening. We were all in good spirits for we'd just taken down a multi-kilo marijuana dealer who nobody in the Narcotics office had even known existed. Before that bust it was very rare for narcotics detectives to ever come across a kilo brick of marijuana. And here, after just 16 hours of good undercover work, we'd confiscated over 45 bricks—108 pounds of marijuana. My wish would soon come true; I'd receive an official letter of commendation, signed by the chief of police. "You done good Bernie!"

The celebration had finally quieted down, and we were all just sitting around chatting about various narcotics cases that we'd been involved in at one time or other. There were many strange stories involving past cases; some funny, some not so. I was sitting on top of my desk just kicking back and relaxing. It had been a good day, and I was feeling great.

All of a sudden Detective Dan walked up and, standing not three feet from me, started yelling at me and cussing me out; "Bernie, you're a fucking asshole!" Then he reached around to the small of his back, brought out a revolver, and shot me point blank in the chest. Bam-bam-bam-bam-bam-bam! As I felt the six rounds thump into my chest. I flew back, head-over-heels, and onto the floor. I lay sprawled out next to my desk clutching my chest. I couldn't focus; my mind was racing. Why? Why had Dan shot me? I had a difficult time breathing. I just lay there unable to move. I was going to die.

There was total silence, and then all of a sudden, I heard laughter. Everyone in the office was laughing. Dan came over, offered me his hand, and helped me to my feet.

"How you doing there, Bernie? Here, have another drink."

I blinked in wonderment. Dan had shot me six times, but lucky for me, the gun had been loaded with blanks![3] After I'd finally composed myself, I joined in with the hysterical laughter. What a rush!

---

[3] Blanks sound and react like live rounds. Flame and wadding shoot out from the gun barrel exactly like a live round, only there's no bullet, just gun powder and wadding. The wadding hurts a little.

Cops have the best dope!

36

Johnny Rotten

A new informant had recently been assigned to me. "Tony" was his name, but he preferred to be called "T."

T was a light-skinned black male around 6' tall in his early 20s. The reason T wanted to become a paid informant soon became apparent. He was highly insecure and needed to feel like he was "important." T was in reality a "wannabe pimp" and dressed accordingly. The green-colored wide-brim hat he always wore matched his greenish jacket, vest, and bell-bottom trousers, which he accented with a pair of worn-out designer white-tip shoes. Yeah, T thought he was cool, all right. The only problem was T purchased all his clothes from Goodwill, a second-hand clothing outlet that catered to people with low-incomes or on welfare.

T wore that bright green outfit day in and day out. During the several months I worked with him, I never once saw him wear anything else, just that ridiculous green pimp-type outfit which made him look like a big black leprechaun. We'd joke around the Narcotics office, calling T a "leprecoon" (of course, never when he was present).

T constantly bragged that he personally knew all the big cocaine dealers in the CD and offered to introduce me to one of them. So I told him to go ahead and set up a meeting. I remember it being a cold, miserable, rainy Thursday afternoon. At 5:45 P.M., T and I entered the Cadillac Grill Restaurant located up on Madison Avenue and took a seat at a table towards the rear. Within minutes a short black male in his late 20s came over and sat at our table. T made the introductions; "Errol, this is my cousin 'Johnny.' Johnny, this is Errol, a good friend of mine."

Now T was black and I was white and here was T, introducing me as his cousin! But Errol never gave a second thought as to how I could be T's cousin. For the next half hour, we made small talk which eventually came around to the reason for this meet. Errol asked me how much cocaine I wanted to buy.

"I need a half-ounce, Errol."

"A half-ounce is gonna cost you $500. Johnny, tomorrow afternoon around four forty-five bring the $500 in a sealed, white envelope to where I work, the Public Defender's Office located at 3rd and James. You know where that's at? You'll see me sitting at my desk. Just walk in, put the envelope on my desk, then walk out. Six-thirty, tomorrow evening you can come by my place and pick up your half-ounce."

"OK if I bring along my girlfriend, Tina?"

"Sure, Johnny. OK with me!"

Friday afternoon while in the Narcotics office, I signed for the $500, placed the money in a white envelope as Errol had instructed, and got ready to make the cash delivery. At 4:35 P.M. I exited the Arctic Building, walked across the street to the S.W. corner of 3rd and James, and entered the Public Defender's Office. Errol was sitting at his desk next to a large window. I went over and placed the envelope on his desk. Errol looked up, said "Hi, Johnny. Here's my address," and handed me a slip of paper. Pocketing the piece of paper, I turned and exited the Public Defender's Office, crossed the street, and returned to the Narcotics office located on the 7th Floor of the Arctic Building.

Back in the office, I smiled at the surveillance detectives. "Well, guys, you see me go in?"

"Certainly did, Bernie. We witnessed you walk into the Public Defender's Office, saw you give Errol that white envelope, and watched you walk back. Damn, this is the easiest surveillance we've ever done!"

The detectives had only had to stand over by one of the windows in the Narcotics office in order to see me deliver the money to Errol. Unbelievable!

Later that evening, I picked up Tina and drove out to Errol's house, which was located on the shore of Lake Washington. There, we picked up the cocaine. Over the course of the next few weeks Tina and I made three more cocaine purchases from Errol. Three months later, an arrest warrant was issued for Errol Bates, charging him with four counts of delivery of a controlled substance, cocaine.

The case never went to court. Being he had worked as an aide in the Public Defender's Office and was well-known and liked throughout the court system, he was allowed to plead to one count of delivery of a controlled substance to a police officer and was given a six-month sentence to be served in the county jail. Errol, of course, lost his good-paying job.

Sunday morning, kicking back at home with Tina. Bobby C. had been charged. From what I understood, Bobby was pleading "No Contest." Basically he was saying that he'd most likely have been found guilty if his case had gone to trial. In return for the no-contest plea, the sentencing judge would probably give him a lighter sentence. Bobby might have to do three years in the State Penitentiary. Could have been a lot worse if he hadn't cooperated.

Juddestin Maya had also been taken down, resulting in a large seizure of 108 lbs. of marijuana plus the confiscation of his truck and camper-trailer.

Tina couldn't stick around any more; too dangerous. Danger aside, her cover was blown and she'd no longer be able to get us near any real dealers. She missed her kids and wanted to know if I could help get her back with them. I promised to get her out of town with some money, and back with her mom and kids.

"Tina, you done good work over the past eight months, and I gotta say that I'm very proud of you. Thanks, hon! No officer or detective in the history of the SPD has ever seized such a large amount of marijuana as we did in the Juddestin Maya case. No one. 45-plus kilos. Wow; that amounts to 108 lbs. The brass were certainly pleased, to say the least, and by the way, I did end up getting my letter of commendation, signed by the chief. Like I said, you done good, Tina."

"Johnny, there's one more guy I can get for you before I leave for Yakima. It should be an easy bust."

"Who's that?"

"'Johnny Rotten.' I met him when I first came to Seattle. Johnny was my methamphetamine connection for a short while. That is, until I decided to work with you guys. He deals meth out of a trailer that he's got parked out by Fall City. I think I can make a buy from him without any problem cause he likes me."

"Yeah, right. They all like you. He's, like, hoping to get in your panties, that's all!"

"Now, Johnny, don't you be getting jealous on me." Tina gave me a hug and a light kiss on the cheek.

"Well, Tina, if you can make a buy from this Johnny Rotten guy, then all we have to do after that is get a judge to sign the search warrant, then go kick his door in. No need trying to introduce me and all that. That's gonna take too long. You make the hand-to-hand buy, we get the warrant right after that, and then Johnny Rotten goes down. Could be another quick caper, just like with Judd. Probably won't take more than 24 hours from start to finish. Boy, that'd be great. Another asshole taken down, and another trailer confiscated! I'll run this by the guys at the office tomorrow. Shouldn't be any problem."

Monday morning Tina and I arrived at the Narcotics office. We sat down with Jerry, Tom, and Sgt. Bert and talked over the possibility of Tina making this buy from Johnny Rotten. It was decided that Tina and

I would drive past Johnny Rotten's trailer later that afternoon and see if he was camped out there. If he was still there, I'd have Tina walk up and try making a buy. Nothing big, just a gram or so. 80 bucks worth of meth would be enough to get our search warrant. Tina'd buy the dope, and I'd run a field test just to make certain that what she bought was in fact methamphetamine. If the test came out positive, that would give us probable cause to get a search warrant. I'd take a portable radio with me, so I could radio in as soon as Tina made the buy and I ran the test. That way Jerry could get going on the search warrant, and then meet Tina and me somewhere up in Fall City. No use Tina and me driving all the way back into Seattle once she made the buy. Hell, we could wrap this up in five or six hours.

We'd need to notify the Fall City Police that we were about to serve a Seattle police narcotics search warrant in their jurisdiction—standard protocol and professional courtesy. They'd do the same for us if they were ever about to make an arrest in Seattle. Kept everybody happy that way and information got shared.

As we exited the office, Detective Dan arrived. "Hey, Bernie, how you doing? Tina, thanks for all the work you've been doing. You've gotten us a lot of good cases lately. The whole squad appreciates it."

"Thanks Dan. Nice to hear that!"

"Tina, Bernie treating you OK?"

"No, Dan, he's mean to me. He gets me drunk, then ties me up and all that."

I looked at Tina and said, "Tina, quiet. Dan don't need to hear about our sex life."

Dan laughed, "Bernie, you sure you're not the one getting tied up by Tina?" Tina responded, "I wish!"

"Hey, Dan, you ever hear of a guy by the name of 'Johnny Rotten?'"

"Yeah, sure. Why?"

"Well, Tina used to buy meth from the guy occasionally. She suggested she try making a buy from him this afternoon. That is, if Johnny's still camped out in Fall City."

Dan laughed, "Come in for a minute, guys. I know this Johnny Rotten guy you're talking about."

Dan went to his desk, pulled out a file, and showed Tina a police mug shot.

"Here, Tina. This the guy you're talking about?"

"Yeah, Dan, that's him. That's Johnny Rotten alright."

"Well, Bernie, about a year and a half ago I had one of my informants make several meth buys from this guy out of his trailer. The judge signed a search warrant, and later that day, we went to serve the warrant. Just as we approached the trailer, Johnny spotted us and flushed the dope. Johnny's always wired on meth, always paranoid, constantly looking out his window every few minutes. Typical tweaker behavior. We did get a small amount of meth on him though. Seems Johnny forgot he had a few grams in his pocket. So yeah, we arrested Johnny Rotten, but because of the small amount of dope we found on him, the judge only gave him three months jail time with credit for time served. Johnny was out in no time."

"Tell you what, Bernie; if you're going to serve a search warrant today, let me know. You know what we can do? If we can get to his trailer when he's not home, I can disconnect his sewer line and put a fishing net on the end. That way if he flushes, we can still get the dope!"

"Damn, Dan, that's one hell of a great idea. Let's do it! You wanna drive up there with Tina and me after lunch? Tina's going to try to make a buy from him this afternoon."

"Yeah, Bernie, count me in. Meanwhile, I'll get the tools I'll be needing. The sewer line is made of plastic, so I can probably cut through it real easy with a hacksaw. Then I'll just tie the net over the end of the sewer line. Hey, man, I can hardly wait to see his face. Is he gonna be pissed!"

"OK, Dan, how about I come by and pick you up around one-thirty this afternoon? That give you enough time to get what you need?"

"Yeah, Bernie. All I need's a hacksaw, a small fishing net, some twine, and oh yeah, a pair of rubber gloves. That should do it."

Come one-thirty, Tina and I picked Dan up in front of the Arctic Building, and we headed east on I-90. Just before the Fall City city limits, I turned right onto a one-lane gravel road heading south. A half mile up the road, I spotted the trailer. It was the only one around.

I drove by slowly. No vehicle parked next to the trailer, no one seemed to be home. I drove several hundred yards past and pulled off the gravel road into some brush. No one would be able to see our vehicle from Johnny's trailer.

"OK, Dan, what do you think? Wanna try it?"

"Yeah, sure, Bernie. What have we got to lose? If he spots me, he spots me."

Dan got out of our vehicle and headed towards the trailer, taking his tools with him. It wasn't more than five minutes before he returned.

"Damn, Bernie, that was easy as hell. The pipe wasn't glued at all. I just sort of wiggled it apart, placed the fish net around one end, and reconnected it. Can't tell the net's there, if anyone should walk by. Being Johnny's not here, let's head on out to Fall City and grab us a burger or something before we start."

Approximately 45 minutes later, Dan, Tina, and I once again drove up towards Johnny's trailer. As we approached, I could see from some distance an old beater vehicle parked next to the trailer.

"How do we get you to the trailer?" I asked Tina.

"Last time a friend dropped me off, and I walked in from the road." She saw that I looked doubtful.

"Look, Johnny, he's a meth-head and probably using right now. That means he's horny as hell. I knock, he opens the door, and all he sees is tits and ass."

"So you think you can handle him?"

"Hell, yeah, Johnny. Not a problem!"

I handed Tina four twenty-dollar bills.

"Here you go, Tina; 80 bucks. Go see if he'll sell you a gram. Dan and me'll back into the brush and stay out of sight. If Johnny asks, just tell him you got a ride with some friends, and you told 'em not to drive up here. Sweet talk him. See if he'll give you a fat one![1] Don't let him keep you too long. Say your friends are waiting down the road, and if you don't return soon, they might come up looking for you."

"OK, Johnny. I won't be long."

Tina exited the GTO and walked up towards Johnny Rotten's trailer. She turned and waved.

"Quite an informant you got there, Bernie. She sure made us some good cases these past few months. The brass were sure happy with that last bust we made, that 45 kilos we got off Judd. Boy, what a dip-shit he was. There we were, looking like two asshole bikers, and he decides to throw us a tea party. Tea and cookies served in fancy cups and saucers! It always amazes me what weirdness some folks do."

"You know, Bernie, if we'd been real bikers, Judd would be dead by now. He'd have gotten two in the head, especially after letting us see all that dope he had hidden in that bench compartment. Dumb. Rule number one is you never, ever let anyone see where you hide your stash; that's just asking to get ripped off. And another thing; bringing us way up here in the woods, like he did. What a perfect place to off the motherfucker and take his dope. Shoot his ass, take all his clothes off, dump him in the brush and drive off with his truck and camper-trailer. No one would know. It would probably be months before anyone found bits and pieces of what was left of him. Most likely, his skull and maybe a rib or two."[2]

"Yeah, Judd was fucking lucky we were cops and not a couple of real biker assholes. Fuck, can you just imagine some real assholes spotting Judd's dope stash, like we did? Even if they weren't going to jack him to begin with, once they saw that huge amount of dope, no doubt in my mind, they'd kill him!"

---

[1] Putting in more than a gram for the price of one.

[2] Taking a person's clothing off after you kill him or her and then dumping the naked body makes it less likely for someone to spot any human remains. A human being's scattered bones are easily mistaken for animal bones, except, of course, the skull. Lots of hungry critters up there in the woods; wolves, coyotes, big-ass hungry bears, mountain lions, rodents. After a day or two, there wouldn't be much left of a corpse. And the bones get scattered for miles.

"OK, here she comes. Yup, she got it; she's smiling."

Tina got in the back of the vehicle.

"Got it, guys. One very fat gram and a half from what I can tell."

I put the GTO in reverse, backed up, and got the hell out of there. Tina handed Dan the small cellophane baggie containing the suspected meth.

"Damn, girl. Talk about a fat gram. Shit, he does have the hots for you, doesn't he?"

"Yeah, Johnny sure wanted me to stay and party with him. He was horny as hell. I could see the outline of his boner through his jeans. He started feeling me up, so I just joked around with him, teased him a bit, and then asked if maybe I could drop by tonight. I told him, "Tell you what, Johnny; if you save a couple grams, I'll come on by later tonight, then you and me can party all night long." Before I got out of there, I told him I'd suck his dick long and hard tonight if he put a little meth on the head. I also asked him if he'd mind if I brought my girlfriend along. He was going nuts listening to me talk that trash. I bet you he's getting himself off right about now! The guy could hardly talk when I left. Ha-ha. What was it you call that, Johnny; pussy something?"

"'Pussy power,' Tina. Good old pussy power! A gal can get anything she wants from any guy if she knows how to use it. Guys are so fucking dumb! Like Bobby. He only let me come up to his apartment cause he had the hots for you. Otherwise, no way he would have let me come up. Yeah, Bobby was hoping to get into your cute little panties."

Dan looked at Tina, "You wearing cute little panties today, Tina?"

"Well, Dan, if you must know, I ain't wearing no panties at all today. I never do! Ha-ha!"

I piped in, "OK, you two, stop with the dirty talk. Let's run the field test."

Dan took an amphetamine field test kit from his jacket pocket, opened it, placed a few crystals of suspected meth into it, closed it back up, pinched and broke the small glass vial in the test kit, shook it around a few times and––bingo! A bright amber color flashed in the test kit. Positive for methamphetamine. It was good shit!

"Dan, you wanna call Sgt. Bert and tell him to go ahead on the warrant?"

"Yeah, sure."

Dan got the portable radio from the glove box, switched the dial to F-2 frequency, and radioed in: "Unit 355, Detective Dan calling Sgt. Bert. Unit 355, over. (355 was the radio code for the narcotics unit.)"

"This is 355. Dan, that you?"

"Ah, yes, Sarge. Test came back positive. You can go ahead with the paperwork. Radio me when you're on your way, over."

"OK, Dan. Understand test was positive. I'll go get the paperwork taken care of. I'll let you know when we head on out your way, over."

"Roger, Sarge. I'll be on the air. Thanks." Turning to me, he said, "OK, Bernie; it's about three-thirty now; how about we go get ourselves a bite at McDonald's? After that, we can go talk to the Fall City Police. Sound good to you?"

"Yeah, sure. It'll be at least an hour and a half before the sarge leaves to come up here. Probably be around six-thirty or seven before he gets here, depending on the evening traffic. That'll be good. That way we can hit Johnny when it's dark. Makes it a lot harder for him to spot us."

This was turning out to be fun, especially for Dan. It was always fun to kick in another asshole's door. We all enjoyed that. But it was even better when it involved some sort of caper, and better yet when it was a second shot at someone who'd outsmarted you before. Must have been fun for Sgt. Bert too. Being a sergeant kept him in the office doing paperwork most of the time. You gotta have fun once in a while, and what's more fun than kicking in a door and arresting some asshole?

We got our bite to eat and then headed on over to the Fall City Police Department. We IDed ourselves and talked with the shift commander, telling him we were in the process of obtaining a narcotics search warrant for a "John Doe" suspected of dealing methamphetamine in the Fall City area. We didn't mention Johnny's name or the location. It would be best not to reveal too much till we were ready to go. One never knew who knew who in the drug world.

At 6:45 P.M. Sgt. Bert radioed in that he and another detective were on their way, and at that moment, were on I-90 just passing through Bellevue. Shouldn't be more than 15 minutes or so before they showed up. At 7:10 P.M. he pulled into the parking lot of the Fall City Police Department.

Introductions were made. Sgt. Bert instructed Dan and me to drive up towards Johnny's trailer, lights off, and if he was home, to pull off the road. Tina got to ride along in the back seat. If Johnny was at home, Dan would radio Bert, who would then drive up and park behind our GTO. Two uniformed Fall City police officers would be on standby at the Police Station until we entered Johnny's trailer and served him the search warrant. The two officers would then drive up and take part in the arrest.

The Fall City Police Station was just a 5-minute drive away from Johnny's trailer. Slowly I drove up towards where the trailer was parked. When I was several hundred yards away, I turned off my headlights and pulled off the road. I could see that the camper had its lights on and that Johnny's car was still parked where we last saw it. Dan radioed Sgt. Bert: "OK, Sarge; he's home." Making certain that the GTO interior dome light was off, Dan and I exited our vehicle, and we all gathered behind Sgt. Bert's vehicle.

"OK, Sarge; your call."

"Here, Dan, you take the warrant since you've arrested Johnny Rotten before. I'm sure he'll be happy to see you. Bernie, you go with Dan. I'll be right behind you guys. Tina can stay here next to the vehicles. OK, Dan, you ready?"

We paused. There's always that moment when I felt the release of the body's adrenalin, just moments before we hit a place on a warrant. The heart starts pumping faster, the body tenses up, the mouth gets dry, butterflies make their presence known.

"OK. Let's do it!" Dan and I jogged at a slow pace towards the trailer; we hunched down. OK. We were right by the trailer door. Dan stepped up and pounded hard on the door.

"Police with a search warrant. Open up! Police. Search warrant!"

Within seconds, we heard the sound of someone flushing the toilet.

"He's flushing the dope, Bernie!"

"Good! Ha-ha. Johnny, you dummy!"

Dan took hold of the trailer door and pulled hard. The door popped open. We rushed in, guns drawn.

"Police. Search warrant. Get on the floor. Let me see your hands!"

Johnny Rotten was secured face down, handcuffed, and searched. We then stood him up and searched him one more time. He was clean! Dan spoke: "Evening, Johnny. Remember me?"

Johnny answered sarcastically, "Yeah, you're the fucking narc who busted me last year. Well, guess what, Officer? Too bad, cause I ain't got no dope in here. I don't use no more, so fuck you!"

Dan showed Johnny the search warrant, then read him his rights. Once again he addressed Johnny; "You sure about that, Johnny? I heard you flush."

"I was taking a healthy shit, Officer. No law against that, is there?"

"No, Johnny, no law against that."

Meanwhile, Sgt. Bert had entered the trailer and was conducting a search for narcotics and related paraphernalia—photographs, address books, or anything that might be of use to us in identifying other drug dealers or drug connections.

"Hey, Bernie. Keep an eye on Mr. Rotten here. I'm going to have a look around outside."

Johnny said, "Well, you ain't gonna find nothing out there, Officer. I told you I ain't got no dope in here."

I was smiling to myself because I saw Dan putting on his gloves as he exited the trailer. Gloves, flashlight ... OK, here we go diving for shit!

Meanwhile, the two uniformed officers from the Fall City Police Department had arrived on the scene and were standing by. Several minutes passed. Then I heard a loud "bingo" from Dan, and he came back into the trailer.

"Hey, Bernie, Sarge; look what we got here!" He was holding up a baggie of white, crystalline powder.

"Hey, Johnny, look what I found in your sewer line! Does this belong to you by any chance?"

"Hey, man, that shit ain't mine! No way, man, that ain't mine!"

"Sorry, Johnny; guess you should have flushed twice."

Dan spoke to Johnny Rotten; "Mister Rotten, you're under arrest for possession of a controlled substance, which is believe to be crystal methamphetamine."

Johnny's jaw tightened up and his face turned beet red as he attempted to break free. His eyes had a wild look and the veins in his neck were starting to bulge. I was glad the guy was cuffed. At the top of his lungs he screamed, "Motherfuckers! Aaahhhh!"

"Sorry, Johnny; we got you good this time. It won't be just a few months' sentence. I believe you're headed to Walla Walla."

Dan took Johnny Rotten outside of the trailer and turned him over to the two uniformed officers.

"Here you go, Officers. You guys interested in making a good narcotics arrest? He's all yours."

The officers nodded and smiled as they took custody of Johnny Rotten. They conducted another search of him before placing him in the back of the patrol unit. Then the officers went back inside the trailer and chatted with Sgt. Bert. Later, Johnny was transported to the Fall City Police Department and placed in a holding cell.

All this time Tina had stayed in the background. We didn't want Johnny Rotten seeing her. Wouldn't have been a good idea.

When we got back to the Fall City Police Station, Sgt. Bert was talking to the shift supervisor.

"Lt. Morrison, I'd like to thank you and your officers for assisting us with the serving of the search warrant. By the way, would your department be interested in taking possession of Mr. Rotten's trailer? It's in pretty good condition, considering it once belonged to a meth dealer."

Lt. Morrison looked at Sgt. Bert, "You serious, Sarge?"

"Certainly am. It's yours if you want it. You can also have that old wreck of a vehicle that he's got parked next to the trailer. Tune it up; might be a good undercover car for your narcotics guys. We'll provide you with a copy of the search warrant, the arrest report, and case number for your paperwork. Let's write this up as a joint police agency narcotics investigation and arrest. Fall City Police Department and Seattle Police Department working together. It's your backyard, so you guys deserve credit for providing us with your full cooperation and assistance."

So that was how, with Tina's help, Johnny Rotten was finally caught and sent to the state pen.

37

Tina

It was getting time for Tina to be heading back to Yakima. Eight months; that's a long time to be with someone. We worked together and even went on vacation together just like a normal couple. Except that our work was dangerous and stressful.

It takes a lot out of a person, living life pretending to be somebody else. I was Johnny Medeiros, the biker, the drug addict, the asshole. Do not fuck with me! I was someone to be feared, especially when I'd had a few drinks. Just leave me the fuck alone. If I don't talk to you first, don't talk to me cause if I don't know who the fuck you are, then you got no business talking to me!

Wasn't that long ago, I remembered being a naive, young police rookie. I hadn't even liked writing someone a parking ticket. I liked everybody, and I wanted everybody to like me. I wanted to be friends with people. I didn't want to always be alone, not belonging. I'd been that way all my life and it sucked.

Now, a few years later, I was playing the role of a hard-core asshole, an outcast from society. I guess it was an easy role for me to play since I'd never really fit in, not in France, not in Hawaii, not in the Navy and not in the police department. I was different.

So I found myself playing the role of this fictional Johnny Medeiros. Or was Johnny the real me and Bernard the fake? When I was a child, I'd sometimes felt there was someone else in my head. A violent person, easily enraged, but someone ready to protect me and take care of me. Maybe that person was the real me.

The next evening, to celebrate our eight months of working together, I took Tina to Sun Ya Restaurant located in Seattle's Chinatown for our final dinner together. "Phillip," my favorite waiter at Sun Ya, greeted us as we entered the restaurant.

"*Sifu*, welcome!" He then showed us to my favorite booth, the very last booth located towards the rear of the restaurant.

"*Sifu*, tonight you like fish?"

I looked over at Tina.

"Any ideas?"

Tina shrugged her shoulders and shook her head, "No, Johnny, it's up to you. Go ahead and order for me."

"Phillip, what you suggest? You pick for us, OK?"

"*Sifu*, rock cod very good tonight; we have fresh in tank. Come look."

We followed Phillip to the front of the restaurant, where there was a huge fish tank containing a multitude of live fish and crabs. Phillip looked at Tina.

"OK, Miss; you choose."

Tina looked at me again; "You mean I get to choose which fish I want for dinner?"

"Yeah, Tina. Those cods' lives now depend entirely on you. So which poor fish are you going to choose?"

Tina took her time eyeing the fish. There must have been at least a half-dozen cod swimming around in the tank. Phillip disappeared into the kitchen and soon returned with a net and a large pan.

"OK, which one you choose, Tina?" She pointed to one of the larger rock cods.

"I want that one. He's nice and fat."

"OK, good choice," said Phillip. Then, standing on a stool, he scooped out the chosen fish.

"*Sifu*, this one good. Very fat, very good!" The cod flipped madly as Phillip scooped it up and placed it in the pan. He then passed the still-flopping cod off to a cook and called out cooking instructions in Chinese. The cook disappeared back into the kitchen area.

"Sifu, I make special for you Hong Kong-style. Very special! I steam with green onion and ginger. How about crab? You want crab, Sifu? I choose big one for you, OK?"

"Yeah, Phillip, go ahead. You choose."

"OK, Sifu. For you I get good one."

Another cook with a large pan waited as Phillip snagged a nice-sized Dungeness crab from the corner of the tank.

"Sifu, I tell you, cook do this one special for you and Missy. Cook fry crab fast in wok; whole crab in oil, ginger, and garlic."

"Phillip, 15 years, I coming here, I never have a bad meal when you make for me!"

"Ha-ha," laughed Phillip. "Yeah. OK, you want drink?"

"Aah, yeah. For me Budweiser in a glass with ice. Tina, how about you?"

"Ah, Johnny, I think I'd like a glass of white wine."

Tina and I went back to our booth.

"You come here often, Johnny?"

"Yeah, Tina, I've been coming here at least once a week since 1970, when I first got hired by the department. Usually every Friday, sometimes Saturdays or Sundays, when they serve *dim sum*, and I always sit in the last booth here on the left where we're sitting now. From this booth I have a view of everything that's going on in the restaurant and can observe who comes and goes."

"Don't you ever go to any other Chinese restaurants?"

"No, I found Sun Ya years ago and made friends with the owner, Mr. Liu, and some of the waiters, like Ma, Phillip, and David. They all treat me good, treat me like family. The food here is good, so why go anywhere else? Nah, Sun Ya is my favorite place in Chinatown. The owner and his wife always greet me with, 'Hi, Cousin,' and Phillip always waits on me like he's my personal waiter. Sometimes I come in here just for a cup of coffee, just to take a break from work. I sit in this booth, and no one bothers me. Nothing else exists; it's just me and this booth."

"Johnny, I noticed that your accent changes whenever you start talking to Phillip." I laughed.

"That's just from growing up in Hawaii around local folks. That's how we talked to each other in Hawaii. We call it 'Pidgin English,' 'Pidgin' or 'broken' English as it's sometimes called. Makes it a lot easier for us locals and Chinese to understand each other. We don't need to use all those big words you find in the so-called 'proper English.'"

"Johnny, they ever give you a discount here?"

I laughed again; "Hell, no! Chinese don't give discounts to nobody. Sometimes I get a free dessert from Phillip, but a discount—never! Friendship is friendship, but business is business. The Chinese don't mix the two. They're good with money. They know how to earn it, but more important, they know how to invest and hang on to it. When I first met Mr. Liu and his wife back in 1970, they were both living in a run-down apartment building on King Street‖——the Milwaukee Hotel. Today they own this Sun Ya Restaurant. They even own the property that Sun Ya sits on. And now they live in a beautiful home on Mercer Island. They did good for themselves, but they both worked hard and sacrificed a lot in the beginning to get where they are now. They're good people, and I'd do anything to help them if they ever asked me. Like I said, they're like family."

Phillip brought out the dinner. Steamed Rock Cod, Hong Kong Style, Dungeness crab, Sun Ya Special

Fried Rice, Chinese greens, and of course, a bowl of steamed rice.

"The Chinese don't put their rice on a plate. Rice gotta be in a bowl. Only white folks put rice on plates, and only white folks put sugar in Chinese tea. Don't ever do that, Tina; it's a big no-no! Chinese tea is very special. You can't taste its delicate flavor if you dump a bunch of sugar in it."

Tina and I took our time eating and enjoying the meal. Every dish was totally delicious and had its own unique flavor. I ordered another round of drinks, sat back, and relaxed. What a wonderful evening. We didn't have to worry about finishing up any more assignments. We were all done.

Tomorrow Tina would return to Yakima to be with her mother and daughters. It had been almost two years since she'd last seen them. Now it was time for Tina to go home. No doubt about it, I was going to miss her. We'd been good for each other, worked good together, just like regular partners. Tina made some great cases for our unit, and I'd enjoyed having her working undercover with me. We'd also shared many a wonderful evening together in bed. Yes, I was going to miss her. But there was always the phone. Tina and I could keep in touch and chat whenever we wanted to.

Dinner over with, Phillip and I exchanged brief conversation. A short while later, Tina and I got up. I paid the tab, left Phillip a hefty tip, and thanked him as we exited the restaurant.

"Johnny, that was really delicious. Thank you very much. Did the department pay for the meal?"

"No, Tina, this time it was my treat."

Instead of getting into the GTO, Tina and I, arm in arm, took a casual stroll through Chinatown. Another habit of mine, always taking a stroll through Chinatown after eating dinner at Sun Ya. I love Chinatown. I've always felt so much at home when I was there. Not just Seattle's Chinatown, but any Chinatown. I was born a French bastard, but over the years, due to being raised in a Chinese family, I'd become a Chinaman in my mind.

Following our stroll, Tina and I drove back to Mountlake Terrace. We didn't have sex that final evening. Instead we made love for the first time since we'd met, some eight months earlier.

Over the years we kept in touch. I visited Tina and her daughters several times, always at her mom's home in Yakima. Tina's two daughters finished school and went on to live successful lives.

Tina passed away in 1990. I miss her to this very day. God bless.

C. I. Tina and "Johnny Medeiros"

38

The Razor's Edge

In 1975 the SPD Narcotics Section had sent one of our police undercover agents to Alaska to work with the Alaska State Troopers Narcotics Special Task Force. The Alaskan oil pipeline was under construction and that had led to a large increase in the flow of cocaine as well as methamphetamine in and around Anchorage.

Through a supervisor in the Narcotics Section, I was informed that our undercover guy in Anchorage hadn't been able to make any significant drug buys. A few marijuana cases was about all. The Task Force in Anchorage had requested the loan of another undercover officer or detective; one who hopefully would be able to do the job.

I'd been a detective for about a year and worked with a number of CIs. I'd also kept working undercover. There was a lot of dope out there to buy and cases to be made. I loved the job, I loved the thrill of it all. I thrived on the danger that comes with undercover work. Living on the edge, running along the razor's edge, then jumping off! How I loved that feeling. So when they asked me if I'd be interested in working undercover in Alaska, I said yes without any hesitation.

The Narcotics Section had been offered a great deal on the purchase of a newly-developed 9 mm. S&W automatic pistol. I'd ordered one and the shipment arrived just before I left for Alaska. Back then patrol officers and detectives were issued .38 caliber S&W revolvers. Undercover officers and detectives in vice and narcotics, however, were allowed to purchase and carry their own automatics.

A week later, I found myself boarding an Alaska Airlines flight bound for Anchorage. I had long hair, wore jeans, carried my detective's badge in my right rear pocket, and my newly-purchased automatic tucked in my belt at the small of my back. Back in 1975 police officers were allowed to carry firearms on their person while aboard an airline flight. There were no pre-boarding security checks to speak of.

Landing in Anchorage, I was met by Lt. "Ray Andrews," Sgt. "James Lee," and Detective "Nolan Henderson." All three were from the Alaska State Troopers Drug Task Force. I was then driven to a secret apartment complex in downtown Anchorage, where I had been assigned a studio apartment unit in the complex. This was to serve as a base of operations during my ten days of undercover work. Then I was photographed and official forms were filled out, all of which I was required to read over and sign. Within the next several hours I was issued an official Alaska State Driver's License and personal identification bearing my undercover alias, "Johnny Medeiros." I was also handed the keys to what turned out to be a beat-up-looking, two-door undercover vehicle. The body was ratty-looking, as dopers' cars usually are, but the engine and mechanics were all in top condition. The vehicle was equipped with a remote-control switch, which, when activated, would automatically open up a garage door on the side of the apartment complex.

Johnny Medeiros in Alaska

Lt. Andrews laid out how he wanted the cases made and reminded me that, as a law enforcement officer, I wasn't allowed to actually consume drugs. To get around having to do drugs, I was instructed to simply say, "Thanks, but I'd rather wait until I'm with my old lady." I kid you not. This is what I was expected to say to the dealers if I was ever offered cocaine or methamphetamine. Like, you know, "Just Say No." Yeah, right!

Preliminaries out of the way, Lt. Andrews brought in the CI. His name was "Bill Darnell." He was an ex-biker, and I'd be working with him for the next ten days. We shook hands.

He was heavier-built than me, sprouting shoulder length hair and a full beard, and he dressed more casually than your typical biker.

Meanwhile, Sgt. Lee and Detective Henderson headed out the door, saying, "We'll be back around six, so you guys be back here then too."

Lt. Andrews continued to brief me. "Bernie, we got a lot of cocaine coming into Anchorage since that pipeline started. Guys working the line are using coke and speed to help them pull those long, difficult hours. They don't just work eight-hour shifts. The job of laying that pipe will soon be over, and they'll all be out of a job, so these guys will take all the overtime they can get."

"Bill" and "Johnny"

"Meanwhile, we have this huge influx of cocaine. We know there's one main guy bringing the stuff in. His name is Lawrence, Hal Lawrence. He's no dummy, though. He won't sell to anyone he doesn't know personally. Always got some flunky selling the cocaine for him. We've managed to get a couple of grams off some guy we arrested last month. We ran it; came back 99.9% pure. That's pharmaceutical grade! "

"The plan is for Bill here to start taking you around to spots where drug dealers are known to hang out. You'll cruise taverns and go-go joints, where Bill will introduce you to some of the low-level dealers he knows, ones that he's bought cocaine or methamphetamine from in the past. You've bought coke in the past, right Bill?" asked the lieutenant.

"I ain't saying nothing," he said, "but if you're asking me if I can get these low-lifes to sell me coke, no problem. I could take Bernie out right now and be back in 20 minutes with whatever amount you want. You give me the money, I'll get you the coke."

"Bernie, you'll be handling all the money. You make the drug buys, not Bill. We want you to be the one testifying in court."

"How much you want us buying, Lieutenant?" asked Bill.

"We've got a budget of $10,000 to spend in the next ten days."

"You're not going to give me the ten grand all at once, are you?" I asked.

"No, we'll start you off with $1,000 cash. You and Bill go out tonight and see what you can do. As of tomorrow you guys will be dealing with Lee and Henderson. I won't be involved with the day-to-day activity. That's for them to handle. I'm the overall supervisor on this venture and will be kept up to date on your progress.

"Can I get fake ID?" asked Bill.

"Bill, everyone in Anchorage knows your name. It would be sorta strange if you suddenly came up with a new name, don't you think?"

"Yeah, right. But after this is over with, can you get me a new ID? A lot of folks here in Anchorage are gonna be really pissed at me. You know? All the ones Bernie and me are gonna cop from. They already shot me in the head once. I'm not looking forward to being a target twice."

"Shot in the head?" I asked. What else hadn't they told me yet?

"Yeah, right in the fucking head with a .357 magnum."

"And you lived?"

"Well, I was in intensive care for a couple of weeks, but I survived. That's why I turned snitch."

The lieutenant turned to me and said, "OK, so you're Johnny Medeiros from now on. Johnny, you and Bill get $40 each per diem for food. That should cover three meals a day. Anything over comes out of your own pocket."

"What about beer and such, Lieutenant?" I asked.

"For that use the buy money that Henderson will hand out to you every day. Just keep track of the money. Every night you need to write out a report on the buys you made during the day. Write it out in longhand, and my secretary will type it up for you. Every morning Lee and Henderson will come up here and go over the details of the buys, your report, and your financial statement."

"Got it."

Lt. Andrews counted out $1,000 from a bank-type pouch and handed the cash over to me. Then he took out $80 from a manila envelope for the food allowance and handed $40 to me and $40 to Bill.

"OK, Bernie. You and Bill hit the streets. Go out and get the feel of things, grab a few beers, get some chow, and be back here at six. Here's the key to the apartment."

Then the lieutenant said to Bill; "Bill, don't mess Bernie up!"

"Don't mess Bernie up," I thought to myself. What's that all about?

Bill replied with a chuckle and a big grin, "Lieutenant, you know me. Not to worry."

The three of us left the apartment. Lt. Andrews went down the far stairwell while Bill and I took another set of stairs that led down to the parking garage. We located our vehicle and got in. I started up the car, drove towards the exit, and then hit the electronic garage door opener. Up it went.

Out into Alaska's bitter cold. I drove off to the location of the bars and clubs, where drugs, sex, and music all converged. I looked over at Bill.

"Show time, Bill. Here we go!"

Bill looked over at me, "So Johnny (Bill had been instructed to call me 'Johnny'), can you drink while working?"

I laughed, "Sure can!"

"How about using drugs? They allow you to do drugs?"

"No way, Bill. I'm not allowed. I can only simulate taking drugs, you know, like make believe, pretend that I'm actually doing the drug."

Bill looked at me with a worried expression.

"How ya gonna do that, Johnny? How the fuck ya gonna simulate in front of dealers who're watching you?"

"Well, the way they taught me back at the Narc office. I scoop up a small amount onto my coke spoon, bring the spoon up to my left or right nostril, bring my other hand up to my nose to close one nostril, and at the same time, cover the spoon, so no one can see what I'm doing. Then I quietly exhale out through my nose to blow the cocaine off the spoon. Now all the cocaine should be gone, so I inhale sharply, loudly, like I'm actually snorting up the coke. Then I start blinking and pinching my nose as I sniff in three or four times without the spoon there and say, 'Damn, that's good shit!' That's what they have us practice. Not using real cocaine, of course. They have us use banitol, some sort of baby laxative. It's a white powder that sort of looks like cocaine and dissolves completely, like real cocaine."

"Yeah, I know the stuff," said Bill. "Heroin dealers use it all the time to cut heroin and coke. Good stuff. Difficult to get nowadays because it's gotten so popular with drug dealers. Government's clamping down. So now, being banitol is difficult to get, guys cut the dope with whatever they can get their hands on. I've even seen guys cut their shit up with rat poison, no shit. Fucking rat poison."

"I don't know, Johnny. That simulating shit they taught you back in Seattle, that might work on some dumb college kid, but these guys out here, they ain't stupid. You're a new face around here. You suddenly appear out of nowhere, you got a ton of cash money to spend, you're buying a lot of dope in a very short period of time... What did they say? 10,000 bucks to spend in a week to ten days? Shit, that's 1,000 bucks per day. Folks are gonna be noticing that. It's gonna be tricky pulling that simulating shit off without getting made as a narc."

"Well, I got this far."

"OK, Johnny, but you're gonna have to be real careful what you say and how you act. Your body language, how you react to dope when you simulate... Shit, Johnny, I don't know. It's no fucking game out here. These folks do not fuck around. They'll whack you at a drop of a hat if they think you're the police. Johnny, you ever do cocaine? I mean do you have any idea exactly what happens when you do coke, how it makes you feel, and what happens to your body in reaction to the cocaine?"

"No Bill, I never did do coke."

"Look, Johnny, when you buy coke these guys are gonna want to see you toot. They don't know you, and they won't trust you unless they actually see you do coke. Damn, Johnny, I just don't know about all this. It's my ass out there, too! Anchorage just ain't that big a place. Everybody knows everybody. Word gets around real quick amongst dopers."

"Another thing; Anchorage is surrounded by tons of open space—the tundra. I personally know of guys that got whacked, then were taken miles out of town and dumped. Left out there. No need to bury the body. Just take it out there five, ten miles out, dump it, and leave it for the wildlife to feast on. We got all types of critters out there, all hungry, especially being it's winter now. Them fucking rodents be hungry as hell. Bears, mountain lions... Shit, we got fucking wolves all over, hundreds of 'em. Big motherfuckers too. Wolves come across some human corpse out there, some sorry motherfucker that got himself whacked, his body still warm... Shit, it's banquet time for the pack."

Bill continued, "The alpha male will get the first helpings. He'll go up to the corpse, carefully move around it, sniffing and all that, and then piss on the body to claim it. He'll look around first, making sure there's no human threat, then he'll start tearing flesh, taking hold of some exposed body part. If the body is clothed, he'll start with the face, ripping and tearing off the soft fleshy parts—nose, ears, tongue, and all that. Then with his powerful jaws, he'll clamp down on the head and crush it. Fucking wolves are huge. They can get an entire head in their jaws, no problem. Crush a human skull with no problem. The alpha male starts by licking at the brain matter. That brain shit must be the best part of the entire body, after the dick and nuts, that is. Most times when a body is dumped out there, the assholes who wasted the motherfucker will take the clothes off and leave him or her completely naked. Leaves less evidence that way. If the cops somehow stumble on whatever remains are left, it usually just amounts to a few bones or bits of hair. If the body's naked, the alpha male starts out by chomping on the dude's dick and nut sack. I shit you not, Johnny; fucking dick and nut sack is some real gourmet eatings for wolves. Got that human urine smell around the dick and nuts."

I winced and shook my head.

"Meanwhile, the other wolves sit off at a distance, whimpering, licking their chops, and watching him tear at the body. When the alpha male is good and ready, he'll allow the rest of the pack to join in. There could be anywhere from five to a dozen wolves in any given pack. Won't take but a short time for the entire body to be devoured. The pack will eat all the flesh and tendons, and then they'll gnaw at the bones, breaking the larger ones apart so they can get the marrow. Dump a warm human body out there, come back the next day, and there ain't no fucking body left to be found."

"OK, I got it, Bill. Be careful or I'll get my nuts and pecker ripped off and eaten by some hungry wolf."

"There, that tavern up ahead, pull over. I've bought coke in that place before. I know a few dealers that hang out there."

I parked by the tavern, and we went inside. The tavern had the usual bar layout: a half-dozen tables and chairs in the front, bar towards the rear. We took a seat further back and against the wall. That's the seat that's favored by both criminals and cops because it allows you to see what's happening.

The music was playing loud on the juke box. On an elevated stage in the front section of the tavern was a cute young white gal dancing without any clothing. No clothing; completely naked.

"Welcome to Alaska, Johnny. This is what it's like in every tavern up here in Anchorage—dancing completely naked!"

I was thinking, "Shit, this is all right. Never seen no naked chick dancing around like that before. Damn!"

A tough-looking gal in tight jeans came over to take our orders. For me, just a beer. Bill ordered a beer and two shots of Yukon Jack. I stared at the gal dancing till the waitress returned with our drinks.

"That's 30 bucks, guys."

"30 bucks?" I asked.

"Beer, five bucks each, Yukon Jack, ten bucks a shot."

I thought it was high for two beers and two shots, but I figured, what the hell, I'm on a $10,000 budget, after all. I handed the gal a crisp fifty-dollar bill and told her to keep the change. I got a great smile and a free titty-shot in return as she bent over and whispered something to Bill. She then turned and walked back to the bar.

"Johnny Boy, you need to try a shot of this Yukon Jack. It's fucking cold out there, and a shot of this will warm you up quick. Keeps your circulation going, just like anti-freeze. Don't wanna freeze your nuts off, right?"

"Well, yeah, I guess not. But Bill, I don't drink that hard stuff. All I drink is beer and wine."

"Wine! Fuck, Johnny; you're suppose to be an addict, right? Or at least pretending to be one, so don't be ordering none of that gourmet wine! Out here it's not fucking Seattle. It's Alaska. It's still the Wild West. Dudes even go around with six-shooters strapped on their hips. It's legal out here. Never know when you're gonna be confronting a pissed-off bear or some other wild critter."

"You know, Johnny, we got the pipeline going in here now. Workers hit town to take a break, get fucked up, buy cocaine to take back to the job site. They need that shit to keep working and making them big bucks. Without coke and speed that pipeline ain't gonna get built on schedule, no fucking way!"

Bill bumped me, "Here's a toast to Johnny from Hawaii. May he learn to walk, talk, and fuck like a real asshole junkie, so as not to get his head blown off, dumped in the woods, and left naked for that alpha male to piss on him and feast on his nuts."

I downed my shot of Yukon Jack and followed it with a huge swallow of cold beer. Wow. Not bad. Not bad at all!

"Fuck, Bill, that's fucking strong stuff. Not bad, actually. Hell, I'm ready for another shot!"

Bill smiled and ordered another round. I paid—another 50 bucks gone. I was feeling slightly buzzed from the alcohol. This was more fun than working undercover in Seattle; a hell of a lot more fun.

"Hey, Johnny, the gal that served us, she says that her guy—the dude sitting over there (Bill pointed out some dark-haired, skinny dude sitting at another table by himself)—she says he's got some coke. What you think? Time for our first buy?"

"OK, Bill. Make the buy. How much you need?"

"I'll buy two grams from him. Two grams, that's 200 bucks. Here, give me four of them fifties you got—hurry up!"

I handed Bill four fifties. He took the bills, got up, and went over to the guy. I watched as they walked into the men's room. Bill returned several minutes later and stood at our table, "OK, Johnny, let's get the fuck out of here!"

I asked, "You got the dope?"

"Yeah, Johnny, I got it. Fuck, Johnny, let's just get the hell out of here!"

Bill and I returned to the car, got in, and drove off.

"Where to, Bill? Let's see what you got!"

"Head out of town, Johnny. Take that exit up ahead and get on the highway."

I was feeling good. Bill had just made our first coke buy. My undercover caper in Anchorage had officially started.

I looked over at Bill. He was looking at the two small cellophane envelopes. He opened up one of them, put a finger inside, pulled it out, and rubbed his gums with the white powder.

"Damn, Johnny, this is fucking good cocaine; damn good!"

Next thing I knew, he'd taken the cap off a ballpoint pen, dipped the protruding part into the envelope, brought the end up to his right nostril, and taken a hit. Bill had just snorted up some of the cocaine that we'd purchased! Confused, I said, "Bill—what you doing? You can't be doing that. You're not supposed to be snorting that coke. We're supposed to turn it in!"

Bill was blinking, his eyes were watering, and his pupils were slightly dilated. He was breathing in and out slowly through his open mouth.

"Johnny, Johnny, Johnny! Not to worry. I needed to make sure the shit was real. Just because it looks and smells like cocaine and gives a freeze, don't mean it's real. I've seen bunk sold as real coke, some kind of shit powder cut with lidocaine to give it that freeze. Fuckers out there got all kinda tricks to make the coke look and smell real. Only way to tell for sure is to snort some of it. It's the only true 'field test,' as you cops say. I just field-tested this cocaine and it's the real thing. Pure, fucking cocaine, Johnny. We just bought ourselves some pure shit! Sgt. Lee is gonna like this, Johnny. First buy and we get 99.9% cocaine."

"Now, we just got to find out who's selling ounces. I'll be checking around with some of the few friends I got left. All the other motherfuckers out there want me dead. Remember, I told you a few months ago I was in the hospital dying after being shot in the fucking head by a .357? All my so-called 'friends' thought I was gonna die, so they jacked my tools and my fucking Harley. They fucking traded my chopper to some biker from California for an ounce of meth. Can you imagine that? Traded my bike for an ounce of fucking speed. Fuck 'em! That's why I went to the Drug Task

Force and offered to snitch. I'm gonna get as many of them fuckers who ripped me off as I possibly can."

Bill went on, "I heard rumors that the head prosecuting attorney wants to run for Attorney-General, and he's going to use this caper, us busting a bunch of dope dealers, as part of his campaign promise. Clean up Anchorage and get rid of the cocaine dealers. So Johnny, whether you know it or not, you're here working undercover, putting your nuts on the line so that some head prosecuting attorney can run his Anti-Drug Campaign for a shot at being elected State Attorney-General. Now ain't that a bunch of crap!"

At 6:00 P.M. Bill and I returned to the apartment and met up with Sgt. Lee and Detective Henderson. Both were pleased with the two-gram cocaine buy that Bill had made and were surprised at the cocaine's purity and how quick Bill was able to make the buy. I was off to a good start. I didn't mention anything about Bill's "field testing," and the shortage apparently went unnoticed. Bill explained to Lee why he made the first buy instead of me, and Lee understood that I needed to get comfortable with my role here in Anchorage. Lee then instructed Bill to go and try to find out where I could buy an ounce or two of cocaine, and handed me $2,000 in cash.

Bill and I left the apartment and drove off to another tavern. There, Bill introduced me to one of his cocaine connections, "Jimmy," a skinny, young cocaine addict. Bill, Jimmy, and I sat at a table drinking beer, and I ordered a round of Yukon Jack for Bill and myself. That Yukon Jack really did warm me up, and I was starting to enjoy the "buzz" I got from its potency.

Bill informed Jimmy that I'd just gotten in from Honolulu, had lots of bucks to spend, and was interested in buying several ounces of prime cocaine. Jimmy was impressed by all this since he was meeting "Johnny Medeiros," a cocaine dealer from "Sunny Hawaii." The weather was freezing in Anchorage, and there was snow on the ground.

Jimmy agreed to locate some "ounces" for me to buy. His fee—$100.

"Not a problem," I said as I peeled off and handed Jimmy a crispy fifty-dollar bill from the fat roll of fifties I now had in my pocket. As the three of us walked out into the parking lot, I saw Jimmy looking down at the fifty-dollar bill he was holding in his trembling little hands.

Bill suggested I show Jimmy my 9 mm. I scoped out the parking lot to make sure no one was close by and, satisfied, I reached around and removed the automatic from the small of my back. I held it low in front of me. Jimmy asked if he could hold it.

"No fucking way, dude," I replied and quickly returned the automatic back to the small of my back. Jimmy asked me if I had $1,200 cash on me. I looked at Jimmy as if I were pissed off.

"Jimmy, what the fuck you think I'm standing here for? Don't be asking stupid questions, OK? Yeah, I got the fucking $1,200 on me."

"Sorry, Johnny, just wanted to make sure."

The plan was for me to go with Jimmy to buy the ounce of cocaine from his connection. Bill would meet up with me later at the apartment. As I drove out of the tavern parking lot, Jimmy asked me if we could go pick up his girlfriend first. I started to grumble, but then figured, OK, what the fuck, why not?

Jimmy directed me to a run-down trailer park located on the outskirts of the Anchorage city limits. Arriving there, Jimmy got out. Ten minutes later, he returned with a burnt-out white female who looked like a junkie.

"Johnny, this is Jenny, my girlfriend."

"Hey, how ya doin', girl?"

Jimmy and Jenny climbed in the back seat of my undercover vehicle, and I drove off towards the highway, leaving Anchorage far behind.

"OK, Jimmy, how fucking far we gotta go to get this ounce?"

"Uh, about a half-hour's drive."

"Fuck! why that far, Jimmy?"

"Cause my guy lives out there, that's why. He don't like coming in anywhere near Anchorage. Too spooked about cops. Just keep driving on this highway, about 30 miles or so. I'll tell you when to turn off."

About ten minutes of driving later, Jimmy asked, "Hey, Johnny, you smoke?"

I smiled to myself. Here we go, here comes the "narc" test. I knew right away what was going on. Jimmy didn't know me; he'd just met me, and even though Bill had told him that I was "cool," neither Jimmy nor Jenny trusted me completely. Nothing unusual about that when you're buying drugs from someone you just met.

Jimmy lit up a marijuana joint, took a hit, and passed the joint to Jenny, who also took a hit. Moments later, Jenny passed the joint to me. I thought, "OK, kids, I'll play your silly, fucking game." I reached back and took the lit joint from Jenny. Looking back towards the highway, I proceeded to take in a big hit. Jimmy and Jenny knew that cops aren't allowed to smoke dope, right? Well, in this particular case, right here, right now—wrong!

I knew if I refused to take that hit, the ounce buy would come to a screeching halt. Not only that; my cover as a drug dealer from Hawaii would be blown. Jimmy and Jenny would make me as a "narc." So yeah, I'd take a hit; I just wouldn't write in my report. The report would state that I was handed a lit joint of suspected marijuana from suspect Jenny and that I took the joint and proceeded to "simulate" smoking the suspected marijuana.

After hitting on the joint, I handed it back to Jimmy and held in the smoke for as long as I could. Then I turned and, facing Jimmy and Jenny, exhaled the marijuana smoke directly into their faces. I smiled and said, "Thanks. That's some pretty good shit!" Jimmy and Jenny were pleased and relieved to see that Johnny Medeiros wasn't a narc. Johnny was just another druggie, just like them.

I'd become very good at simulating smoking a joint. I'd demonstrated it in front of juries many times in the past whenever I had to testify. I was also good at simulating snorting cocaine from a coke spoon. I'd gotten the sounds down pat. I could blink my eyes, rub my nose, and look lost and confused as the pretend rush hit my brain. I'd even got the dialog down pat: "shit, damn, fuck, wow," etc., as I bent over while shaking my head slightly back and forth. Then I'd exhale a few times, as if trying to catch my breath, I'd blink a few more times, rub my nose once again, and my demo was over. Then I'd return to being "Detective Bernie Lau of the Seattle Police Department" testifying in court. The judge and the jury were always convinced, pleased, and entertained by my demonstrations. One Judge Goodfellow even wrote a letter in which he stated that "Detective Bernie Lau testifying in my courtroom always makes his demonstrating of drug use simulation look so realistic; he truly is an expert witness in the field of narcotics use."

As I continued driving, I started to feel the effects of the marijuana. Everything seemed to have slowed down. It seemed like it was taking a hell of a long time to drive to wherever the dope man lived. Just as I was about to complain, Jimmy directed me to pull into a rest stop ahead. I did as instructed and parked.

"Johnny, the money. I need the money now; give me the twelve hundred!" I took the bankroll out of my pocket and slowly counted out $1,200, all in fifty-dollar bills, a total of 24 fifties. I was having a difficult time focusing. I handed the money over to Jimmy, who counted it for himself. Satisfied, Jimmy and Jenny got out of the car, walked over to the pay phone, and made a call. Jimmy came back and instructed me to go park at the far end of the rest area.

"Jimmy, I gotta piss!" I said.

"OK, Johnny, go ahead and piss, but make it fast."

Getting out of the car, I felt unstable. Fuck, I was stoned. I had to lean on the car to regain my balance. I wasn't comfortable, not one bit. Pretending to be fucked up is one thing, but actually being fucked up is another matter and not fun at all.

I somehow made it to the men's restroom. Leaning up against the urinal, I took a long and much-needed piss. That over with, I shuffled back to the car. I got in and drove slowly over to the other end of the parking lot. Engine off, I slumped down behind the steering wheel, put my head back, and quickly fell asleep. I don't know how long I dozed, but suddenly Jimmy and Jenny were getting back in the car.

"OK, Johnny, let's head out. Hurry up and get the fuck out of here."

I started the car and drove back towards Anchorage. "Jimmy, you got my dope?"

"Yeah, Johnny, don't worry about it!"

"I ain't worried, Jimmy. Just want to make sure you got it."

I glanced back. Jimmy showed me a baggie of white powder.

"OK, good. Where to now?"

"Drive us back to the trailer park. Don't forget Johnny; you still owe me 50 bucks!"

"OK, damn it. You'll get your 50 when we get there."

Eventually, we arrived back at the trailer park. I pulled off into a darkened spot and parked. Peeling off another 50, I handed it to Jimmy, who in turn handed me the baggie of cocaine.

"Johnny, this here's pure cocaine. If you decide to be getting more, tell Bill, and I'll hook you up again."

"OK, I'll see how I like it first. If I like it, I'll tell Bill to get a hold of you. Jimmy, ain't there anyone closer in town? I don't like driving way the fuck out of town, not when I'm fucked up. Wasn't just the smoke; I also eat valiums and pain pills."

"I know this guy who's closer, but I don't know if he'll deal with you. This guy don't trust nobody!"

"Hey, man, I'm cool. You know that."

"Yeah, I know that, but he don't know you. I'll be talking to him in case you be wanting more."

I drove back to the apartment and let myself in. I spotted Bill laying back on the couch, looking fucked up to the max. Great! Bill noticed me and attempted to sit up, "Hey, Johnny, you get the coke?"

"Yeah, Bill. Right here. Why?" I showed Bill the baggie. Bill suddenly came alive, "Johnny, how about kicking me down just a pinch?"

"No can do, Bill. I need to put it all into evidence. Besides, the baggie's sealed. I don't want to open it. The sergeant won't like it if I open up the baggie."

"Aw, c'mon, Johnny. You got to at least see if it's coke, see if it's any good! Sergeant won't know if the baggie was sealed or not when you got it. Just tell him that Jimmy opened it and took a little for himself. You give Jimmy any kick down?"

"No, I didn't. Just gave him the 100 bucks."

"Well, I'm sure his guy kicked him down some."

I looked over towards the low table in front of Bill and spotted a spoon, a syringe, a glass of water, a short section of rubber tubing, and a small paper bindle.

"Shit. What the fuck you been doing Bill? What's going on?"

"Aw, no big deal, Johnny; I just slammed some girl (heroin). I'm not doing too good right now. I'm not shitting you. I feel like I might OD from the hit I just did!"

"What you talking about, Bill? What if the sergeant shows up, are you nuts?"

"Johnny, the sergeant won't be back here till morning, remember? They told you that. C'mon, Johnny, I'm serious. If I don't get a little bit of cocaine to counteract the heroin, I might fucking OD. I ain't bullshitting you. All I need's a pinch. I really need some coke, and fast. I ain't feeling good; I'm getting sick!"

Bill did look sick. Annoyed and disgusted, I opened up the sealed baggie and gave Bill a very small amount of cocaine. I can't say exactly how much I gave him as I didn't know much about cocaine back then. I'd never done cocaine and didn't know what a gram actually looked like.

Taking the cocaine that I handed him, Bill quickly put it onto the spoon, then added a few drops of water, which dissolved it immediately. Next, he drew up the liquid into a syringe, tied off his left arm above the elbow, and proceeded to insert the needle into a vein. He then carefully pulled back on the plunger and drew blood into the syringe, allowing it to mix with the dissolved cocaine and water. Slowly he pushed the plunger down. Next thing I knew, he was breathing deep and heavy. Then suddenly he was wide awake, smiling, and talking up a storm.

I knew I had just made a huge mistake. Bill now had something that he could hold over my head any time he wanted to. (It was illegal for me to give him cocaine.) It hadn't even been twenty-four hours since I'd been introduced to him, and he'd already played me. I'd fucked up big time.

I felt uneasy. Why had I been so naive as to have given him cocaine in the first place? This whole thing was messed up; everything was happening way too fast. Up to this moment, I'd enjoyed playing the role of a "junkie." But suddenly, it wasn't fun any more. Things were not turning out the way they were supposed to.

"Bill, this is total bullshit. I'm not comfortable with you staying here, so you need to leave, like right now!"

I threw him out of the apartment and went to bed, but first I took two valiums to help me fall asleep.

39

First Toot

The next morning I woke up early and quickly wrote up the paperwork on the ounce buy. An hour or so later, Lee, Henderson, and Bill showed up. Apparently Bill had told them about my ounce buy from Jimmy. Both detectives were excited and pleased as I turned over the baggie of suspected cocaine along with my report on the buy. I didn't mention Bill slamming heroin or me giving Bill any of the cocaine I'd purchased. My cocaine evidence and my reports were gathered up and turned over to Sgt. Lee. No one said anything about the baggie being unsealed.

Detective Henderson instructed Bill to go out and start spreading the word around that "Johnny Medeiros" had flown into town a few days ago from Hawaii and was looking to buy ounces of top-quality cocaine. Put the word out that "Johnny" had big bucks to spend for quantity buys, that sort of thing. Sgt. Lee then handed Bill $150 cash for "tavern expenses."

"Here, Bill, go spend the money! Buy drinks for your drug dealer buddies. Just get the word out on 'Johnny!'"

"Got it, Sarge. Thanks."

Bill quickly exited the apartment. Sgt. Lee turned to me.

"Bernie, how about coming out to my place tonight? I'll show you some of our famous Alaskan hospitality. We can all relax at my cabin while Bill does his thing. How do you like your bear meat cooked, Bernie? You ever have bear steaks?"

"Bear steaks?" I wasn't sure I'd heard correctly.

Sgt. Lee laughed, "That's right. Bear meat."

Sergeant Lee drove Detective Henderson and me out to Lee's log cabin, located about 20 miles out of town.

Like a lot of police officers working vice or narcotics, Sgt. Lee was divorced, as was Detective Henderson. During the drive, we talked about our lives. About working vice and narcotics details and the fact that cops are never home nights, which makes it difficult to keep a marriage together.

Once at the cabin, Detective Henderson and I kicked back, drinking beer, as Sgt. Lee cooked up some of that bear meat he'd been talking about. It tasted "different" but not bad. Lee talked about living in Alaska, where there was no need to be buying meat from the local supermarket.

"Just step out the back door, and shoot something big. You'll have meat for a long time. Lot of big critters walking around out there in the Alaskan wilderness just waiting for you to shoot and eat 'em. But you better spot them before they spot you cause it works both ways."

Detective Henderson shared a joke he'd heard recently. Two hikers were heading down a trail, when one hiker spotted a bear up ahead with her two cubs. The hikers heard a grunt and saw Mama Bear coming towards them at breakneck speed. Instantly one of the hikers dropped his pack, pulled off his boots, and put on a pair of Nikes. The other hiker said to him, "You fool, you can't outrun a bear." Jumping up with his Nikes tightly laced, the second hiker turned to his friend and said: "Yeah, I know, but I only have to be fast enough to outrun you!"

As the night wore on, more food was served and eaten, more beer was consumed, and more jokes and laughter were shared. Much later that evening, Sgt. Lee asked to see my new Smith & Wesson 9 mm. stainless automatic. I removed it from the small of my back, released the clip, ejected the round from the chamber, and handed him my gun. He was immediately taken with it.

"Bernie, I'll give you 300 bucks for that automatic. 300 cash, right now! What do you say?"

"Aah, well, Sergeant, thanks, but I don't know. I mean, I just bought it. I've only had it for a week. I didn't even have a chance to shoot nobody with it yet." We all laughed.

"No, seriously, Bernie. I'll give you cash money right now!"

"I dunno, Sergeant. I really like my new 'nine.' I had to wait six months on a special order from Smith & Wesson to get it."

"OK, Bernie, would you trade?"

"Well, that depends on what you got to trade."

Sgt. Lee told me to wait a few minutes as he crawled up into the cabin's attic. Moments later, he returned, holding a small briefcase. He laid it on the kitchen counter and opened it. I looked down in awe.

"Damn, Sarge! Where the hell did you get this little beauty?"

"Never mind, Bernie. It don't matter where I got it. All that matters is that I got it, and I'm willing to trade it for your nine. So you wanna trade?"

I stared at the contents of the briefcase. It was perfectly crafted, expert workmanship all around. I picked it up, felt its heft, cracked it open, then snapped it shut again. I thought for a few minutes; should I or shouldn't I? I really hated to give up my automatic, but what the heck, I wasn't going to find a deal like this anytime soon. I reluctantly decided to trade.

Sgt. James Lee of the Anchorage State Troopers Drug Task Force traded me a double-barrel 12-gauge shotgun with a sawed-off stock for my 9 mm. automatic. Total length of the weapon was a mere 14 inches. I couldn't believe it; a 14-inch sawed-off shotgun!

This shotgun was in fact a highly illegal weapon. Should the ATF (Alcohol, Tobacco and Firearms) folks catch me with it in my possession, cop or no cop, I'd be in a world of trouble. I'd be looking at possible federal penetentiary time. This was no small matter! Still, I decided to trade.

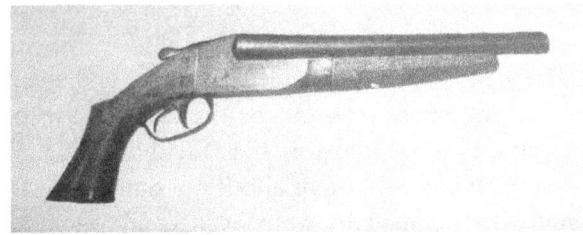

Sawed-off shotgun

Sgt. Lee placed the shotgun into a police evidence envelope and wrote across it in bright red lettering, "Evidence—Case Pending." Lee then sealed the open ends of the envelope with red evidence tape and had me initial over the evidence tape.

"Here, Bernie. This way you shouldn't have any problem taking it back to Seattle with you."

I was surprised and confused, to say the least. Here an Alaska State Troopers Drug Task Force Detective Sergeant had just traded me a highly illegal firearm and acted like it was no big deal! I guess they conducted police business a little differently in Alaska. Hey, who was I to judge?

Over the next few days Bill introduced me to several small-time cocaine dealers that he knew. I'd buy a gram here, several grams there, that sort of thing. All small buys. Being most of those dealers knew Bill from past dealings, they had no qualms about selling to me. An ounce of cocaine was at that time (mid-1970s) selling for around $1,200, so I made certain that I always had at least several thousand dollars cash on me at all times.

At several buy locations, the instant I set foot into a dealer's house, apartment, or camper, a sample of cocaine would immediately be offered to me. I quickly realized that "simulating" wasn't at all possible. In fact, I had one dealer who actually held a coke spoon under my nose and watched to make sure that I snorted the cocaine off the spoon. There was absolutely no way I could fake it. If I refused the offered sample, my cover would have been blown and the word would have immediately gone out that "Johnny" was a narc. After that, I'd no longer be able to buy cocaine in the Anchorage area. Plus my safety and Bill's safety would have been at risk. So yes, there were occasions when I did in fact snort small amounts of cocaine. I'm talking about an amount no larger than a match head (and usually of poor quality).

Most dealers just wanted to test me to see how I'd react when offered their sample of cocaine. It was normal for cocaine dealers to offer such samples to buyers. This sampling served two purposes: one was to check to see if the buyer might be a narc since it was illegal for a narc to actually sniff cocaine. But also, the cocaine buyers themselves would logically want to sample the cocaine before making a purchase. If you're shelling out hundreds or even thousands of dollars for cocaine, it's only common sense that you'd want to test the quality first. Who would purchase several thousand dollars of cocaine before first checking out its quality? Answer: someone who wasn't using their own money to make the buy (narcs).

Several days later, Bill informed me that Jimmy had a line on a mid-level cocaine dealer. "Great!" I thought, "Now, maybe we're getting somewhere." Bill arranged for me to meet Jimmy at a go-go club that featured a simulated lesbian act live on stage. He mentioned that he didn't know this particular coke dealer that Jimmy was talking about. That didn't matter to me; I was in Anchorage to buy cocaine from big dealers, if possible, and this was a chance to do so. I was excited!

About 11:00 P.M. that evening Bill and I met up with Jimmy at the agreed location. Jimmy spotted us, walked over to our table, and started talking.

"Johnny, I called this guy I know yesterday and again today, trying to set this whole thing up. I explained to him that I had someone named 'Johnny' from Hawaii, who was interested in buying several ounces. The guy wasn't interested; he told me that whoever this 'Johnny' was, he'd need to buy at least three ounces. I told the guy that I'd say the cost for two was $2,500, even though the price was actually $1,100 per ounce, meaning that they'd make an extra $300 on the sale of two ounces."

Bill started in, "You little fucker; don't be pulling that shit. If the price is $1,100 per ounce, then that's all Johnny'll be paying. That's pure bullshit, Jimmy!"

Jimmy cut in, "They won't go for it, Bill. They're not going to sell two ounces for $2,200 to someone they don't know. I told them I'd say the price was $2,500 for two ounces, and the guy finally agreed to it."

I looked over at Bill, "It's OK. If it's pure, I'll gladly pay $2,500. Shit, an ounce of coke in Honolulu goes for $3,000 to $4,000, and we're not talking about pure, we're talking cocaine that's been stepped on (cut or diluted with some other product). $2,500 for two ounces of pure cocaine is a good deal any day of the week. No problem, Jimmy. I'll gladly spend $2,500 on this buy. A sale is a sale. A few more bucks in price isn't a problem."

"OK, Johnny," said Bill, "Just trying to save you some money, that's all."

Jimmy went on, "Johnny, this dealer is real cagey. He trusts me, but no way is he gonna let me and the two of you walk into his apartment, not knowing who you are. It has to be me and only one of you guys. It's Johnny or you Bill, but not the both of you."

Jimmy looked over at Bill, "Look bro', I need to make something off this deal. $2,500 is the cost of the dope, but I figure $300 for my fee for introducing one of you isn't asking for all that much."

Bill was about to come down on Jimmy, but I cut in, "Jimmy, tell you what; I'll give you $100 per ounce for your troubles, so that's $200 total. I give you $100 now and another $100 after we do the deal, agreed?"

"Johnny, I'd really like to get $300, man. Can't you just throw in an extra hundred? I mean this guy sells top quality. Plus he don't sell to just anyone. He's real cautious. By the way, this guy is a 'brother.' He's black!"

I didn't like what I was hearing. Black drug dealers, not good. (In Seattle we had a lot of black drug dealers. They normally stuck to selling heroin and were always paranoid. They trusted no one, especially white guys!)

"Sit tight, Jimmy," I said and motioned for Bill to follow me into the men's restroom.

"What's up, Johnny?"

"Bill, black dealers are fucking dangerous. I don't know, man. Just me and Jimmy going in there ... I'm not comfortable with that! If things go wrong, then what? Damn it, fuck, man, I just remembered, I traded my 'nine' to the sergeant for ... never mind! Anyway, I no longer have my auto. Fuck!"

"Johnny, I understand your concern, but if you stand this guy up, you don't show up after all this going back and forth, this guy's gonna think something's not right, maybe make you for a narc. Johnny, you gotta make the buy. You can't back out now!"

I thought it over. I really wasn't comfortable with buying from some "brother." However, backing out wouldn't be a good idea, either. On the other hand, if all went well and I ended up actually buying two ounces of pure cocaine ... Man, wouldn't that be great? OK, I could do this. I'd go in there, act calm, pay the twenty-five hundred, get the two ounces, and then get the hell out.

"OK, Bill. Fuck it! I'll do it. If I get my ass blown away, so be it!"

I returned to our table. Bill would stay there and wait for Jimmy and me to return. Jimmy asked me for his $100 in advance. I peeled off two fifties and handed them to him.

"OK, Jimmy, let's get this over with."

Jimmy and I left the club in the undercover vehicle. As I drove, he directed me to an apartment complex located a half a mile away.

"Jimmy, this guy OK? I mean, I honestly don't like dealing with blacks. It's not worth it. They're too unpredictable, too dangerous. Several years ago back in Hawaii some black dealer found out that he'd sold dope to an undercover cop, a cop fresh out of the Honolulu Police Academy. The dealer found out where the cop lived, went to the officer's apartment late one evening, and blew him away with a sawed-off shotgun as he was sleeping on the living room couch. That was fucked-up, man. I mean, I don't like cops and all that, but killing a cop over a dope deal is fucked-up. Honolulu cops ended up shutting down all the prostitution and gambling activity in Honolulu and Waikiki. Shut it down completely. It wasn't long before the shooter was identified, located, and apprehended. "5-O" (Honolulu cops) caught him. He ended up getting life cause Hawaii ain't got no death penalty."

"Johnny, the guy's cautious, but once he gets to knowing you, he's OK. He's actually easy-going. We go in there, you lay down the money, take the dope, and leave. Shouldn't be any problem."

As I drove, Jimmy pointed out a run-down, two-story apartment building. I pulled into the parking area and parked. We got out of our vehicle, walked up a flight of steps, and found the apartment. I still wasn't at all comfortable, not one bit. Jimmy knocked. Seconds later, the door opened slightly.

"What you boys want?"

Jimmy explained that he'd called earlier and had been told to come on over. A skinny black gal, maybe 22 years old, opened the door and motioned us in, all the while looking Jimmy and me over with suspicion, never once taking her eyes off us. We walked into the apartment, where I observed a "nappy-haired" young black female laying back on a couch. She must have been around 14 or 15 years old. Looking towards the open kitchen area, I saw a black male, perhaps in his

40s, sitting at the kitchen table. Nobody was paying attention to Jimmy; all eyes were on me.

The black male told Jimmy to take a seat in the living room and then motioned me to take a seat at the kitchen table next to him. I sat next to him as instructed. I didn't dare say a word.

"What your name boy? Who you?"

In a shaky voice, I responded, "Johnny. I'm Johnny!"

"Johnny, my boy Jimmy here tells me you be from Hawaii. That right? What island you from? Hawaii got lots of islands, which one you from?"

I answered, "Hawaii—I mean, Honolulu, on Oahu."

"Yeah, I know, I know Honolulu, I been there long time ago when I was in the service. So tell me, Johnny from Honolulu, how come you ain't got no tan, if you from Hawaii, like you say? Where's your damn tan?"

"Aah, I don't go to the beach. I sleep most of the day. I do my business at night."

"And so what, why you fly all the way up here for? You a long way from home, ain't you? What you be doing up here in Alaska?"

"I flew up here to buy, aah, you know, to buy cocaine. Cocaine in Hawaii cost a lot. It's priced too high. Plus it's hard to get good stuff; too much cut!"

Jimmy, still sitting on the couch, started to say something, but the guy raised a hand and interrupted him, "Hey, Jimmy, you just sit there and keep your fucking mouth shut. I don't need to be hearing nothing from you! I'm having me a conversation with Johnny!" Jimmy went silent.

"Stand up, Johnny!"

I stood slowly. He ordered the older black gal to come over and search me.

"Make sure this here Johnny boy ain't got no pistola or some Hawaiian spear on him."

The gal searched me—arms, waist, legs. She came up empty. A gun wouldn't have been a problem. I was, after all, supposed to be a drug dealer. I figured he was looking for a wire.

"He ain't got nothing!"

"Good. Sit your ass back down, Johnny. You toot?"

"I do every once in a while, but I try keeping my head clear when I'm doing business."

"So you're telling me you don't toot?"

"No, I didn't say that. I do coke sometimes, every so often, but when I travel or do business, I try not to. Flying around with ounces hidden in your carry-on or on your person, well, you need to be careful. You can't look fucked up!"

"You got my money, Johnny? Jimmy here tells me you wanted two ounces, that right?"

"Yeah, two, if it's pure, like Jimmy said."

"Let me see my money, Johnny. You got my twenty-five?"

I really wanted to get it over with. This guy was being cautious, asking me an awful lot of questions. I wasn't comfortable. I reached into my right front pocket and pulled out a roll of fifties and hundreds. I counted out $2,500 and put the money on the table in front of him. He picked up the stack of bills and counted it himself. As the dealer moved his right hand to pick up the cash, I noticed a small automatic pistol that had previously been hidden by his large hand. Seeing that he had a gun didn't exactly sit well with me. Now all I wanted to do was get my two ounces and get the hell out of there. I wasn't at all comfortable being here and dealing with this black dealer who had a gun.

"Good, it's all here. Tell you what, Johnny. I got what you looking for, but first, you need to do a sample right here in front of me."

"Like I said, when I'm doing business or traveling, I . . ."

Hearing this, the guy placed his hand over the automatic and looked up at me.

"Johnny Boy, you don't toot in front of me, you don't walk out of this apartment. You understand?"

Then he called to the older black gal in the living room, "Hey, girl, bring Johnny Boy here a sample. Let him decide for himself how good my stuff be."

The gal walked into the kitchen, went over to the kitchen counter, brought back a small mirror about 12 inches square, and placed it directly in front of me. On the mirror were two three-inch lines of what appeared to be cocaine; pure, white powder that sparkled under the light. Next to the lines was a blue four-inch-long cut-off soda straw.

"Here you go, Johnny Boy. Free sample. It's on the house. You wouldn't want to be buying something you didn't sample first, now would you?"

I knew what was going on. This guy didn't trust me, didn't know me. To him I was just some white boy, new in town, with money to spend, and even though Jimmy had said that I was cool, that didn't mean anything to this guy. I looked over at him, smiled, and picked up the straw. I bent over close to the mirror, held one end of the straw up to my nose, closed off one nostril, put the straw at the end of one of the lines of cocaine, and inhaled sharply.

The cocaine hit my brain! My eyes watered, my pupils dilated, my teeth froze as the taste of ether entered the back of my throat. I leaned back in my chair and blinked several times as the rush hit me. It was more powerful than anything I'd ever experienced before.

The man smiled and asked, "So how's my stuff, Johnny Boy?"

As I sat back in the chair, an indescribable feeling overcame me. I'd never felt so wonderful, so alert, so invincible, so awake, so damn good in my entire life. I shut my eyes, took in a deep breath, and slowly let it out. I didn't have a care in the world, not one. Everything felt fine. It didn't matter to me that I had in fact crossed a line. I didn't care. I felt better than I'd ever felt before in my entire life. I thought to myself, what could be so wrong in feeling this way? What was so wrong about feeling good? What was so wrong with doing cocaine?

The dealer went on, "My coke's the best in town, Johnny, because this here shit is as pure as it comes. I don't cut it. See here, Johnny, the way I look at it, when you get a product that's pure like this, the best quality available, why the fuck would anyone want to mess with it? It's like fine liquor. Now, if you got VSOP Courvoisier, the good stuff, would you want to dilute it? Hell, no. No fucking way. With me it's the same thing. I don't dilute my cocaine, I don't step on it. It stays as pure as the day I got it. Now, what folks do with it once it walks out that door, well, that's no longer my concern. But what you get from me will always be pure fucking cocaine!"

The guy reached back behind him, opened up a drawer, and handed me a large baggie containing what appeared to be two ounces of cocaine. I took the baggie and was about to stuff it down the front of my trousers, when he said, "Johnny Boy, before you leave, how about kicking down a bit of that fine powder for me and my girls here, just a couple of grams? We'd appreciate that. You see, Johnny, I can't be using or giving my shit away. Not good business. So how about it, Johnny; kick me down some?"

My mind was clearing, but I still felt great. I knew that I wasn't allowed to actually do cocaine, and I also knew that I wasn't allowed to give anyone cocaine once I'd bought it. But how the hell could I refuse this guy's request? I knew it was normal practice to kick down some cocaine to the seller. Kicking down was part of any cocaine transaction and was expected of the buyer. I wasn't about to piss this guy off. Anyway, what's a gram or two, I thought? A couple of grams taken from two ounces, what was the big deal, anyway?

I took out a silver cobra spoon out of my jacket pocket and scooped what seemed to be about a couple of grams of cocaine out of the baggie and onto the mirror. That done, I carefully resealed the baggie and shoved it down the front of my jeans. The dealer was pleased. He looked up and smiled; "Thanks, Johnny Boy. Appreciate it!"

The two black gals in the living room hurried over to the table and started chopping up the cocaine with an old razor blade and making lines. I shook hands with the dealer and turned to leave. Jimmy and I walked out of the apartment and down to my vehicle.

I headed back to the club where I'd left Bill waiting, driving cautiously. All the while Jimmy was bugging me for some of the cocaine I'd just bought. Fuck,

I was becoming agitated. Jimmy was messing with my cocaine high!

And now Bill would want some cocaine too! I wasn't in a position to refuse either of them. If I didn't kick down some coke, then I was an asshole. But worse, the suspicion of me being a narc would start all over again. When you'd just bought a couple of ounces of cocaine, you were expected to kick down to the people you were with. How could I pretend to be an addict, a dope dealer and at the same time not act like any addict or dope dealer would? It just wasn't possible! Yes, the brass, the powers that be in the police department, the prosecutors, the judges ... all those normal, everyday folks in law enforcement expected me to abide by their rules. I couldn't do drugs, I couldn't give drugs to anyone, I couldn't do this, I couldn't do that ... I was only allowed to "pretend" to live a drug dealer's lifestyle, but I wasn't actually allowed to do what they would normally do.

Those folks who made the laws and the rules of behavior weren't the ones who had to go into drug houses to buy drugs. They weren't the ones who had to hang out with addicts, drug dealers, perverts, and prostitutes on a daily basis. They weren't the ones who'd be courting danger with the scum of the earth, all for the purpose of producing the desired stats that passed for victory in the "War On Drugs."

I pulled into the parking lot of the tavern. Jimmy and I went in and walked over to Bill's table. Bill started in on me immediately; "Johnny, you get the coke? Let me see it. Where is it?"

"Slow down, Bill. Yeah, I got it, but I can't show it to you right here in front of everyone."

Jimmy interrupted, "Johnny, don't forget me. C'mon, you gonna let me have some too, right?"

"Will you guys just gimme a fucking second? Fuck, man!"

I ordered what was now my usual; Yukon Jack with a beer back. Jimmy looked over at me, "Johnny, can I get a drink too?"

"Jimmy, buy your own fucking drink. I gave you 100 bucks before we left, remember? Here, here!"

I took two fifties out and handed the bills to Jimmy.

"Here's the other hundred I owe you. Pay for your own damn drink." Jimmy reached over and took the money.

"What about kicking me down some of that cocaine, Johnny? Can I have some? I'll even buy some off you!"

"Jimmy, I told you to shut the fuck up! God damn it, just shut up! Jimmy, if you give me a damn, fucking minute, I'll kick you down some, but not here. Wait till we get back in the car. Can I at least have my drink first?"

Boy, when you got cocaine available, everyone goes nuts. What the fuck, man. Why couldn't they just wait a few minutes? But in time, I'd find out that, no, folks can't wait. When cocaine is available, they want it right now, in front of everyone if need be. They don't care.

Drinks came. I sat back and took my time drinking. Jimmy quickly finished his beer. Bill didn't order anything. He was just sitting there, impatiently waiting for me to kick him down some coke. I was still feeling the effects of the cocaine that I'd done earlier. It had felt good, but now, because of being bugged for a kick-down, I was starting to get agitated.

I finished off my shot of Yukon Jack, gulped down my beer, got up, and walked out of the club with Jimmy and Bill two steps behind me. I got in my car. Jimmy got in the back seat, Bill in the passenger seat. Bill was holding a cellophane wrapper he'd taken off a pack of cigarettes. Jimmy had a scrap of paper. They were both holding their hands out to me, like a couple of beggars.

I took a deep breath and exhaled. Damn it, I really didn't want to do this! OK, fuck it. I pulled out the baggie from the front of my trousers. Bill's eyes went big when he saw it.

"Johnny, that's a whole lot of fucking coke you got there!"

Bill held out his cellophane wrapper, and I scooped a small amount into it from the baggie.

"That all you gonna give me, Johnny? C'mon, just a bit more. You got a lot there."

"Just take what I give you, damn it, and put it away."

Jimmy had his arms hanging over the seat, waiting for his kick down. I put a small amount of cocaine into his scrap of paper. Jimmy carefully folded the paper into a bindle, thanked me, and quickly got out of the car, bindle held tightly in his hand.

"Thanks, Johnny. See me next time you get to needing more."

I started the car and drove off to the undercover apartment. I didn't say a word to Bill. I was feeling pretty uncomfortable about all this. Once again in the apartment, I started writing up my report. I'd called Sgt. Lee from a pay phone just moments earlier and informed him of the two-ounce buy that I'd just made. Lee told me that he and Henderson were presently tied up, so they couldn't come over for at least two hours.

Bill and I entered the apartment, and I went in the bathroom to take a much-needed piss. As I came out of the bathroom, I saw Bill with a damn needle in his arm. He was slamming the cocaine I'd given him!

"Bill, fuck this. I can't stay here while you're shooting up. No way! I'm going for a drive. I'll be back in an hour or so."

I got in the car and headed out of town. I couldn't believe this shit. What the fuck was going on? A little over an hour ago I'd done my first big line of pure cocaine. Now Bill, my confidential informant, was in an Anchorage police undercover apartment shooting up the same cocaine that I'd recently purchased. And to top it all off, my two supervisors were presently busy.

I was starting to come down off the cocaine high. I felt agitated and depressed. The longer I drove out of town, the more depressed and sick I felt. I felt like I had the flu or something. Up ahead, I spotted a rest stop. I pulled into the parking area and drove to the back of the lot, totally out of view. I didn't want to see anyone, I didn't want to talk to anyone; I just wanted to be left the fuck alone. All of a sudden the good feeling I'd been experiencing was gone and was rapidly being replaced by depression. I started to feel nauseous. I parked, turned the engine off, and rolled the windows up. I'd never felt so messed up and totally confused in all my life. What was happening to me?

I was a cop, damn it. I was there to do undercover drug buys, arrest drug dealers, and throw them in jail. I was there to fight crime, to fight drugs! But I suddenly found myself coming down off a cocaine high that, not long ago, had made me feel better than I'd ever felt in my life.

I felt like shit. What I probably needed was to do a small hit of that cocaine. "Just this once, I'll do a hit to get this feeling to go away, then I'll be OK. Just this one time, then I'll feel fine again." I had to meet up with Lee and Andrews in about an hour. I couldn't let them see me coming down off cocaine. I needed to have my shit together, I needed to be grounded.

I scanned the parking area, making sure no one else was around, pulled out the baggie, and sank down in the front seat. I felt into my jean jacket and located my coke spoon. My cobra snake cocaine spoon was one of a kind; there wasn't another like it in the entire world. (I'd had it custom-made from my own design.) The cocaine was sitting in my lap. I looked around to make sure no one was watching, then carefully opened up the baggie and dipped my spoon into the shiny flakes of pure cocaine. I looked around one last time before bringing the coke spoon up to my right nostril. I took in a deep breath, looked away, and exhaled. I paused, and then in one deep snort I inhaled the cocaine off the spoon.

There was a momentary burning sensation in my nose, but I didn't care. "Pain don't hurt," I always say. My brain got hit by the sudden intake of pure cocaine. My depression, my drug-sick feeling, my nausea instantly disappeared! Just that quick, it was gone. I felt great once again. I couldn't remember why I'd felt so down just a few seconds ago. All it took was a tiny amount of cocaine, maybe an amount the size of two match heads, to get me feeling good again.

I breathed in deeply as I wiped away the snot running out of my nose. Again I dipped my spoon into the cocaine and took a hit; this time into my other nostril. Wow, this cocaine was truly a miracle drug! It had the ability to take me from utter depression, from being an undercover cop on the verge of tears, to, several seconds later, feeling fine, happy, confident, and once again ready to "fight crime!" Go fight those damn drug dealers, Detective Bernie Lau. Buy their dope, arrest 'em, lock 'em all up, and throw away the key! That's what I was there to do!

I looked down at my watch. Time to head back to the undercover apartment and turn the cocaine over to Sgt. Lee. Before I drove back, however, I felt I needed to take a little cocaine off the top for myself, "just in case." I might need a tiny bit if my depression returned. I took out a $50 bill from the money I had left, folded it into a bindle, and then shoveled off about a gram's worth of cocaine into the bindle. I double-wrapped the bindle with another $50 bill, then stuffed it into my right sock, shoving it way down so that it was actually under my foot. Just having that cocaine near and available ("in case I needed it") allowed me to relax.

On the drive back I started thinking. What if Sergeant Lee said something like "Bernie, this here baggie containing an alleged two ounces of cocaine looks a bit short. How come?" I'd answer, "Hey, Sergeant, I gave the dealer man 2,500 bucks, and he gave me this here baggie he claimed was two ounces of pure cocaine. You say it's short—take it up with the dealer! You realize, Sergeant, that I couldn't actually weigh it when I bought it. So no, I don't exactly know if it's actually two ounces or not! Oh, by the way, that highly illegal shotgun you traded me, how much did you say it weighed?"

Bill had something over me because I'd given him some of the cocaine that I'd purchased. I now had something on Sgt. Lee because of that shotgun he'd stupidly traded me. My undercover assignment in Alaska was getting confusing!

Driving back to the apartment, I stopped at a service station and bought myself a 40-ounce bottle of fortified beer. Beer always helped in fighting those negative feelings that creep up at times. And I always carried a handful of valium and a dozen pain pills with me.

The great part of being a narc was that we were allowed to have drugs on our person because if the bad guys searched us, finding drugs on us gave us more credibility. Sometimes I even jaywalked right in front of Seattle cops, just to have a jaywalking citation written up on me. I'd keep a stack of those tickets in my wallet in case anyone ever looked through it. No, the Seattle cops writing me jaywalking tickets never recognized me. How could they? My personality, my demeanor was no longer that of a Seattle police officer. In my own mind I wasn't a "cop." I was "Johnny Medeiros," biker asshole and "pretend" addict!

Deep down, however, I wasn't so sure about the "pretend" part. I felt I was changing, but because of the change, I was getting better and better at fooling the bad guys and getting them to sell me dope. Yeah, fooling the bad guys was getting easier, but was I also fooling myself?

I unscrewed the cap off the 40-ounce beer, popped two valiums and a demerol, and washed them down with several large swigs. Ah. OK. Now I was ready to face the sergeant.

Sgt. Lee and Detective Henderson were in the apartment when I got there. Lee asked where I'd been.

"Just went for a drive, Sarge. This undercover stuff can be stressful at times! I needed some fresh air and time alone."

"Where's Bill?"

"I got no idea where he's at. He was here when I left. Probably went back to the tavern."

"So what about the buy, Bernie? It go down OK?"

"Yep, went down fine. No problem."

I removed the baggie from the inside of my trousers and placed it on the table. Lee picked up the baggie and looked at me with a big shit-eating grin on his face.

"Damn, Bernie, you did good. You did real good!"

Lee took the baggie of cocaine, placed it in a large evidence envelope, and sealed the edges with red evidence tape. I signed my initials, date, and serial number across the tape in three different places, then handed the envelope back to the sergeant.

"We'll get this into evidence and pick up your report in the morning."

"Good. I'm beat. I need to crash." The beer, valium, and demerol were starting to take effect.

After they left, I sat down and wrote out my report on the two-ounce buy, without, of course, mentioning me doing those two lines of cocaine. I didn't sleep at all that night; the cocaine in my system kept me awake. Come morning I dragged my butt out of bed, not feeling good at all. I'd forgotten how long it had been since the last time I'd eaten anything, and a night without sleep didn't help. I felt shitty.

I suddenly remembered the cocaine I had hidden in my shoe. Ah, yes. I'd taken some from the baggie, "just in case I needed it." Well, "just in case" was in fact right now. I needed a "wake-up call!"

I carefully removed the bindle from my sock, scooped out some of the cocaine onto the kitchen table, and using my official Alaska State Drivers License in the name of "John Abel Medeiros," I proceeded to crush up the flakes of cocaine. Several minutes later, I had there in front of me two neat one-inch lines of cocaine awaiting my attention. Being I had no straw available, I rolled up one of the fifty-dollar bills, and proceeded to quickly snort both lines.

There was no longer any pain in my nose as I snorted the cocaine. My eyes, however, started to water, and my nose began to run. I stood straight and took in a deep breath. Aah, yes! How I was getting to love that feeling of instant relief. I was no longer tired or hungry. I felt great again and ready to go out and fight that "War on Drugs."

Suddenly, I thought to myself, "Bernie, what the fuck are you doing?" "Johnny" cut into my thinking: "Shut the fuck up dude! I got things to be doing today, like getting me another gun!"

Yes, it was time for "Johnny" to re-arm himself. Time to go buy him a gun. Walking around buying dope while unarmed wasn't at all healthy! Way too dangerous. Stupid actually; especially up here in Alaska.

In the State of Alaska a person could simply walk into a gun store, show the clerk some form of Alaska State identification, pick out the handgun or rifle he wanted, plunk down the required cash, and walk out with the gun. There was no waiting two or more weeks while the gun dealer ran a police background check.

I chose a pre-owned .41 Magnum Smith & Wesson revolver, and handed the clerk the $75 asking price. I thanked him, tucked the revolver in the small of my back under my jean jacket, and walked out of the store. Buying a gun took all of 25 minutes. The .41 caliber revolver in the small of my back bulged out a bit, but I didn't care. Fuck it! This was, after all, Alaska, where everybody owned a gun or two. I was just happy to once again be "armed and dangerous."

I was walking back to the undercover apartment. It was a beautiful, winter day in Anchorage. When I'd gotten out of bed that morning, along with doing those two lines of cocaine, I'd washed a couple of valiums and a pain pill down with the remaining fortified beer. The combination of the three "medications" helped start my day on a mellow note. Bill was off doing whatever he was doing, and truthfully, I didn't care. I was by myself enjoying the peace and quiet of early morning.

Several yards up ahead, walking towards me, I spotted a white male, about 30 years of age, walking with what appeared to be his girlfriend. Cute gal, perhaps, but I could tell that she was the "high-maintenance" type. White gal, well-dressed, too clean, too pure, too stuck up ... not my type.

Not wanting to walk near them, I crossed to the other side of the street and kept walking, minding my own business. Beautiful, sunny day, the winter air was fresh, the morning birds were chirping ... BAM! I was suddenly slammed up against a parked car. Just like that, nothing said, no warning.

"Police. You're under arrest!"

What the hell?

"Under arrest! What the fuck for?" I yelled back.

"You got a permit for that gun, boy?"

Boy? Had this motherfucker just called me "boy?" Oh, hell, no! No fucking way!

Well, it turned out that the asshole was a police officer on his way to work. As I'd walked past him, he'd turned and spotted the bulge in the small of my back, and knowing that the bulge was most likely a gun—and probably to impress his "high-maintenance" gal friend—he slammed me up against a car and placed me under arrest for carrying a concealed weapon without a permit. Damn it; seemed Lt. Andrews had forgotten to get me one of those permits. Oh well, asshole drugs dealers don't usually have concealed weapons permits!

Anyway, I wasn't worried. I was actually enjoying my present encounter with "Anchorage's Finest." When I first arrived, I'd been told that if I ever got arrested, I was to say nothing about who I was or what I was doing in Anchorage. I was instructed to just have the arresting officer call a number that was written down on a piece of paper that I carried with me, tucked in my wallet. So I didn't resist. However, I did mouth-off to the officer. You know, the usual "You motherfucking asshole." Stuff like that.

A patrol unit soon arrived, and I was placed, still handcuffed, in the back of the patrol vehicle.

"What's your name, boy? Where you from?"

"Boy." The guy was sure working hard at being an asshole. I said nothing except, "Call this number and ask for Sgt. Lee." Now, that alone should have made the cop back off a bit, at least till he talked to the sergeant.

Arriving at the Anchorage Police Station, I was placed in a holding cell, still handcuffed. Looking the way I did, sort of like "Charlie Manson," I must have been absolutely terrifying to those officers.

The duty sergeant came over, eyeballed me sitting there in the cell, and made some derogatory remarks, all the while snickering and having fun at my expense.

"I gotta piss." I said.

"You hold it a while, asshole," he replied.

In one sense, it was funny as hell and I was enjoying it. To me it was all just one big game. When else could you act and talk to a cop as if you were really an asshole, and actually get arrested, handcuffed, and thrown into the back of a patrol vehicle, then placed into a holding cell at the local police station, and made fun of by the duty sergeant and his fellow officers, all the while they not knowing that you were actually also a police officer?

I must have sat handcuffed in that holding cell for close to an hour. The officer who arrested me would come over every so often to smirk at me and make some childish little remarks that were designed to piss me off. In response I pretended to be pissed off and talked a bunch of shit back to him. I was, after all, pretending to be an asshole, so I needed to act the part.

Eventually, Sgt. Lee arrived with Bill and came over to the holding cell. Sgt. Lee just looked at me, shook his head, and smiled.

"Hey, Johnny, you been a naughty boy again!"

Within minutes the duty sergeant appeared, opened up the holding cell, removed my cuffs, and led Bill and me to the coffee room. He didn't yet know who Bill and I really were. Sgt. Lee followed us into the coffee room.

"Sarge, I gotta piss real bad."

"OK, Johnny; you just sit tight. You'll be out of here before long, no problem. I just need to talk with the duty sergeant and sort all this out. I won't, however, reveal that you're a cop! Let them wonder what the hell is going on, and who the hell you might be. I know they're dying to find out."

Lee then went back to the duty sergeant's office and closed the door behind him. I walked over to the door of the coffee room and peeked out. Bill asked, "What's the matter, Johnny?"

"I gotta piss bad, Bill, really bad. I asked them idiots to let me have a piss, but all they kept saying was for me to 'just hold it in!' Well, I can't hold it any longer! I gotta piss!"

I walked over to the coffee pot which was only halfway full. I picked it up, took the coffee pot with me, and walked over to the far corner of the coffee room.

"Bill, go ahead and keep an eye out for me, will ya?" Bill stood next to the door, acting as my lookout.

I looked at Bill one last time, then I took my dick out of my jeans and proceeded to take that much-needed piss right into the coffee pot.

"I hope these assholes like their coffee good and strong!" I stated, as I pissed.

Yeah, I know; that wasn't a very nice thing to do to my fellow police officers. But, hey, what the hell—it was fun!

Looking back, I can now see that while working undercover in Anchorage, I really started to get caught up in my undercover role. The more I worked at "pretending" to be an asshole and a drug addict, the more I was becoming that person. My way of thinking, my attitude, my way of looking at life in general, even my way of looking at my fellow police officers was changing. I no longer thought of myself as a police officer. Day by day, I was taking on the personality and character of "Johnny Medeiros." Johnny Medeiros, my pretend buddy, my friend, my protector, and the asshole drug addict that I so enjoyed making believe was me.

The titty bars, the buys, processing evidence, filing reports ... it all went on for another week. I bought several more ounces of pure cocaine from several dealers. I also bought an ounce of heroin. In all I purchased illegal drugs from 13 separate individuals. Hal Lawrence, the main supplier of cocaine in the Anchorage area, would soon be stopped on an arrest warrant, and two ounces of pure cocaine would be discovered in his vehicle. He ended up serving nine years in a federal penitentiary.

Over the next four months, I traveled back and forth between Seattle and Anchorage in order to give testimony in federal court against those individuals that I'd purchased cocaine and other illegal drugs from. All were either found guilty or pleaded guilty in order to receive a lesser sentence. I'd purchased cocaine and other illegal drugs at least twice and often three times from most of those 13 individuals. That amounted to 25 or so separate hand-to-hand undercover drug buys, all done in a short period of ten days. During those ten days, I spent over $10,000 in cash and racked up 112 hours of overtime. I often worked 16 hours a day, pushing myself to the limit. All of the law enforcement individuals concerned were happy with the work I'd done.

Truth of the matter is that I started getting burned out while working undercover those ten days in Anchorage. I'd been offered cocaine, and in order to keep my cover and hopefully stay alive, I'd chosen to snort. Not your ordinary, low-quality cocaine, but rather, 99.9% pure pharmaceutical grade. I'd been confronted with, "an offer I couldn't refuse!" as there was no way the black cocaine dealer was going to allow some white boy from Hawaii who he didn't know to walk out with two ounces of pure cocaine without first witnessing him do a line or two. That wasn't going to happen! So I'd gotten a taste of cocaine, and I'd liked how it made me feel.

I'd never felt so good in my entire life. On cocaine, nothing mattered; everything was fine. Fine, that is, until I started to come down off the cocaine high. My undercover stint in Alaska was the start of my eventual drug use and medical retirement. Over the next eight years of continued undercover work, I'd pay a heavy price.

Informant Bill Tarniff was paid over $1,000 cash and given an airline ticket out of Alaska for his assistance in introducing me to local drug dealers in Anchorage.

As for my pissing in that coffee pot ... yeah, OK, I shouldn't have done that. But, hey, it was just payback for them taunting me and treating me like an asshole. The arresting officer had his fun talking shit to me, and so I decided to have my own fun. Nothing was ever said about that spiked coffee. Maybe they didn't even notice it.

40

Little 'Ho'

Each time I ventured out into Seattle's decadent streets as an undercover narc, looking to buy drugs, I first needed to transform myself from a law-abiding Seattle cop into a biker-type asshole drug dealer and addict. Buying drugs while pretending to be a junkie was my job. Buying drugs and making court cases against Seattle's drug dealers, perverts, and assholes. Before doing so, however, I needed to be 100% convincing in every aspect of my undercover personality. My life depended on it. If I ever got made as an undercover cop, I'd more likely than not end up with a bullet in the head, maybe two.

It takes more than just "pretending" to be convincing in the role of a drug addict. I, Detective Bernard Lau, needed to actually believe deep down inside that I was in fact that asshole, a biker puke, a drug addict, and yes, sometimes even a sick, slimy, sexual pervert. I had to become those anti-social personalities, and I accomplished this by first transforming myself into the person I called "Johnny Medeiros." Johnny Medeiros wasn't just pretending, making believe, or playing a role. He was in fact an asshole, a biker puke, and a drug addict. And over a period of a few years, I, Bernie Lau, would become an asshole, a biker puke, and a drug addict just like my mentor, Johnny Medeiros. Johnny Medeiros was every disgusting thing that I wasn't. But he was what kept me alive as I worked those dangerous undercover assignments in and about Seattle's drug-infested, crime-ridden neighborhoods.

I was driving to the Narcotics office early one Friday morning, southbound on 3rd Avenue. As I passed Madison Street, I happened to glance down towards 1st Avenue. There in the distance, I noticed a blonde female crossing the street. I knew instantly that she was a prostitute, a new 'ho' in town. Long years of experience had given me a sixth sense.

I checked into the Narc office, met Detective Paul, and then we went downstairs and had breakfast. I had coffee, crispy hash browns, two eggs sunny-side up, and toast. We chatted over pending and future cases, then Paul went back to the office, while I indulged in one of my favorite pastimes: cruising the streets of Seattle, looking for trouble.

I was walking along 1st Avenue, and the closer I got to Pike Street, the more I became Johnny Medeiros. That was the part of town where the action was, the action Johnny liked. The scum of the earth congregated there: pimps, 'ho's, sluts, drug dealers, perverts, and child molesters. There were gays looking to pick you up, offering rock-bottom prices for blow jobs, theaters showing dirty movies around the clock, classics like "Deep Throat" and "The Devil in Miss Jones." Yeah, I loved this area. It was alive. Never boring, always something going on. My kind of place.

As I neared 1st and Union, I spotted the cute blonde I'd seen earlier on my way to work, standing on the corner. I saw that she didn't look quite as good up close as she had from a distance of several blocks. She was young and still sort of cute, but her face had the tell-tale signs of early aging brought on by drug abuse and days gone without sleep. Working the streets of Seattle as a prostitute was starting to take a toll on her. I figured she was probably 17 or 18 years old, but she looked much older.

Crossing Union Street, I walked up to her and said, "Hey, how you doing?"

She smiled and answered, "Hi! So what's up? Nice day, eh? You looking to party?"

I noticed she still had all her teeth. Even though she looked burnt-out, she was still sort of cute.

"Yeah, maybe!"

"I'm Sue. So you looking for a date or what?"

"Could be; depends how much you asking and what I get for my money."

"Well, for a blow job and a fuck, I charge 30 bucks. No anal though, nobody fucks me in the ass, no way. And another thing: I spit. I don't swallow. So you interested?"

"Yeah, sure. Know any place we can go?"

"Uh, yeah. There's a hotel just up the street, rents rooms by the half hour. Five bucks for a half hour and you get a towel with the room. Safe. No cops, no problems. So you wanna go?"

"OK, why not?"

We walked north on 1st Avenue, past the Pike Place Market, and continued for several more blocks until we got to a run-down, two-story hotel. We climbed up two flights of darkened stairs. At the top of the landing I bumped into an old guy hanging around in the shadows. I handed him a five-dollar bill. Taking the money, he handed me a towel.

"Half hour, Mis-tah, you got only half hour!"

He then handed Sue a key; "Room-num-ba-tree, Missy!"

We walked down the hall to door number three. She unlocked the door, and I followed her in, checking out the room as I went. It was tiny, damp, and mildewed and had just enough space for a small, soiled mattress that rested on bare box springs. No sheets, no pillows—fucking nasty! The toilet was located down the hall. I thought, "Well, what do you expect for five bucks? Certainly not a presidential suite."

Sue started to undress while I stood at the foot of the bed watching her, observing her firm, tiny titties. I smiled to myself. I liked what I saw. No stretch marks, no sagging boobs. Great. My type of gal. Her face wasn't all that hot, but her body was just fine.

Totally naked, Sue sat on the filthy mattress and bounced up and down. She looked up at me and said, "Hey, you gonna take your clothes off or what? Don't just stand there; get your clothes off, damn it. Time's a-wasting. We only got a half hour, you know!"

"Sorry," I replied. "I was just zoning on your tight-ass body. You got a fine body there, girl!"

"Yeah. Thanks. Money first, Johnny! 30 bucks. I get paid first. Business before pleasure, you know."

I took out my wallet and counted out $30: two tens and two fives. I handed Sue the money and she quickly stuffed it into one of her dirty socks. I reached around to the small of my back and removed my automatic. Carefully I laid the gun down on a chair next to the bed.

Sue frowned and asked, "What the fuck you need a gun for? You some kind of stick-up man?"

"Nope. The gun's my insurance policy. Some punk-ass motherfucker tries to jack me, I pull out my 'insurance policy' and do what I gotta do. I don't take no bullshit from nobody!"

"You ever kill anybody?" she asked.

Still undressing, I answered. "Yeah, but he was an asshole and had it coming. Tried to sell me bunk, didn't wanna give me my money back. It was only 40 bucks, but you know, it's the principle of it all; you let some punk-ass motherfucker jack you, word gets out, you lose respect. From then on, you're just another chump. I told the asshole to give me my money back, but he got in my face, talking that ghetto shit. Next thing I know, the dumb fuck pulls a knife on me. Oh, hell, no! Big mistake dude! I took my gun out and shot the motherfucker right in his face. Died right there on the spot. I got my money back, picked up the knife, and walked away. 40 bucks, that's what it was all about; 40 fucking dollars. Dumb fuck!"

Now totally naked as well, I stood at the foot of the bed holding my hard on. Damn, my dick was hard! Sue looked up and smiled; "OK, come over here, Johnny Boy, so I can suck your dick!"

"Aah, you got any condoms?" I asked, as Sue reached out for my throbbing hard on.

"Nope, but don't worry; I'm clean. See, I got busted down in L.A. a few weeks ago for O&A. Up in the jail they ran some sort of STD test on me. My test came out positive; I had the fucking clap. You know—VD. The nurses gave me a buncha shots and now I'm OK. Really, I'm fine. I know I'm clean cause I ain't got no more discharge or nothing like that oozing out of my pussy. It's as clean as can be. Here, look; see for yourself!"

Sue leaned back on the mattress, spreads her legs wide, and exposed her tiny, pink pussy to me. Shaking my head, I took a step back. Ah, hell, no. I didn't need to be looking at her damn pussy!

"So you ain't got no condom, that what you saying?"

"No, man, I ain't got no damn condoms. So what? You won't fuck without a rubber? Is that it! I ain't giving you your money back, if that's what you're thinking. OK, how about I jack you off? I'll make you get your nut that way!"

"Nah, that's OK. Go ahead and keep the damn money. It's not that big a deal."

Sue's mentioning her STDs and all that nasty discharge talk had killed my mood and my throbbing hard on. I went limp—total bummer!

"How about we go shoot some pool. That be OK with you instead of fucking?"

"It don't matter to me, Johnny. It's your money. Fuck or shoot pool; it's all the same to me."

Sue rolled off the bed and started to get dressed, leaving the $30 stuffed in the sock. Safe a place as any, I guessed. Money, drugs, etc.—a lot of gals carry that shit in their socks. Cops might stop and check your ID, even run your name for warrants, but unless they have a very good reason ("probable cause"), they can't just go ahead and start searching you or ask you to take off your shoes so they can search your socks.

I put my jeans back on and tucked my automatic into the small of my back. It was wrapped with rubber bands, so it wouldn't slide down into my pants, and I always wore a jean jacket cause it hid the gun.

We left the run-down hotel and headed down 1st Avenue. Two blocks up, on Union Street, we entered a pool hall, grabbed a table, and started shooting pool. For the next hour we played for two bucks a game. I ended up losing five games in a row. Fuck! Oh, well; it was only city money.

Now fully frustrated, I handed Sue her two fives. "OK, here's your ten, I gotta go." The little 'ho'd just made 40 bucks off me and didn't even have to fuck for it!

"OK, Johnny, bye. Maybe I'll see you around."

"Yeah, maybe."

"Next time I see you, I'll try having some condoms with me."

"Yeah, OK. Maybe we'll have us some fun next time."

"You know, Johnny, you really missed out because I suck dick real good!"

"I bet you do, sweetheart. But you don't swallow, right?"

"Well, Johnny, depends on how much you're willing to pay. All us girls have a price, you know. For 100 bucks, I'll swallow, but if you wear a rubber, that can't happen, right?"

"Guess not. By the way, how much for anal? Every gal's got a price."

"For you, Johnny, $2,000, and you'd be the first."

"Well, that's kinda outta my price range. See you around!"

"Yeah, OK. I'll be around."

I walked back to my undercover GTO, parked in a Diamond lot. Looking up at the sign, I mumbled to myself, "A buck twenty-five per hour! Damn! Price just keeps going up. Used to be 75 cents, not that long ago!"

As I drove off, "Johnny" faded away, and once again, I was Detective Bernie Lau. Damn, this working undercover was fucking cool! Here I was driving a seized GTO, I never had to dress up, and I got lots of spending cash from the city any time I needed it. I was allowed to drink while on the job, I carried a gun and a badge, and I could fuck 'ho's whenever I wanted. Well, OK—as long as I didn't get caught. I knew cops weren't supposed to be fucking 'ho's or doing some of the shit that I did, but it wasn't really me who was doing it. It was Johnny.

The more drug arrests made, the happier the brass were because lots of stats made them look good. And I was willing to do whatever I had to do to get them those stats. I wanted to be the best damn undercover narc ever in the history of the SPD. I wanted to feel worthy. I was tired of always feeling like a fuck-up. All my life I'd felt out of place, like I wasn't wanted, like I didn't belong. All I wanted was to somehow be accepted for who I was. I knew I hadn't been the brightest kid around. I'd struggled constantly to do better, but I couldn't seem to break the curse I was under. I was tired of always being put down.

With Reggie I was a huge disappointment. In the Navy I was a poor excuse for an electrician. Even as a cop in uniform I was still made fun of and sometimes falsely accused of doing things that I didn't do. Any sort of criticism would make me physically sick for weeks on end.

When I started working undercover, I felt free for the first time in my life. I could go out with no one looking over my shoulder, no one out there to criticize me or cut me down. I was Detective Bernie Lau, narc. I was leading a dangerous life that few if any of the 1,200 officers in the SPD would be willing to lead. Just being a cop was dangerous; being an undercover cop was like walking the razor's edge. And I loved it. I thrived! It was my entire life.

41

Concerned Citizen

Several weeks later, I spotted Sue again at 3rd and Pike. As I approached her, I noticed that her left eye was swollen shut and her lip was cut and puffy. She saw me coming and quickly walked the other way. I caught up, took hold of her left arm, and spun her around.

"Sue, what the fuck happened? Who did this to you?"

"It's OK, Johnny. It's nothing really. Don't worry about it; I'll be fine. It was all my fault, anyway."

"What do you mean 'your fault?'"

Seeing what some asshole had done to Sue's face, Johnny got angry and clenched his fists.

"Fuck that, Sue. I'm not letting this go. Tell me what the fuck happened. Who did this to you? I'm serious; I'm not walking away till you tell me what happened!"

Pedestrians walking by looked over at us, probably wondering what was going on, maybe thinking that I'd done this to her. I paid no attention to them. I didn't give a fuck! I didn't care what they thought of me or what they said to me because at that moment I wasn't that messed-up-in-the-head Bernie Lau; I was the confident asshole Johnny Medeiros, who didn't give a damn about how other people felt or what they said. Johnny couldn't have cared less. And what a wonderful feeling that was!

Sue took hold of my arm and started pulling me away from the gathering crowd and down towards 1st Avenue.

"Come on, Johnny, let's just go. Can we get out of here, please? We don't need this. Johnny, I need a drink real bad. My face hurts!"

"Yeah, yeah, OK. Fuck it. Let's go."

We walked towards the Pike Place Market and ended up at 1st and Union in front of the Union 101 Tavern. Going inside, we grabbed a table against the far wall. The waitress came over and I ordered a beer and a shot of Yukon Jack. Sue ordered a double rum and coke. Drinks came. I hit my shot of Yukon Jack and chased it with a couple large swigs of beer. Sue downed hers quickly.

"Damn, girl, slow down. Don't drink so fast!"

"Sorry, Johnny, but my face really hurts. Can I have another, please? Another double!"

"Yeah, sure." I ordered another double rum and coke.

"OK, now tell me what the fuck happened. Who did this to you?"

"OK, Johnny, I'll tell you. I live with this guy, Ronnie. He's got a room above the Paramount Theater up on Pine. You know, that brick building that's also a theater?"

"Yeah, I know the building."

"He's not really a bad person," Sue continued, "but when he drinks, he gets mean and hits me. Otherwise, he's OK."

"OK? I don't think so, Sue. Him being drunk ain't no fucking excuse for beating up on you. He's a chicken-shit, punk-ass motherfucker as far as I'm concerned! Any guy beats up on a woman is a fucking punk! Damn it girl, look what he did to your face!"

"Is my face really that bad, Johnny? It is, isn't it?"

"Fuck, yes, it is. Your face is fucked up!"

Sue started crying. Damn it! I hate it when gals start crying. I can't stand it.

"Sue, stop your crying or I'm leaving!" She still kept sobbing, but not as much.

"I don't know what to do, Johnny. I try being nice to Ronnie. I give him all the money I make. I give him sex whenever he wants. Sometimes when Ronnie's friends come over, I even have sex with them because he tells me to. If I say no, Ronnie or his friends start hitting me. I do whatever he tells me to do, but sometimes, he still gets angry and hits me. I can't take his beatings any more. What do I do, Johnny? I'm too scared to go back up there. I know that he's gonna start hitting me again. I hurt so bad right now, I just can't take another beating! How can I make him stop hitting me? How can I make him happy?"

Johnny took hold of Sue's hand.

"Look, Sue, you can't make this asshole happy no matter what you do, no matter how good you are to him, no matter how much money you make for him, or how much pussy you give him and his friends. He's always gonna whop up on you no matter what. It's a control thing. Ronnie needs to always remind you that you're his property to do with as he pleases. It's never going to stop, Sue. It's only going to get worse. Just look at you, and here you're, what, 18 years old?"

"I'm really only 16. I made 16 three months ago. I ran away from home. My mom and I didn't get along. She's an alcoholic, and when she drinks, she gets angry and starts hitting me. She's constantly yelling at me for no reason and cutting me down, telling me I was a mistake, and that I ruined her life. So finally, I couldn't take it any more and ran away. I ended up in LA, then Oakland. After that, I took a bus to Seattle."

"Ronnie saw me get off the bus and offered me a place to crash. A few days later, he bought me some nice clothes and said I could stay at his place for as long as I wanted to. At first, he was real nice to me and treated me good. Then a week or so later, he said I had to repay him for the clothes and for all the food I'd eaten and also for him letting me sleep at his place. I didn't have no money, so he told me to get out there and sell my ass, told me to start tricking. He pushed me out the door and told me not to come back till I'd made a couple 100 bucks. I mean, what else could I do? I don't know anyone in Seattle. He told me not to try running away cause he'd find me and hurt me bad."

I finished my beer and ordered another Bud with a shot of Yukon Jack. I sat back looking up at the dark ceiling, feeling no pain. Sue had no idea that Johnny was actually an undercover cop and, I figured, the less she knew, the better for everyone. I knew about guys like Ronnie from experience. His thing was runaways. He befriended them, gave them a place to stay, and then turned them to a life of drugs and prostitution.

Bernie was a dreamer who'd have liked to change the world and make it a better place for kids like Sue. Johnny Medeiros was a hardened realist who knew you couldn't change the world. It is what it is! Society expected Officer Bernie Lau to arrest Ronnie for assault and battery. But Ronnie would make bail in a day or two, locate Sue, and that would be the end of her. She'd never live to see the inside of a court room. If he didn't kill her himself, he'd have someone else do it. She'd turn up dead, maybe from a "drug overdose." In the world of prostitutes and pimps, a "hot shot" of heroin was the quickest way to get rid of a problem. A runaway kid or a prostitute overdosed, and no one really cared. It wouldn't even make the evening news.

The only way to deal with someone like Ronnie was to come down to his level. You had to scare the shit out of him and make him believe that if he didn't do what you "advised" him to do, there would be immediate and dire consequences. Let him know without a doubt that it was "do as he was told or else!"

I made small talk with Sue.

"So where are you from?"

"Spokane."

"When did you split?"

"About seven months ago."

"You think you'll ever go back to your mom?"
"No way."
"You got any other family you can go to?"
"Yeah, I got a sister in Spokane."
"You think she might be willing to help you out?"
"Pro'bly. Yeah."

As I sat drinking my beer, I was slowly formulating a plan. I took my last swig and smiled to myself. I knew what had to be done. I got up and walked over to the pay phone.

"Hey, Roy. Johnny here. Feel like having some fun?"

"OK. What's up? Where you at?"

"I'm down at 1st and Union. I need you for some back-up in dealing with an asshole pimp who likes beating on 16-year-old runaways. You in the mood for a little fun and excitement?"

Roy was a fellow undercover cop who I'd worked with on occasion when dealing with similar situations. Doing what needed to be done to protect Seattle's law-abiding citizens from scum and dangerous predators, like this Ronnie guy, and protecting frightened, helpless victims, such as Sue, when our courts' legal process failed to do so. I knew Roy could be trusted to keep his mouth shut, no matter what. He'd never rat out a fellow cop. It was all part of the infamous "Blue Code of Silence," which was: "No matter what, you keep your mouth shut!"

I told Sue to sit tight for an hour or so cause I needed to go take care of some personal business. I handed her a twenty-dollar bill and walked off. I headed over to Pine Street and continued on for six blocks. Soon I entered the underground parking garage of the Roosevelt Hotel located at 6th and Pine.

"Hey, Roy. Thanks for meeting up."
"No problem. So what's up?"

I explained the situation to Roy about meeting Sue a few weeks ago and about her predicament.

"OK, but why this gal? What makes her so special?"

"I don't really know, Roy. Guess I'm just soft-hearted. Look, she's only 16. She's just a kid! She don't know nothing about the streets. She'll most likely end up a heroin junkie before long, and we all know it's downhill from there. I'd just like to give her a second chance. After all, isn't being a cop all about helping people? To 'Serve and Protect,' as the saying goes?"

"There you go again, trying to rescue another lost soul. When you gonna learn that you ain't some sort of comic book super hero going around saving every 'damsel in distress' that crosses your path? You ain't Superman, you know!"

"Well, actually, Roy, I was thinking more along the lines of Batman. He works nights, and I really dig that cool outfit he wears. Oh yeah, and Batman lives in a cave. You know how much I like caves!"

"Bernie, you're messed up. You know that, don't you? Let's get serious for a moment. What you wanna do about this Ronnie asshole?"

"Well, I say we pay him a visit, scare the shit out of him, and give him till sundown to get his pimping ass out of town."

"You screwing this gal, Bernie?"
"No, not really."

"'Not really.' What's that supposed to mean? Damn it, Johnny, she's only 16 years old. That ain't cool; you can't go round fucking 16-year-old kids!"

"I didn't. Honest, Roy, I didn't have sex with her. I almost did, but I didn't because she didn't have any condoms! Look, Roy, this gal's beat up pretty bad. Whatta you say? Wanna help me run this punk-ass outta town?"

"OK, I'll help you out. By the way, she know you're a cop?"

"Hell, no. I ain't that dumb. She don't need to know shit!"

"Good. Keep it that way. I'll give "Sly" a call. He's always ready for some fun."

"Yeah, good idea. I don't know how big this monkey is. He could turn out to be a gorilla."

"Well, no problem. Sly's no small monkey himself, and you know that egg foo young shit, right?"

"It ain't egg foo young, Roy. It's aikido."

"Yeah, OK. It all looks the same to me. You say this Ronnie guy lives above the Paramount?"

"Yeah, next block up, Apartment 702. Oh yeah, I almost forgot. Sue mentioned that he keeps a gun under the mattress in the bedroom, some kind of small gun with a pearl handle."

"OK, good to know."

I went back to the Union 101. Sue was still sitting in the back of the tavern. Her drink was empty. She saw me coming and said; "Johnny, can I have another?"

"Yeah, OK. Why not?"

I ordered another rum and coke for her and another beer for myself. No more Yukon Jack; I had work to do. Sitting down next to Sue, I said; "Sue, me and a pal of mine are gonna take care of this problem you got."

"What are you gonna do, Johnny? How are you gonna do that? I don't want Ronnie looking for me later. He'd kill me! He's big, you know, and he can be real mean. I've seen him fuck guys up."

"So I just gotta get someone that's bigger and meaner."

"Who are these guys, Johnny?"

"Look, Sue, I'm here to help ya cause Ronnie fucked your face up. You just turned 16, ran away from home, and you don't know a fucking thing about the real world. You've survived so far by tricking, but you keep this shit up, and in a couple of years you'll be just another burnt-out, skinny, alcoholic, strung-out little 'ho', like all the rest of 'em. You'll be old, ugly, and toothless. You doing drugs yet?"

"Ronnie gives me quaaludes. Makes it easier for me to trick. I really don't like tricking, but I have to be making money for Ronnie."

"You don't need to be making money for nobody, Sue, especially for that motherfucker. You doing any other drugs?"

"Well, Ronnie lets me chase the dragon[1] every few days. But I get real sick when I do that. I get sick to my stomach, but after a while, everything gets like a dream. I like that feeling. It makes you feel like everything's peaceful-like."

"God damn it, Sue! He's turning you into a junkie. Can't you see that? That way he's got you right where he wants you. You get strung out on heroin, you may as well fucking shoot yourself in the head. It'd be a lot less painful. Look, I'm going to take care of Ronnie. While I'm gone, I want you to sit your ass down in that donut shop on the corner. Guy who runs it's called Guenter. He helps runaways, but he also fucks them, so be careful."

"Too late, Johnny. I already know him and he's one of my regulars."

"Damn him! Anyway, just sit your ass down there and stay put until I get back. Eat donuts or something. And don't be talking about all this to nobody. Nobody, not a fucking word. Shouldn't be more than a couple hours till I get back. Here's ten bucks."

I didn't know if she'd even be there when I got back. Fuck it. All I could do was try. I drove up Pike Street, turned north on 6th Avenue, and pulled into the Roosevelt Hotel underground parking lot at the end of the block. Two levels down, I spotted Roy and Sly standing outside their seized undercover vehicle, a brownish Porsche. I pulled into the empty stall next to them, got out, and stretched.

Roy was wearing a black leather coat. Sly had on a military-type field jacket. I had on my usual funky, falling-apart jean jacket and a welder's cap worn backwards. Roy stood at 6'2" tall. Sly was only 5'10", but he weighed around the two-fifty mark, and there wasn't an ounce of fat on him. He was a power lifter. Altogether, we looked like some kind of wrecking crew. No way like cops.

"Hey, Roy, how ya doin? Sly?"

"Hi, Bernie. So what we got going, here? Something about some 16-year-old hooker getting smacked around?"

"Yeah, her pimp really did a number on her. Messed her up pretty bad. Busted-up lip, black eye, chipped tooth ... She used to be pretty good-looking

---

[1] Narcotics are placed on a piece of tin foil which is heated, then the user inhales the vapors.

before that. She's only 16. It just ain't right for someone to be putting her out at her age. Plus he's starting her on smack, just chasing the dragon, but before long that dragon will be a monkey on her back for the rest of her life."

"You say this Ronnie dude lives above the Paramount Theater?"

"Yeah. Apartment 702."

"So how you wanna work this?"

"I figure we go up and knock on his door, say something like 'Office Manager, sir. I need to have a word with you.' He opens the door, we barge in, grab him by the arms, put his ass down on the floor, Roy puts a gun in his face, and informs him that it's time for him to get his pimping ass out of town. We don't say who we are. We don't mention Sue or anything about prostitutes for that matter. For all he knows, we're just a bunch of concerned citizens who don't want his kind doing business in Seattle."

"Sounds good, but what if he decides to fight?"

"Well, Roy, we got Sly, here. Think you can handle him, Sly?"

"No problem. I can bench over 300 lbs. This boy won't be no problem. I hope he decides to fight."

"Cool. What about guns? That gal mention anything about Ronnie having a gun?"

"Yeah, she said he keeps a small, silver automatic with a pearl handle under the mattress in the bedroom."

"OK, good to know. But let's try to do this without shooting him. Might be difficult to explain ... though not impossible. We could just say we got a tip from an informant that this guy Ronnie is dealing drugs out of his apartment, and we just wanted to go talk to him about it."

"Yeah. No a problem. Nothing unusual there. Hell, let's just shoot his ass and get it over with. Rehabilitate the motherfucker."

Roy shook his head.

"No, let's not. This Ronnie is a minor asshole, not worth all the paperwork, the news media, the shrink, the desk job for a week or so till the shooting review board goes over it ... Too much bullshit. Save it for some major dirtbag who needs rehabilitating."

"Yeah, you're right, Roy. But if he pulls a gun, what then?"

"Well, yeah, if he pulls a gun, then he dies. OK, let's do this. I'm getting hungry. How about Tai Tung afterwards?"

"Sounds good. Let's do it."

The three of us went over to the Paramount Apartments, entered the lobby, and took the elevator to the 7th floor. I knocked on the door of 702. No peephole—good. No one answered, so I knocked again, harder this time. A voice came from inside the apartment, "Who's there?"

Roy responded, "Apartment Manager. Gotta talk to you about the rent!"

From inside the apartment again; "Fuck you man, I paid the damn rent a few days ago!"

"Sir, that was last week's rent. You need to pay for this week's rent!"

"Fuck you, man. Go away, leave me alone. I'll pay tomorrow."

"Ah, sir, no can do. You need to pay the rent right now, or I'll call the cops."

"OK, hold on. I ain't dressed. Damn, this is bullshit!"

After about a minute, the door opened. Standing in the doorway was a tall black man with a large afro, wearing a suede vest, a flowery, long-sleeve shirt, and sunglasses.

"Who the fuck are you guys?"

Roy stepped aside. Sly stepped up to Ronnie, placed both hands on his chest, and shoved him hard. Ronnie went flying backwards and fell on his ass. Quickly he got up, turned, and started for the bedroom. Sly said, "No you don't, motherfucker," and grabbed Ronnie's right arm at the wrist and elbow. Ronnie was making a fist with his left hand just as Roy grabbed his left arm. Ronnie hunched down, trying to break loose, but Roy and Sly had him secure. I walked up in back of him, grabbed a hold of his afro with my right hand, and pulled his head back until he was looking up at the ceiling. I made a fist with my left hand, raised my arm high above my head, then struck downwards with a hammer-fist blow to his nose.

Roy and Sly let go, and he fell to his knees, screaming, "Fuck! You fuckers broke my nose!" Blood was gushing from his nose. Roy and Sly stood silently next to Ronnie as I checked under the mattress. I felt the gun. I flipped the mattress off the bed, and there was the pearl-handled automatic just as Sue'd described it. There was also a lot of cash and a photograph.

I picked up the photograph and stared at it, shaking my head in disbelief. It was a 5 x 7 showing Sue sitting on the floor, handing Ronnie a large amount of cash and looking into the camera with a big smile. Ronnie was posed standing over Sue, one hand on his hip and the other reaching for the money. He had a smirk on his face. I showed the photograph to Roy and Sly. We shook our heads as we looked down at Ronnie, who was holding on to his bleeding nose.

I went into the bathroom, got a towel, and threw it to Ronnie. He didn't say a word, just held the towel to his nose. Roy winked at me, reached under his leather jacket, and took out his Browning 9 mm. automatic pistol. He squatted down at Ronnie's right side, placed the barrel of the Browning automatic to Ronnie's right temple, and pulled back the hammer. He said not a word. Ronnie panicked.

"Don't kill me, man. Please don't shoot. You can have all my money. I got some dope too in the kitchen drawer. Take it. You can have it. Take it all; I don't want it. Please don't kill me. Who are you guys? What did I ever do to you? Man, I don't wanna die. Don't kill me!"

Roy spoke in a calm, low voice, still holding the automatic to Ronnie's temple.

"Listen up, asshole. There's a Greyhound Bus leaving for L.A. in an hour. You got a choice: fucking die right here, right now, or be on that bus. I really don't give a fuck if you live or die. I'd just as soon shoot your black ass as have to look at you, but if I shot you, I'd have to clean up the mess, so I'm gonna let you go on one condition."

"What's that? What condition?" asked Ronnie, his voice shaking.

"Like I said, you get your ass out of Seattle, and you never come back. That's the deal. Now give us your wallet."

Ronnie reached back with his right hand, took out his wallet, and handed it to Sly. Sly went through Ronnie's wallet, took out the contents, and placed them on the kitchen table. Then he rifled through the ID cards, selected a few, and stuffed the rest back into the wallet. He handed a California State ID card to Roy and threw the wallet back to Ronnie. Roy carefully lowered the hammer of his automatic and put it back in his jacket. Looking at the ID, he asked; "So your name's Ronald Jefferson Carter, that right?"

"Yes, sir. That's me."

"OK, what about this address on your ID card? Who lives there?"

"That's my mom's house in Oakland."

"Your mom still live there?"

"Yes. Why you asking about my mom?"

"Well, Mr. Carter, if some time later me or my crew hear about you being back in town, we're gonna pay your mom a little visit. Just to talk to her, of course."

"Please don't mess with my mom. She didn't do anything."

"Up to you, Mr. Carter. It's all up to you. Now, go get your face cleaned up."

Ronnie got up slowly and went into the bathroom. Sly was standing watch over him. Five minutes later, Ronnie came out of the bathroom, still holding the towel to his nose. On the kitchen table was all the money found under the bed, several knotted-up balloons, some foil with black residue, a cut-off straw, and a paper bindle with white powder inside.

"What's in the balloons, Ronnie?" asked Roy.

"Uh, heroin. Just heroin."

"Just heroin. Well, you take all that 'just heroin' and flush it down the toilet."

"Please, can't I just keep just a few at least. I need that shit. I need it or else I'm gonna get sick."

"Too bad, Ronnie. Heroin ain't good for your health. That shit'll kill you."

"Please, sir, just the bindle then. Please."

"OK, Ronnie, just the bindle. Everything else gets flushed."

Sly took the dozen or so tied balloons into the bathroom, threw them in the toilet, and motioned for Ronnie to flush them. Ronnie was trying to think of how to save the heroin. He started to mumble something, but too late; Sly reached over and flushed the toilet. Ronnie looked like he was about to cry as he watched the balloons go down.

"OK, Ronnie," said Roy, "Time for you to get the fuck out of our town. Go back to where you came from and don't ever set foot in Washington State again. You can take the money on the table and that one paper bindle."

"Where's the rest of my money?" asked Ronnie. "I had more than that."

"You wanna die or go home?"

Ronnie picked up the cash off the kitchen table, then the bindle, which he carefully placed in his wallet.

"Now what?" he asked.

"Walk your ass down to the bus station, buy a one-way ticket to L.A. or Oakland, get on the fucking bus, and don't ever come back to Seattle." Roy motioned to Sly.

"This man will be watching you until you leave. He's got a gun too."

As he was heading out the apartment door, Ronnie stopped and looked at Roy.

"Just who the fuck are you guys, anyway? I mean, who are you? You guys can't just go around doing this shit, fucking with whoever you want."

"Listen up, asshole. Me and my friends here, we be working for the Sanitation Department, so our job is to keep trash like you off our streets and the fuck out of Seattle. We don't allow drug-dealing, pimping types like you to reside here in our fine city and dirty up our streets, so you need to be on the next bus out of town."

"I got a right to be here. It's a free country!"

"You're absolutely correct, Mr. Carter; it is a free country and that's what gives us the right to keep trash like you out of here! Go back to Oakland cause you're not welcome here, and it ain't because you're black, it's because you're fucking trash! We got a lot of fine, upstanding black folks living here in Seattle, trying to earn a decent living and raise their kids in a good environment. We don't need pimps and drug dealers like you fucking up our fine city."

"What about my ID and the rest of the stuff?"

"We keep those. That way I have your address just in case I need it later."

"That shit ain't right, man. You can't just keep my shit."

"Uh, yes, we can. But if you don't like it, you can always call the police. I'm sure they'd be interested to hear your story. Go ahead and call."

"Ah, fuck you guys."

Sly walked up to Ronnie and looped a braided leather cord around his right wrist.

"Hey, what the fuck, man. What's this shit?" Ronnie tried to pull his arm back.

"Now, don't be starting no shit just because we allowed you to live another day. Start mouthing off, and I'll personally pop you one on that fucked-up nose of yours."

Ronnie automatically put his left hand over his nose and winced. Just touching it was extremely painful.

"My associate here got you on a leash just to make certain you don't run. He'll escort you to the bus station and stay with you till the bus leaves. Try anything stupid, and I assure you you'll regret it."

"This guy ain't said a word. Neither has that other peckerwood there. Don't they know how to talk? They dumb or something?"

"Now be nice, Ronnie. There's nothing for them to talk about. You won't be having any conversation with your escort. Just keep your mouth shut and everything'll go just fine."

"So now you got me on a damn leash, like a fucking dog."

Sly motioned for Ronnie to keep moving, and they left the apartment. I took the photo out of the inside of my jean jacket and looked at it again. Roy took it from me, stared at it for a few moments, and shook his head.

"Yeah, that's sick. No matter what she's done, she's still somebody's daughter. I'd sure hate for her parents to see this picture. It'd kill them."

"Yeah. A parent's worst nightmare."

Paul handed the picture back to me and I put it in my jean jacket.

"Well, Bernie, that didn't go too badly."

We looked down at the cash on the kitchen table.

"So how much we got here, Roy?"

"Total was $875. I let dummy keep 400. That leaves us 475. Figure you give Sue 50 bucks now, get her a room till tomorrow, then put her on a bus to Spokane. Give her the rest of the money just before she leaves town. Give her the cash now, and she'll just get it taken away from her. If she knows she's got money coming to her, she'll stay put in her room till morning."

"Yeah. I'll put her up in the Roosevelt. I know the desk and security guys there. I'll have them keep an eye on her."

"What say you go take care of getting Sue set up with a room now, and we'll meet later at Tai Tung, say around eight?"

"Sounds good. Sly should be freed up by then."

"Yeah, I think I'll go keep him company just in case."

"What about the gun?"

"I'll just keep it locked up safe for now. Never can tell when it might come in handy. Why, you want it, Bernie?"

"Nah. Lock it up."

Roy and I left the apartment. He headed for the bus station, and I went towards 1st and Pike, back to the donut shop. Sue was sitting next to the window. When she saw me, she started to say something, but I said, "Later, not here. C'mon, let's go."

She got up and followed me up Pike Street. She wanted to know everything. I told her to wait till we were off the street and in the hotel room. We went in the side entrance of the Roosevelt Hotel and up to the front desk.

"Hi, Ed." (I knew the front desk clerk.) I winked and put my finger on my lips. "Ed, my name's 'Johnny.' I need a room for the night for this young lady here. She'll be leaving on the bus first thing in the morning."

"Yes, sir. Let me see what we have available. We have a single on the 8th Floor, nice room, good view facing Pine Street."

"Got anything on the upgrade?"

"Uh, let's see. Ah, yes. I have a suite available on the top floor, very nice, and with a much better view, of course."

"OK. I'll take it. Why don't you let me take the young lady up to her room, and then I'll come back down and finish checking her in?"

"Very good, Mr. . . . Johnny."

"It's Medeiros, Johnny Medeiros."

"Very good, Mr. Medeiros. Room 2002. Take the elevator to the 20th Floor, turn right."

He handed me the key. I checked the room number and took Sue up to the suite. We went inside.

"Wow, this is nice. Huge. What do you think, Sue? OK for one night?"

"Damn, Johnny. This is beautiful. How many nights can I stay?"

"Just tonight, Sue. So don't be getting comfortable. Tomorrow morning your ass gets put on the bus to Spokane, period! Today I ran Ronnie out of town; tomorrow I run you out of town. And don't come back."

"Johnny, this huge room must cost a fortune! Who's paying for all this? And who are you, anyway? I mean, what kind of work do you do? I'm confused about all this. One day you're a 30-dollar trick who don't wanna fuck; a week later, you and your friends are running my pimp out of town and putting me on a bus to Spokane. What's the story?"

"Sorry, Sue. Can't talk about it. It's not your concern. Just think of me and some guys I know as 'sanitation engineers.' Clean-up guys, so to speak. But like I said, it's not your concern, so don't be asking me questions. As for the money, I took some of Ronnie's cash. I'll use it to pay for the room, and there'll be a bit left over for you when I put you on the bus in the morning."

"Really? How much? Tell me!"

"You'll have a hundred or so, but not until tomorrow."

"Johnny, I don't believe it. Ronnie would never let anyone take his cash!"

"Well, he didn't exactly have a say in the matter. Or maybe I should say he had a choice, and he chose to leave town. Look, I'm not going to talk about Ronnie. Forget him. He's gone. What's happening now is you're getting on the bus out of Seattle. I gotta go now and take care of some things. I'll be back around ten tonight. Maybe then we can talk, but not about what went on today. That's over and done with. Why don't you take a long, hot bath, turn on the TV, and kick back."

"Can I use the phone?"

"Absolutely not. Tomorrow morning, OK, you can call your sister and let her know you're coming. Until then, no phone calls. I'll tell the front desk not to turn on your phone. If you're hungry, call the front desk. You can order some food from next door."

"What about booze? Can I get something to drink? I could use a drink."

"When I get back, we can go downstairs and have a few drinks, but not till then, understand?"

"Yeah, OK. I guess I don't have a choice."

"I'm going now. Remember: stay in the room. No phone calls, no visitors. You mess up, I'll just drop your ass and walk away, and you won't get no money."

"How much did you say I was gonna get tomorrow? How much total? Tell me!"

"Nope, that's for tomorrow morning. Now, I gotta go. Bye!"

I took the elevator back to the lobby and walked over to the front desk. Ed was still on shift.

"Hey, Ed."

"Hi, Bernie. So what's going on?"

"OK, Ed, listen up; this is important. First of all, this Sue gal, she don't know I'm a cop, she don't know my real name, she don't know nothing about me and that's how it's gotta stay, OK? And don't be calling me 'Bernie.' I'm 'Johnny Medeiros.' All right?"

"Yeah, no problem."

"Ed, how much for the suite? I wanna pay for it now."

"Aw, don't worry. It's covered."

"No, Ed. The money isn't coming from me. I can't explain, but it's not my money. So how much?"

"You sure? It's no problem."

"No, Ed. I pay for the room. You can give me a discount, though."

"OK. That reticular suite runs $76 a night. How about we say 30 bucks? That covers the hotel's actual cost."

I took out two twenties and a ten. "Here, Ed. 30 for the room and 20 for you."

"Johnny, you don't need to do that!"

"Like I said, it's not my money. Now don't be a fool; take the 20. You can earn it by making sure Sue don't go nowhere. And don't hook her phone up. Here's another 20 in case she orders food. Remember, she stays put in her room, no phone calls, no visitors. OK?"

"OK, Johnny. I'll keep watch on her. I'll let security know too."

"Thanks. I'll be back around ten tonight. Gotta run now. Bye."

I drove up to Chinatown, parked, and went into Tai Tung. The owner, Harry, came over and told me that Roy and Sly were in the back room, so I went and joined them.

Tai Tung restaurant in Chinatown (recent photo)

"Hey, Roy, Sly. Been here long?"

"Nope, just ten minutes or so."

"You guys order yet?"

"Nope, just a couple of beers."

Roy looked over at me. "What do you suggest, being you're a Chinaman and all that?"

"Tell you what, Roy. I'll make it interesting."

I called Harry over to the table. "Harry, tonight, you order for us, OK? Special stuff, you know; none of that egg foo young shit. That's for white folks!"

"OK, Baa-nee. I get you chicken feet, fried fish lips, and some Chinese greens, OK?"

"You do that, and these guys here'll arrest your skinny Chinese ass and send you back to China!"

"OK. I only make joke. Not worry. I get good dishes for you guys. Not *lofan* (Caucasian) stuff; only good Chinese dish. OK?"

"Good. Oh yeah, and a Bud for me in a glass on ice."

"OK, I get right away."

"Sly, our boy get on the bus OK?"

"Yup, no problem. He sure wanted to know who the fuck we were. I didn't say one word the whole time."

"Good. Sue don't know either."

"Hey, Bernie, you can't be doing this shit again, OK?"

"Yeah, OK. I just felt sorry for her, that's all."

"Bernie, you feel sorry for everybody. But like I said, no more doing this shit. It's too risky. The world is filled with 'ho's in distress. We can't help 'em all. It's not our job."

"OK, no more. I promise."

Harry of Tai Tung (recent photo)

Food came. Clams with Black Bean Sauce, some kind of smoked crispy duck, pork, mixed Chinese greens, and Special Fried Rice. What a meal. We feasted and discussed the day's events. Ronnie ended up paying for the dinner and drinks.

After dinner, I went back to the hotel and let myself in the room. Sue was crashed out on the bed, buck-ass naked. Damn. Tight little body. Wished she were a bit older, say like three years older. Without waking her, I took a shower. I didn't feel like driving home and back in the morning, so I decided to spend the night. Naked, I got under the covers.

I had no desire to cuddle up with Sue. To me she was just a stupid little tramp who'd run away from home and gotten involved with some asshole of a pimp who liked to thump on 'ho's. If it hadn't been for her face being so fucked up, I probably wouldn't have bothered to help her. 'Ho' or no 'ho,' no gal should be beaten like that. OK, I told myself, I helped this one. Now that's it. I gotta knock it off. I can't go on getting personally involved with the underdogs. It's not healthy to feel like that. There are too many underdogs!

Middle of the night Sue woke up and we talked. I didn't feel like preaching to her. I refused to talk about Ronnie or the day's events. I didn't care what she did once she got on the bus.

She offered me a blow job. Then she offered me pussy. Then "anything, Johnny, anything you want. I'll even do anal for you. I got rubbers." Maybe she wanted to repay me for getting her out of her nightmare. But no. Much as I enjoyed looking at her tight-ass little body, I declined the offer. Wouldn't have felt right about it, her being only 16.

Next morning I took Sue next door for breakfast and then gave her the remaining 300-plus dollars left over. I gave her a quick hug and put her skinny ass on the bus. As the bus pulled out, I waved goodbye.

Good luck, Sue. Don't be coming back!

42

New Sheriff in Chinatown

San Francisco had recently experienced the "Golden Dragon Massacre," where five people had been killed in a gun battle between rival gangs at a restaurant in Chinatown. All of the five people killed had been innocent bystanders. This provided the impetus for San Francisco and other U.S. cities with large Asian populations, like Seattle, to set up gang units within their police departments.

As usual the department brass were more than happy to let me do my own undercover thing. I began hanging around Seattle's Chinatown at all hours of the day and night. I'd even go down there during my off-duty hours. For me it was the perfect job assignment since I preferred to be around Chinese folks.

During the weeks and months that followed, I began to get to know most of the Asian youths that hung in Chinatown. Some of them had come to Seattle from Hong Kong. A few had escaped the Chinese mainland. Some, along with family members, had fled Vietnam as refugees during the war. The Vietnamese youths along with a few ethnic Chinese kids had formed a gang that was going around demanding protection money from local merchants, restaurant owners, and Chinatown's underground gambling establishments. It was either pay up or get your windows smashed.

In one Chinese movie theater, all the seats in the theater had been slashed. The theater owner, knowing that I was an undercover police officer, pulled me inside and showed me the damage.

I got pissed. Those kids were nothing more than a bunch of street punks. They were taking advantage of the frightened local Chinese population through threats and intimidation. The Chinese were vulnerable to this kind of shakedown because, being somewhat of a closed community, they didn't normally run to the police for help or protection.

I'd been adopted into a Chinese family, my last name was Chinese, and over the years my way of thinking had become Chinese. I felt that it was my responsibility to do something for the Chinese community.

Since becoming a Seattle police officer in April of 1970, I'd often eaten at the Sun Ya Restaurant. The restaurant owner was a Mr. Liu. Being the Chinese characters for Liu and Lau are similar, we quickly became friends. He called me "cousin," and out of respect, I called him "boss." Liu and I would often sit and chat over tea in one of the rear booths of the restaurant.

Early one Saturday morning around 2:30 A.M. I received a panicked phone call from Mr. Liu.

"Cousin, god damn Vietnamese waiting for rob me, they across street right now, what I do? You come help me?"

I calmly answered, "No problem, boss, I'll be right there. You stay in restaurant and wait for me, no go outside. I be there real quick!"

I leaped out of bed, grabbed my loaded double-barrel sawed-off shotgun off the bedroom wall and raced out the door. Adrenalin pumping full force, I got into my undercover GTO and sped off towards Chinatown. Within 12 minutes I pulled into Sun Ya's parking lot and screeched to a halt. Shotgun in hand I jumped out of my vehicle, walked over towards the four Vietnamese punks, pointed the shotgun directly at them, and with total confidence and in a calm, low voice, stated, "You punks stay away from this restaurant! The owner is 'family' so you leave him alone! Any of you ever threaten him or anybody else in Sun Ya or cause any damage, I'll come looking for you, and I'll blow your asses away. Now, you guys get the fuck out of here!"

The four Vietnamese punks were caught totally off guard. Maybe too they were unnerved by the sawed-off shotgun pointed at them. They nodded their heads indicating that they understood me, and without saying a word, they turned and headed off into the darkness of the night like a bunch of frightened rats.

Meanwhile, Mr. Liu had come out of the restaurant and had been observing me talking to the four punks. Punks now gone, I walked back to the parking lot, greeted him, and shook his hand. He spoke, all the while gazing down at my shotgun, "Thank you, cousin, thank you very much. God damn Vietnamese—they was going rob me, so I call you. Thank you for coming fast!" I smiled as I spoke, "No problem, boss, anytime you need help you call me, OK? I come help you right away."

I followed Mr. Liu as he drove off and headed home. Once he arrived, I got out of my vehicle, walked over to say goodbye, and shook his hand. As we shook, he handed me some money. I raised my hand, "Boss, thank you, but money not necessary. We family, so I help you, money not necessary!" Mr. Liu insisted I take the money, and I knew that if I refused to accept his "thank-you money," he'd feel highly insulted. He'd feel like I was too proud to accept his "thank you." Still saying "Not necessary, boss," I took the money and quickly pocketed the bills. I had no choice. I made a slight bow to Liu as a sign of respect, returned to my vehicle, and drove off.

As I slowly drove home, I relived in my head the events of the past few hours. It had all been exciting as hell, and it felt great that I'd personally been able to come to the rescue of a friend who was an important and highly-respected member of Seattle's Chinatown community. I'd fearlessly stood up to the Vietnamese punks, all the while pointing that sawed-off shotgun of mine in their faces. Yeah, I'd scared the shit out of them and it felt good, damn good!

The following day I asked around and was given the location of the place where the Vietnamese punks hid out; their "rat's nest" as I called it. Some individuals in Chinatown were now willing to talk to me and provide information. Word spread quickly throughout the community that I was willing and able to help out and would take care of whatever needed taking care of, and that even though I was a police officer, I could be trusted!

The rat's nest was located in Canton Alley, connecting King and Jackson, and turned out to be the rear storage room of a Chinese benevolent society. All alone, standing in front of the door, I made a fist with my right hand and pounded hard three times. The door swung open immediately. I stood straight and, with total confidence, walked in before anyone could utter a word of protest. There were six young Asian males present in the room ranging in age from 18 to maybe 23 years old. Against the wall was a soiled mattress on which lay a young totally naked Vietnamese girl. It looked as though I'd interrupted a gang bang in progress. The girl looked up at me, but said nothing, her face without expression. Being she didn't look frightened and didn't ask for help, I ignored her.

Looking around the dimly-lit room, I quickly recognized the four individuals that my shotgun and I had confronted the night before. I walked up to the taller of these four and shook his hand.

"You remember me from last night, right?" He looked at me surprised and confused.

"Yes, I remember you last night, you have shotgun last night, but now you no have!"

I looked him in the eye and replied, "I no need shotgun now!"

Looking around the room at his fellow gathering, he boasted, "We know gung fu, what you think about that?"

I just looked at him and smiled, "Ah, yes, gung fu very good; but I know *chin na*! You know *chin na*? Police in China use *chin na* for capture punks like you. Here, I show you!"

I took hold of his left arm and applied a painful wrist lock. He immediately went to his knees. I transferred to a finger lock and applied pressure while holding him securely with only my right hand. He started to yell out. Meanwhile, the other guys standing around didn't know what to do. Should they attack me all at once? I applied even more pressure to the finger lock, and the guy started screaming.

Still keeping the finger lock applied, I looked down at him. I smiled and said, "OK, I tell you what; if you can get out of this lock I give you $100 cash. $100 if you escape. Go ahead, try! I hold you only by one finger!"

He attempted to pull his hand out, he tried to stand up, but it was impossible for him to do so. I had him completely under my control. Finally, I released the finger lock. He turned away and started to massage his hand and finger. He didn't say a word.

I spoke, "OK, all you guys know who I am, you know where I work. (By now, they'd figured out that I was a cop.) I'm *Sifu*! From now on, you guys don't mess with my friend from Sun Ya. You leave those people alone! Any of you cause trouble, I come back with my partners, arrest all of you, and deport everyone back to Vietnam, you understand?"

They all nodded their heads and quietly said "yes." I stood straight and strolled out the door without looking back. I headed off to Sun Ya for *dim sum* and a cold Bud on ice. Boy, I loved my job!

43

Internal Investigation

Out of a clear blue sky, word came down that the Narcotics Section was being investigated. There were no details as to who was under investigation or why we were being investigated. It was just, "Hey, you hear? We're being investigated by IIS (Internal Investigation Section)."

What the hell was going on? What had any of us in the unit done to bring on an internal investigation? All we knew was that we were all being investigated. The Narcotics Section quickly went into "stress mode." An internal investigation was serious stuff!

The IIS sergeant heading the investigation was Sgt. Dundee, a tall, red-haired Australian. Over the years I'd heard of this individual, this Sgt. Dundee, and what I'd heard wasn't good. Word was he was a prick and not to be trusted. Dundee had come over from Australia some years prior, become a U.S. citizen, and in time, got himself hired on with the SPD.

Yeah, Dundee was a cop, but a cop that couldn't be trusted; an asshole, really. He was one of those "by the book or else," supervisors. You know; accept a free cup of coffee, and he'd nail your ass to the wall.

In good police work it's sometimes necessary to accept a free cup of coffee or even a free meal. You make personal contact with a bar or restaurant owner, in time he just might give you valuable information on criminal activity taking place in the area. It's sort of like having a confidential informant. In return, should this bar or restaurant owner have any problems with certain individuals, well, that's what the police were there for—to "Serve and Protect."

The investigation began with each of us detectives assigned to the Narcotics Section being called up to the IIS office (which, by the way, was located one floor up from our section). One by one we were called in for an "interview." A better word than "interview" would be "interrogation."

It was my turn to be interviewed. Upon entering the IIS office, I was instructed by Sgt. Dundee to take a seat. From behind his large desk he formally introduced himself.

"Detective Lau, I'm Sgt. Dundee. I'm in charge of this investigation, and I'll be the sergeant conducting all interviews. I'm now going to ask you some questions regarding suspected criminal activity within the Narcotics Section. Do you mind if I tape record this interview?" (Federal law states that if an interviewee isn't under arrest, permission must first be granted by the person being interviewed before the interview can be taped.) Hell, yes, I minded. I wasn't a dummy. In a taped interview an individual's emotional reaction to the questions being asked is also recorded and can later be used against him or her in subsequent interviews.

I looked him in the eyes and stated, "Nope, you ain't got my permission!"

He looked surprised and said, "Well, I'm going to have to do a lot of writing!"

I looked at Dundee again and responded, "Well, Sarge, start writing."

I wasn't the least bit frightened or intimidated by this guy as I'd never been caught doing anything wrong in my entire police career, and I'd never been written up for any infraction.

The first question he asked me was, "Detective Lau, I want you to tell me about illegal activity that you observed while working in the Narcotics Section."

Say what? Was this guy for real? This red-headed peckerwood of a sergeant wanted me to rat on my fellow detectives? No way! I looked at him and said, "Sorry, Sergeant. I've never seen anyone do anything wrong while working in the Narcotics Section."

Sgt. Dundee looked upset and agitated. He kept up the same line of questioning for the next ten minutes, but my answer was always the same. "Nope, I didn't see that take place. Nope, sorry, I don't know anything about that, etc." Finally, totally frustrated and red in the face, Dundee informed me that the "interview" was over with and that I could leave.

Without saying a word, I got up, left the IIS office, and returned to the Narcotics office, where I immediately reported to Sgt. Joe and my fellow detectives what questions I'd been asked. I advised them not to allow Dundee to tape record their interviews.

The investigation lasted an entire year. Confidential informants who had previously worked for the Narcotics Section were supposed to be located by IIS detectives and then interviewed by Sgt. Dundee. Somehow the log book listing the informants' true names and addresses as well as the one containing records of money paid to them for information both came up missing.

It turned out that the witch hunt into possible criminal activity within the Narcotics Section conducted by the SPD's Internal Investigation Section was due to an ongoing personal vendetta between a certain ranking major assigned to the chief's office and the captain running the Vice and Narcotics Division.

As a result of the year-long investigation and the personal stress the it caused, several detectives' marriages fell apart. One of the detectives' wives died of a heart attack. And in the end, no one in the Narcotics Section was brought up on criminal charges or accused of any misconduct.

44

Benjamin Ng

In late January of 1983 homicide detectives contacted me and asked if I knew the whereabouts of a young Chinese individual named Benjamin Ng. Story was, for years two elderly Chinese women had grown mung beans in the basement of their homes in order to make money to live on. One of these two women was the grandmother of Benjamin. A week earlier Ng's grandmother and her friend had been murdered and $1,000 in cash, which was kept in a tin can on top of the kitchen refrigerator, was stolen. Someone had tied them up and wrapped duct tape around their heads, covering their mouths and noses. Both women had suffocated and died.

Homicide wanted me to locate Ng. The next day I spotted Ng driving around Chinatown westbound on King Street in front of Tai Tung Restaurant. I stepped out from the sidewalk and stood in the middle of South King Street, blocking the path of Benjamin's vehicle, and displayed my detective's badge. Benjamin stopped. I yelled out "Police Officer, keep your hands on the steering wheel," radioed the homicide unit, and minutes later, detectives were on the scene. They took Benjamin into custody for questioning. He was later released due to lack of any physical evidence or witnesses connecting him to the two murders.

A few days after that, Benjamin saw me in Chinatown and invited me to have dinner with him. As we sat at a table at the Atlas Cafe, he ordered Clams with Black Bean Sauce and a few other side dishes. We made idle talk for a while, then the topic changed. Benjamin attempted to convince me that he hadn't killed the two old ladies and didn't know anything about the murders. Homicide had clued me in that Benjamin's vehicle, a GTO, had been purchased recently, so I asked him where he'd gotten the money. He gave me some bullshit story about gambling winnings which I didn't buy.

A week or so later, I was having dinner by myself in a quiet, out-of-the-way restaurant in Chinatown, where I could enjoy my meal without being bothered by anyone. I sat back in the booth and sampled the hot pepper oil and yellow Chinese mustard. I always did that: a sip of cold beer, a scoop or two of the very hot pepper oil mixed with the Chinese mustard, then another sip of cold beer. That was my ritual as I waited for my food to arrive. Soon the waiter brought over the rock cod I'd ordered. Looked damn good. He returned to the kitchen and brought out the rest of my order: steamed *lop chong*, baby *bok choy* and, of course, steamed rice. You just can't enjoy a Chinese meal without a bowl of steamed rice.

First, I ate the eyes of the rock cod; very good for your health, so they say. Next, I ate the cheeks of the fish. Located just in front of the gills, it's the tenderest part of the fish. After that, I ate the rest. I took my time and enjoyed it. Meal finished, I ordered a shot of warm brandy in a snifter and sat back.

I was still enjoying my brandy, when an elderly Chinese gentleman entered the restaurant. He walked towards me and stopped at my table. "*Sifu*," he made a slight bow of respect towards me and then started in, "Very sorry. I don't wish to interrupt your dinner, but there is something important that I must speak to you about."

I half-stood and welcomed him to sit. He declined and remained standing.

"You know Ben Ng, and you know what he did to his grandmother and her friend."

I nodded, "Yeah, I know."

"We ready to offer to you $25,000 if you can take care of Ben Ng for us."

I stayed calm inside, but my thoughts were racing. I thought to myself, "I can't believe what I'm hearing. Here I am presently sitting in a restaurant, where I've just enjoyed a great meal. I now have a Chinese elder standing at my table, offering me $25,000 cash money to 'take care' of Ben Ng." Me, a white guy (but, of course, with a Chinese mind), being offered such a task. What an honor, really. I was blown away. I looked at the elder and replied, "Thank you, but I must think about your request. I'll think about it and let you know soon."

That said, the elder bowed slightly, turned around, and exited the restaurant. A hit on Ben Ng. Me kill Ben Ng. Sure, I could do it—no problem. I knew Ben Ng, and he knew me. All I'd have to do would be to go up to him next time I spotted him in Chinatown. Ben was in Chinatown every day. I'd just walk up to him as he was parking or getting into his vehicle. I'd ask him to show me what type of hand gun he was carrying. (Ng always carried a handgun on his person.) He'd reluctantly take out his gun to show me. I'd immediately take out my own gun while yelling out "Ben—drop your gun, drop your gun!" I'd simply shoot him twice in the chest. I'd kill the little fucker right there on the spot, and I'd get away with it!

As mentioned, I'd always felt more comfortable with the Chinese community than with the white community. Yes, I was indeed white, but for as long as I can remember, I've always seen myself as Chinese. However, I was still a cop, and if something went wrong with me killing Ng, my life would be over with. If found guilty, I'd be sent to a federal penitentiary to serve a life sentence. Cops don't fare well locked up and serving time among criminals. Criminals, perhaps, that I'd arrested in the past. I was emotionally torn as I wanted more than anything else to help out the frightened Chinese community.

For reasons unknown to me at the time they were indeed frightened of Benjamin Ng. I later learned that Ng and some of his partners had been going around to numerous underground Chinatown gambling establishments demanding protection money.

45

Off the Edge

A short time after the conclusion of the internal investigation of the Narcotics Section, Sgt. Dundee was reassigned from the IIS Division to Narcotics. He hadn't been able to pin any illegal activity on any of the detectives in our section, so the brass decided to have him watch us. Soon after, many personnel in the Narcotics Section, including me, were transferred to Criminal Information. To our surprise and disgust we found that Dundee had been transferred there too.

During one of our normal Monday morning unit meetings, as we sat around drinking coffee, Dundee went over the cases from the previous week. At this particular meeting, however, he went to the section's locked safe and removed a large scrapbook containing typed and handwritten notes detailing information about the private sexual activities of a high-ranking State of Washington official. The "private sexual activities" were said to involve sex with numerous underage males.

I was aware that keeping a secret police file on any individual concerning their political, sexual, or religious activities was highly illegal. It was in fact a federal crime to do so. Keeping such information on one of the most powerful individuals in Washington State ... well, that could be suicidal to one's career. I wanted no part of it.

In past years, what was formerly called the "Intelligence" unit had gotten into serious trouble because of keeping files on politicians. Several detectives had been transferred back to the Patrol Division and the unit itself had been broken up (and reconstituted as "Criminal Information"). There'd been hell to pay.

It turned out that those particular files had been nothing more than Seattle newspaper articles that had been clipped out and saved over the years. That's all they were: just a collection of newspaper clippings. What Sgt. Dundee was now so proudly displaying and instructing all of us to read would lead to much severer consequences, should the file ever be made public. Heads would certainly roll. Many fine police officers would end up not only losing their careers and pensions, but possibly going to federal penetentiary.

I just sat there and kept my mouth shut, but the enormity of it all registered fully. I was dumbfounded. How could this be happening? It was, after all, not that long ago since Dundee had been an IIS investigator, hounding the detectives in the Narcotics Section. Now here he was instructing all of us in the unit to read illegal files.

The scrapbook was being passed around and was about to be handed to me, but I raised both hands and refused to take it. I scooted my seat back and allowed it to be passed on to the detective sitting next to me. I wanted no part of it. A short time later, the scrapbook, having been passed around and briefly examined by most of the detectives in the unit, was handed back to Sgt. Dundee, who then placed it back in the section's safe and stated, "You guys just let me know whenever you want to read it."

Several weeks later, Detective Don Phillips from the gambling unit and I were assigned to sit in surveillance on a bookie's house located on the outskirts of Lynnwood. We were instructed to keep an eye out for individuals going into or leaving the residence while a search warrant was being written up. This particular house was said to be the location of a large gambling operation. We were sitting in our pickup truck located perhaps a block away, making small talk as we kept an eye on the residence. Like the good old days, I decided to pop open a chilled Budweiser which I'd brought along. Over the years while working undercover narcotics I'd gotten into the habit of drinking a beer or two while on duty. Drinking beer was part of my cover.

The location where we were doing the surveillance was a heavily-wooded area far outside the Seattle city limits, where there were few houses. Two guys sitting in an old pickup truck parked in the woods, drinking a beer. Wouldn't look at all suspicious.

Suddenly, out of nowhere, Sgt. Dundee appeared by the side of our pickup truck. There he was just inches from the passenger window where I was sitting and drinking my beer. I looked at him and said; "You're one sneaky son of a bitch, aren't you, creeping up on us like that?" Dundee didn't say a word; he just turned and walked off.

Later that afternoon after we'd all returned to the Narcotics office, he approached me and handed me a typed memo. "What's this?" I asked. "Just read it and sign it," he said. The memo read:

> "On such and such a date and location, I Detective Bernie Lau, was observed by Sgt. Dundee, drinking a beer while on surveillance and while on duty. Should this ever take place again, I am hereby notified that disciplinary action shall be taken against me. Signed _____"

I looked at the memo, then back at Dundee. I couldn't believe what I was reading. "Johnny Medeiros" was supposed to be able to drink beer on duty! He'd done it for years! All at once, I snapped emotionally. I started shaking uncontrollably, I gritted my teeth and my face flushed with rage. As I crumpled up the memo with both hands and threw it at Dundee, I yelled out; "You motherfucker, I will throw you out the fucking window, you ever mess with me again. You hear me, you son of a bitch? Fuck you!!" I then turned to one of the detectives that was sitting near by and said; "Munson, get me the fuck outta here right now. I can't take this guy's bullshit any longer. Drive me the fuck home."

Without saying another word to Sgt. Dundee or the other detectives sitting near by, I turned and started to walk out of the office. On the way out, however, I happened to spot the "secret scrapbook" lying on Dundee's desk. I picked up the file, tucked it under my arm, and continued walking out of the office as I mumbled under my breath; "Dundee, you hypocritical son of a bitch, you write me up for having a fucking beer on duty, and yet you keep this highly illegal file for us to read. You two-faced motherfucker. Fuck you, Dundee!"

Neither Dundee nor any of the other detectives uttered a word as I walked out of the office. No one spoke, not even Detective Munson. He just followed me out. I'd expected Sgt. Dundee to try and stop me from walking out with the scrapbook, but he didn't. He just stood there frozen, not knowing what to say or how to respond to my explosive outburst. Everyone present remained speechless, as it wasn't at all like me to suddenly flip out and become so enraged and threatening.

Shaking and crying uncontrollably, I instructed Detective Munson to drive me to my doctor's office, which was located in the town of Mountlake Terrace. I was having an emotional breakdown and was in need of immediate medical help. At the clinic the doctor examined me and took my vital signs.

"Mr. Lau," he said, " if you don't retire soon, you'll die from a stroke or a heart attack. Your blood pressure is dangerously high. I'm going to give you a sedative injection to calm you down and relax you."

He then prescribed several high-dosage antidepressants for me to start taking on a daily basis.

Following the doctor's recommendation, I immediately went on medical leave. Several days later, I started seeing Dr. Liebert, a clinical psychiatrist.

I'd seen a psychiatrist before, after returning to Seattle from my undercover assignment in Alaska with my newly-discovered taste for cocaine. Initially my occasional cocaine use hadn't interfered with me doing my job, but I knew deep down that it was something I'd have to get under control sooner rather than later. So I'd gone to see the department shrink, Dr. Berberich, and told him about my using cocaine. His initial response was "Oh, c'mon, Bernie. Not you!" (I knew Dr. Berberich personally. He often dropped by the Narcotics office just to chat with us.)

For several months Berberich treated me with counseling and clinical hypnosis. The therapy seemed to work for a while, but eventually, I went back to occasional cocaine use. Cocaine somehow made me feel normal, grounded, and relaxed.

Months later, I decided to try a different department psychiatrist, a Dr. Smythe. The first thing he did after I'd introduced myself and explained my drug problem was to hand me a packet of sugar and say "Here. Go ahead and show me what you'd do if this was actual cocaine!" With no hesitation I ripped open the packet and emptied the contents onto a table. Then I took out my driver's license and went through the ritual of making "lines" of cocaine.

Cocaine users become very good at this. First, you spread out the cocaine, moving it around the surface of the table. Eventually, you make several two- to three-inch lines, side by side, which are then snorted by with the aid of a straw or a rolled-up dollar bill. This ritual is actually fun for the user.

After I'd done this, Dr. Smythe seemed satisfied that I was most likely an actual cocaine user since it's difficult to fake that kind of ritual.

Again I was treated with clinical hypnosis, once a week for a month. At the beginning of the second month, I went in for my usual appointment, but when I got to the doctor's office, I was told that he was no longer with the department. I was told that he had "resigned."

Later, I learned that Dr. Smythe had gotten into a domestic altercation with his girlfriend, who was living with him at the time, and in anger, she'd locked him out of his own apartment. He'd gone into a rage, kicked in the door, and threatened her with bodily harm. She called the police. When they arrived, she told the responding officers that he'd roughed her up and threatened her and that he had an ounce of cocaine in his night stand. The officers searched for and found the cocaine. Smythe was arrested and booked on a drug possession charge. Being the girlfriend also lived in the apartment, the officers hadn't needed a search warrant.

It later occurred to me that there might have been a reason he'd made me go through the ritual of making lines of cocaine when I first met him. He may have thought that I'd been sent undercover to investigate him for cocaine use as there'd been rumors within the department of him possibly being involved with drugs.

So now, I was going to see Dr. Liebert. I told him that since returning from my assignment in Alaska, I'd occasionally used cocaine. I told him that I didn't know what had happened to me, I didn't know why my personality had changed so drastically over the years, and I added that I was confused and frightened. When I'd first started working undercover, I hadn't used any drugs. I'd been a good, law-abiding police officer. Now I no longer felt like a cop; I felt like an outsider in the department.

I expected Liebert to give me some answers to my questions about what was going wrong, but the only thing he ever said was to warn me that I'd be arrested and put behind bars if I were ever caught using drugs. Here he was, a highly-paid psychiatrist who specialized in police officers as patients, yet with all his professional schooling and clinical knowledge, he didn't seem to know how to help me.

I also told him about the illegal secret scrapbook that contained information on a high-ranking state politician (and mentioned the politician's name). I told him that I had possession of the scrapbook and that it was locked up in my safe deposit box. Upon hearing all that Liebert became highly agitated, and in a shaky voice, warned me not to say another word about it as he didn't want to know anything about the book or its contents. He fully understood how destructive the book could be if it were made public.

Then I told him about being offered $25,000 to kill Benjamin Ng, and that even though the policeman part of me knew that it was wrong, I had the strong belief that I was the only one who could help the Chinese community. Once again, the only thing Dr. Liebert could come up with was a warning that if I was found out, I'd be arrested and put behind bars, and how, as a police officer, could I even think of killing someone for money?

I kept on seeing Dr. Liebert once a week, but continued to get no help with resolving my inner issues. However, he did give me additional prescriptions for medication to help me deal with my severe depression, my anxiety, and my personality disorder.

One night around 2:00 A.M. I received a call from one of the detectives working homicide, asking if I knew the whereabouts of Benjamin Ng. I responded that Ng was most likely staying with his girlfriend. I asked the detective what was going on, and he told me that Ng and two other individuals had just killed 13 people at an after-hours gambling club called the Wah Mee.[1]

At first, I thought the detective was kidding, I asked, "What'd he do, use a machine gun or something?" The detective answered, "No, Bernie. Ng and his two pals hog-tied everyone, robbed them, then went around and shot each individual in the head so there'd be no witnesses."

I asked if I could come down and view the scene of the killings, and the detective said I could.

I quickly drove downtown. There were police cars with lights flashing at all the major intersections leading into Chinatown. I parked several blocks away and walked over to the crime scene. The officers securing the perimeter recognized me and allowed me to enter the cordon. I headed towards Maynard Alley just off King Street and walked into the Wah Mee via the large double-door entrance.

By now I expected the bodies to have already been removed by the coroner, but that was not the case. Just inside the main door and to the left was the dead body of the doorman. He'd been shot through the chest. Walking into the main area of the club and to the right, I saw numerous men and one female, hog-tied and killed by gunshot wounds to the backs of their heads. In all 13 bodies, all killed by Benjamin Ng and his two buddies.

A 14th individual, a male, had been shot in the neck but had somehow survived and been able to free himself. This lone surviving witness was presently being treated at Harborview Hospital and was under heavy police guard.

Slowly, cautiously I walked around the 13 bodies, trying to identify anyone that I might have known. There, lying before me on the ground, hog-tied, shot in the head, with blood oozing from head wounds, with vomit spilling from their mouths, trousers defecated in, I did recognize people I knew.

Soon I was sick to my stomach and on the verge of throwing up. I needed to get out of there. In my mind I was responsible for those 13 bodies that now lay in the

---

[1] The Wah Mee Club was a clandestine gambling club.

Wah Mee Club. Had I only shot Benjamin Ng as I'd been asked, I could have prevented those deaths. Confused, with tears streaming down my face, I walked slowly out of the Wah Mee and away from Chinatown.

Entrance to the Wah Mee Club as it appears today

Epilogue

April 25, 1983—I went into the personnel office of the Seattle Police Department and stood before the desk of Lt. Henderson.

"Hi Bernie, sorry to see you go! You've been a good cop. You caught a lot of bad guys and seized a lot of dope. If I remember correctly, in one of your undercover cases you seized several ounces of pure Mexican Tar Heroin with a street value of half a million dollars. A half million bucks Bernie; that's big. It was one of the largest heroin drug seizures to date for this department. And you were able to arrest the two dirt bags who brought the stuff in from Mexico. That bust and seizure certainly made the chief happy; real happy. You know, Bernie, it's a shame; they kept you working undercover way too long. Anyway, now I gotta ask you for your gun and your badge, so please unload your firearm and lay it on the desk."

Slowly I reached back around and removed my service revolver from its holster. I carefully unloaded the gun and placed it on the Lieutenant's desk.

"Now the badge, Bernie. Sorry, but you gotta turn in your badge too."

I reached around to my right rear trousers pocket and pulled out my badge holder. Flipping it open, I stared down at my detective badge, the badge I'd wanted so bad since I was 16 years old. Everything I'd gone through all these years, all I'd worked so hard for; it had all been to earn that detective's badge. And I'd done it; I'd made detective in just four years.

I unclasped the badge from its holder, looked down at it one last time, and slowly placed it on the desk next to my service revolver. Lt. Henderson reached over, took the gun and badge, and put both in the top drawer of his desk. Standing up, he reached out and shook my hand.

"Best of luck to you, Bernie."

I exited the Public Safety Building via the main entrance and stood there looking across 5th Avenue, staring at the Municipal Building, the building where thirteen years earlier I'd been sworn in as a Seattle police officer. That day had been the happiest day of my life. Today would be the saddest.

Alone, confused, depressed, and shivering from the cold, I just stood there in the courtyard, getting soaked and having absolutely no idea what to do next or where to go. Moments earlier I'd been a Seattle cop, a detective. Now I stood all alone without a badge, without a gun, without anything. If you're not a cop, you're nobody; you're just "little people."

I didn't have the energy or the desire to walk up the hill to where my car was parked, so I headed down Cherry Street towards the waterfront. I continued walking aimlessly for hours, first along Western Avenue, then up Pike Street, back down Pine Street, then over towards the Pike Place Market, all the while trying to figure out what had gone so wrong. All I'd ever wanted in life was to be the best damn undercover detective in the history of the Seattle Police Department. What had happened to me? What had happened to my police career?

In April, 2006, I received my monthly copy of the Seattle Police Journal and read of Detective Mike Tipton's death. Mike, the son of a Seattle police officer, had also retired on disability after eight years on the force. He was found dead in his cabin in the San Juans about a month after he'd died. A line from his obituary struck home with me, "Not unlike other undercover police officers of that era, he soon lost his own identity, which presented an enormous conflict within him and which ended his police career."

It was only after reading this article that I finally understood what had happened to me. Years of undercover work had changed the naive young recruit from Hilo. Bernie Lau had shown up eager for the dance, and the Devil had partnered him in the guise of Johnny Medeiros, the anti-social biker puke asshole. Most people have a Johnny Medeiros lurking somewhere inside them, but they manage to keep him bottled up. In my case Johnny Medeiros was essential to my survival. I needed him and he, of course, took advantage of that. I lost control of my identity.

That I had gotten into this situation in the first place was perhaps no accident either. From childhood, I'd always been an outcast seeking acceptance. Under the right circumstances I'd take risks if I thought it would gain me approval. Add that to a natural love of risk and danger, and you get someone who may gravitate towards being a cop or in the military.

Apparently even otherwise normal and healthy people can be turned into something else by posing as something they're not for long periods of time. But even before I became a narc, I may have had problems. I believe it began when I was a very young child and I wasn't always taken care of properly with who knows what effect on my later development. My difficulties with learning may have been partially owing to inherited ADD/ADHD (undiagnosed until much later) combined with Reggie's misguided attempts to mold my character. Much later, after being a cop for many years, I was diagnosed with bipolarity and personality disorder. The personality disorder was a result of my long stint as an undercover detective, but bipolarity is at least partially inherited.

As a result of these and probably other factors as well, I became a cop who was lonely and confused. I was a substance-dependent outsider who had anti-social thoughts and occasionally exhibited uncontrollable anti-social behavior due to a personality disorder involving loss of identity. The SPD doctor certified that I qualified for medical retirement.

As for the "secret file" that I'd taken from Sgt. Dundee's desk as I stomped out of the office during my meltdown several months prior, it had been my intention to drive down to Olympia, the state capital, and hand the entire file over to the state authorities. But after thinking it over, I realized that if it were ever made public, many good police officers, detectives, and ranking officers within the SPD's Narcotics, Vice and Criminal Information Sections would certainly be arrested, lose their careers, and possibly end up serving lengthy prison terms in a federal penitentiary, so I later returned the file to a lieutenant working in the Criminal Information Section.

Seattle Police Department
Certificate of Retirement

Awarded to:

Detective

Bernard M. Lau

In recognition of **15** *years of dedicated service to this department and to the citizens of the City of Seattle.*

Date **April 25, 1983**

Chief of Police

Glossary

ADD (also "ADHD"—Attention deficit hyperactivity disorder) Symptoms may include inattention, distractibility, disorganization, procrastination, forgetfulness, lethargy, hyperactivity, or impulsiveness.

Aft Towards the rear of a vessel.

Aikidoka (Japanese) Someone who practices aikido.

Aloha shirt (also "Hawaiian shirt") A printed, short-sleeved, collared style of shirt originating in Hawaii.

Arrest technique A method of immobilization that minimizes harm to a captured suspect.

Ashram (Hindi) A Hindu religious hermitage.

Asshole A citizen who creates a problem for a police officer.

ASW (Anti-submarine warfare) A branch of naval warfare devoted to finding and destroying enemy submarines.

Bindle A piece of paper folded so that it makes a safe container for a drug in powder form, such as cocaine.

Bipolar disorder Mood swings from manic to depressive.

Bird dog A kind of vehicle tracking device.

Bokken (Japanese) A wooden sword used in practicing martial arts.

Booking sergeant A sergeant in charge of registering and incarcerating newly-arrested suspects.

Budo (Japanese) A term designating martial arts created after the Meiji Restoration (1868).

Bunk Fake narcotics.

Burn (n.) Fake narcotics (v.) Sell fake narcotics to someone.

CD (Central District) In the 1970s it had the highest percentage of African-Americans of any Seattle neighborhood.

CI (Confidential informant) Someone who reveals information that is supposed to be secret.

COB (Chief of Boat) An enlisted sailor on a submarine who serves as the senior enlisted advisor to the commanding officer.

Chain of evidence (also: chain of custody) Documented management of evidence to be used in trials.

Chasing the dragon Inhaling the smoke from heated narcotics placed on a piece of tin foil.

Chin na (Chinese) Arrest techniques.

Cold-copping Buying illegal drugs from someone you've just met for the first time.

Cop (v.) Get or buy.

ComSubPac (Commander Submarine Force, U.S. Pacific Fleet) The principal advisor to the Commander, United States Pacific Fleet on submarine matters.

Conning tower A raised platform on a submarine from which an officer can give directions to the helmsman.

Corpsman A medical care-giver in the U.S. Navy.

DSHS Department of Social and Health Services (Washington State).

Dan (Japanese) "Degree," as in "first degree black belt."

Dispatch See "Radio dispatch."

Dojo (Japanese) A practice hall for martial arts.

Dolphin insignia A uniform breast pin worn by U.S. Naval personnel who are qualified to crew submarines.

E-3 Petty Officer Third Class—the lowest ranking non-commissioned officer in the Navy.

Eurasian A person with one Asian and one European (Caucasian) parent.

FTO (Field training officer) A patrol officer who takes the recruit along on patrol as part of the recruit's training.

Forward Towards the front of a vessel.

Field testing Testing a substance suspected of being narcotics while undercover.

Galley The kitchen of a vessel.

Girl Heroin.

Hakama (Japanese) A traditional divided skirt (or baggy trousers) for formal wear.

Hand-to-hand buy Illegal drugs sold directly to a narc.

Haole (Hawaiian) A person of Caucasian descent.

Hapuu (Hawaiian) A tropical tree fern found in Hawaii.

Hash oil An evaporated solution of tetrahydrocannabinol and other compounds produced from cannabis.

Home invasion The act of illegally entering a private occupied residence.

Hot bunking Sharing a bunk bed in shifts.

Hot shot A lethal injection of drugs.

Hype A heroin addict.

Hydrophone An underwater microphone.

Indecent liberties Non-consensual sexual contact.

Jack (v.) Steal.

Jonesing Symptoms of drug withdrawal.

Jujutsu (Japanese) Traditional unarmed fighting techniques.

Kick down (v.) A drug buyer shares drugs with a person involved in a drug transaction.

Kyu (Japanese) Rank. In martial arts, used for ranks below black belt.

Lid An ounce of marijuana.

Local A non-white native of the State of Hawaii.

Lofan (Chinese) Caucasian.

Meth-head A user of methamphetamine.

Misogi (Japanese) Shinto purification ceremony.

MK V (Mark V) A model of standard diving dress used in the Navy.

Mochi (Japanese) Traditional confection made of pounded rice.

NCIC National Crime Information Center.

Nage (Japanese) In aikido, the one who throws.

Narc Undercover police officer, usually in the narcotics unit.

Nidan (Japanese) Second degree black belt in Japanese martial arts.

O&A Offering and Agreeing (to an act of prostitution).

P2P Phenyl-2-propanone, used in the manufacture of methamphetamine.

Pan Head An overhead-valve Harley-Davidson engine introduced in 1948.

Papa Hotel Code name for Pearl Harbor.

Pen reg(ister) An electronic device that records all numbers dialed from a particular telephone line.

Petty Officer A non-commissioned officer in the U.S. Navy.

Pidgin (also Hawaiian Pidgin English, Hawaiian Creole English) An English creole language used by Hawaiian locals.

Poi dog Hawaiian term for a mixed-breed dog.

Rack Bunk bed.

Radio (dispatch) The police department personnel who manage dispatching of patrol cars.

Randori (Japanese) A kind of aikido practice where several persons attack one.

Rat An informer.

Recruit Someone who has been accepted into the Seattle Police Academy and is undergoing training.

Rehabilitate Kill (a criminal).

Rigged for red When the interior of a submarine is illuminated only by red-colored lights. This is done at night so that sailors conducting periscope operations don't have to wait for their eyes to adjust to the darkness.

Roll call Inspection and briefing of police officers before they begin shift.

Rookie Someone who has been serving as a police officer for two years or less.

Sail A tower-like structure on the dorsal side of a submarine containing the conning tower, periscope, radar and communications masts.

SCUBA (Self-Contained Underwater Breathing Apparatus) A set of equipment for underwater diving.

SPD Seattle Police Department.

Second Class Diver The lowest of four levels of deep sea diving qualifications in the U.S. Navy.

Seiza (Japanese) The formal way of sitting with one's legs folded underneath one's posterior.

Sensei (Japanese) Teacher.

Shinto The indigenous religion of Japan.

Shodan (Japanese) First degree black belt in Japanese martial arts.

Shore patrol Naval ratings temporarily assigned to make sure that sailors on liberty don't misbehave.

Sifu (Chinese) "Master," "teacher." Used as a general term of respectful address.

Slam (v.) Inject narcotics.

Snitch Informant.

Snitch jacket Information or rumor that a person is a snitch.

Snorkel (v.) To run a submarine's engines while submerged, using a long tube-like device to supply the necessary air.

Speed Methamphetamine.

Steinke hood An inflatable life jacket with a hood used in escaping from a disabled submarine.

Step on (v.) Cut or dilute drugs.

Subase Naval Submarine Base.

TM (Transcendental meditation) A meditation technique popularized by Maharishi Mahesh Yogi (1914- 2008).

Tatami (Japanese) Straw mats used in traditional rooms, including martial arts training halls.

Toot (v.) Sniff cocaine.

Tracks Marks in a junkie's arm from repeated injection of drugs.

Turtleback The after deck of a submarine.

Tweaker A habitual user of methamphetamine.

UDT (Underwater Demolition Team) U.S. Navy divers skilled in demolition and underwater construction, merged with SEALS by 1983.

Uke (Japanese) In aikido, the one who takes the fall.

UW University of Washington, the largest university in Seattle.

UWPD University of Washington Police Department.

Ultraviolet powder Various powders used in forensics that are visible only under a black light.

VUSCA Violation of the Uniform Substance Control Act.

Victimless crime A crime that doesn't result in violation of another person's rights.

Watch commander Supervisor of the Patrol Division.

WestPac Western Pacific Ocean.

XO (Executive officer) Second in command on a naval vessel.

Zulu quiet Code word for making as little noise as possible in order to avoid detection by the enemy.

Appendix A: Fake I.D. Cards

State of Washington Concealed Weapons License

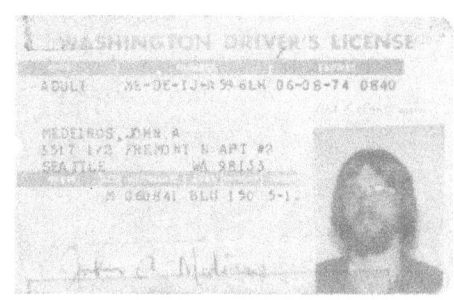

J. A. Medeiros' Washington State Driver's License

Johnny Medeiros' Alaska State Driver's License

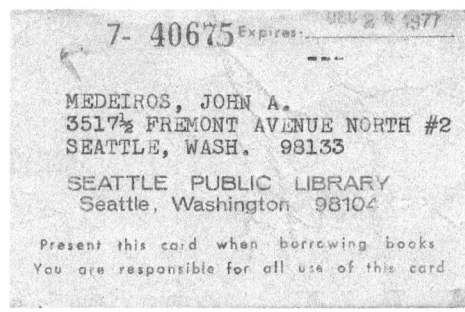

Johnny Medeiros' library card

Appendix B: Dr. Liebert's Letter

JOHN A. LIEBERT, M.D., P.S.
27 - 100TH AVE. N.E.
BELLEVUE, WASHINGTON 98004

TELEPHONE (206) 455-5850

March 11, 1983

Mr. Ray Schork
Seattle Pension Board
Bitterman Building
4th & Jefferson
Seattle, WA 98104

Dear Mr. Schork:

This letter is in regard to Bernard Lau who is applying for medical retirement from the Seattle Police Department. Mr. Lau has been in treatment with me since last fall. He sought help because of inability to control himself and mood disturbance. Mr. Lau was very active in undercover work both in Chinatown and narcotics. Due to his success in this field he became increasingly confused about his own personal identity until he began experiencing alien feelings of an antisocial nature. These feelings enhanced his undercover role but made it impossible to function as a law enforcement officer. His very complex family and cultural background made him particularly vulnerable psychologically to losing his personal self concept. He was a French war baby adopted by a Chinese American military officer after World War II. Although fluent in English and French, he is strongly identified with his oriental culture. This has created conflict with him during his work in undercover assignments, particularly when it involved conflict between Western and Oriental cultural values. The recent homicide in Chinatown was nearly devastating to him, and he is unlikely to ever be able to return to any law enforcement assignment. Currently he is improving on a high dosage of antidepressant medication. He maintains marginal psychological adjustment by intense concentration on martial arts and Buddhism.

He is totally disabled for law enforcement and, I believe, his claim for service connection is very legitimate. It is extremely unlikely that his current condition would have occurred without the excessive investment he made in multiple antisocial roles. It was to the point, he said, that the only giveaway for his real identity was his normal teeth, uncommon he states, in the subculture he mingled with on his assignements. This is a complicated matter; so, please feel free to call me if there are questions about this case.

Psychological testing by Dr. Berberich is in concurrence with my findings. You may wish to confirm this by calling Dr. Berberich.

Sincerely yours,

John A. Liebert, M.D., P.S.

CPSIA information can be obtained
at www.ICGtesting.com
Printed in the USA
LVHW062131150523
747094LV00022B/460